BANKRUPTCY AND THE U.S. SUPREME COURT

In this illuminating work, Ronald Mann offers readers a comprehensive study of bankruptcy cases in the Supreme Court of the United States. He provides detailed case studies based on the Justices' private papers on the most closely divided cases, statistical analysis of variation among the Justices in their votes for and against effective bankruptcy relief, and new information about the appearance in opinions of citations taken from party and amici briefs. By focusing on cases that have neither a clear answer under the statute nor important policy constraints, the book unveils the decision-making process of the Justices themselves – what they do when they are left to their own devices. It should be read by anyone interested not only in the jurisprudence of bankruptcy, but also in the inner workings of the Supreme Court.

Ronald Mann has been a commercial law professor at Columbia University for the last ten years. Previously he has taught at the University of Texas, the University of Michigan, and Washington University in St. Louis. He has also argued bankruptcy cases in the Supreme Court while working in the Office of the Solicitor General, and he has clerked for Justice Powell in the United States Supreme Court.

Bankruptcy and the U.S. Supreme Court

RONALD J. MANN
Columbia Law School

CAMBRIDGE
UNIVERSITY PRESS

CAMBRIDGE
UNIVERSITY PRESS

One Liberty Plaza, New York, NY 10006, USA

Cambridge University Press is part of the University of Cambridge.

It furthers the University's mission by disseminating knowledge in the pursuit of education, learning, and research at the highest international levels of excellence.

www.cambridge.org
Information on this title: www.cambridge.org/9781316613238
DOI: 10.1017/9781316673034

First published 2017

Printed in the United States of America by Sheridan Books, Inc.

A catalogue record for this publication is available from the British Library.

Library of Congress Cataloging-in-Publication Data
Names: Mann, Ronald J., 1961- author.
Title: Bankruptcy and the U.S. Supreme Court / Ronald J. Mann.
Other titles: Bankruptcy and the US Supreme Court | Bankruptcy and the United States Supreme Court
Description: Oxford [UK] ; New York : Cambridge University Press, 2017. | Includes bibliographical references and index.
Identifiers: LCCN 2017009672 | ISBN 9781107160187 (hardback)
Subjects: LCSH: Bankruptcy–United States. | Bankruptcy–United States–Cases. | United States. Supreme Court. | BISAC: LAW / Banking.
Classification: LCC KF1524 .M269 2017 | DDC 346.7307/8–dc23
LC record available at https://lccn.loc.gov/2017009672

ISBN 978-1-107-16018-7 Hardback
ISBN 978-1-316-61323-8 Paperback

Contents

List of Figures — *page* ix
List of Tables — x
Preface — xi

Introduction — 1

PART I SETTING THE STAGE — 5

1 **Literature Review** — 7
- 1.1 The Political-Science Perspective: From "Attitudinal" to "Constrained" Decisionmaking — 8
- 1.2 The Legal Academic Perspective on Bankruptcy: A Case Study in Textualism — 11
- 1.3 The Role of External Knowledge in Judicial Decisionmaking — 13

2 **Data and Methods** — 16
- 2.1 Defining the Subject — 16
- 2.2 Quantitative Analysis — 17
- 2.3 Qualitative Analysis — 18

3 **Congress and The Bankruptcy Code of 1978** — 24

4 **By the Numbers** — 31

PART II THE HARD CASES — 37

SECTION A – MISSED OPPORTUNITIES: CONGRESS, THE COURT, AND THE BANKRUPTCY CLAUSE — 39

5 **From *Marathon* to *Wellness*: Assessing the "Public[ity]" of the Bankruptcy Power** 42

5.1 Introduction 42
5.2 Setting the Stage: From Referees and Summary Jurisdiction to the Comprehensive Bankruptcy Vision of the Code 43
5.3 A Jaundiced View of Bankruptcy: *Marathon* 48
5.4 Retrenchment Extended from Article III to the 7th Amendment: *Granfinanciera* 56
5.5 *Marathon* Consolidated: *Stern v. Marshall* 65
5.6 The Court Blinks: *Arkison* and *Wellness* 68
5.7 The Irrelevance of Bankruptcy to Constitutional Doctrine 76

6 **Sovereign Immunity and the Bankruptcy Power: From *Hoffman* to *Katz*** 79

6.1 Introduction 79
6.2 Setting the Stage: From *Fitzpatrick* to *Union Gas* 79
6.3 Applying the Rules: *Hoffman* 83
6.4 An Interpretive Interlude: *Nordic Village* 91
6.5 Congress Talks Back: *Katz* 94
6.6 The Unfortunate Irrelevance of Bankruptcy to Constitutional Doctrine 96

SECTION B – INTERPRETIVE STRATEGY: THE COURT, THE SOLICITOR GENERAL, AND THE CODE 98

7 **Bankruptcy versus Labor Law: *Bildisco*** 99

7.1 Introduction 100
7.2 Labor Politics in the 1980s 101
7.3 The Legal Context of *Bildisco* 102
7.4 The Court's Decision 107
7.5 *Bildisco*'s Aftermath 118
7.6 A Postscript on GM and Chrysler 121
7.7 Conclusion 123

8 **Bankruptcy versus Environmental Law: *MidLantic*** 125

8.1 Political Background 126
8.2 Bankruptcy Abandonment under the Act and the Code 128
8.3 The Factual Setting 129
8.4 *Midlantic* at the Supreme Court 133

8.5 The Role of the Solicitor General 142
8.6 The Legacy of *Midlantic* 145

9 **Bankruptcy versus Criminal Law: *Kelly*** 146
9.1 Criminal Restitution and Victims' Rights 146
9.2 Background 148
9.3 The Supreme Court's Decision 150
9.4 The Aftermath 156

10 **Setting Text against Tradition: *Ron Pair*** 158
10.1 The Factual Setting 158
10.2 The Legal Setting 159
10.3 *Ron Pair* in the Lower Courts 161
10.4 *Ron Pair* in the Supreme Court 162
10.5 Explaining *Ron Pair* 168
10.6 The Aftermath: *Rake v. Wade* and Its Rejection 171
10.7 Conclusion 172

11 **Bankruptcy and State Sovereignty: *BFP*** 174
11.1 Introduction 174
11.2 Foreclosure as a Fraudulent Conveyance 175
11.3 *BFP* in the Lower Courts 180
11.4 *BFP* in the Supreme Court 184
11.5 Conclusion 191

PART III AMICI AND THE COURT 193

12 **The Supreme Court, the Solicitor General, and Statutory Interpretation** 197
12.1 Agency Cases 198
12.2 Tax Cases 200
12.3 United States Trustee Cases 200
12.4 Sovereignty Cases 202
12.5 Secured Credit Cases 202
12.6 Bankruptcy Interests 206
12.7 Summary 207

13 **Learning from Amici** 210
13.1 The Contributions of Amici 211
13.2 The Court's Own Contribution 221

PART IV CONCLUSION **231**

APPENDIX A: The Supreme Court's Bankruptcy Cases 239

APPENDIX B: Available Papers of the Justices 242

APPENDIX C: References to the Hard Cases 245

APPENDIX D: Sources of the Court's Citations 246

APPENDIX E: Sources from the Solicitor General and Other Amici 247

Bibliography 249

Index 259

Figures

2.1 Justice Scalia's Memorandum in *Owen v. Owen* — *page* 21
2.2 Justice O'Connor's Memorandum in *Norwest Bank Worthington v. Ahlers* — 22
4.1 Supreme Court Bankruptcy Decisions (1981–2014) — 32
4.2 Voting in Non-Unanimous Cases, by Justice — 34
5.1 Powell Argument Notes (*Marathon*) — 51
7.1 Rehnquist Memo (*Bildisco*) — 116
13.1 Powell Bench Memo (*Bildisco*) — 226
13.2 Bankruptcy and Foreclosure Rates (2003–2015) — 236

Tables

12.1 SG Participation and Outcomes in Secured Creditor Cases *page* 205
12.2 Pro-Bankruptcy Outcomes, by Federal Interest in Case 208
A.1 The Supreme Court's Bankruptcy Cases 239
B.1 Papers of the Justices (By Case) 242
B.2 Papers of the Justices (By Justice) 243
C.1 References to the Hard Cases 245
D.1 Sources of the Court's Citations 246
E.1 Sources from the Solicitor General and Other Amici 247

Preface

My work on this project has proceeded for so long that the number of people to whom I owe gratitude is surely longer than I can name in this context. To mention just a few, I should start with the tireless work that Samuel Lemley did collecting and organizing the papers of the Justices and presenting them on the Web site. I would thank Loring Veenstra on the same account had he not also worked so hard on the project as to justify his status as a collaborator. Jennifer Wertkin and Marty Witt at the Columbia Law School Library also deserve special thanks for their indefatigable efforts to help me obtain the relevant papers from the Library of Congress. John Jacob, the archivist of the Lewis F. Powell Jr. Archives at the School of Law at Washington and Lee University, also deserves special thanks for his prompt responses to my numerous inquiries about the contents of those papers.

The work of collecting and organizing the papers would not have been possible without a generous grant from the Endowment for Education of the National Conference of Bankruptcy Judges. Their support of empirical research about bankruptcy is a remarkable testament to the oft-overlooked care and thoughtfulness with which bankruptcy judges operate the system that this book examines.

So many people have provided so much input at so many different times that I cannot possibly list them all. I should, though, single out Greg Dovel, Roy Englert, Richard Lazarus, Deborah Malamud, Tom Merrill, Henry Monaghan, Bob Rasmussen, Jim Rogers, and Gil Seinfeld.

Finally, any thanks I can offer to my family are wholly inadequate. They have tolerated my intermittent obsession and procrastination on this project for longer than I care to admit. The intellectual contributions of my spouse, Allison, to this project go far beyond any call of collegial or familial responsibility.

Introduction

I can pinpoint almost to the hour when my thoughts first turned to the subject of this book: Thursday morning, October 9, 1986. I was a law clerk for Justice Powell, and the Supreme Court had heard arguments the previous day in an obscure bankruptcy case captioned *Kelly v. Robinson*, in a month in which the Court also heard arguments in the landmark *McCleskey v. Kemp* (1987), which upheld the constitutionality of the death penalty despite statistical evidence of a pervasive racial bias. The issue in *Kelly* was whether a bankruptcy filing discharged the debtor's obligation to pay restitution imposed as part of a criminal sentence. I had worked hard preparing for this case and had provided the Justice with a detailed bench memorandum explaining my view that the language of the statute compelled the conclusion that the bankruptcy discharge absolved the debtor of the obligation to pay restitution. The basic point was that restitution is compensatory in nature and thus is not properly considered a "penalty" exempted from discharge under Bankruptcy Code Section 523. Because I had focused on commercial law courses in my law school studies, including multiple courses involving the Bankruptcy Code, I felt well qualified to examine the question. My confidence was buttressed by the knowledge that the other eight law clerks working on the case shared my view, including, among others, Dan Bussel (now a successful bankruptcy professor at UCLA) and my colleague at Columbia Eben Moglen.

I was anxious and excited when I entered the Justice's office to discuss the case. It was the first argued case I had discussed with him, and so I did not know what to expect. As always, he was most gracious. He had read my memorandum with care, annotating it throughout. He waited patiently and attentively through my brief presentation summarizing my views of the statute. When I was finished, he smiled and nodded approvingly. He then told me that he was sure my statutory analysis was meticulous, but that he was just as sure that his colleagues would not decide that a bankruptcy court had the power to absolve a state criminal sentence. I left his office doubtful at best that he could be right – the statute seemed so clear.

Not surprisingly, the expectations of the Justice were more accurate than those of his young law clerk. At the conference the next morning, the Justices decided by a 7–2 margin that the Bankruptcy Code did not discharge the restitutionary obligation. The opinion was assigned to Justice Powell. His opinion explained that the tradition of federal deference to the state criminal process was so important that only the clearest possible language could convince the Court that Congress intended to interfere with the enforcement of the sentence of a state criminal court. Because the language of Section 523 was not incontrovertible, the Court concluded that the Bankruptcy Code should not be interpreted to interfere with the state criminal process. Justice Marshall, joined by Justice Stevens, offered a stinging dissent emphasizing the stark tension between the Court's conclusion and the plain language of the statute. Despite what I regarded (and still regard) as its direct inconsistency with the language of the Code, the decision sank like a small pebble into the United States Reports, leaving not a ripple of controversy.[1]

Kelly is a useful starting point not only because of its prominence in my professional consciousness but also because it underscores the themes that have motivated me to write this book focusing on how the Justices interpret the Bankruptcy Code. Perhaps the easiest answer, the one I hear most commonly in conversations with other lawyers who have clerked at the Court, is that the Justices don't care about these cases: they didn't become judges to interpret obscure provisions of federal statutes like the Bankruptcy Code. They are there for the big questions: the First Amendment, the death penalty, abortion, affirmative action, gay marriage, and the other leading issues of the particular era in which they serve. Probably the most famous example of this perspective is the oft-cited anecdote in which Justice Blackmun complained about receiving an undue share of tax cases, which he regarded as "dogs" (Wasby 1993, 70–71).

But the "they just don't care" explanation withstands little scrutiny. For one thing, it seems inconsistent with my own personal experience – admittedly anecdotal. If the Justices did not care about these cases, why would they take the trouble (as in *Kelly*) to reject the advice of their clerks? The path of

[1] Justice Marshall did, in a sense, get the last word. When a similar question (the dischargeability of restitution orders in Chapter 13 cases) reached the Court several years later in *Pennsylvania v. Davenport* (1990), Justice Marshall wrote for the Court, limiting *Kelly* and holding that those orders can be discharged in Chapter 13 (over the objection of Justices Blackmun and O'Connor from the *Kelly* majority). I discuss *Kelly* and *Davenport* in more detail in Chapter 9.

least resistance in such cases would be to accept the legalistic resolution of the controversy and agree to a brief opinion explicating that point (presumably largely written by law clerks). The attention of the Justices to these cases is evident from Justice Powell's notes, added in red down the side of his conference notes in an early environmental bankruptcy case: "None of us has a clear rationale for deciding this case. I've rarely heard such divergent and unclear views by all of us" (OKOV002).

But Justice Powell's correct expectation that the Court would pay no heed to the settled view of the law clerks at least suggests a principled framework for issue resolution. Whatever that framework is (and that is the central topic of this book), it is the antithesis of apathy. Indeed, the *Kelly* anecdote suggests a framework far removed from abject submission to the text of the statute. To put it another way, saying that the Justices don't care about a particular class of cases tells us nothing about how they decide them: Whether they are important or not, the Court still reaches decisions in those cases. What this book attempts to understand is how they reach those decisions in bankruptcy cases. If there is a discernible pattern of issue resolution in bankruptcy cases, that suggests that the Justices do care about those cases. More empirically, the case studies that occupy the bulk of this book demonstrate that the Justices in fact care deeply about these cases. The files are replete with back-and-forth negotiations about the precise wordings of opinions, changes of position after the initial decision, and substantial changes in doctrinal approach over time. Those are not the features of apathetic and disinterested decisionmaking.

My project, then, is to open up the black box of the Court's decisionmaking, to understand as best as I can what the Court actually does when it decides cases under statutes like the Bankruptcy Code. The core of the book is a set of case studies analyzing several of those cases in detail. For each of those cases, I have collected all of the available papers of the Justices (which I have cataloged, imaged, and archived online at www.bksct.net). I have collected all of the briefs of the parties and as much as I can locate of the records of proceedings in the lower courts. I have corresponded with law clerks that worked on each of those cases. Finally, I have searched news archives for information about the parties to the dispute, all with a view to developing as rich and broad an understanding as possible of the disputes, the competing policy interests, and how the Justices resolved them. It is my hope that the case narratives proceed at four distinct though overlapping levels. Collectively, the different levels of analysis reflect the different goals I hope the project advances.

- At the highest level of generality, I am trying to show where courts look for knowledge in an area in which positive law provides little guidance and where political preconceptions have little power or salience. As Posner (2010, 47) emphasizes, this is an important question for the still underexamined topic of judicial reasoning. As I explain in Chapter 2, it also advances the extensive literature on the Court's decisionmaking.

- At a second level, the case studies illustrate how courts interpret statutes when they have limited guidance from reliable external sources. By moving beyond the simple labels of "textualist" and "purposive" to a narrative that provides a richer institutional framework, I hope this study advances conceptions of statutory interpretation.
- At the level of bankruptcy policy, the primary focus of the book's narrative, the case studies show how the Court's decisions systematically have underenforced the Bankruptcy Code. Faced with ambiguous statutory language and a conflict with other state, federal, or constitutional interests, the Court in almost every close case has ruled against a broad application of the Bankruptcy Power. Given the increased importance of appropriate responses to financial distress in our ever-more volatile economy, the infirmity of the Court's bankruptcy instincts have handicapped the Code's ability to fill the constitutional role set out for it. The view that the bankruptcy system should play a powerfully positive view in our society is of course not a common one. It is not, however, completely unprecedented, as a glance at the recent work of David Skeel (2009) will demonstrate.
- Finally, at the lowest level of generality, the narratives of the individual cases are compelling. From the shockingly toxic pollution presented in *Midlantic* to the rare-coin fraud behind *BFP*, the Court's bankruptcy cases provide a fascinating glimpse at the world of commercial and financial failure.

A brief word about the authorship of the project is also appropriate. Loring Veenstra worked extensively on Chapters 7, 8, and 10. For that reason he is listed as the coauthor of those chapters and the collaborator on the book as a whole. He bears no responsibility for any errors of judgment or omissions in the remainder of this work.

PART I

SETTING THE STAGE

1

Literature Review

I am not the first to consider the sources of Supreme Court decisions. Is my approach an arbitrary personal predilection drawn entirely from my anecdotal recollections? Or can I justify it as a contribution to the disparate efforts in the literature that explains Supreme Court decisionmaking? The purpose of this chapter is to put the case studies in context by exploring existing academic approaches to Supreme Court decisionmaking and relating them to the framework I use for understanding the Court's bankruptcy jurisprudence.

For analytical purposes, I perceive much of the existing literature as starting from one or the other of two polar opposites: the legal perspective that the statutory law for the most part controls decisions; or the political-science perspective that the political predilections of the Justices for the most part control decisions. However interesting that controversy might be, it is largely off to the side of the work I present here. Because this work emphasizes influences that are neither strictly legal nor strictly attitudinal, it is in tension with both of those perspectives. But that tension is of little importance, because this project does not aim to reassess those perspectives. My goal is not so much to understand what types of information are more (or most) important to the Justices, but rather to understand the sources of the information on which they rely. The existing literature is important to my inquiry – I cannot understand how Justices obtain the relevant information without understanding what information is likely to be important to them. But it is important primarily as the background against which I write; I have no need to stake out any particular position on the major issues that previous scholars have analyzed so divisively. Because my strategy is to isolate the cases in which neither legal nor policy information is likely to be immediately dispositive, the relative weight that the Justices give the different types of information is much less important than the basic idea that their decisions rest on various types of information not immediately apparent even to a trained observer.

1.1 THE POLITICAL-SCIENCE PERSPECTIVE: FROM "ATTITUDINAL" TO "CONSTRAINED" DECISIONMAKING

The idea that something external to the legal materials plays an important part in Supreme Court decisionmaking is an old one. It has been a dominant theme in political-science literature on the subject since the 1940s work of Herman Pritchett. His seminal book on *The Roosevelt Court* (1948) examines the pattern of voting in non-unanimous decisions of the Supreme Court from 1937 to 1947. Presenting only the simplest of descriptive statistics, Pritchett draws detailed portraits of the individual Justices, illustrating that their attitudes in different subject-matter areas made them predictably more or less likely to fall on particular sides of controversies.

It is not surprising that policy views are an important part of the Court's doctrinal work. It is central to the work of mainstream judicial writers of traditions as far removed from each other as Cardozo (1921) and Posner (2010). But implicit in Pritchett's work, and explicit in the later attitudinal work, is the conception of "policy" inputs as preexisting perspectives held in the minds and personalities of the individual Justices. Thus, the most prominent strand of the political-science literature in this domain has expanded Pritchett's analysis into a large-scale quantitative argument that the attitudes of the Justices are, in substance, the only important determinant of Supreme Court decisionmaking. The leading proponents of this view in its strongest form are Jeffrey Segal and Harold Spaeth.[1] Although the early work of Segal and Spaeth (1993) was largely anecdotal, it has grown over time to include a database of all of the Supreme Court's merits decisions since 1953 and is now the foundation for nearly all quantitative studies in the field. Chapter 2 uses that database as the foundation of its introductory quantitative discussion of the Court's bankruptcy decisions.

Segal and Spaeth use the database to estimate the importance of judicial attitudes quantitatively (Segal and Spaeth 2002, ch. 8). Specifically, they use newspaper editorials at the time of each Justice's appointment to derive an index of each Justice's place on a liberal/conservative continuum. They show an impressive correlation (0.76) between votes and the Justices' individual ideological indices, and provide a regression model documenting a statistically significant relation between the index and the votes. More dubiously, Segal and Spaeth argue that they can demonstrate the irrelevance of law by

[1] Strangely enough, as many political scientists have moved on to institutionally richer modes of analysis, much of the most recent work in this area has come from legal academics (George 1997; Martin et al. 2004; Miles and Sunstein 2006; Sunstein et al. 2006).

showing that the predictive power of their model is enhanced only slightly by the addition of a series of variables accounting for the different facts of the cases that should be relevant as a doctrinal matter (whether there was a warrant, whether the search involved a car, etc.). Their absolutist perspective is well captured by Spaeth's description of law as "a low form of rational behavior [akin to] necromancy or finger painting" (Spaeth 1979, 64).

Although the Supreme Court database that Segal and Spaeth originated is without a doubt the dominant tool for quantitative analysis of Supreme Court decisionmaking, it has come under increasing scrutiny in recent years as scholars express concerns about the methodology by which the database codes decisions as "liberal" or "conservative." For example, Judge Richard Posner and his co-authors have created a modified database reflecting recoding of a large number of decisions based on Judge Posner's sensibilities about what should count as "liberal" and "conservative" (Landes and Posner 2009; Epstein et al. 2013). More ambitiously, Anna Harvey argues (2013) that the methodology for defining decisions as liberal and conservative reflects an inherent "confirmation" bias in the minds of those making the coding decisions. She goes on to present (2014) a book-length analysis of a new methodology for assigning conservative/liberal codes based on whether the decision upholds or invalidates a decision adopted during a time of a Democratic or Republican majority in Congress. Whatever impact that methodology might have in the political-science literature, it is of limited use for this project because it does not extend to statutory cases.

A closely related body of scholarship, building on the work of Murphy (1964), emphasizes strategic interactions among the Justices themselves: circumstances in which Justices cast votes that do not reflect their sincere preferences. That literature, rooted in game theory, seems to me less a reaction to the Segal–Spaeth premise that only attitudes matter than an explanation of how rational Justices would act if Segal and Spaeth were correct (Posner 2010, 30). That work has been particularly prominent in the last few decades (see McNollgast 1994; Knight and Epstein 1997; Wahlbeck et al. 1998; Maltzman et al. 2000; Arrington and Brenner 2004; Hammond et al. 2005; Daughety and Reinganum 2006; Bonneau et al. 2007). More recently, it has entered the law-review literature (Jacobi and Sag 2009), as legal academics have used it as part of the "New Legal Realism" movement (Miles and Sunstein 2008).

The polar opposite of Segal and Spaeth is a wholly positivist perspective, that legal decisionmaking applies a self-contained set of principles to texts, producing determinist results wholly independent of the individual views of the actors involved. Although it dominates the legal scholarly debate (discussed in the next section), that perspective has not played a major role in the scholarly debate among political scientists. Rather, the intra-disciplinary challenges to Segal and Spaeth have come for the most part from two fronts: those who argue that their notion of "attitude" is impoverished and those who argue that an adequate model of decisionmaking must accept the importance not only of judicial attitudes, however defined, but also of law itself.

On the first front, many scholars have emphasized the broader institutional backdrop against which the Court operates: The Court's decisions reflect not only the preexisting attitudes of the nine Justices, but also the views of Congress, the executive, state political systems, and even nongovernmental elites. Law necessarily exists within a network, including those parties and any others with substantial interests in the content of the law. Essentially, the law represents the alignment of all of those contested interests. From that perspective, the stability of any particular alignment is a function of the apparent costs of reopening the "sealed object"; stare decisis is a doctrinal vessel for managing those costs. The positive statutory and constitutional law obviously is one of the most important constraints, but its strength in any particular context varies directly with the strength of other competing interests in the topic at hand.

Again, there is nothing new about this idea. Even Pritchett could note this reality and quote Dooley's aphorism about the Court's propensity for following "th' illiction returns" (Pritchett 1948, 8–9, referring to Dunne 1901, 26). In modern years, this is reflected in the American Political Development Tradition, which includes an entire volume of detailed case studies about particular Supreme Court decisions (Kahn and Kersch 2006), a book-length study by Powe (2009) emphasizing the importance of nongovernmental elites, and numerous careful empirical studies. Within that tradition or working alongside it, political scientists in the last twenty years have gone a long way toward documenting and quantifying the role of the multifarious interests that constrain the Court in its determination and development of legal rules (Cross and Nelson 2000; Caporale and Winter 2002; Bergara et al. 2003; Hume 2014; Owens 2010; Segal et al. 2011). For my purposes, that work is primarily cautionary. Specifically, I need to distinguish between the ability of elites to influence decisions strategically (the Court is disciplined to follow the views of elites because of a fear of retribution) and the ability of elites to influence decisions by providing information that shapes the Justices' independently developed legal views (the Court's decisions take account of factual information that elites provide to it).

The second broad reaction to Segal and Spaeth has accepted that law independently constrains the influence of attitudes, whether they come from the Justices' preexisting dispositions or from some sense of the desires of powerful actors external to the Court. Although the interaction of attitudes and external influences has been an important theme of work for years (Lim 2000; Richards and Kritzer 2002; Bartels 2009; Posner 2010), the 2011 publication of Bailey and Maltzman's *The Constrained Court* makes that interaction the foundation for a comprehensive synthesis of the attitudinal, legal, and elitist perspectives. Using a newly developed methodology for comparing the ideal policy points of actors in the judicial, executive, and legislative branches, Bailey and Maltzman provide compelling empirical evidence that the attitudes of the Justices are substantially constrained by both law (legal principles) and politics (signals from the executive and Congress).[2] By integrating the various perspectives into a single quantitative model, their work largely redefines the debate for all future writers in the area. They provide a relatively moderate structure against which I can situate my project, which I hope is sufficiently capacious to appeal both to political scientists and legal scholars.

1.2 THE LEGAL ACADEMIC PERSPECTIVE ON BANKRUPTCY: A CASE STUDY IN TEXTUALISM

Despite its relative obscurity as a subject matter when compared to more salient topics like abortion, affirmative action, and civil rights, the decisionmaking frame of the Supreme Court's bankruptcy decisions has spawned a substantial literature in the law reviews. That literature is almost entirely separate from, and largely uninformed by, the extensive literatures discussed above. For the most part, the law-review literature on bankruptcy decisionmaking has started from the premise that, for better or worse, the Supreme Court's bankruptcy decisions are predominantly textualist (see Carroll 1993; Cuevas 1994; Effross 1992; Rasmussen 1993; Schwartz 2001; Tabb and Lawless 1991). The best example in this tradition is Rasmussen (1993). Analyzing the Supreme Court's twenty-eight bankruptcy decisions from 1986 to 1993, he concludes that the text almost always drives the decisions, with limited departures in cases that involve important governmental interests. Interestingly, Rasmussen reads the decisions of lower courts (principally the federal courts of appeals) as being much more "dynamic" in their interpretive strategy – more likely than the Supreme Court to read the text in light of the underlying policies and purposes of the statute. Rasmussen vigorously criticizes the Court for its failure to articulate a coherent bankruptcy policy (Rasmussen

[2] Pacelle (2015) follows in that vein, providing an updated statistical analysis that underscores the effects of congressional majorities on the Court's decisionmaking process.

1993, 565–571). Ultimately, however, Rasmussen concludes that textualism works better at the Supreme Court than a dynamic approach. He contends that few of the cases would have been decided differently under any approach, that the harm of following the text to a bad policy decision is relatively small (principally because Congress can repair the damage), and that textualism is valuable because it saves the Court's resources for more important and difficult cases (Rasmussen 1993, 595–597). Schwartz (2001) offers a slightly different take on the problem, arguing that the Court's emphasis on predictable textualism has prevented it from developing coherent policies or goals in its bankruptcy cases. Finally, complementing Rasmussen's work, Bussel (2000) surveys the court of appeals bankruptcy decisions that claim to adopt textualist reasoning and finds that they are more commonly reversed by statute than other decisions; the work suggests both that wholly textualist decisions are more likely to be pernicious and that their ill effects easily are remedied by statute.

Writing more recently, Dembart and Markell (2004) review seventy bankruptcy decisions of the Court from the adoption of the Bankruptcy Code in 1978 up to 2004. They come away with a perspective parallel to that of Schwartz, i.e. that the Court systematically has abjured the adoption of any coherent policy and instead emphasized the "plain meaning" of the statute. More than Rasmussen, however, and perhaps reflecting Markell's position as a judge himself, Dembart and Markell emphasize the ease with which the authors of opinions easily can cloak themselves in the plain meaning of the statute to justify decisions that the language of the statute does not compel. Thus, among other cases, Dembart and Markell (2004, 391) emphasize the inconsistency of Justice Scalia's opinion in *BFP* (the subject of Chapter 11) with the language of the Bankruptcy Code. They also emphasize the apparent dominance of policy in *Bildisco* and *Midlantic*, the subjects of Chapters 7 and 8 (Dembart and Markell 2004, 392). Lawless takes a similar perspective. Although he had argued earlier that the Court's decisions are inordinately textualist (Tabb and Lawless 1991), Lawless (1996) embraces the difficulty of the textualist interpretation, criticizing the Court as unreasonably favorable to the Government and institutional creditors and insufficiently attentive to broader bankruptcy policies.

Tabb (1987) offers the only substantial effort to situate the Court's bankruptcy decisions as a group against broader patterns of decisionmaking. He provides detailed discussions of the Court's first nine decisions under the Bankruptcy Reform Act and suggests a number of "principles of decision" other than pure textualism that might explain those decisions. In general, however, he concludes that the Court applies none of the principles he discusses consistently across all of the cases.[3] Still, his frank recognition that textualism alone provides a poor explanation of the pattern of results stands out against the other writing in the field.

The inadequacy of textualism as an explanation for the Court's decisions is not simply a straw man that I aim to debunk. Rather, it is a premise from which I start, central to the motivation of this project: Although the Court emphasizes the text as a matter of course in all statutory cases, even the Court acknowledges the importance of other factors in many cases. To be sure, that idea is not novel. It is central in the voluminous literature about statutory interpretation – the backdrop against which the legal scholars situate their work. The point of this project is to tie the way in which the Court weighs policy against text to the specific institutional framework in which a case arises. That tie is to my knowledge absent from the legal literature about statutory interpretation, presumably because it makes no sense within the purely legal tradition to assert that the "correct" answer to a legal question is (or should be) influenced by issues of external institutional design.[4]

1.3 THE ROLE OF EXTERNAL KNOWLEDGE IN JUDICIAL DECISIONMAKING

This, then, is my point of departure – to focus on the source of information, of knowledge, on which the Court draws when it decides routine cases about which the Justices lack strong preconceptions. The principal study of that question to date has involved the importance of amici – nonparties who voluntarily provide information to the Court. Generally, that literature documents the importance of the information those parties provide – its importance to the Court's decision (see Caldeira and Wright 1988; Collins 2007, 2008). That is especially true when the information comes from particularly reliable parties, like the Solicitor General in the Department of Justice (Provine 1980; Kearney and Merrill 1999; Bailey et al. 2005; Owens and Wohlfarth 2014). Indeed, Black and Owens (2014) provide persuasive statistical evidence that the Solicitor General's participation actually influences the Court's decisions. In most of that literature, though, the theory is that the information provided by the

3 Because Tabb wrote so soon after adoption of the Bankruptcy Reform Act, he had a much smaller universe of decisions to examine. Moreover, because he did not yet have access to any of the Justices' papers, his discussion of the cases rests almost entirely on the opinions of the Court. As we will see in the case studies that follow, the published opinions often tell little of the story of the Court's decisionmaking process.

4 Pildes (2013) comes close to this problem, asking whether the Court's decisions should rest on institutional design (in theory) or institutional capacity (in fact).

brief is simply that the case is important to the party in question – there is rarely discussion of underlying legal or policy arguments that would bring the amicus effect closer to a legalist conception of decisionmaking (Epstein and Knight 1999). Only in the last few years have scholars begun to consider the possibility that amici might influence the analytical structure of the opinion (Collins et al. 2015; Larsen and Devins 2016). Because this study rests on a firm distinction between a strategic effect of that information (discussed above, depending entirely on the identity of the advocate) and the direct value of the information as inputs for the decisionmaking process, that literature provides a baseline for the work I undertake in the closing chapters of this book.

To explore how the judicial process integrates the available information into the decisions that it produces, I delineate three separate stages of analysis. First, how much room does positive law leave unresolved? Although positive law might provide a compelling answer in many (perhaps most) disputes, it will rarely be dispositive in cases that reach the Supreme Court; the cases that divide the Court closely should be those where positive law is *least* dispositive. Thus, several scholars in recent years, most successfully Bailey and Maltzman (2011), have emphasized how other factors are especially likely to come to the fore in cases in which law is indeterminate (Maltzman and Wahlbeck 1996; Johnson et al. 2012; Epstein et al. 2013). If we accept the legal skills of all the Justices, then any case that divides the Justices closely is one on which the legal materials themselves are not definitive. In that vein, Sunstein et al. (2006, 130) document the limited importance of attitudinal norms when political salience is limited.

The second step is to consider the sources to which the Justices turn when legal constraints are relaxed. Although attitudes and predispositions are certainly part of the process – something all would admit even in the absence of the compelling statistical demonstrations of the attitudinalists – there is much more. I argue here that the Justices, seeking to resolve cases as best as they can, search in close cases for expertise to which they can defer, at least in part to minimize the risk of unforeseeably disruptive decisions that are not compelled by legal doctrine. Expert federal agencies, for example, are likely sources for the Justices seeking guidance in resolving difficult cases. Eskridge and Frickey (1994) discuss the difficulties of deciding when to defer to agencies.

The third and final step is how to incorporate the information and expertise brought to bear on the question into a final and definitive ruling. Here, the problem is one of judgment, constructing a coherent narrative of legal doctrine that incorporates the knowledge and expertise the Justices have gleaned from external sources. Aggregating those sources into a single lucid framework is of course not an easy, or inevitably successful, task (Jasanoff 1990; Whiteman 1985). Indeed, with this Court, as with supreme courts in other nations, the preliminary question of identifying the point on which the case will turn is itself a delicate one (Latour 2010). Most often (and always in the cases at the heart of this project), the question can be viewed as one of accommodation of disparate and incompatible interests.

As applied to the context of this project, the central question in the case studies typically will be which of a pair of competing interests will prevail: the interest in a broadly effective bankruptcy proceeding or the opposing interest seeking to escape invalidation in bankruptcy, whatever that interest might be (labor policy, environmental policy, criminal enforcement, state autonomy, and so forth). Analyzing the resolution of that question across a range of close cases, the book presents an "information-based" explanation that the absence of a reliable and articulate advocate of bankruptcy policy – the absence of a crucial information resource – has led to a course of decisions in which the bankruptcy policy gives way for the most part to the opposing interest.

2

Data and Methods

The question of how the Justices determine their votes in cases that lack notable salience or political importance is not only multifaceted but also one as to which there is little direct evidence. To be sure, the literature summarized in Chapter 1 includes a rich history of quantitative studies which provide techniques and data that certainly can shed some light on the subject. But for an inquiry that ultimately seeks to analyze the Justices' actual motivations, a purely quantitative study seemed inadequate. As a result, a thorough study would mix methods, including elements of both quantitative and qualitative inquiry.

2.1 DEFINING THE SUBJECT

The first task is to define and justify the boundaries of the inquiry. My selection process is the opposite of the method in much of the existing literature. It is well recognized that one of the weaknesses of the attitudinal literature is its "preoccupation with politically charged cases," an exaggerated impression of the "permeation of American judging by politics" (Posner 2010; Friedman 2006 (arguing that the emphasis on votes instead of opinions overstates the meaning of votes in hard cases)). Instead of analyzing the most controversial cases (where preexisting policy attitudes are most likely to be important), I want to identify cases where preexisting attitudes are relatively unlikely and where law is similarly indeterminate. By identifying the cases least likely to be resolved by the statutory text or preexisting attitudes, I can most readily examine the process by which the Court acquires and processes the information that would be likely to inform policy. Metaphorically, my goal is to remove the "noise" introduced by overpowering legal and attitudinal effects so that I can observe the routine underlying processes of information collection and processing – just as scientists can examine gravity waves only by insulating their apparatus from the noise of the everyday environment.

For this study, I have chosen the Court's cases evaluating the Bankruptcy Code of 1978. Although the statute has sufficient economic and social significance to produce a steady diet of cases before the Court, it is not among the issues that are politically salient or controversial to the Court. This reduces the likelihood of strong preexisting intuitions at the Justice level (Nash and Pardo 2011 (documenting lack of ideological bias at the court of appeals in bankruptcy cases)).

To give the study coherence, I begin with the adoption of the Bankruptcy Code of 1978. As Chapter 3 explains in more detail, the Code's adoption was a watershed event, substantially rewriting American bankruptcy law, generally to extend relief much more broadly than had been the case previously (Skeel 2003). The adoption of the new statute rapidly brought the Court a relatively large set of cases presenting parallel questions about how to fit the new form of relief into the background of existing bankruptcy law and the array of state and federal policies that the new statute affected. This study examines the universe of the Supreme Court's cases under that act, which first reached the Court in October Term 1981. Appendix A lists the universe of those cases, eighty-two as of the fall of 2015.

2.2 QUANTITATIVE ANALYSIS

The wealth of quantitative analysis of Supreme Court decisions discussed in Chapter 1 provides a ready set of tools for analyzing the cases in this study. I start with a dataset of the eighty-two cases identified in Appendix A. In addition to basic identifying information, the principal variable of interest is a new hand-coded variable that classifies the decisions based on the effect of the decision on the scope of the bankruptcy power. Specifically, I code a case as "broad" if it broadens (or broadly interprets) the relief available in bankruptcy and as "narrow" if it narrows (or narrowly interprets) such relief. So, for example, a case that denies the ability of a bankrupt to abandon contaminated property would be coded as narrow, while a case allowing discharge of debts arguably incurred by defalcation would be coded as broad.[1] The general idea is to capture the extent to which the Justices give credence to the importance

[1] Few of the cases are difficult to code under that conception. When in doubt (occasionally in cases like *Timbers of Inwood Forest* that involve disputes among creditors that are wholly internal to the bankruptcy process), I assess whether the decision positively (or negatively) affects the assets available to the estate. Appendix A displays the coding for all of the cases in the dataset.

of Congress's adoption of the Code (or the constitutional Bankruptcy Power that justified Congress's action) by interpreting the Code to establish a more robust system of relief.

I merged the dataset of Supreme Court bankruptcy cases with the Segal–Spaeth Supreme Court Database, including Quinn-Martin and Segal–Cover ideology scores. I also added to that dataset the "salience" scores of the cases (all available at the web site for the Supreme Court Database), which score a case as salient if it is mentioned on the front page of the New York Times when it is decided or in the Congressional Quarterly. Using the resulting database, I can examine the extent to which the decisions (or votes) in bankruptcy cases map onto traditional estimations of "conservative" and "liberal," and also the extent to which the decisions (or votes) favor a broader or narrower bankruptcy system. For comparative purposes, I collected parallel data for the securities and tax cases dating back to 1954 (the starting point of the Supreme Court Database).

2.3 QUALITATIVE ANALYSIS

Because the ultimate goal of the project is to understand the Justice-level motivations for the votes in individual cases, the quantitative analysis summarized above is inherently limited. Accordingly, I decided at the earliest stage that the project also would include detailed studies of particular cases, using the Justices' papers to broaden the information beyond the information available from the Court's published opinions. Of course I am far from the first scholar to use the Justices' papers as a resource; some of the most important books discussed in Chapter 1 rely heavily on those papers (Knight and Epstein 1997; Maltzman et al. 2000), but the political science literature that uses those papers has grown far beyond the context discussed there (Corley 2008; Johnson et al. 2006; Owens 2010; Wahlbeck et al. 1999).

Legal scholars also have used those papers frequently. Much of that literature focuses on the decisions of a particular Justice (Greenhouse 2006 (Harry Blackmun); Hutchinson 1998 (Byron White); Jeffries 2001 (Lewis Powell); Purcell 2000 (Louis Brandeis); Schwartz 1983 (Earl Warren); Stern and Wermiel 2010 (Bill Brennan)), or, occasionally, to examine doctrinal developments in a particular area (Pritchard 2002; Pritchard and Thompson 2009). The effort here – to understand the Court's decision-making process itself and the influences on it – is closest to the work by Richard Lazarus (2007; 2011) on the Court's environmental decisions, although it also resembles in some ways work by Black and Owens (2014) (analyzing the influence of the Solicitor General), Maltzman et al. (2000) (documenting the importance of strategic decisionmaking by the individual Justices), and Schwartz (1997) (analyzing the shifting role of the Chief Justice from the 1970s to the 1990s).

More generally, the attention to qualitative case studies as an alternative or supplement to quantitative work has become increasingly common in the political science literature, especially in work about the Supreme Court. To mention just a few of the most prominent, that methodology has been particularly successful in work from Howard Gillman (2001), Mark Graber (1998), Thomas Keck (2007), and Keith Whittington (2001). Indeed, as emphasized in Chapter 1, the American Political Development Tradition is founded on case studies (Kahn and Kersch 2006). To offer one salient example of direct relevance to this project, Keck (2007) compares the political alignments that supported the enactment of statutes with the presumed political alignments of Justices that voted to invalidate statutes, concluding that a large share of the invalidations can be explained only on the basis of a "legal sensibility," as opposed to any "partisan platform."

The question in each case is whether the internal papers reliably shed light on anything that cannot more easily be determined from the final published opinion. In particular, because the papers come from the files of a particular Justice, the risk that they will be self-justifying or reflect the single perspective of one Justice rather than the Court as a whole is apparent. Those problems do not undermine the value of the papers for what I am doing here. For the purposes of this work, some of the most important documents in the files are the documents that represent the views of particular Justices: the drafts that show how opinions developed over time, the documents they circulate among each other seeking changes to opinions, and the missives to and from their clerks discussing the issues they find important. Those internal documents provide a valuable glimpse at the differing perspectives of the various Justices and their clerks, as well as how the positions shifted through the decisionmaking process. As prior scholars have recognized (Maltzman et al. 2000), the Justices' papers are valuable sources for that type of information.

The papers also provide a valuable window on the sort of questions that the Justices consider during the process of reaching a decision. When we think of the making of law as the combination and reconciliation of disparate information, a central part of the process is the identification and selection (to use the term of Latour 2010) of the "moyen" – the point of decision on which the case will turn. It is commonplace that legal reasoning requires that law at least appear to be a "delicately knitted lace" that is seamlessly interwoven with the social institutions out of which it arises (Latour 2010; Pritchett 1948, 47 (discussing the importance of reconciling continuity and adaptability)). That necessity, in turn, makes it incumbent on the Justices to understand the institutional background into which their decisions will be placed.

The papers of the individual Justices often provide a far richer resource for that inquiry than the final published opinions. Among other things, they often document an interplay between legal and extra-legal concerns that is not evident from the published opinions. For example, the papers related to *Owen v. Owen*[2] include a remarkable note by Justice Scalia, to whom the opinion in that case had been assigned. In the process of drafting the opinion, he apparently determined that the law imposed an insuperable constraint to writing an opinion explaining the result that all nine of the Justices had supported when they first discussed the case. He commented:

> I was as firm as any of you in my opinion that the judgment in this case had to be an affirmance. I have found it impossible, however, to write it that way. The principal difficulty is that the case-law [on a relevant point] is unanimous . . . I am unwilling to contradict this unanimous line of authority; and I cannot find a way to distinguish this authority. OWEN009.

The files from *Norwest Bank Worthington v. Ahlers*[3] provide a similar example of the way in which law provides a constraint to concerns related to broader social policies. The Court in that case rejected a plan for the reorganization of a family farm, but the opinion did include a substantial passage acknowledging the plight of family farmers. In her note joining Justice White's opinion, Justice O'Connor commented that she "particularly appreciate[d] your inclusion [of] a recognition of the plight and worth of the family farm. While we can't help solve the problem, at least we acknowledge it" (NBWA021).[4]

Given the goals of the undertaking, it is ambitious to think that it can succeed even with access to the Justices' papers, but almost pointless even to try without them. Because at the time this study was designed none of those papers were available beyond October Term 1993, I terminate the case studies at that point (with the 1994 decision in *BFP v. Resolution Trust Corporation*). As a basis for the case studies, I collected all of the available papers of the Justices that relate to any of the eighty-two cases in the dataset, scanned all of the individual documents in the files of the Justices, assigned each document a standardized document identification code, and then posted them online

[2] 500 U.S. 305 (1991).

[3] 485 U.S. 197 (1988).

[4] On his copy of the note, Justice Blackmun added a wry comment: "Still running for high public office?" (NBWA021).

Supreme Court of the United States
Washington, D. C. 20543

CHAMBERS OF
JUSTICE ANTONIN SCALIA

December 3, 1990

Re: No. 89-1008 - Owen v. Owen

MEMORANDUM TO THE CONFERENCE:

I was as firm as any of you in my opinion that the judgment in this case had to be an affirmance. I have found it impossible, however, to write it that way. The principal difficulty is that the case-law interpreting the phrase "impairs an exemption to which the debtor would have been entitled" is unanimous, with respect to the federally listed exemptions, to the effect that a lien excluded from an exemption nonetheless impairs it. I am unwilling to contradict this unanimous line of authority, since lien avoidance for the most important federal exemptions is nonexistent on any other assumption; and I cannot find a way to distinguish this authority from cases involving state exemptions.

I hope you may agree with me, but otherwise the opinion will have to be reassigned.

Sincerely,

FIGURE 2.1 Justice Scalia's Memorandum in *Owen v. Owen* (OWEN009).

at www.bksct.net.[5] For each case, the site includes a timeline, constructed by arranging in chronological order all of the papers of all of the Justices. Because the individual documents are identified by date, type, and chamber of origin, they should permit ready reference for future scholars. For the purposes of this project, citations to papers available at that site use the web site's document identification codes.

The next problem was to decide which cases to examine in detail. Bankruptcy cases rarely present high-profile policy questions likely to speak to Justice-level predispositions, and in many cases the statutory text or relevant doctrine will be sufficiently clear that resort to external information will not be important to the decision. Information external to the statutory text obviously will be most important when the legal doctrine is not directly dispositive (Richards and Kritzer 2002; Bartels 2009 (analyzing the

5 A generous grant from the National Conference of Bankruptcy Judges supported that work.

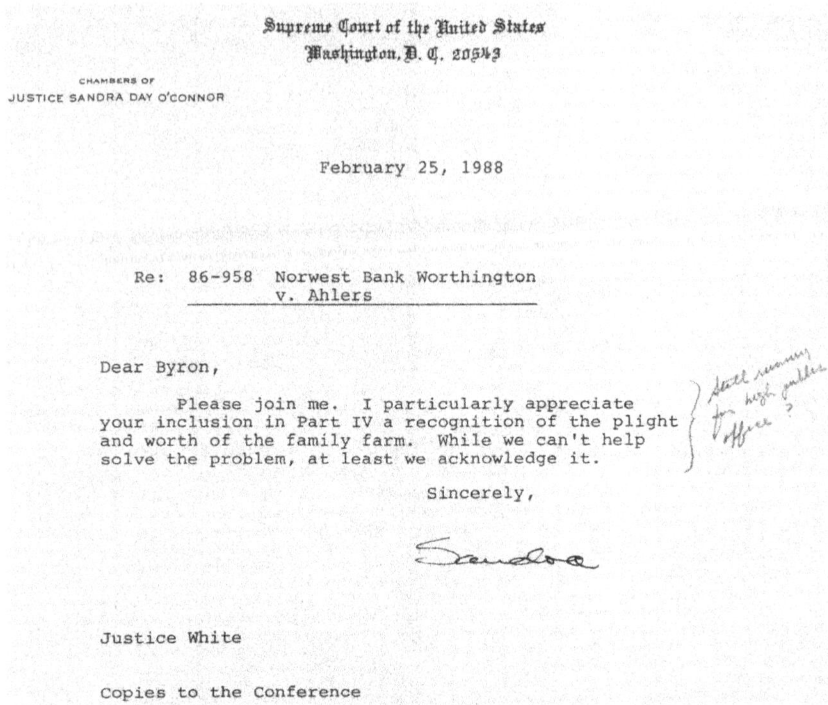

Supreme Court of the United States
Washington, D. C. 20543

CHAMBERS OF
JUSTICE SANDRA DAY O'CONNOR

February 25, 1988

Re: 86-958 Norwest Bank Worthington v. Ahlers

Dear Byron,

Please join me. I particularly appreciate your inclusion in Part IV a recognition of the plight and worth of the family farm. While we can't help solve the problem, at least we acknowledge it.

Sincerely,

Sandra

Justice White

Copies to the Conference

FIGURE 2.2 Justice O'Connor's Memorandum in *Norwest Bank Worthington v. Ahlers* (NBWA021). Justice Blackmun's handwritten comment reads: "Still running for high public office?"

"constraining" power of doctrine)). Recognizing the difficulty of identifying any objective (or positive) measure of ambiguity (Farnsworth et al. 2010), I follow Pritchett's example of studying cases in which the Justices disagree. In that respect, the work resembles Gebbia-Pinetti (2000) (descriptive analysis of interpretive methodologies in non-unanimous bankruptcy cases). To emphasize the cases in which the law is least likely to be dispositive, I decided to present case studies for all of the cases in which the Justices are closely divided (either 6–3 or 5–4). The last of those cases for which papers are available is the 1994 decision in *BFP v. Resolution Trust Corporation*.[6] Chapters 5 through 8, 10, and 11 present case studies of each of the close cases through and including

6 Interestingly enough – after ten closely decided cases in the twelve years leading up to *BFP* – there was not another such case until 2004, far too recent for any of the Justices' papers to be available.

BFP. Although it mars the elegance of the project design, I add a discussion in Chapter 9 of the relatively "easy" decision in *Kelly v. Robinson*, decided by a 7–2 vote, both because it is such an excellent example of my thesis and because of its role in the development of this project.[7]

7 I have collected and studied the papers in all of the cases that are not unanimous, but consider in the detailed case studies only the more closely divided cases. Where appropriate, I refer to the papers in those other cases. I should add that I excluded the 5–4 decision in *Pioneer v. Brunswick* because it involved neither the constitutionality of the Code nor interpretation of the Code itself, but rather interpretation of the Bankruptcy Rules (promulgated by the judiciary) that govern the rights of creditors that fail to file a timely proof of their claim. Although it was a closer call, I also excluded the 6–3 decision in *PBGC v. LTV Corp.*, which seemed to me much more a decision about ERISA than a decision about the Bankruptcy Code.

3

Congress and The Bankruptcy Code of 1978

A brief recounting of the Code's adoption sets the stage for the quantitative and qualitative analysis of how the Court has treated the Bankruptcy Code. The extent of Congress's effort in designing the Bankruptcy Code can hardly be overstated. Unlike recent legislation in the area, the Code was not produced by the partisan designs of a single party or drafted to satisfy the interests of particular businesses (Jensen 2005; Whitford 2007). On the contrary, the Code was the end point of a decade of attention. The process began with the 1968 hearings of a subcommittee of the Senate Judiciary Committee investigating the utility of appointing a Bankruptcy Commission (Tabb 1995; Skeel 2003, 136–41). Based on the information collected in those hearings, Congress proceeded with the 1970 appointment of the Commission on the Bankruptcy Laws of the United States.[1] The commissioners were appointed by the President, President of the Senate, the Speaker of the House, and the Chief Justice. The President appointed two distinguished bankruptcy experts (Harold Marsh, the Chairman, and Charles Seligson). The President of the Senate appointed a pair of Senators, the Speaker of the House a pair of Congressmen, and the Chief Justice two experienced judges, Edward Weinfeld (from New York) and Hubert Will (from Chicago). The Executive Director (and presumably the principal draftsman of the Commission's work) was long-time Michigan Law Professor Frank Kennedy.

The Commission spent two years producing a detailed report recommending wholesale changes to almost every aspect of the bankruptcy system in this country (Commission on the Bankruptcy Laws of the United States 1973). Among other actions undertaken, the Commission authorized a series of studies of the operations of the existing system, it held several conferences with

[1] The discussion that follows draws heavily on the lucid discussion by Klee (1980), Skeel (2003), and Block-Lieb (2012).

important stakeholders around the country, and it enlisted the services of a distinguished list of scholars from business and law faculties, as well as noteworthy research institutes like the Brookings Institution and the American Bar Foundation. In stark contrast to the National Bankruptcy Review Commission of the 1990s (for which then-Professor Elizabeth Warren was the Reporter), the 1970s Commission report was almost entirely unanimous, devoid of partisan divides. The sole exception was a brief dissent by Judge Weinfeld (of the Southern District of New York), who argued that the reforms the Commission advocated could be accomplished without the new tier of judges that the Commission recommended. The breadth of the Commission's vision is plain from the structure of its work as a response to three problems Congress emphasized in the Joint Resolution (P.L. No. 91–354) that authorized the creation of the Commission: a radical upturn in bankruptcy filings; a shared sense among participants that the system was functioning poorly; and the vast expansion of credit since the design and enactment of the then-extant Bankruptcy Act of 1898.

Even more importantly, the work of the 1970s Commission (unlike the work of the National Bankruptcy Review Commission) set the framework for legislation. Although I discuss below Congress's studied rejection of the judicial and executive framework that the Commission recommended, much of the structure, and even the language, of the Bankruptcy Code of 1978 finds its source in the Commission's 1973 report. Preoccupied with the question of whether the judges would be appointed for life with the constitutional protections of the federal judiciary (the subject of Chapter 5), Congress largely approved the sweeping extensions of bankruptcy relief that the Commission proposed as a response to the marked upturn in credit and financial distress during the twentieth century. With no dispute about the pressing need for "the modernization of the bankruptcy law" (House Committee on the Judiciary 1977, 3), both Houses of Congress adopted the Code by voice votes. President Carter signed it into law in November of 1978. It took effect, for the most part, on October 1, 1979.

Looking back from the present day, it is difficult to convey the importance of the Code's adoption. Perhaps the most salient indicator of the long-term vision behind the reform is the point noted by Tabb (1995), that this is the only major revision of the bankruptcy laws not enacted as a response to a severe depression. It is only a small exaggeration to suggest that the Code in substance created the architecture of the bankruptcy system as we know it. It should illustrate the point adequately to summarize the structure of what the Commission proposed and Congress created.

Surely the most important innovation of the Commission's report was its recommendation for a bankruptcy agency, in the Executive Branch, to be known as the United States Bankruptcy Administration (Commission Bill §§ 3–101 to 3–403. Commission on the Bankruptcy Laws of the United States 1973; Kennedy 1973). The Commission on that point followed the lead of a detailed 1971 Brookings Institution study, which based its call for an administrative agency on an empirical study of cases under the old Act[2] (Stanley and Girth 1971). The Commission explained that "a great part of the work of the bankruptcy system is administrative rather than judicial in character," and that separating those functions from the more conventional dispute-resolution functions would enhance both the objectivity of the judges (by removing them from day-to-day administration) and the efficiency of the system (by limiting the tasks that the judges needed to perform) (Commission on the Bankruptcy Laws of the United States 1973, 5–8). Related to that point, the Commission recommended the creation of a new set of judges – specialist judges, with the constitutional status of the existing federal judiciary, who would decide all of the issues arising in bankruptcy cases, subject to review by the district and appellate courts (Commission Bill §§ 2–101 to 2–210).

Aside from the thorny problem of constitutional status, Congress accepted the need for new judges whole-heartedly. Congress did not, however, go so far as the Commission recommended to regularize the administrative process. Congress acknowledged the need to separate the administrative and judicial roles (House Committee on the Judiciary 1977, 89–91), crediting the common complaint that "the bankruptcy court is the only court I appear in in which the judge is an interested party" (House Committee on the Judiciary 1977, 91). But instead of a separate federal agency, Congress chose a much less ambitious system of United States trustees, to be appointed in each of the federal judicial districts, together with a minor officer in the Department of Justice to supervise the trustees, the predecessor of what is now the Office of the United States Trustee (House Committee on the Judiciary 1977, 100–112). By creating a group of trustees to administer the individual estates, separate from the judges that adjudicate disputes about them, Congress thought it had resolved the problem of the self-interested decisionmaker that had plagued procedures under the Act.

2 Although it is surprising from our vantage point - after three decades of the Code - the call for an agency at the time was commonplace (Skeel 2003, 77 (discussing various early calls for an agency)).

It well might be that the chances of Congress at that time creating any major new agency were scant. The SEC (probably the closest parallel) was created almost a half-century earlier in response to a firestorm of outrage at harms the entire nation suffered that were attributable, to some degree, to ill-functioning securities markets.[3] No such emergency faced the Congress that considered the report. On the other hand, as Rafael Pardo and Kathryn Watts emphasize, "the Bankruptcy Code is one of the few major federal civil statutory regimes administered almost exclusively through adjudication in the courts – not through a federal regulatory agency" (Pardo and Watts 2012, 386). The result is to have the final decisions about the direction of the bankruptcy system made by the appellate federal judges – generalists – rather than by informed specialists in an agency. More generally, the decision to operate the system through courts rather than an agency comes at the cost of the various potential benefits that usually justify the choice of an agency as the most effective tool for implementing complex policy on the ground: accountability, uniformity of outcome,[4] accessibility and transparency, prospective clarity, and flexibility in responding to unforeseen situations and issues (Pardo and Watts 2012, 423–445). Indeed, although it was not apparent at the time, hindsight suggests that the rejection of the agency has pushed the system down an adversarial path that is much more expensive, especially in large business reorganizations, than the more "inquisitorial" system that might have accompanied an expert agency (Bussel 2016).

In any event, Congress's decision to reject the agency proposal rested at least in part on the firm opposition of the bankruptcy judges to that proposal (Skeel 2003, 143–145). From a cynical perspective, the opposition could be viewed as a classic instinctive reaction on the part of officials anxious to protect their "turf," though presumably the individual actors sincerely doubted the effectiveness of the proposed agency. Although this was by far the most important departure from the Commission's vision (in part because the creation of the agency was the most notable feature of that vision), it received relatively little attention in congressional deliberations; apparently judicial opposition made it a "non-starter" even before Congress began deliberations. From the perspective of this project, though, this relatively quiet moment

3 Moreover, as Ernst (2014) documents so persuasively, even during the Great Depression it required remarkable effort to manage the successful creation of the SEC and other New Deal agencies.

4 The triviality of many of the Supreme Court's bankruptcy decisions would lead the casual observer to think that the Court's exercise of its certiorari jurisdiction is an adequate mechanism for ensuring uniformity. That is plainly not the case. For example, one Federal Judicial Center study concluded that "bankruptcy law is less settled than in other areas of law–and ... it affects judges' work" (McKenna and Wiggins 2002, 635).

was the single point on which all later events turn. This is the point to wonder about the shape of the path not taken: What would the bankruptcy process look like if Congress *had* accepted the result of the Commission's considered deliberations instead of rejecting them out of hand? I am not alone in the structural inquiry. Pardo and Watts recently presented an incisive plea (2012) for a resuscitation of the administrative model, though so far as I know their call has received little or no attention in the policy-making community.[5]

Putting to the side the "personnel" question – agency versus judges versus pseudo-judges – the Code also comprehensively recast almost every aspect of the relief available in bankruptcy. As the Commission recognized, the inadequacy of consumer relief was one of the main factors motivating Congress's creation of the Commission (Commission on the Bankruptcy Laws of the United States 1973, 9). The Commission proposed two chapters for consumer relief (the existing Chapters 7 and 13), both of which were markedly more generous than relief available under the old Act. Among other things, the Commission recommended (and Congress adopted) a broader discharge for debtors in Chapter 7 and a provision for wage-earner plans in Chapter 13 without the consent of creditors. Emphasizing the "tremendous rise" in consumer credit since World War II (House Committee on the Judiciary 1977, 116), Congress followed the Commission's lead by broadening eligibility and relief for both of the consumer chapters, emphasizing an effort to avoid creditor "techniques that enable them to avoid the effects of a debtor's bankruptcy" (House Committee on the Judiciary 1977, 117).

Probably even more important were the changes for business bankruptcies, which one study characterized as "the most ambitious effort yet to shift the concept of bankruptcy law from a legal mechanism for liquidating a company to an enabling mechanism for company rescue, [an] emphasis [that] would eventually propagate across the world" (Halliday and Carruthers 2009, 2; Carruthers and Halliday 1998). Emphasizing that the lethargic pace of procedures under the old Chapter XI had made companies reluctant to use the system until liquidation was the only option, the Commission recommended relief that would be both more expeditious and more effective (Commission on the Bankruptcy Laws of the United States 1973, 14).

5 Littwin (2011) provides a provocative cautionary note. Comparing the relative success of the judicial process of Chapter 7 with nascent administrative processing, she suggests that in fact the judicial process has done quite a good job, avoiding many of the pitfalls that have made administrative claims systems frequently ineffective.

Accepting that perspective, Congress responded with a new vision of Chapter 11 that gave debtors more control over the process, a broader stay of creditor collection efforts during the bankruptcy, and more effective powers to recover pre-bankruptcy payments to creditors (Skeel 2003, 160–183). Those changes removed the primary role the Securities and Exchange Commission previously had played in the reorganizations of major businesses. Admittedly, the SEC's efforts were not regarded as effective; they surely contributed to the limited use of the old Chapter XI. All in all, those changes have transformed the institutions for restructuring failed businesses, with Chapter 11 now being the presumptive locus of relief – even for companies as central to the economy as General Motors and Chrysler.

Perhaps the most impressive testament to the success of the Code it is durability. To be sure, it has been amended more than twenty times, most recently by the Bankruptcy Technical Corrections Act of 2010. And some of those amendments have been quite important. The Bankruptcy Amendments and Federal Judgeship Act of 1984 reshaped the role of the bankruptcy judges (responding to the decision in *Marathon* discussed in Chapter 5) and significantly eased the availability of relief under Chapter 13. Most recently, the Bankruptcy Abuse Prevention and Consumer Protection Act of 2005 (universally referred to as "BAPCPA") sharply truncated the relief available to consumers, imposing a "means test" that limits the bankruptcy discharge to relatively impecunious filers. But the basic architecture of Chapters 7, 11, and 13 that was founded on the Commission's Report and implemented in the Code continues in force to this day.

As I suggest above, one of the major claims of the book is that the Court systematically has interpreted the Code too narrowly. One interesting piece of evidence that underscores Congress's perspective on that problem comes from the occasions on which Congress has decided to reject the Court's decisions in this area.[6] By my count, there are four such cases: *Rake v. Wade*,[7]

6 I rely for this discussion on the data collected by Dan Bussel and presented in Bussel (2000). My list omits two of the decisions that he lists as overruled (NLRB v. Bildisco & Bildisco, 465 U.S. 513 (1984) (analysis modified by 11 U.S.C. § 1113); United Savings Ass'n v. Timbers of Inwood Forest, 484 U.S. 365 (1988) (result undermined by 11 U.S.C. § 362(d)(3)), because the statutory amendments do not seem to me to directly reject the Court's holding (although they probably would change the result on the facts of the cases in question). I should mention that Dan Bussel served as a law clerk for Justice O'Connor on *Kelly v. Robinson*, the subject of Chapter 9.

7 Rake v. Wade, 508 U.S. 464 (1993) (permitting post-filing interest even if prohibited by mortgage documents), superseded by 11 U.S.C. §§ 1123(d), 1222(d), 1322(e) (all barring the collection of such interest). I discuss *Rake* in connection with my extended discussion of *Ron Pair* in Chapter 10.

Davenport,[8] *Nordic Village*,[9] and *Hoffman*.[10] In three out of those four cases, Congress overruled a decision interpreting the Code narrowly, substituting a broader rule that the Court had rejected. The only exception (*Davenport*) is itself interesting, because it cut back substantially on the narrow reading of the Code in *Kelly v. Robinson*, the subject of Chapter 9. In that context at least, the Court's hesitant sensibility matched Congress's ill-expressed intent.

8 Pennsylvania Dep't v. Davenport, 495 U.S. 552 (1990) (allowing discharge in Chapter 13 of certain restitution obligations), superseded by 11 U.S.C. 1328(a) (prohibiting such a discharge). I discuss *Davenport* in connection with my extended discussion of *Kelly v. Robinson* in Chapter 9.

9 United States v. Nordic Village, 503 U.S. 30 (1992) (holding federal government immune from suit in bankruptcy), superseded by 11 U.S.C. § 113 (abrogating immunity). I discuss *Nordic Village* in detail in Chapter 6.

10 Hoffman v. Connecticut Dep't, 492 U.S. 96 (1989) (holding state government immune from suit in bankruptcy), superseded by 11 U.S.C. § 113 (abrogating immunity). I discuss *Hoffman* in detail in Chapter 6.

4

By the Numbers

Turning at last to the Supreme Court's bankruptcy decisions, some descriptive statistics about the Court's bankruptcy jurisprudence illuminate the domain of the project. Since enactment of the Bankruptcy Code in 1978, the Supreme Court has adjudicated eighty-two cases involving the constitutionality or application of that statute (eighty cases with full argument and two "per curiam" summary reversals). This is about 2.5 percent of all of the civil cases the Court has adjudicated during the relevant time period (from October Term 1982, when the first case reached the Court, through the most recently concluded Term of the Court). As Figure 4.1 shows, the cases have not come evenly over time, but have trended upward and downward with three distinct peaks of activity. The earliest peak came from about 1989 to 1996, with the first set of major issues reaching the Court under the Bankruptcy Code. The second peak, from 2002 to 2004, is a little harder to understand, but presumably reflects the sharp upturn in bankruptcy filings about that time. The third peak, if it can yet be called that, is the upturn in cases the last several years, reflecting for the most part issues raised by the enactment of BAPCPA in 2005 and the Great Recession that followed close upon its heels.

I start with the two-part thesis explored by the book as a whole: First, that the institutional structure of the Code (specifically – Congress's decision *not* to vest administration of the bankruptcy process in an administrative agency) leaves the Court systematically underinformed about the importance of the Bankruptcy Power and the relief it provides. Second, that this vacuum leads the Justices to underweight that interest when they decide cases involving bankruptcy issues. The first place to look, at the level of the Court as a whole, is the extent to which the Court has decided those cases in a way that gives an expansive interpretation of the Bankruptcy Code. There is some subjectivity in that determination, but by my coding of the cases, the Court has voted for an expansive interpretation of the Bankruptcy Power in thirty-two of the cases,

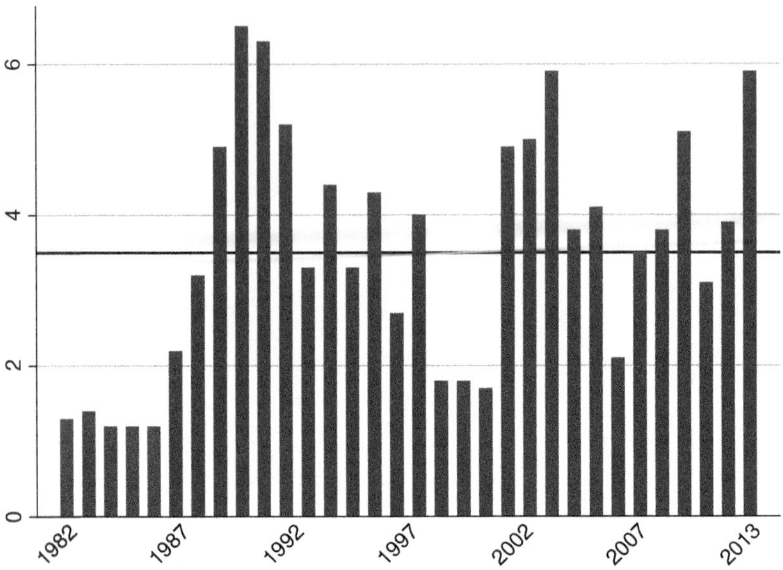

FIGURE 4.1 Supreme Court Bankruptcy Decisions (1981–2014). Source: Author's calculations from United States Reports and Supreme Court Reporter, matched to data from annual Harvard Law Review Supreme Court issues. Figure shows rolling three-year average percentage ratio of plenary bankruptcy decisions to all plenary civil decisions. Reference line indicates mean share from 1981 to 2014.

about 39% of the time. Because close cases are the ones in which the law is likely to be least determinative, those are the cases in which any disposition toward or against a broad reading of the Code could be seen most clearly. Looking at just those cases with at least three dissents, the Bankruptcy Power fares even worse: only five of the nineteen close cases (26%) interpreted the Bankruptcy Power expansively, and four of those five came in the last dozen years: close cases in the first twenty years of the Code's existence were decided against the Bankruptcy Power more than 90% of the time (eleven of twelve cases).[1]

In light of the emphasis in existing scholarship on attitudinal motivations for the votes of the individual Justices, it is instructive to look not only at the Court's decisions, but also at the votes of the individual Justices. I start by considering the extent to which the traditional liberal–conservative indices in the political science literature explain the votes in these cases.[2] Though

[1] The list of cases in Appendix A shows the coding of each of the cases.

[2] I used the traditional Segal–Spaeth coding for the results of the cases. For the ideology of the individual Justices, I estimated separate models using the Quinn–Martin ideology scores and

those ideology scores relate closely to the liberal–conservative coding of votes in the Supreme Court Database as a whole, they do not relate significantly to the voting in the subset of bankruptcy cases that I consider. Indeed, the coefficient in a logistic regression for the bankruptcy sub-sample is less than one-fifth of its size for the database as a whole. Thus, however useful liberal–conservative ideologies are in general, they provide no significant explanation of the pattern of "liberal" and "conservative" votes in bankruptcy cases.[3]

I also examined the salience of the cases, using the New York Times and Congressional Quarterly salience data that accompanies the Supreme Court database; those data score a case as salient if it is mentioned on the front page of the New York Times when it is decided or in the Congressional Quarterly. Although about 13% of all Supreme Court decisions are salient under the (more generous) New York Times data, only one (1.3%) of the bankruptcy cases is – the decision in *Bildisco* that is the subject of Chapter 7. Interestingly, the votes in that case break down in accordance with the traditional measures of ideology used in the attitudinal literature, with the four most conservative Justices on one side of the case and four of the five most liberal Justices on the other side. Only Justice Stevens crossed lines to join the then Associate Justice Rehnquist's majority opinion; as Chapter 7 explains, Justice Stevens forced a substantial narrowing of Rehnquist's opinion as a condition of his vote.

I next turned to examining whether metrics of political ideology relate to any propensity to narrow the Bankruptcy Power. The question here is whether there is a relation between traditional metrics of "liberal" and "conservative" ideology and a predisposition in favor of (or against) the Bankruptcy Power. Again, using my coding of the cases as broadening or narrowing the reach of the Code, the data suggest no significant relation between political ideology and votes for (or against) the Bankruptcy Power.

The last step was to explore the possibility of any noteworthy attitudes among individual Justices, whether related to "conservatism," "liberalism," or something else not captured in the data. To that end, I estimated the rate of broad-bankruptcy votes, by Justice.[4] The first panel of Figure 4.2 displays

the Segal–Cover ideology scores. The text discusses the Quinn–Martin results, which do not differ substantially from the Segal–Cover results.

3 For purposes of the models discussed in this paragraph, each Justice's vote in a particular case is an observation, the explanatory variable is the Justice's ideology score, and the dependent variable is whether the vote is in the direction that is coded as "liberal" or "conservative. As a robustness check, I also run all analyses against the parallel dataset used in Epstein et al. (2013). They do not differ in any material way from the analyses I present here.

4 Following the lead of Pritchett (1948), the figures are based solely on cases that were not unanimous. As you would expect, parallel calculations that include unanimous cases display even less variation from the mean.

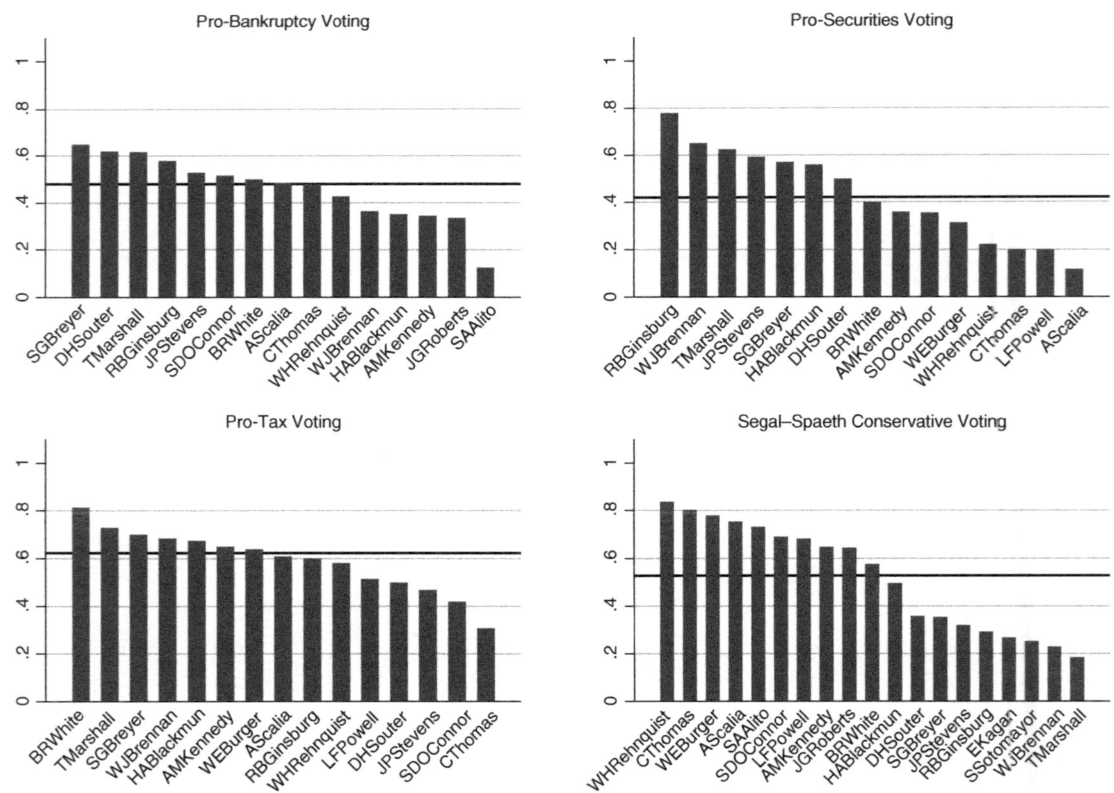

FIGURE 4.2 Voting in Non-Unanimous Cases, by Justice. Source: Supreme Court Database and author's calculations. Reference lines indicate mean likelihood of indicated vote among all Justices. Justices with fewer than six qualifying votes omitted.

the results of that analysis. At the individual vote level (as opposed to the decision level), the mean level of broad-bankruptcy votes is almost exactly 50% (as the reference line indicates). Even though many of the Justices participated in relatively few non-unanimous bankruptcy cases, the great majority of the Justices are clustered quite close to the mean, with few departing from the mean by more than 10%. None of the Justices are remarkably pro-bankruptcy; Justice Breyer tops the list with such votes in only 65% of the cases, followed closely by Justices Souter and Marshall (both at 62%). To the extent any Justice stands out with a marked predisposition, it is possible that Justice Alito is developing such a perspective, with pro-bankruptcy votes in only 13% (1/8) of the non-unanimous bankruptcy cases.

For comparative purposes, I also made similar calculations in securities and tax cases. If my thesis about the role of institutional support in leaving the Justices relatively agnostic about the Bankruptcy Power is correct, I would expect the strong presence of the Securities and Exchange Commission and the Internal Revenue Service to be reflected in stronger dispositions for (or against) broad interpretations of the securities (or tax) laws. The agency could be expected to present the best case for strong regulation, leading to a fuller exploration of the issues those cases raise. The second panel of Figure 4.2 lends some support to that hypothesis, as the pattern of votes in the securities cases is more disparate than it is in the bankruptcy cases. So, for example, three of the Justices vote in a "pro-securities" direction at a rate more than 20% above the mean; Justice Ginsburg's pro-securities perspective is remarkable (78%), with Justices Brennan (65%) and Marshall (63%) next in line. Similarly in the other direction, four of the Justices vote in a pro-securities direction at a rate more than 20% below the mean, led by Justice Scalia (12%), with Justices Powell (17%) and Thomas (18%) and Chief Justice Rehnquist (22%) close behind. The third panel of the figure summarizes parallel data for tax cases. Interestingly, they are not nearly so disparate as the securities votes. Still, the outliers are considerably farther afield from the mean (62%) than the bankruptcy outliers. Justice White stands out on the high side (81%), while several Justices seem to have staked out remarkably anti-tax perspectives, led by Justice Thomas (31%) and Justice O'Connor (42%).

To put those figures in context, the fourth panel of the figure illustrates the rate of conservative/liberal voting by the Justices in all their cases during the same time period. In that figure, only two Justices (White and Blackmun) are within ten percentage points of the mean. The outliers on that panel are far from the mean, resembling the outliers in securities voting much more than they do the outliers in the bankruptcy voting. On the high end, Chief Justice Rehnquist voted in a conservative direction in 85% of his cases and Justice

Thomas in 82%; on the low end, Justice Marshall voted in a conservative direction in only 18% of his cases, Justice Brennan in 23%.

Given the small number of observations, though, there is only so far the quantitative analysis can take us. As intriguing as those figures are, what they suggest is the need for a more detailed qualitative inquiry, to which the remainder of the book is devoted.

PART II

THE HARD CASES

We turn now to the heart of the project: studies of particular cases. Recognizing the arbitrariness of selecting any small group of cases, we have settled on nine cases to study in detail. As emphasized above, the principal factor driving our selection was the desire to identify a group of cases in which the Justices are relatively free of legal, institutional, and strategic constraints. On the first point, the close division of the Justices in their resolution of these cases provides an excellent proxy for the indeterminacy of the legal doctrine. It well may be that most of the cases that reach the Supreme Court are sufficiently close to bear an important element of indeterminacy, but those that are closely divided even at that level are paradigmatic examples of a lack of binding legal constraint. As for institutional and strategic constraints, the premise is that the focus on a topic of little policy salience to Congress or the Justices themselves resolves those issues adequately; the previous chapter pointed out that only one of the Court's eighty-two bankruptcy decisions ranks as "salient" by conventional criteria. In a policy backwater such as bankruptcy, the likelihood of institutional "pushback" from Congress or strategic repercussions among the Justices in later cases seems quite unlikely. No set of cases is perfect, but we believe that the case studies below provide an unparalleled laboratory for studying how the Justices resolve cases in which they have broad freedom to act.

Although we say much below about those decisions, we leave much unsaid. The question naturally arises of how we came to shape the narratives that we offer. For the most part, we have been guided by interest in the Court's framing and resolution of the issues before it: What the Justices take for granted, what the Justices regard as difficult to contest, and what the Justices regard as debatable. The resulting narrative emphasizes the process by which the Court sifts through the materials that come to it to formulate a ground for decision.

Although these cases typically come to the Court with some claim of a circuit conflict, it is apparent that the Justices have a free hand in identifying a suitable path of decision. It is always open to them to resolve a case by selecting a view not adopted by any of the lower courts or by answering a question that was not the basis of the decision under review. Those alternatives are not purely hypothetical. Rather, as the case studies below illustrate, the Justices retain considerable doubt about the path of decision deep into the process of crafting opinions. It is the identification of that path that the case studies attempt to illuminate, the process by which the Justices as a group abstract from the mass of possible legal rules and outcomes find a path of decision that suits the Court's interests. As those chapters show, the path is informed by not only the briefs and lower court decisions but also broader sources of information both internal to the process (such as the oral argument and amicus briefs) and external (the practical and expert knowledge of the Justices).

Section A – Missed Opportunities: Congress, the Court, and the Bankruptcy Clause

I start with a section about the breadth of Congress's enumerated power "To establish … uniform Laws on the subject of Bankruptcies throughout the United States." Although the case studies underscore the Court's hesitancy to give a broad reach to that power, the point is neither that the text of the Clause compels any particular answer to the cases that the Court has confronted nor that any historical practice provides strong guidance. Rather, I explore the extent to which the Court's cases involving the Code consider the *possibility* that the Court should give any weight to the framers' decision to provide an explicit enumeration of Congress's power in the area.[1]

Early cases had suggested that Congress had all but plenary power under the Clause.[2] So, for example, when the Panic of 1837[3] drove Congress (in the 1841 Act) to break sharply with tradition by introducing a discharge without the permission of creditors,[4] Justice Catron forcefully concluded that "all

1 For those interested in the history, I highly recommend Nadelmann (1957), who provides a detailed discussion of the debates related to the introduction and drafting of the Clause, as well as the contemporary litigation out of which the apparent need for the Clause arose.

2 Those who find the actions of the earliest Congresses instructive will find it notable that Congress put bankruptcy legislation near the top of its early priorities, considering bankruptcy bills in each of the first six Congresses, culminating with the Act of 1800. John Marshall himself was involved with the efforts to draft successful bankruptcy legislation (Haines 2003, 174–175, 186).

3 Combining a careful analysis of the files from cases under the Act with contemporaneous records about the filers, Balleisen (2001) offers a compelling narrative of the financial upheaval to which that Act responded.

4 The novelty of the 1841 Act is not easy to appreciate from the vantage point of the twenty-first century. To get a flavor of the sensibility of the time about the starkness of the changes, consider the strident discussion of the many differences between that act and all preceding acts in England or this country, offered by the district judge whose decision invalidating the statute was rejected by Justice Catron. Nelson v. Carland, 1 How. (42 U.S.) 265, 269-76 (1843) (Catron, J., dissenting (quoting the district court opinion in detail)).

intermediate legislation, affecting substance and form, but tending to further the great end of the subject – distribution and discharge – [is] in the competency and discretion of congress."[5] Similarly, two generations later, when the Court faced legislation that forced secured creditors to accept reorganizations that altered their rights in their collateral (then known as "compositions"), the Court had no trouble in concluding that congressional enactments in the area would pass constitutional muster. As Jim Rogers explains, the Court settled by the time of the Great Depression on the view that "the principal source of substantive limitations on bankruptcy legislation is the bankruptcy clause itself, and hence the constitutionality of a statute adopted under the bankruptcy clause depends only on whether the measure falls within the scope of the powers conferred by the bankruptcy clause"[6] (Rogers 1982, 998).

When it came to the Bankruptcy Code, however, the Court took a sharp and skeptical turn. The Court's critical perspective was evident from its first three encounters with the Code, in which it considered various aspects of the transition from the Act to the new Code. The first of the three was trivial enough – a "per curiam" opinion[7] holding that the enactment of the Code did not require the dismissal of cases then pending under the Act.[8] The next two decisions, however, retreated from the broad understandings of the Clause that had driven the Court's earlier activity in the area. One, the closely divided decision in *Marathon*, is the centerpiece of the next chapter. The other (*United States v. Security Industrial Bank*)[9] limited the application of one of the Code's exemption provisions to post-enactment transactions, avoiding a constitutional question that would have been insubstantial under the Court's earlier analysis of the Clause (Rogers 1982, 1013–1021).

To situate the Court's reaction to the Code in a broader perspective, the two chapters that follow discuss the Court's constitutional analysis in two distinct areas, both of which unfold in a series of closely divided cases. The first involves the question that has divided the Justices in *Marathon*

5 In re Klein, 1 How. (42 U.S.) 277 (C.C.D. Mo. 1843). The inclusion of the decision in the United States Reports, although it is a decision of the Circuit Court rather than the Supreme Court, suggests its contemporary importance. So far as I am aware, this is the only lower court decision to appear in the United States Reports since 1801.

6 Thomas Plank offers a much narrower reading of the Clause, but it rests not on the Court's early decisions nearly so much as on the argument that practice in Britain and the Colonies was quite narrow, coupled with the view that nothing in the Framing suggested any intention to broaden the contemporary practice (Plank 1995).

7 A "per curiam" opinion ordinarily is a brief opinion that the Court issues without full briefing or oral argument, typically because it believes that the matter at hand is so plain that careful deliberation is unnecessary.

8 Central Trust Co. v. Official Creditors' Committee, 454 U.S. 354 (1982).

9 459 U.S. 70 (1982).

and its progeny, whether Congress can give bankruptcy judges a broad and comprehensive adjudicatory authority even though they operate with neither the independence of life tenure nor juries. The second involves the question of whether Congress has the power to abrogate the sovereign immunity of States that become involved in bankruptcy proceedings because of claims that debtors hold against them.

In both areas, the Court's early cases invalidated the relevant parts of the Code. In more recent years, however, faced with repeated expression of Congress's intent to implement a comprehensive and effective system, the Court has acquiesced, albeit grudgingly, in Congress's exercise of its authority under the Clause. As those chapters emphasize, only rarely have the Justices (much less the Court) in their evaluation of the Code considered the possibility that the Bankruptcy Clause's place in Article I might distinguish the subject from more general congressional enactments. Rather, their evaluation of those problems has progressed almost entirely through the application of bodies of doctrine developed in other contexts under the pressure of policies of little or no relevance to any distinct problems of the bankruptcy system. If anything, their reluctant acceptance of Congress's broader perspective suggests that the Justices do not find the area sufficiently important to justify a sustained confrontation with Congress.

5

From *Marathon* to *Wellness*: Assessing the "Public[ity]" of the Bankruptcy Power

5.1 INTRODUCTION

The story begins with the enactment of the Code itself. Because the Code established a quasi-judicial bankruptcy process operated without jury trial by judges that were not appointed under Article III, the Code immediately presented the Court with a fundamental constitutional question – whether Congress had the power to establish that process. Starting from a clean slate, a variety of interpretive approaches would come readily to mind. For example, noting the prominence of the Bankruptcy Clause in Article I (Art. 1, § 8, cl. 4), the Court could have concluded that Congress's power to define the mode of proceedings for bankruptcy carried with it an implicit control (or at least a relatively free hand) over the question whether those proceedings would be "legal" (with Article III judges and jury trials) or "administrative" or "equitable" (without). For example, the Court has given Congress quite a free hand in defining the jurisdiction of military courts under Art. I, § 8, cl. 13, which grants the power "[t]o make rules for the government and regulation of the land and naval forces."[1] The Court has given a similarly capacious reading to the parallel phrase in the same Clause as the Bankruptcy Power, which grants uniform authority over naturalization.[2]

[1] Consider, for example, Solorio v. United States, 483 U.S. 435 (1987), which upheld Congress's power to bestow military jurisdiction on a crime committed by a member of the armed forces even though the crime had no connection with the defendant's military service. The cases discussed in this chapter, by contrast, deny Congress the authority to extend the bankruptcy process even to matters that are closely related to the bankruptcy.

[2] "Over no conceivable subject is the legislative power of Congress more complete than it is over the admission of aliens" (Kleindienst v. Mandel, 408 U.S. 753, 766 (1972)). Indeed, Justice Scalia takes the view that the courts lack any authority whatsoever to constrain the exercise of Congress's power over naturalization (Miller v. Albright, 523 U.S. 420, 452–60 (1998) (concurring opinion)).

Alternatively, the Court might have considered the practical need for expeditious and conclusive resolution of the financial affairs of bankrupts as an important factor in its analysis of the constitutional right to a jury trial and an Article III judge. Balancing the importance of making the bankruptcy laws effective and efficient against intrusions on other constitutional values, the Court could decide in a relatively flexible way whether any particular exercise of the Bankruptcy Power intrudes unduly on those other values.

Still another possibility would have been that the Court make an exclusively historical inquiry: analogizing twenty-first-century insolvency proceedings to the nearest eighteenth-century precursor and applying the jury status of the precursor to the modern insolvency proceeding. Although the last alternative seems as a doctrinal matter the least plausible, it comes closer to the Court's choice than any of the others. The overall theme of importance for my narrative is whether it is purely a coincidence that this is the choice that gives the least weight to the needs of the bankruptcy system.

To situate the choices of the Justices in context, the story proceeds in four parts: background on the role of jury trials and referees under the Act; the Court's initial confrontation with the Bankruptcy Code in *Marathon*, which limited Congress's power to define the terms of judicial appointments; the Court's decisions in *Granfinanciera* and *Stern*, which extended and consolidated the analysis of *Marathon*; and finally the more recent decisions in *Arkison* and *Wellness*, in which the Court largely bowed to the practicalities of the system and retreated from the disarray that a vigorous application of *Stern* would have exacerbated. The availability of internal papers from the Justices bolsters the discussion of *Marathon* and *Granfinanciera*; the absence of those materials for the later cases leaves me with only the public materials on which to base my account.

5.2 SETTING THE STAGE: FROM REFEREES AND SUMMARY JURISDICTION TO THE COMPREHENSIVE BANKRUPTCY VISION OF THE CODE

In this area as in the chapters that follow, Congress did not enact the Bankruptcy Code against a clean slate. On the contrary, Congress and the Bankruptcy Commission worked against the backdrop of a prominent and apparently definitive decision suggesting at least the likelihood of broad congressional power to design administrative proceedings unhampered by either a jury trial or the requirement of an Article III judge.

5.2.1 *Setting the Judicial Baseline: The Bankruptcy Act and* Katchen v. Landy

The relevant provisions of the Bankruptcy Act of 1898 establish the baseline from which the Commission and Congress worked.[3] Rejecting the precedent of considerably broader grants of power in the short-lived nineteenth century bankruptcy statutes, the first permanent statute, adopted in 1898, divided the Bankruptcy Power into two heads – a "summary" power to be exercised by the referee expeditiously without procedural or jurisdictional constraints; and a "plenary" power accompanied by the processes of conventional litigation (such as jury trials and Article III judges). The summary jurisdiction was for the most part exercised by administrative officers known as "referees," who were not Article III judges and did not conduct jury trials. The other big players under the Act were "trustees," who took control of the assets of the debtor and handled distributions from those assets to creditors.

Referees routinely resolved disputes about the disposition of property that was held by either the court itself or the bankruptcy trustee. Among other things, that involved evaluating and rejecting claims creditors made to the assets of the estate. The summary jurisdiction did not, however, extend to affirmative actions to recover property for the estate from third parties, even when brought by the trustee. Thus, proceedings involving property not held by the court or the trustee fell within the "plenary" jurisdiction, which (the Court early on held) only the district judge could exercise.

The Court's 1966 ruling in *Katchen v. Landy* brought the interplay between that framework and constitutional constraints into focus. *Katchen* involved a commonplace bankruptcy problem, a dispute between an officer of a bankrupt company (Katchen) and the company's trustee in bankruptcy (Landy). In that case, the officer (Katchen) had secondary liability on a series of notes that the company had issued before bankruptcy. Shortly before the company filed for bankruptcy, Katchen used funds from the company's trust account to pay down the notes. Predictably enough, after the bankruptcy filing Katchen was forced to make payments on the guaranteed notes from his own funds.

The dispute involves the offsetting claims of Katchen and the trustee Landy. For his part, Katchen made two claims against the company's estate in bankruptcy: one for rent the bankrupt company owed to him, and one for reimbursement for the payments he had made on the guaranteed notes from

3 The discussion that follows draws heavily on the lucid descriptions of Skeel (2003) and Brubaker (2012).

his own funds.[4] Landy, in turn, filed a "preference" action in the bankruptcy proceeding,[5] seeking to force Katchen to return to the estate the funds that he had taken from the company's trust account. The district court and the court of appeals held that Landy could force Katchen to return the money.

The case reached the Supreme Court on a surprisingly simple question: whether the referee could adjudicate the action against Katchen in the first instance. Katchen argued that the Seventh Amendment guaranteed him a right to a jury trial. If he was correct, because the referee was not an Article III judge that could conduct a jury trial, the referee would have had no authority to consider the complaint against him. Like the lower courts, the Justices rejected that claim. Justice White wrote for a 7-2 majority, with only Justices Black and Douglas dissenting.

What is most important about the case is not the Court's strong majority for centralizing these disputes in the bankruptcy court. Rather, it is Justice White's concerted emphasis on the relevance to that question of ensuring a functional bankruptcy process. His opinion is redolent with the sentiments established during his time in the Justice Department that he had left only four years earlier. Indeed, the opinion is an example of the skepticism characteristic of his entire career, dubious that vaguely worded constitutional provisions should stand in the way of efficient government (Hutchinson 1998). In this case, that skepticism produced an opinion that hammers again and again on the theme of the importance of facilitating an effective bankruptcy system. For example, he emphasized Congress's desire that the Bankruptcy Act would lead to relatively inexpensive administration of the estates of bankrupt firms:

> It is equally clear that the expressly granted power to allow, disallow, and reconsider claims, which is of basic importance in the administration of a bankruptcy estate, is to be exercised in summary proceedings and not by the slower and more expensive processes of a plenary suit. ... This is essential to the performance of the duties imposed upon it. ... The whole process of proof, allowance, and distribution is, shortly speaking, an adjudication of interests in a res, and thus falls within the principle ... that bankruptcy courts have summary jurisdiction to adjudicate controversies relating to property

4 Longstanding principles of commercial law allow a guarantor to recover from the original borrower payments that the guarantor makes on obligations of the borrower; in legal terms, the guarantor has a right to "reimbursement" from the borrower (American Law Institute (Suretyship) 1996, § 22).

5 A "preference" is a payment that improperly favors ("prefers") one creditor to another. The trustee under the Act (as under the Code) often could recover those payments for the benefit of creditors in general.

> within their possession. (382 U.S. at 329–330 (citations and quotation marks omitted)).

To be sure, Justice White also contended that the result was consistent with the language of the Bankruptcy Act. Thus, after emphasizing the importance of giving a broad reach to the referee's summary jurisdiction, he pointed out that there "is no contrary indication" elsewhere in the Act and that "[i]f anything, the other provisions of the Act support the view that [these kinds of] objections are to be summarily determined."

That discussion is noteworthy for this project, not because it is unusual for Justices to write with such verve, but rather because it will appear rarely, if ever, in the opinions discussed in the case studies that follow. To reiterate: Justice White's approach to the Act in *Katchen* started from the principle that it is important to give a broad reach to the Bankruptcy Power, read the Act through the lens of that principle, and thus justified a conclusion that validated the authority of the referee.[6] No Justice offered a word of disagreement with the analytical frame; Justices Black and Douglas stated only that they disagreed "for the reasons stated in the dissenting opinion" in the court of appeals.[7]

5.2.2 *Congress's Move*

As previously discussed in Chapter 3, Congress soon turned to a full-scale revision of the bankruptcy laws, the effort that eventually would lead to the Bankruptcy Code. The Commission's recommendation that Congress replace the often-biased referees with an administrative agency and a group of specialist federal bankruptcy judges quickly became the focal point of Congressional deliberation. Specifically, the Commission contemplated that the jurisdiction of those courts would extend both to controversies arising out of proceedings under the Code and also to controversies between a trustee in bankruptcy and any third party (Commission on the Bankruptcy Laws of the United States 1973, I, 7).

6 Ray Warner (1989) provides a comprehensive analysis of *Katchen* as a matter of constitutional interpretation, situating it against the Seventh Amendment cases that preceded and followed it.

7 Judges Phillips, Lewis, and Breitenstein dissented from the en banc opinion of the Tenth Circuit affirmed in *Katchen*. The majority opinion by Judge Phillips argued that because the claim of the creditor was "legal," rather than "equitable," he was entitled to a jury trial under the Seventh Amendment (Katchen v. Landy, 336 F.2d 535, 540–43 (10th Cir. 1964)). The dissent criticized as unfair the advantages the trustee would reap from proceeding in the bankruptcy forum without the need for a jury trial.

In its discussion of the jurisdictional reforms, the Commission emphasized the problem at issue in *Katchen*, viewing "the most important objection to the present dispensation [as] the division of labor between the bankruptcy court and other courts" (Commission on the Bankruptcy Laws of the United States 1973, I, 88). The Commission detailed the practical problems associated with that division: delay (because ordinary court processes proceed in a much more leisurely fashion than bankruptcy courts), expense (because ordinary court processes are much more laborious than the expedited proceedings typical of bankruptcy courts), and the immense efforts historically wasted on litigation about jurisdiction (with *Katchen* providing a salient example). The Commission justified the broad grant of jurisdiction by direct reference to the Bankruptcy Clause, and saw no reason to expect the Court to be any less receptive to this arrangement than it had been to previous congressional legislation in the area (Commission on the Bankruptcy Laws of the United States 1973, I, 87–92).

When Congress turned to the task of implementing the Commission's proposal, it was accepted as a given that it would create a new set of bankruptcy judges to handle the adjudicative functions previously handled by referees. The only question was whether it would give those judges Article III status (which carries with it a constitutional guarantee of life tenure and protection against diminution in salary). The first drafts of what would become the Bankruptcy Code did not give the judges Article III status (H.R. 10792 & S. 4026, 93rd Cong.). But when critics argued that the Constitution might require Article III status, subsequent drafts were amended – not to limit the power of the judges, but simply to give them Article III status (H.R. 6, 95th Cong. See Trugman 1984; Klee 1980). Appalled at the notion that the prompt addition of 200 new Article III judges would dilute their power, the Judicial Conference responded with what fairly might be described as horror. Although one obvious tack was to promulgate a resolution opposing the bill, a second approach, more accommodating to the commitment of Congress to the enterprise of bankruptcy reform, was to argue that the Constitution would permit Congress to enact the bill without giving the judges Article III status.

After considerable deliberation on the question, Congress ultimately decided to adopt the Commission's separate bankruptcy court, but not to give the judges Article III status. The outcome was hardly foreordained. The House Report considered the problem in remarkable detail, emphasizing the same issues that motivated the Commission; the House Report's own discussion of the topic ran to more than forty printed pages (1977, 9–52), with an additional twenty-five pages of letters from the nation's most distinguished constitutional scholars offering advice on the constitutionality of the various alternatives available to Congress (1977, 63–87). Agreeing that the disputes raised by bankruptcy required judicial attention, Congress dismissed out of hand the idea that the massive caseload in question could be assigned to existing district judges. Taking account of the gravity of the judge's responsibility and the constitutional doubts about lesser status, the House Report strongly recommended Article III status. When the bill (H.R. 8200, 95th Cong.) came up for debate, however, an amendment on the floor removed the Article III status by a narrow vote (Klee 1980). Of importance to our topic, the representatives supporting the amendment apparently acted with advice from the Judicial Conference; they supported their argument with, among other things, a letter from then-Chief Justice Burger, indicating that there was no constitutional need for Article III status.

When the Senate took up consideration of the topic (S. 2266, 95th Cong.), it received testimony from representatives of the Judicial Conference (sitting Article III judges) urging the view that the Constitution did not require Article III status for the bankruptcy judges that the Commission contemplated. Concerned about the constitutional problems, and influenced by continued vociferous lobbying from the Chief Justice, the Senate, like the House, enacted legislation that did not grant the judges Article III status. In the end, then, the Code as adopted grants the broad jurisdiction recommended by the Commission, but withholds Article III status from the judges who exercise it (Countryman 1985).

5.3 A JAUNDICED VIEW OF BANKRUPTCY: *MARATHON*

When Northern Pipeline Construction Co. became one of the first companies to take advantage of the new provisions of Chapter 11 of the Code, nobody would have expected anything noteworthy to come out of the bankruptcy. Founded in 1967 in Northern Minnesota, the company grew by the late 1970s into a major builder of natural gas distribution networks.[8] At the time of the bankruptcy, Northern Pipeline was involved in a contract dispute with Marathon Pipeline, which had led to litigation in a federal district court in Kentucky. When Northern Pipeline's bankruptcy filing stayed the Kentucky litigation, Northern promptly filed an adversary proceeding against Marathon in the bankruptcy court (all as set forth in the new Code). Predictably enough, Marathon challenged the jurisdiction of the bankruptcy

[8] The web site of the firm's successor NPL, now based in Arizona, provides the historical information. http://www.gonpl.com/01_whoWeAre/history.asp.

court. The bankruptcy judge rejected that argument, but the district court accepted it, holding the Code's jurisdictional provisions unconstitutional.[9]

At the time, numerous cases were considering the constitutional question. Purely by happenstance, the *Marathon* matter was the first case that squarely presented the question to the Justices. Because the district court had held the jurisdictional provisions of the Code unconstitutional, and because the Supreme Court had not previously held any Act of Congress unconstitutional for vesting adjudicatory authority in an Article I Court, it was no surprise that the Court agreed to plenary review.[10]

The limited role that the specific grant of authority under the Bankruptcy Clause played in the Court's deliberations on the question whether to review the case is notable.[11] The earliest analysis of the case in the files is the "pool" memo, prepared by a law clerk for one of the Justices to be used by a group of Justices who pooled resources for the purpose of determining whether the Court should hear the case. In this case, for example, the pool memo was written by a law clerk for Justice Blackmun; it was then circulated to all of the Justices in the pool, who read that memo in connection with the decision whether to review the particular case. The pool memos are particularly valuable here, because they can be treated as displaying a relatively pure doctrinal analysis, as unaffected by policy predispositions as any of the materials in the Justices' files.

What is important about the pool memo in this case is what it doesn't say – it situates the dispute entirely within the existing cases about Congress's power to establish tribunals under Article I. It does not even mention the Bankruptcy Clause (NPMT002, 047). Similarly, the "bench" memorandum prepared for Justice Blackmun by his clerk[12] does not mention the Bankruptcy Clause (NPMT048). Justice Powell's private notes from the meeting at which the Justices collectively considered whether to review the case (usually referred to as the "Conference") do not suggest any substantial discussion and indicate

9 Brief for Appellant, Northern Pipeline Construction Co. v. Marathon Pipeline Co., Nos. 81–150, 81–546, at 3–4; Brief for Appellee, Northern Pipeline Construction Co. v. Marathon Pipeline Co., Nos. 81–150, 81–546, at 2–3.

10 At that time, Title 28 provided for direct appeals of district court decisions in such cases.

11 In this particular instance, though not in any of the later case studies, a previous scholar (Mund 2004) has examined the papers. My emphasis is quite different, as her study centered on the strange role that Chief Justice Burger played, first in urging Congress not to grant Article III status and then in trying (without success) to convince his colleagues to find that arrangement valid.

12 Ordinarily, one of the clerks in each of the Justices' chambers prepares a "bench" memorandum for the Justice to summarize the issues for the Justice as an aid in preparing for the argument (which is when the Justices go on the "bench").

that all nine Justices agreed that the case warranted full briefing and argument (NPMT003, 004).

When the case came to the Court, the attorneys before the Court did not ignore the idea that the Bankruptcy Clause gave Congress broader power in this area. Indeed, Justice Powell's argument notes indicate that he was particularly impressed with the argument of Rex Lee (the Solicitor General), arguing in support of the statute, that "bankruptcy *requires* judicial action," that "Art[icle] I Sec[tion] 8 is one of [the] few Art[icle] I provisions requiring this," and that "bankruptcy *always* has been treated separately and apart from the judicial system generally" (NPMT005, Justice Powell's emphasis). The transcript documents Lee emphasizing that the Code was "Congress' most comprehensive effort in this century ... to deal with bankruptcies" (NPMT115:3). Responding to the concern that Lee's argument had no limiting principle, Lee pointed the Justices to the text of Article I, Section 8, noting that none of the other clauses "is linked quite so directly to the resolution of private disputes as ... bankruptcy" (NPMT115:11).

But the discussion at the oral argument was the high-water mark of that topic. The emphasis on the Bankruptcy Clause had little weight among the Justices when they met to consider the case at the Conference.[13] Most of the Justices appear to have focused on how closely the case resembled *Palmore* (an earlier case about Congress's power to establish courts for the District of Columbia).[14] Justices Brennan and Stevens in particular emphasized the idea that Congress's authority over territories is a special and limited exception to Article III (NPMT006, 045). As far as the record indicates (from the notes of Justice Powell and Justice Blackmun), only Justices White and Powell attributed any similar significance to the Bankruptcy Power. Justice Powell was the lone voice emphasizing that Article I "expressly authorizes Congress to enact bankruptcy laws" (NPMT006); he also pressed the view that "[w]e have long since departed from the notion that only Article III courts can decide important issues." For his part, Justice White, as you would expect from his writings in *Katchen*, suggested that bankruptcy was a "strange world"

[13] Ordinarily, the Justices meet in Conference within a few days after the oral argument to reach a tentative decision on the case (as they will have met earlier when they decided to review the case). No clerks or other outsiders are present. All of the Justices state their views of the case. After the Conference, the most senior Justice in the majority (usually the Chief Justice) assigns the opinion to one of the Justices who voted for the outcome favored by a majority of the Justices. The vote at the Conference is not the actual decision; the actual decision occurs (and is announced) when all the Justices have agreed to opinions justifying the result.

[14] Palmore v. United States, 411 U.S. 389 (1973).

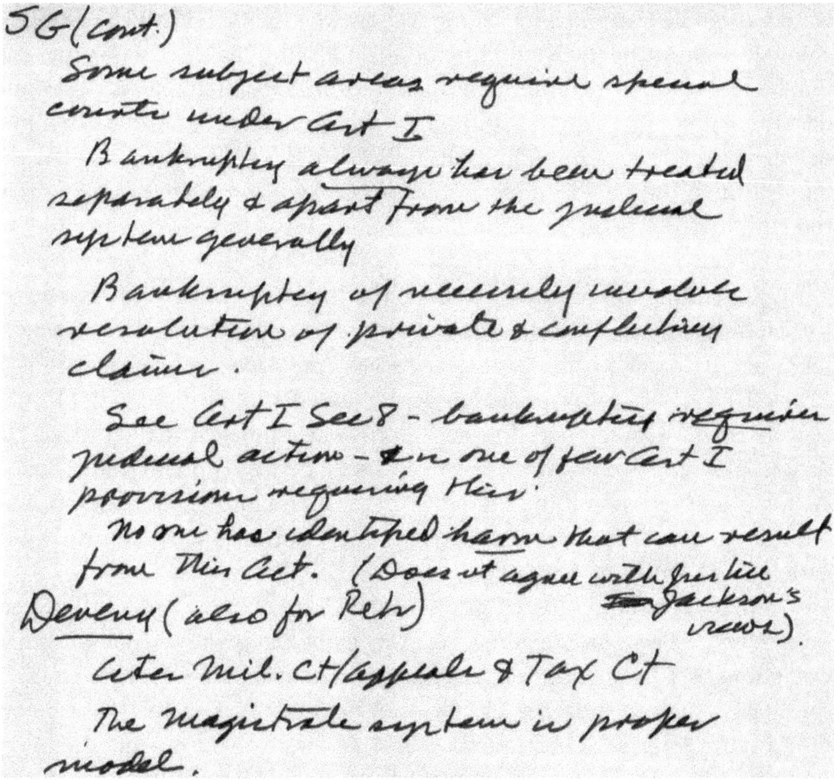
SG (cont.)
Some subject areas require special
courts under Art I
Bankruptcy always has been treated
separately & apart from the judicial
system generally
Bankruptcy of necessity involves
resolution of private & conflicting
claims.
See Art I Sec 8 – bankruptcy requires
judicial action – is one of few Art I
provisions requiring this.
No one has identified harm that can result
from this Act. (Does not agree with Justice
Jackson's views).
Deveny (also for Resp)
Cites Mil. Ct/appeals & Tax Ct
The magistrate system is proper
model.

FIGURE 5.1 Justice Powell's Argument Notes from *Northern Pipeline v. Marathon* (excerpt). NPMT005. Justice Powell's notes read as follows: "SG (cont). Some subject areas require special courts under Art[icle] I. Bankruptcy *always* has been treated separately & apart from the judicial system generally. Bankruptcy of necessity involves resolution of private & conflicting claims. See Art. I Sec. 8 – bankruptcy *requires* judicial action – is one of few Art I provisions requiring this. No one has identified *harm* that can result from this Act. (Does not agree with Justice Jackson's views). Deveny (also for Resp). Cites Mil. Ct [of] Appeals & Tax Ct. The magistrate system is proper model."

that "needed special" rules, rather than the "barren" public rights approach Justice Brennan articulated (NPMT045).

Justice Powell's notes from the Conference indicate five clear votes to hold the Code unconstitutional – Justices Brennan, Marshall, Blackmun, Stevens, and O'Connor (NPMT006). The majority grew to six on the following Monday, when Justice Rehnquist circulated a note indicating that he also would vote in that direction (NPMT008, 063, 085). At the same time, because Chief Justice Burger had not expressed a view on the case, it was not clear who would assign it. The following Monday, however, the Chief Justice circulated a note indicating that he would support the constitutionality of the statute and that he had asked Justice Brennan (the senior Justice in the majority to invalidate the statute) to assign the opinion (NPMT007, 064, 084). Justice Brennan decided to draft the opinion himself (NPMT065, 083). The following day the Chief Justice[15] assigned the dissent to Justice White (who had spoken most forcefully at the Conference about the importance of the bankruptcy process) (NPMT009, 086).

In the drafting of opinions, however, the Justices became more fractured. Justice Brennan undertook to use the case as a vehicle for a broad expression of his concerns about the ability of Congress to limit access to the protections of Article III.[16] That view resonated in particular with the strong views of Justice Stevens at the Conference; Justice Stevens had opined that the purpose of Article III would "go down the drain" if the Code were upheld (NPMT006). Echoing that sentiment, the opinion Justice Brennan circulated began with a lengthy paean to the importance of an independent Judiciary, enshrined in Article III (NPMT044, 089, 116).[17]

Turning to the Bankruptcy Code – which did not bestow Article III protections – Justice Brennan categorized existing cases that permitted congressional exceptions as falling into three categories: territorial courts for areas outside the States (such as the District of Columbia and areas in the West before they became States), courts-martial, and cases involving so-called "public rights," a category based on the 1856 decision in *Murray's Lessee v. Hoboken Land & Improvement Co.*[18] By using those categories, Justice Brennan submerged entirely the congressional grant of authority over bankruptcy. Moreover, because bankruptcy plainly did not involve territorial courts or

[15] By convention, the senior Justice in the minority assigns the writing of the dissent, just as the senior Justice in the majority assigns the writing of the opinion for the majority. In this case, because the Chief Justice was in the minority, and because the Chief Justice is for this purpose always senior to all of the other Justices, Chief Justice Burger was expected to assign the dissent.

[16] Charles Tabb provides a useful and considerably more detailed summary of Justice Brennan's opinion. Tabb 1987, 489–491.

[17] I do not doubt Justice Brennan's sincerity. To an outsider, though, it would be easy to believe that the perceived advantages of independence are closely related to the prestige associated with the federal judiciary. It does not require a great deal of cynicism to think that Justice Brennan's assessment of that question was just as influenced by the dilution of that prestige as Chief Justice Burger's opposition to a statute granting Article III status to the bankruptcy judges. Mund (2004) provides a detailed study of Chief Justice Burger's activity furthering his view during Congress's deliberations about the enactment of the Code and the Court's deliberations about *Marathon*.

[18] 18 How. 272 (1856).

courts-martial, he left the Code to stand or fall on a technical question of the vague boundaries of the archaic "public rights" doctrine. Justice Brennan's next step was to relate that category to the traditional principle of sovereign immunity, a move that limited "public rights" to disputes to which the government is a party. Because the Government was not a party to the adversary proceedings at issue in *Marathon* (a contract dispute between a debtor and a creditor), Justice Brennan concluded that the public rights doctrine could not apply.

Justice Brennan also firmly rejected the idea that the bankruptcy courts could be justified as an "adjunct" to the district courts, which did have Article III protections (NPMT044:24-33). Justice Brennan rejected that argument because the case involved rights that Congress had not itself created. It was one thing for the Court (as it previously had done) to tolerate Congress's creation of rights that would be adjudicated in the first instance by agencies that did not possess Article III protections; Justice Brennan thought it quite different to extend that rule to common-law claims and the like, rights that Congress had not created (NPMT044:28–29). The Court had approved the use of magistrates in an earlier case, but Justice Brennan concluded that adjuncts were permissible only when "the district court judge alone acts as the ultimate decisionmaker" (NPMT044:29). Accordingly, Justice Brennan reasoned, the jurisdictional provisions of the Code were unconstitutional.

Justices Stevens (NPMT013, 041, 068, 090, 120) and Marshall (NPMT038, 092, 125) promptly joined Justice Brennan's opinion, apparently without requesting any changes. Justice Brennan responded by circulating a second draft (NPMT040, 091, 117) with only two changes of any substance. The first added a somewhat hyperbolic claim that affirmance of the Code would "threate[n] to completely supplant our system of adjudication in independent Art. III tribunals with a system of 'specialized' legislative courts" (NPMT040:22). The second (perhaps hoping to attract Justice Blackmun's inexplicably delayed agreement) added a footnote with a detailed approving reference to a concurring opinion Justice Blackmun had written in a 1980 case called *Raddatz*.[19]

At that point, Justice White circulated a draft for his dissent. In that draft (NPMT039, 060, 109, 129), he vociferously rejected the "pigeonhol[ing]" of prior precedents apparent in Justice Brennan's opinion (NPMT039:2). As Justice White saw it, "[w]hether fortunate or unfortunate, at this point in the

[19] United States v. Raddatz, 447 U.S. 667 (1980). The offhand introduction of the reference is notable because, as we will see by the end of the chapter, *Raddatz* will turn out to be quite important in later decisions in the area.

history of constitutional law that question can no longer be answered by looking only to the constitutional text" of Article III (NPMT039:2). Analytically, Justice White's disagreement with Justice Brennan started from his categorization of prior cases, which in Justice White's view (sharply favorable to congressional discretion) grossly misread the earlier cases. He was most powerful in his criticism of Justice Brennan's determination that the existing exceptions from Article III constraints were limited to "exceptional" constitutional powers, where Congress's authority was "plenary." Why, Justice White asked, were the congressional powers over the military and the District of Columbia and other territories any more "exceptional" or "plenary" than congressional powers over other matters (such as bankruptcy)? (NPMT039:11–13).

Ultimately, Justice White concluded, after reviewing the blizzard of previous cases approving congressional discretion, there "is no difference in principle between the work that Congress may assign to an Art. I court and that which the Constitution assigns to Art. III courts" (NPMT039:21). In his view, the proper role of the Court was to treat the Article III mandate as "one value that must be balanced against competing constitutional values" (NPMT039:22), including congressional authority under Article I. Under that test, he found the Bankruptcy Code clearly constitutional, offering three distinct reasons: appellate review by Article III courts, no risk of aggrandizement of the political branches (given the limited political significance of bankruptcy matters), and the practical needs of Congress to modernize the bankruptcy system.

Of relevance to my general thesis, his explanation of congressional necessity did not mention the Bankruptcy Power a single time. His outrage related to congressional expertise in general, not anything particular to bankruptcy. Thus, notwithstanding Justice Powell's references to the Bankruptcy Power at Conference, the Bankruptcy Clause had no place in Justice White's discussion. Rather, he presented arguments that justified congressional power under Article I in general. So, for example, his principal argument was that Congress constitutionally can assign the adjudication of questions of federal law to Article I courts. Because all determinations about the obligations to and by debtors, and among their creditors, are part of the "restructuring of debtor-creditor relations . . . at the core of the federal bankruptcy power," they all should be regarded as matters of federal law, whether state or federal law provided the rule of decision (NPMT039:3-4). Like his opinion in *Katchen* (on which he relied in part), his opinion emphasized the unitary nature of the process and the long historical tradition of bankruptcy process extending to these kinds of disputes (NPMT039:4–8). I can only speculate whether an opinion by Justice Powell would have emphasized the textual argument from the Bankruptcy Clause more strongly.[20]

When Justices Powell (NPMT015, 035, 075, 094, 128) and the Chief Justice (NPMT014, 037, 093, 126, 127) promptly joined Justice White's dissent, the vote count had reached 3–3.[21] But when Justice Brennan circulated a third draft without substantial revisions (NPMT036, 059, 095, 118), Justice Blackmun joined (NPMT016, 034, 074, 096, 138). At that point, the central question was whether Justice Brennan could retain the fifth and sixth votes against the Code from the Conference (Justices Rehnquist and O'Connor).

But that was not to be. Just a few days later, Justice Rehnquist circulated his opinion (NPMT018, 062, 098, 122, 139). Unsure of his vote at the Conference, he eventually settled on affirmance, finding the Code unconstitutional. He did not, however, accept Justice Brennan's reasoning, but rather concurred only in the judgment (so that Justice Brennan's opinion did not gain a majority). Specifically, Justice Rehnquist declined to address the "pigeonholing" framework that organized Justice Brennan's opinion. In his memorable phrase, he explained that he saw no reason to decide whether the Court's earlier "cases in fact support a general proposition and three tidy exceptions, as the plurality believes, or whether instead they are but landmarks on a judicial 'darkling plain' where ignorant armies have clashed by night, as Justice White apparently believes them to be" (NPMT018:3).

Justice Rehnquist rested his vote directly on the nature of the particular dispute at issue – a dispute involving damages for breach of contract that was "the stuff of the traditional actions at common law tried by the courts at Westminster in 1789 [and] aris[ing] entirely under state law" (NPMT018:2). Because resolution of such disputes was, in his judgment, the core business of Article III courts, it was impermissible for Congress to assign that type of dispute to an Article I court. Two days later, Justice O'Connor sent a note indicating that she expected to join the concurrence, "[w]ith the few changes we have discussed" (NPMT101). The second draft that Justice Rehnquist circulated the next day (NPMT021, 103) included several revisions emphasizing the impropriety of reaching out to decide a broader question when a narrow ground of decision was available. That opinion produced a final brief opinion from

[20] The files reveal less than they usually do about the views of Justice Powell. In particular, the *Marathon* file includes neither a bench memorandum nor a memorandum stating his personal views (which he often dictated before he received a bench memorandum from his clerk). When he reviewed Justice White's draft dissent, he noted a single typographical error and wrote on the top of the first page a simple note "Reviewed; Join; A strong opinion."

[21] The file includes a detailed tally sheet (NPMT017) on which Justice Powell noted, apparently in his own handwriting, the date of each Justice's action with respect to the various drafts circulating.

Chief Justice Burger, who wrote separately to emphasize that the holding of the Court was the narrower analysis of Justice Rehnquist's opinion, not the broader analysis of Justice Brennan's plurality (NPMT031, 061, 102, 108).

The salient point is that Justice Rehnquist's opinion, like those of Justices Brennan and White, treated Article I as a unitary authorization of congressional power, devoid of any consideration of Congress's authority over bankruptcy. Justice Powell's concerns, apparently voiced at the Conference, did not make it into the opinions rapidly prepared at the end of the Term.[22]

5.4 RETRENCHMENT EXTENDED FROM ARTICLE III TO THE 7TH AMENDMENT: *GRANFINANCIERA*

In response to *Marathon*, Congress amended the Code to confine the authority of bankruptcy judges even more narrowly, broadening their subordination to the district courts. All seemed to assume that this resolved the Article III problem addressed in *Marathon*, but the Court soon enough faced an apparently unrelated case, considering the right to a jury trial in bankruptcy proceedings, *Granfinanciera, S.A. v. Nordberg*. Against the backdrop of *Katchen*, this should have been an easy case. *Granfinanciera* arose from the 1983 bankruptcy of Chase & Sanborn Corporation, a long-lived coffee wholesaler that apparently invented the practice of packaging coffee in tin cans. After more than a hundred years of profitable operations, the firm's financial structure was largely destroyed in just a few years by the criminally fraudulent behavior of a Colombian national named Alberto Duque Rodriguez, who destabilized the company through a series of fraudulent loan transactions in the early 1980s.[23]

In the bankruptcy court, the trustee (respondent Nordberg) sought to recover almost $2 million dollars in allegedly fraudulent conveyances from two Colombian entities, one of which had been nationalized by the Colombian Government while the case was in the bankruptcy court. Rejecting the defendants' requests for a jury trial, the bankruptcy court ruled that the payments in fact were fraudulent and entered judgment in favor of the bankrupt's

[22] The Court starts a "Term" each year on the first Monday in October. In recent decades, it has heard oral arguments twice each week from October through April (seven months). With rare exceptions, it concludes the Term by the first week of July, announcing by that date decisions in all of the cases argued that Term. The desire to issue opinions by the end of the Term often leaves less time for deliberations on cases argued late in the Term (like *Marathon*, argued in April) than on those argued early in the Term. October Term 1981, during which the Court decided *Marathon*, was Justice O'Connor's first Term on the Court.

[23] Nordberg v. Arab Banking Corp. (*In re* Chase & Sanborn Corp.), 904 F.2d 588 (11th Cir. 1990).

estate. After the Eleventh Circuit affirmed, the Supreme Court granted review to determine whether the Seventh Amendment required a jury trial for the fraudulent conveyance claims. The Supreme Court reversed, holding 6–3 that the Seventh Amendment required a jury trial. The Court distinguished *Katchen* as applying only when the defendants themselves submitted claims in the bankruptcy process.[24]

5.4.1 *The Doctrinal Terrain*

The doctrinal holding in *Granfinanciera* is far less important than the path the Court took to reach it and the considerations that motivated the Justices. What is most obvious is that the central concern of *Katchen* – the importance of designing a sensible and effective bankruptcy system – is nowhere to be found. On the contrary, the Justices for the most part aligned themselves based on their views about the proper method of analyzing the Seventh Amendment, preconceived views they brought to the field of this dispute from prior cases in which they had debated them.

In a series of prior cases under the Seventh Amendment, the Court's jurisprudence for assessing what types of issues Congress could assign to administrative tribunals that would not provide a jury trial (a Seventh Amendment question) steadily converged with the Article III "public rights" doctrine (the focal point of the *Marathon* plurality). The first of the major cases in the Seventh Amendment line was the 1977 decision in *Atlas Roofing*, decided five years before *Marathon*.[25] In an opinion by Justice White, a unanimous Court approved Congress's delegation of challenges to OSHA enforcement orders to an administrative law judge inside the Occupational Safety and Health Review Commission – a venue that did not offer a jury trial. Although the proceedings included actions to collect penalties, Justice White rejected the analogy to a suit for a money judgment, the classic proceeding at the core of the right to a jury trial in civil cases. He explained that Congress was free to use non-jury procedures, "[a]t least in cases in which 'public rights' are being litigated e.g., cases in which the Government sues in its sovereign capacity to enforce public rights created by statutes within the power of Congress to

24 Firm pronouncements in hindsight are necessarily imprecise, but it seems likely that informed contemporary observers regarded this as a substantial truncation of *Katchen*'s reach. Ray Warner, for example, concluded shortly before *Granfinanciera* that *Katchen* validated affirmative claims by the trustee because the bankruptcy forum was, for Seventh Amendment purposes, entirely equitable (Warner 1989, 35–42 (characterizing *Katchen* as establishing a "niche" in Seventh Amendment jurisprudence that protected the "specialized court of equity")).

25 Atlas Roofing Co. v. Occupational Safety & Health Comm'n, 430 U.S. 442 (1977).

enact."[26] It was that somewhat tautologous reference to public rights in the Seventh Amendment context on which Justice Brennan relied in part for his opinion in *Marathon* that public rights included *only* government actions.

The second case was *Union Carbide*.[27] That case, which divided the Justices more closely, involved procedures under FIFRA.[28] Among other things, FIFRA required manufacturers to submit research data to the EPA about the environmental effects of pesticides. Because often many manufacturers would submit applications related to the same chemicals, it was convenient for later filers to rely on data earlier filers already had submitted. FIFRA permitted this, but required the later filers to compensate the earlier filers for the costs of generating the required data. After several years of extensive litigation among manufacturers and the EPA about the value of data shared under that provision, Congress modified FIFRA to provide that, in the absence of agreement among the submitters and users, the value of the data would be determined by binding arbitration. In part because the arbitration involved disputes among private parties without direct involvement by the Government, the lower courts held that the provision could not be reconciled with *Marathon*.

Writing for a majority of five, Justice O'Connor rejected that view and found the FIFRA arbitration scheme permissible under Article III. She offered a much more flexible perspective than the rigid rule Justice Brennan had articulated in *Marathon*. She explained that "practical attention to substance rather than doctrinaire reliance on formal categories should inform application of Article III," and rejected the idea that "the identity of the parties alone determined the requirements of Article III" (483 U.S. at 587). She recast the public rights doctrine as little more than a proxy for concerns about encroachment on the judicial powers, explaining that it was "simply a pragmatic understanding that when Congress selects a quasi-judicial method of resolving matters that could be conclusively determined by the Executive and Legislatives branches, the danger of encroaching on the judicial powers is reduced" (483 U.S. at 589). Looking to the practicalities of FIFRA, it was enough for her that "[r]emoving the task of valuation from agency personnel to civilian arbitrators ... surely does not diminish the likelihood of impartial decisionmaking, free from political influence." Although the same could have been said about the aspects of the Code condemned in *Marathon*, she offered

26 430 U.S. at 450 (odd punctuation as in original).

27 Thomas v. Union Carbide Agricultural Products Co., 473 U.S. 568 (1985).

28 The Federal Insecticide, Fungicide, and Rodenticide Act.

the plurality opinion in *Marathon* as support for that analysis (483 U.S. at 590).

None of the Justices who had joined the *Marathon* plurality accepted that explanation. Justice Brennan (joined by Justices Marshall and Blackmun) wrote separately to concur in the judgment.[29] For that group, the sole question was whether *Union Carbide* involved a public right. Emphasizing that the dispute at issue in *Marathon* was wholly private, Justice Brennan reasoned that the dispute in *Union Carbide*, albeit among private parties, involved a public right because it "arises in the context of a federal regulatory scheme that virtually occupies the field." In his view, "[t]his case … involves not only the congressional prescription of a federal rule of decision to govern a private dispute but also the active participation of a federal regulatory agency in resolving the dispute." Because the case "involves the exercise of authority by a federal government arbitrator in the course of administration of FIFRA's comprehensive regulatory scheme, … it partakes of the characteristics of a standard agency adjudication" (483 U.S. at 600–601).

5.4.2 *Deliberations over* Granfinanciera

The simplest way to see the legal issues at stake in *Granfinanciera* is to start from the views of the law clerks. The pool memo (from Justice Scalia's clerk) perceives the case as raising an archetypical conflict between two constitutional provisions: the Bankruptcy Clause in Article I, Section 8, and the jury trial right in the Seventh Amendment. He characterizes the court of appeals opinion as relying on "the proposition that Congress's bankruptcy power includes the power to convert what were historically legal actions into equitable actions by bringing them within the core of bankruptcy proceedings" (GRAN001:7). He then goes on to say that this "sounds somewhat strange since the 7th amend[ment] was ratified after Article I and since this would seem to be the very evil the 7th amend[ment] was designed to guard against" (GRAN001:7). He notes language in *Katchen* that would support that result, and suggests the conflict is thus significant, but recommends that the Court wait for further development of the issue in the courts of appeals. The clerk annotating the memorandum in Justice's Blackmun's chambers was similarly ambivalent, suggesting that Justice Blackmun might wish to call for the views of the Solicitor General (GRAN001:7).[30]

[29] Justice Stevens wrote separately, but did not reach the Article III question. He concluded that Union Carbide did not have standing to challenge the administrative scheme.

[30] The files, oddly, contain no information about the Court's decision to review the case, except for Justice Blackmun's notation on the pool memo that he would vote either to "join three"

The only bench memorandum that has survived comes from Justice Blackmun's clerk, who takes a view similar to the pool memo, reasoning that the core issue in the case was whether Congress had the power to assign a cause of action for monetary damages (historically a "legal" action for which the Seventh Amendment required a jury trial) to a specialized forum in which no jury trial would be available. The clerk viewed this as a hard question under the Court's existing cases. On the one hand, *Katchen* provided strong support for an affirmative answer in the bankruptcy context. On the other hand, the intervening decision in *Atlas Roofing* suggested that this was permissible only for the somewhat elusive category of "public rights." Ultimately, she concluded that the Court's more recent decision in *Union Carbide* had recognized broad congressional control over this forum choice when Congress exercised Article I powers like its bankruptcy authority. As she put it:

> I am reluctant ... to conclude that Congress may not properly take the view that the coherent functioning of the bankruptcy scheme requires that the same forum be used to create a plan of reorganization and to draw together the funds and property that belong within its purview. The whole reason for the revision of the bankruptcy laws that resulted in the 1978 and 1984 statutes [responding to *Marathon*] was the perceived inefficiencies of the prior system. I am wary of concluding that this Court's judgments on this issue should trump those of Congress. (GRAN002:30)

The highlight of the oral argument was an extensive interchange between counsel for Granfinanciera (Adam Lawrence) and Chief Justice Rehnquist[31] about the resemblance of the case to *Katchen*. The colloquy started with a courteous inquiry: "How do you deal with the case of *Katchen v. Landy*?" (*Granfinanciera* Transcript at 21). The ensuing rejoinder was much more pointed: "But *Katchen* did say the bankruptcy court without a jury could adjudicate that preference" (*Granfinanciera* Transcript at 22). Rejecting Mr. Lawrence's explanation, the Chief Justice emphasized that "*Katchen* doesn't depend, at least as I read the opinion, on the fact that there was a res in the possession of the trustee. There was simply a submission of a claim" (*Granfinanciera* Transcript at 23).

At the Conference, however, a majority of the Justices saw *Katchen* and *Union Carbide* as much less persuasive. Chief Justice Rehnquist and Justices Brennan, Stevens, Scalia, and Kennedy (a bare majority of five) concluded

(that is, he would agree to review the case if three other Justices wished to do so) or to call for the views of the Solicitor General.

31 By the time of *Granfinanciera*, with the resignation of Chief Justice Burger, Justice Rehnquist had become Chief Justice, with Justice Scalia joining the Court as the junior Associate Justice.

that the Seventh Amendment required a jury trial. Although some of the Justices (like Scalia) seemed to have thought the case easy solely on historical grounds, the conference notes suggest considerable doubt about the outcome. Justice Stevens characterized the case as "hard" and suggested that "[w]hat Congress has done makes a lot of sense" (GRAN007). In addition to Justice White (the author of *Katchen* and *Atlas Roofing*), Justices Marshall, Blackmun, and O'Connor (the author of *Union Carbide*) concluded that a jury trial was not required. Still, with a clear majority of five, the Chief Justice assigned the case to Justice Brennan (to whom he also had assigned the most recent Seventh Amendment case two years earlier, *Tull v. United States*).

A comparison of the vote shifts from the time of *Marathon* to this case suggests how unsettled several of the Justices were about the law in this area. Of the three who had voted to uphold the Code in *Marathon*, only Justice White remained on the Court; Chief Justice Burger and Justice Powell had been replaced during the intervening years by Justices Scalia and Kennedy, both of whom voted to require a jury trial. The case was close only because three of the Justices who had held the Code unconstitutional in *Marathon* (Justices Marshall, Blackmun, and O'Connor) were satisfied, in light of *Union Carbide* and *Katchen*, that a jury trial was unnecessary in this context.

5.4.3 *The Opinions*

In the end, however, the concerns about practicality that troubled Justice Stevens played little role in the final decision. Justice Brennan circulated an opinion a few months later (in late March) (GRAN008, 042), which earned a prompt joinder only from Justice Kennedy (GRAN012, 046, 092). The Chief Justice (GRAN014, 048, 089), Justice Marshall (GRAN045, 093), and Justice Stevens (GRAN011, 044, 091) all sent notes indicating that they would await further developments. The Chief Justice's note suggested no cause for concern: he suggested that he would have given "at least as broad – if not a broader – swath to the right to jury trial than your opinion does" (GRAN014). Nor did Justice Stevens's note give much pause – he suggested he "expect[ed]" to join Brennan's "fine" opinion but that he would wait to read the dissent "before finally coming to rest" (GRAN011).

A notable feature of Justice Brennan's opinion was the arguments he found appropriate to justify his decision that a jury trial was not required. He firmly situated the framework of analysis within the historical regime he had emphasized a few years earlier in *Tull*; the first question for him was whether the case would have been "legal" or "equitable" in 1791. If so, the second question would be whether Congress permissibly might assign the case to a non-Article

III adjudicatory body without a jury. Because the trustee sought to recover monetary payments, the historical argument against a jury trial was obviously weak, and ultimately persuasive to none of the Justices.[32]

The harder question, on which the Justices divided, was the extent of Congress's authority to design a non-jury proceeding for the fraudulent conveyance action. Here, Justice Brennan took the opportunity to further his long-standing perspective about the breadth of the jury trial right. Rejecting the flexible approach applied by the *Union Carbide* majority (with which he had disagreed vehemently), Brennan offered the stark doctrinal rule that "[u]nless a legal cause of action involves 'public rights,' Congress may not deprive parties litigating over that right of the Seventh Amendment's guarantee to a jury trial" (GRAN008:17). Discussing the public rights doctrine, he concluded (repeatedly quoting his concurrence in the judgment in *Union Carbide*, which now would become the rule of the Court) that the crucial question was whether "Congress ... has created a seemingly private right that is so closely integrated into a public regulatory scheme as to be a matter appropriate for agency resolution" (GRAN008:19). By conceiving of the public rights doctrine in terms connotative of the New Deal – redolent of "regulatory schemes" and "agency resolution" – Justice Brennan confined congressional leeway much more narrowly than Justice O'Connor's opinion in *Union Carbide* had suggested. And most importantly, it tied the jury trial right doctrinally to the "public rights" doctrine Justice Brennan had articulated for the Article III requirements in *Marathon*.

To be sure, that frame of analysis left little reason for the decision in *Katchen* to uphold the exercise of summary jurisdiction by a quasi-adjudicatory bankruptcy referee. The referee of course was not an Article III judge, but at the same time it surely was not an "agency" "resolving" the problems of "regulatory schemes." The most that Justice Brennan could do was to suggest that the now-defunct referee regime fell within the exception at least in cases that were decided under the referee's summary jurisdiction (a convenient limitation since it described a forum that no longer existed) (GRAN008:21–23).

At that point, with only two committed votes to reverse, the case stagnated for a month until Justice White circulated his dissent in early May (GRAN016,

[32] For a sustained argument that under Colonial practice the jury trial right did not attach to fraudulent conveyance actions for the benefit of the estates of bankrupts, see Plank (1998) 616–20.

049, 078).[33] GRAN016, 049, 078. Although almost as long as the majority opinion, Justice White in truth added relatively little to the analytical posture of the case. As in *Katchen*, he did not consider the importance of bankruptcy or the Bankruptcy Power. Unlike the writer of the pool memo, his opinion did not cite the Bankruptcy Clause or consider its weight against the Seventh Amendment. Rather, his two points were extensions of his perspective in *Katchen* that Congress has broad power to determine the appropriate forum for a modern proceeding. So, he first made the obvious point that the decision was difficult to reconcile with his opinion for a 7–2 majority in *Katchen*. *Katchen* stated directly that there is no jury trial right for claims to recover preferences.

More importantly, he also reiterated *Katchen*'s justification for its holding: "that Congress had committed the determination ... to bankruptcy proceedings." That rationale of course applied in *Granfinanciera* just as much as it had in *Katchen*. Second, he challenged the Court's limitation of his opinion in *Atlas Roofing*. From Justice White's perspective, *Atlas Roofing* was cut from the same cloth as *Katchen*, and reflects a broad vision of congressional capacity to design administrative processes. The Court's refusal to defer to that vision reflected an immoderately narrow understanding of what is and is not "'integrally related' to the essence of bankruptcy proceedings" (GRAN016:6 (quoting the test developed in Justice Brennan's opinion)).

With Justice White's opinion on the table as a counter to Justice Brennan's opinion, decision of the case proceeded rapidly. Justice Brennan responded two days later with a substantially revised version of his opinion answering Justice White's challenges (GRAN018, 038, 052). Essentially, this draft dug in its heels on the doctrinal limitation of Congress's "forum choice" power to "public rights," repeatedly specifying that the draft recognized congressional power to send cases to jury-less fora, so long as the cases involved "public rights." The disingenuity of Justice Brennan's claim that this was a "lesson" of *Atlas Roofing* (GRAN018 17n.10) is obvious from the directly opposite understanding Justice White had of that opinion (which he had authored for a unanimous Court).

What is most important is the lengthy section Brennan added in this third draft to explain *Katchen*. At this point, he contended that *Katchen* was wholly irrelevant because the defendant in that case had made a claim against the estate. Because the defendant in *Granfinanciera* had made no claim against the estate, resolution of the dispute was not "part of the process of allowance ... of claims," as it had been in *Katchen* (GRAN018:24). That was factually

[33] Justice Brennan did circulate a second draft of his opinion in late March, but it made only stylistic changes (GRAN013, 047).

true, but irrelevant to the broad language Justice White had employed in *Katchen* (and *Atlas Roofing*) and on which he relied in his dissent. Presumably it was apparent to all (if the first draft of his opinion had not already made it clear) that Justice Brennan was proposing to limit *Katchen* more or less to the factual and statutory context in which it had arisen and to overturn the analytical framework he unsuccessfully had opposed in *Union Carbide*. With only four members of the *Union Carbide* majority still on the Court, that goal did not seem out of reach.[34]

The recently released files of Justice Brennan include a note from Justice Stevens (GRAN053), offering to join the opinion if Justice Brennan would delete a single arguably intemperate sentence from a footnote.[35] When Brennan responded later that day with a brief note – "It's out!" – Justice Stevens immediately joined, without even waiting for a revised draft (GRAN019, 050, 079). Similarly, although Justice Marshall had voted for a contrary result at the Conference, he noted his willingness to join on his copy of the third draft (GRAN038) and promptly did so (GRAN024, 057, 083). The only explanation for Justice Marshall's shift is an emphatic "NO" that he wrote on the first page of the draft of Justice White's dissent that he reviewed (GRAN037). Because Justice Marshall had joined Justice Brennan's opinions in *Marathon* and *Union Carbide*, his decision to join his opinion here presumably surprised his colleagues less than his suggestion at Conference that he would join Justice White's view. And Justice Rehnquist at this point also joined (GRAN022, 056, 082), giving Brennan a majority for his opinion by mid-May.[36]

On the other side, Justice Blackmun decided to write a separate dissent, perhaps responding to his clerk's view that Justice White's dissent "duck[ed]" important issues and was too "caustic" for Justice Blackmun's taste (GRAN017). Justice Blackmun's opinion articulated a more nuanced approach to the intersecting questions, and shows the first recognition in the Court's deliberations of the major undertaking the enactment of the Code was for Congress (GRAN025, 058, 084). In his view, the historical record was ambiguous about the "legal" and "equitable" nature of eighteenth-century

34 Of the six votes for Justice O'Connor's *Union Carbide* opinion, Chief Justice Burger had been replaced by Justice Scalia and Justice Powell had been replaced by Justice Kennedy. Besides Justice O'Connor, the remaining holdovers were Chief Justice Rehnquist and Justices White and Blackmun.

35 The sentence in question read: "Without wishing to sound immodest, we do not fancy ourselves connivingly reticent or willfully stupid."

36 The lone remaining vote in the majority was Justice Scalia, who circulated a separate concurrence in late June taking an even broader view of the Seventh Amendment. Disdainfully rejecting the analysis of the*Union Carbide* majority, he argued that the public rights exception is available only for disputes to which the Government is a party (GRAN033, 069, 076).

litigation predecessors to bankruptcy (GRAN025:1-2). For Justice Blackmun, that ambiguity weighed in favor of permitting Congress to allocate the modern action to a juryless forum: Congress should get "the benefit of the doubt" (GRAN025:2). Emphasizing the difficulty of the task the Court set Congress when it invalidated the jurisdictional provisions of the Bankruptcy Code in *Marathon*, he concluded that

> it would be improper for this Court to employ, in its Seventh Amendment analysis, a century-old conception of what is and is not central to the bankruptcy process, a conception that Congress has expressly rejected. To do so would, among other vices, trivialize the efforts Congress has engaged in for more than a decade to bring the bankruptcy system into the modern era. (GRAN025:3)

His conclusion provides the clearest statement of a bankruptcy policy interest in the entirety of the Court's deliberations:

> [G]iven the significant federal interests involved, and the importance of permitting Congress at long last to fashion a modern bankruptcy system which places the basic rudiments of the bankruptcy process in the hands of an expert bankruptcy tribunal, I cannot say that Congress has crossed the constitutional line on the facts of this case. ... There was no need for us to rock the boat in this case. (GRAN025:5.)

When Justice O'Connor (the author of *Union Carbide*) joined Justice Blackmun's dissent (GRAN027, 061, 086), the voting was complete.

5.5 *MARATHON* CONSOLIDATED: *STERN V. MARSHALL*

After a gap of twenty years, the Court came to revisit the bankruptcy boundary problem in *Stern v. Marshall*.[37] As Justices Brennan and White were the only holdovers from *Katchen* to *Granfinanciera*, only Justices Scalia and Kennedy remained from the *Granfinanciera* Court when the Justices turned to *Stern*.

The case was remarkable as one of the rare instances in which a tabloid-headline dispute managed to reach the Supreme Court – indeed, this one reached it twice. The case arose from the estate of the fabulously wealthy J. Howard Marshall II. The dispute over his estate pitted his son (Pierce Marshall) against Howard's spouse Vickie, a former Playboy playmate sixty-two years younger than her husband. Even before Howard died, Vickie sued Pierce, claiming that he had defrauded Howard into excluding Vickie from

[37] 131 S. Ct. 2594 (2011).

his will. After Howard died, the state courts in Texas confirmed the validity of Howard's will excluding Vickie from any bequest. For Vickie's part, she sought bankruptcy relief in California. Pierce sued her in that proceeding for defamation, contending that she had defamed him in her allegations about Howard's estate. Vickie, predictably, responded by asserting truth as a defense to the defamation action and presenting a counterclaim for tortious interference with the expected bequest from her husband. After a trial in the bankruptcy court (without a jury), Vickie prevailed both on Pierce's claim for defamation (which was dismissed) and on her tortious interference claim, for which she received a judgment of $425 million. The Ninth Circuit overturned that judgment based on its holding that federal jurisdiction over the dispute was excluded by an implicit "probate" exception, but the Supreme Court unanimously reversed.[38]

More importantly for the present discussion, Pierce also interposed the argument that the bankruptcy court had never had jurisdiction over Vickie's counterclaim. Given Pierce's consent to the bankruptcy court's adjudication of his affirmative claim, the district court upheld the bankruptcy court's authority over Vickie's counterclaim. On appeal, however, the Ninth Circuit held that the bankruptcy court did not have authority to resolve Vickie's counterclaim because it was not so closely related to Pierce's claim in the bankruptcy as to make it necessary to resolution of Pierce's claim against the estate. The Court affirmed by a 5–4 vote, with both of the *Granfinanciera* holdovers (Scalia and Kennedy) joining a majority opinion that found *Granfinanciera* controlling.

Chief Justice Roberts posed the constitutional question starkly: He firmly rejected the argument that the statute did not authorize bankruptcy adjudication of Vickie's tortious interference claim and conceded that Pierce consented to that adjudication. What was left was the crisp question of whether Congress had the authority to authorize adjudication of the counterclaim in a case in which the defendant had interposed a claim against the estate and consented to bankruptcy court adjudication. In light of the line drawn to explain *Katchen* in *Granfinanciera* – the referee could adjudicate the estate's claim against Katchen because Katchen had presented a claim against the estate – Pierce's affirmative claim against the estate would have seemed to make adjudication of Vickie's claim against him an easy one for the bankruptcy process. Yet the Court rejected the bankruptcy court's jurisdiction to resolve the claim.

38 Marshall v. Marshall, 547 U.S. 293 (2006).

The Chief Justice went straight to the definition of the "public rights" over which the Justices had divided in *Granfinanciera*. The Court rejected the line that Justice Brennan had drawn in *Granfinanciera* (related to consent) and instead looked to the source of the underlying claim (a line of reasoning much closer to the analysis of Rehnquist's *Marathon* concurrence).[39] Working from that perspective, the Court noted that *Katchen* had permitted the adjudication of a federal-law claim against a creditor of the estate, and that *Marathon* and *Granfinanciera* had rejected the idea that a bankruptcy court could adjudicate a state-law claim brought against a party that was not a creditor of the estate. This case (state-law claim against creditor) plainly fell between *Katchen*, on the one hand (federal-law claim against creditor), and *Marathon/Granfinanciera*, on the other (state-law claims against third parties). The Court chose to put *Stern* on the *Granfinanciera* side of the line, barring adjudication of a state-law claim brought against a party that was a creditor of the estate.

The Chief Justice had to acknowledge that prior cases (most obviously *Thomas v. Union Carbide* and *CFTC v. Schor*) had extended the public rights doctrine to include some cases in which the Government was not a party. But reminiscent of the analysis added in the third draft of Justice Brennan's *Granfinanciera* opinion, the Court limited those cases to situations in which the claims were resolved by "an expert government agency" and were also "essential" to the agency's "regulatory objective." Because the claim here was a dispute between Vickie and Howard, arising under state law, it was, in the Court's view, not a "public" matter: "Congress has nothing to do with it" (131 S.Ct. at 2614). To complete the apotheosis of Brennan's rejection of *Union Carbide*, the Court emphasized: "We deal here not with an agency but with a court" (131 S. Ct. at 2615). The message to Congress could not have been clearer: If Congress had delegated these problems to an expert agency (as the Commission recommended), it would have been much easier for the Court to tolerate the in-bankruptcy adjudication (Pardo and Watts 2012, 417–418).

The Court firmly rejected the idea that Pierce's affirmative presentation of a claim against the estate was relevant. It discarded entirely the emphasis on that point in *Katchen* (and *Granfinanciera*), emphasizing the point that

39 Perhaps the most interesting aspect of *Stern* is the shift in ideological divisions. In *Marathon*, Justices Brennan, Marshall, and Blackmun were strong advocates for preventing incursions on Article III. By the time of *Stern*, Chief Justice Roberts and Justice Scalia have taken that side, with Justices like Ginsburg and Breyer calling for a more flexible interpretation in dissent. At least in part, I would attribute the division to the relative preference of the Chief Justice and Justice Scalia for more hard-and-fast rules and Justices Ginsburg and Breyer for more fact-intensive and flexible standards.

the presentation of a claim *vel non* by Pierce does not in any obvious way change the character of the claim against Pierce.[40] The problem, however, is that once presentation of a claim is rejected as relevant, it becomes for all practical purposes impossible to distinguish the case from *Katchen*, decided under the Act.

For those interested in the Bankruptcy Power, the Court addressed the importance of the bankruptcy process dismissively, in the closing pages of the opinion, offering the standard canard (131 S. Ct. at 2619 (quoting *Chadha*)) that "[i]t goes without saying that 'the fact that a given law or procedure is efficient, convenient and useful ... will not save it if it is contrary to the Constitution.'"[41] And even in dissent, Justice Breyer pitched the matter primarily in terms of existing precedents. He relied primarily on the holdings in *Thomas* and *Schor* extending the "public rights" doctrine to disputes between private parties. In his view, those cases made the key inquiry whether the adjudication in this case threatened encroachment on the judicial branch. From that framework, it was critically important that Article III judges supervise bankruptcy judges. Only when he came to the fifth of his five reasons for disagreeing with the majority did Justice Breyer offer an expansive discussion of Congress's explicit constitutional authority over the bankruptcy process and the importance to that process of having plenary control of disputes among claimants to and against the estate (131 S. Ct. at 2628-29). Here, as in *Granfinanciera*, the Bankruptcy Clause made its way into the discussion barely at most, as the implied basis of an unanswered gesture in dissent, with no sense that it played any role in the Court's assessment.

5.6 THE COURT BLINKS: *ARKISON* AND *WELLNESS*

Two unsatisfying features of *Stern* led to considerable chaos in its application "on the ground" in the bankruptcy courts. The most obvious problem was the

40 The apparent importance of the claim/no claim distinction after *Granfinanciera* is evident from Langenkamp v. Culp, 498 U.S. 42 (1990). In that case, the Court in a brief "per curiam" reversed a Tenth Circuit decision holding that a trustee could recover a preference from a creditor that had *not* filed a claim without a jury trial; even the *Granfinanciera* dissenters (White, Blackmun, and O'Connor) agreed with that conclusion.

41 Casey and Huq (2015) view *Stern* as a decision consistent with an efficient design for the system, based on their view that "[a]djudicating claims that the estate has on outsiders is not an essential element of bankruptcy's procedural aggregation." The argument is intriguing, but to an outsider the analysis seems quite flexible. So, for example, what does it mean that the practitioners and judges to whom I speak think (as they generally do) that any sensible person *would* want estate claims on outsiders adjudicated inside the bankruptcy process?

imprecision of *Stern*'s test defining the boundaries of the bankruptcy court's authority. The case did not explicitly overrule *Katchen*, but the decision's reasoning called into question a considerable part of the jurisdiction bankruptcy courts had exercised during the decades that had intervened since *Marathon*.

Perhaps even more problematic was the matter of consent. Although the claimant in *Stern* had not specifically consented to the adjudication by the bankruptcy court of the claim in question, he had consented to the adjudication by the bankruptcy court of closely related claims, and he did not raise the jurisdictional challenge until quite late in the proceedings – after he had lost the trial proceeding. Read broadly, then, *Stern* at least suggested that a bankruptcy court could not adjudicate so-called *Stern* claims even with the consent of the affected parties. In a world in which the Court has blurred the line between claims that are and are not under the bankruptcy court's control, consent is an efficacious tool for parties (and courts) seeking a predictably reliable litigation process; taking consent off the table as a tool for managing the process seemed particularly unsettling. Those problems led to a pair of quick followups to *Stern*. Ultimately, the efforts to work through the practicalities of implementing *Stern* led to a substantial retreat from its starkest implications.

5.6.1 Executive Benefits Insurance Agency v. Arkison

In hindsight, the first of the followup decisions turned out to be relatively unimportant. *Executive Benefits Insurance Agency v. Arkison*[42] presented an adversary proceeding in the bankruptcy of a small insurance agency (Bellingham). Shortly before its bankruptcy, Bellingham conveyed most of its assets to a related company, Executive Benefits Insurance Agency (EBIA). The trustee in Bellingham's bankruptcy (Arkison) filed suit against EBIA to retrieve the assets, claiming that the transfer had been a fraudulent conveyance. The parties disagreed in the bankruptcy court about EBIA's right to a jury trial on that claim, but the bankruptcy court granted summary judgment for EBIA (avoiding the need for a jury trial) without ruling on the question of its own authority.

When EBIA appealed to the district court, the district court reviewed the record *de novo* ("from anew," without deference to the bankruptcy court's decision), concluded that the bankruptcy court was correct, and entered judgment for the trustee Arkison. *Stern* was decided while the case was pending in the Ninth Circuit; EBIA promptly filed a motion seeking to have the entire

[42] 134 S. Ct. 2165 (2014).

proceeding dismissed. When the Ninth Circuit rejected that motion, the Court granted review.

In the Supreme Court, the parties conceded that the claim against EBIA was a *Stern* claim, beyond the bankruptcy court's independent authority.[43] Accordingly, the case presented a useful vehicle for addressing what you might think of as the retroactivity of *Stern*: how courts should apply *Stern* to litigation that had taken place before the decision. At least in theory, a rigorously retroactive application would have invalidated any adjudication of a *Stern* claim not yet final on appeal by the date of that decision. Because the bankruptcy court process often takes several years, especially in the reorganizations of large businesses, such a ruling would have wreaked considerable havoc. Justice Thomas's opinion for a unanimous Court in *Arkison* shows no Justice contemplating such a confrontational application of *Stern*. Rather, the Court retreated, taking two steps to facilitate a practical framework for the application of *Stern*.

First, the Court took a detour to address a point that, though not directly presented by the case, was of great interest to the lower courts: how bankruptcy and district courts should adjudicate *Stern* claims going forward. Justice Thomas explained that the Bankruptcy Code had established separate adjudicatory proceedings for "core" and "non-core" proceedings. Under the Code's framework, bankruptcy courts adjudicate core proceedings largely untrammeled by district court supervision, with conventional appellate review after the fact.[44] Non-core procedure, by contrast, calls for the bankruptcy court to submit proposed findings of fact and conclusions of the law to the district court for *de novo* review.

From a systemic perspective, *Stern* had rejected the line that Congress had drawn between core and non-core claims: The process Congress designed for core claims was adequate for "true" core claims, but it could not extend to the statutory core claims governed by the holding of *Stern*. The question, Justice Thomas explained, was what a bankruptcy court should do with such a claim now, in the absence of any constitutionally appropriate statutory procedure. One obvious possibility was that the Court could have held bankruptcy courts powerless to address those claims at all; as suggested above, that holding presumably would have brought with it broad-scale invalidation of pre-*Stern* adjudications. With no disagreement, Justice Thomas rejected

43 The concession was understandable in light of the holding in *Granfinanciera* that a bankruptcy court without a jury could not constitutionally adjudicate a fraudulent conveyance claim.

44 Technically, the district court has authority under the Code to withdraw any such matter from the bankruptcy court, but in practice that was (and is) uncommon.

that approach as surely inconsistent with Congress's intent. Rather, he concluded, bankruptcy and district courts should treat *Stern* claims as non-core proceedings and adjudicate them on that basis – applying *Stern* as effectively rewriting the statute to shift the Code's core/non-core line to match the constitutional boundary.

However useful that discussion was as a matter of advice for the future, it did not directly address the validity of the pre-*Stern* proceedings in *Arkison*, in which the bankruptcy court had adjudicated the dispute in the first instance. The parties agreed that the dispute involved a *Stern* claim, but the parties also agreed that the district court had afforded the bankruptcy court's findings *de novo* review.[45] The problem, then, was that the bankruptcy court wrote an opinion purporting to grant summary judgment instead of entering proposed findings of fact and law, as a bankruptcy judge would have done under the standard non-core process. Can appellate courts ignore what is now seen – in the post-*Stern* milieu – as an inappropriate arrogation of authority by the bankruptcy court? Justice Thomas's response to that problem was as accommodating as his response to the first question. The Constitution did not entitle EBIA to an initial adjudication by the district court; it would be enough for an Article III court to give EBIA's claim a fresh look unencumbered by deference to the bankruptcy court. Because the district judge provided that review, the Court found EBIA's complaint unavailing. The bankruptcy professionals that have to live with the Court's pronouncements breathed a sigh of relief.

5.6.2 Wellness International Network v. Sharif

Although *Arkison* displayed a considerably more accommodating tone than *Stern*, it left unresolved many of the practical problems in its application. Most obviously, it provided no additional guidance on how to reconcile the competing formulations of *Marathon*, *Granfinanciera*, and *Stern* defining the constitutional boundaries of the bankruptcy court's authority. And it did nothing to resolve the question of consent: Can a bankruptcy court provide a binding adjudication with the consent of the parties? The decision a year later in *Wellness International Network v. Sharif*[46] went a long way toward solving both of those problems, largely by retreating from the implications of *Stern*.

45 That process is not unusual and had nothing to do with the peculiarities of *Granfinanciera*. Because a summary judgment resolves a proceeding based solely on the documentary record, appellate courts ordinarily use *de novo* review to assess the decision of a lower court that grants or denies summary judgment.

46 135 S. Ct. 1932 (2015).

Wellness arose from the bankruptcy of Wellness International Network. Several years before its bankruptcy, Wellness fell into a dispute with Sharif over a distribution agreement. The dispute ended up in a federal court, where Sharif's obstructionist behavior led to a $650,000 award of sanctions for Wellness. When Wellness attempted to collect the award, Sharif filed for bankruptcy. Although Sharif had listed $5 million in assets on a loan application shortly before the filing, the financial statements that he provided in the bankruptcy suggested that he had no substantial assets. On inquiry, Sharif explained that he had transferred those assets before the bankruptcy to a trust that he administered for the benefit of his mother and sister.

Wellness responded with a complaint asking the court to deny Sharif's discharge because of his conduct in disposing of his assets and also seeking a declaration that the assets purportedly conveyed to the trust in fact remained the property of the bankruptcy estate, available to pay Wellness's claim against Sharif. When the parties agreed that the dispute was a core proceeding, the bankruptcy court proceeded to adjudicate it. After what the Supreme Court would characterize as "[a] familiar pattern of discovery evasion" (135 S. Ct. at 1941), the bankruptcy court issued judgment against Sharif on all counts.[47] Sharif promptly challenged that ruling in the district court.

Where *Stern* punctuated the adjudication of *Arkison* in the court of appeals, Sharif had not yet filed his brief in the district court when the Supreme Court announced its decision in *Stern*. The initial brief that he filed nevertheless did not challenge the bankruptcy court's authority. When Sharif tried to raise that issue in an untimely supplemental brief, the district court held that the issue had been waived; the district court in due course affirmed the bankruptcy court. The court of appeals agreed with the district court that Sharif's behavior ordinarily would have amounted to waiver of his *Stern* objection. It reasoned, though, that the claim to recover assets from the trust was a *Stern* claim, noting that the trust was not a creditor in the Sharif bankruptcy. Writing before the Supreme Court's decision in *Arkison*, the court of appeals treated the bankruptcy court as wholly without authority to decide such a claim. Reasoning that Sharif could not waive such a foundational constitutional defect in the bankruptcy court's authority, the court of appeals accordingly dismissed the proceeding against the trust.[48]

47 Justice Sotomayor's experience as a former trial judge (the only Justice with such experience at the time) apparently informed her willingness to condemn Sharif's behavior so unambiguously. That perspective doubtless put her in an attitude of sympathy toward the judges in the bankruptcy and district courts burdened by Sharif's erratic actions.

48 727 F.3d 751 (7th Cir. 2013).

In the Supreme Court, the parties briefed the case largely on the issue of consent. Specifically, the question was whether consent of the parties could give a bankruptcy court authority to adjudicate a claim outside its constitutional authority. A favorable ruling on that point generally would have permitted the bankruptcy courts to return to business as usual – adjudicating all matters that arise in the cases before them – at least so long as the parties accept adjudication by the bankruptcy court. Given the congestion of district court dockets, the general disinterest in bankruptcy matters that district courts display, and the practical likelihood that rejecting the bankruptcy judge as a suitable adjudicator will adversely influence the bankruptcy judge's continuing control over the main proceeding, it would be fair to expect that consent would be forthcoming with regularity.

A solid majority of the Court accepted that approach, concluding that consent could give a bankruptcy court authority to adjudicate *Stern* claims. Shifting sharply from the analysis of the majorities in *Marathon*, *Granfinanciera*, and *Stern*, the Court's analysis rested for the most part on the limited risk of congressional aggrandizement. Writing for six of the nine Justices, Justice Sotomayor explained that separation of powers concerns are at their nadir when a litigant waives the "personal right" to an Article III adjudication; the individual decision is "at most a '*de minimis*' infringement on the prerogative of the federal courts" (135 S. Ct. at 1943). The Court analogized the bankruptcy judges to magistrates, where the Court has permitted consent to justify the adjudication of a wide variety of issues. Suggesting that the authority Congress has granted bankruptcy courts extends only to "a narrow class of common law claims as an incident to the bankruptcy courts' primary, and unchallenged adjudicative function," the Court rested its holding on the absence of any "indication that Congress gave bankruptcy courts the ability to decide *Stern* claims in an effort to aggrandize itself or humble the Judiciary" (135 S. Ct. at 1945).

It is hard to disagree with the Court's view that the risk of aggrandizement is slight, but that had been equally true when the same argument had been pressed by Justice White (dissenting in *Marathon*) and Justice Breyer (dissenting in *Stern*). The earlier decisions – with little sympathy for the practical imperatives of the bankruptcy system or any sense of deference to Congress's authority to assess those imperatives in the first instance – had directly rejected the significance of the limited risk of aggrandizement.

The weakness of the analogy to magistrates is notable. To be sure, the bankruptcy judge's authority theoretically depends on a voluntary decision by the district court to refer the matter to the bankruptcy court. But reference in the bankruptcy context is nothing like it is in the magistrate context.

District courts for the most part refer issues to magistrates on a "retail" basis – particular issues arising in a case resting on a case-specific assessment. Even when district courts routinely refer certain types of issues (like discovery disputes) to magistrates, they rarely cede control over an entire case. In the bankruptcy context, by contrast, the "reference" is no more practically crucial than the Queen's assent to enactments of the British Parliament.[49] Standing orders, substantially identical throughout the nation's bankruptcy courts, operate on a "wholesale" basis, referring all aspects of all bankruptcy filings to the bankruptcy courts. It is only the unusual features of a particular controversy that raise any possibility that a district court would consider the possibility of adjudication of any aspect of such a case in the first instance.

The extent to which *Wellness* presages a trimming back of *Stern* will not be clear for years, but it is hard to doubt that the Court as an institution has turned back from the battle against Congress its earlier decisions had instigated. The vote shifts from *Stern* to *Wellness* provide a useful illustration of the Court's reevaluation of the problem. The opinion in *Wellness* was written by Justice Sotomayor and joined by the other three dissenters from *Stern*. Chief Justice Roberts (the author of *Stern*) offered a stirring rejection of the Court's analysis, almost apocalyptic in its tone.[50] Appalled by the majority's elevation of aggrandizement to analytical centrality[51] as well as the related characterization of the Article III right as "personal," he could not accept the view that personal agreement could alter constitutional lines of authority.[52] However well documented his argument that the Court's opinion was not faithful to the analysis of *Stern*,[53] it did not persuade; Justice Sotomayor gained a majority for her opinion only because of the joinder of two of the

49 The analogy is less fanciful than it might seem. The Queen's routinized assent is a formality that acknowledges the Queen's continuing position as the sovereign of the United Kingdom without interfering with Parliament's independent decisionmaking; the district court's reference is a formality that acknowledges the district court's post-*Marathon* responsibility for exercising the Judicial Power vested by Article III without interfering with the bankruptcy courts' independent adjudicatory activity.

50 "'If there is a principle in our Constitution more sacred than another,' James Madison said on the floor of the First Congress, 'it is that which separates the Legislative, Executive, and Judicial powers.' A strong word, 'sacred'." 135 S. Ct. at 1954.

51 "In [none of our earlier] cases did the branches' willing embrace of a separation of powers violation weaken the Court's scrutiny. To the contrary, the branches' enthusiasm for the offending arrangements sharpened rather than blunted our review." 135 S. Ct. at 1955.

52 "[In *CFTC v. Schor*,] the Court held that Article III confers *both* a 'personal right' that can be waived through consent *and* a structural component that safeguards the role of the Judicial Branch in our tripartite system (my emphasis)." 135 S. Ct. at 1956.

53 "There was an opinion in *Stern* that turned heavily on consent: the dissent." 135 S. Ct. at 1957.

Stern majority (Justices Kennedy and Alito) to join her and the other *Stern* dissenters.

As if the shift in analytical approach and firm embrace of the validity of consent were not striking enough, the opinions as a group also offer good reason to foresee a sharp truncation of the breadth of claims to which *Stern* applies in the first instance. Because the Court held that Sharif's consent would resolve any concern about the bankruptcy court's authority, the Court had no occasion to decide whether *Stern* governed the claim against the trust.[54] Chief Justice Roberts, however, did address that question (because he rejected consent as irrelevant).[55] Joined by Justice Scalia, he oddly concluded that the claim against the trust was not a *Stern* claim, offering a strikingly narrow understanding of his own opinion in that case. As discussed above, the claim in *Wellness* resembles the fraudulent conveyance claims at issue in *Granfinanciera* and *Arkison*: a creditor challenges a pre-bankruptcy conveyance by the debtor, hoping to bring the dissipated assets back into the estate. In this case, however, the attorney had treated this as an "alter ego" claim – alleging that the trust had no cognizable separate existence because it was nothing more than an alter ego of the debtor. Chief Justice Roberts found that narrow distinction enough to avoid *Stern*. To *Stern*'s author, an alter ego claim that did not "depriv[e] third parties of property within their otherwise lawful possession and control" (135 S. Ct. at 1954) was not the kind of common-law action to which *Stern* extended.

If an analytical distinction that slender is enough to avoid *Stern*, it is fair to say that the Chief Justice and Justice Scalia, at least, envision quite a narrow understanding of the litigation *Stern* removes from the bankruptcy court. The six Justices in the majority did not address that question, but presumably they would not press for a broader reading of *Stern* than the Chief Justice: after all, four members of the *Wellness* majority thought *Stern* itself went too far. Presumably they would welcome the Chief Justice's voluntary limitation of it. Following on the strong vindication of adjudication by consent in the bankruptcy courts, that aspect of *Wellness* should encourage the courts of

54 The Court did not decide whether Sharif's conduct amounted to consent. Rather, it remanded the case for consideration of that question by the court of appeals. Justice Alito offered a brief concurrence on the point, emphasizing his view that only express consent could vitiate a *Stern* claim in the first instance. In this case, however, he would have held as a matter of law that Sharif had forfeited any right to press the claim by failing to present it properly to the lower courts.

55 Justice Thomas filed a separate dissent, which if anything reflected an even more visceral abhorrence of the idea that consent could justify the exercise of the Article III Judicial Power by an Article I tribunal.

appeals to think twice before concluding that routine adversary proceedings fall beyond the bankruptcy court's authority.

In the end, then, *none* of the Justices decisively rejected the process in *Wellness*. Although the Chief Justice styled his opinion a "dissent," his view on the case as a whole was that the decision of the court of appeals should be reversed; the bankruptcy court decision should be reinstated because the case did not involve a *Stern* claim at all. The result: A claim all but indistinguishable from the claim in *Granfinanciera*, and yet a disposition in which no Justice finds the bankruptcy court powerless to adjudicate the claim. As with the earlier cases, though, Congress's authority under the Bankruptcy Clause finds no place in the analysis. The only reference to the Clause is a suggestion by Justice Thomas, near the end of a "dissent" parallel to the opinion of the Chief Justice, that the Clause's "grant [of authority] is informed by historical understandings of the bankruptcy power." He reaffirmed the idea that Congress's "power to establish bankruptcy courts" is limited to "jurisdiction akin to that of bankruptcy commissioners in England, subject to review traditionally had in England" (131 S. Ct. at 1967). The only weight he gave the Clause was to suggest the remote possibility that a historical practice of consent (not documented by the parties in *Wellness*) could be used to justify consent as relevant in the modern context.

5.7 THE IRRELEVANCE OF BANKRUPTCY TO CONSTITUTIONAL DOCTRINE

So where does that leave us? The operating thesis of this chapter is that the Court's blind spot about the importance of bankruptcy in the Constitution's scheme of regulation causes the Court systematically to underweight that interest when it confronts other interests of weight. As with the other chapters in the book, the evidence falls far short of proof. I do think, however, that this chapter provides two separate data points to support that hypothesis: one relates to the Court's framing of the question before it, the other to the shifting perspectives of individual Justices.

On the first point, none of the cases under the Code address in any substantial way the conflict between Article III and the Seventh Amendment, on the one hand, and Article I's Bankruptcy Clause, on the other. The Bankruptcy Clause was not mentioned, even in passing, in *Marathon* or *Granfinanciera*, and appears only as an aside in the dissent in *Stern* and in a brief passage near the end of Justice Thomas's dissent in *Wellness*, consigning it to a static historical view that gives Congress no authority to broaden the bankruptcy system to accommodate modern commerce. The limited discussion of the

Clause may seem like a small point, except that from an antiseptically legal perspective, the point is such an obvious one: As discussed above, the conflict between those powers was emphasized by the Government in its support of the statute in *Marathon* and the primary justification offered in the pool memo in *Granfinanciera* for the importance of the case.

The second point relates to the shifts over time in the views of individual Justices. Because the cases discussed in this chapter occur so far apart, only a few Justices have enough continuity for a perceptible pattern; and for none of the Justices does bankruptcy seem relevant. I mention here only Justices White, Brennan, and Scalia. Justice White's reaction to these cases follows directly from his general constitutional perspective, flavored by his experience in the Justice Department:[56] nothing in Article III or the Seventh Amendment is sufficiently specific to justify invalidating a congressional enactment designing a modern administrative process. That is plain from Justice White's consistent votes in all of the relevant cases to uphold congressional authority over challenges from either Article III or the Seventh Amendment.

Similarly, Justice Brennan's perspective in *Katchen* and *Granfinanciera* reflects his developing judicial personality much more than anything about bankruptcy. In his early days on the Court, he was much more willing to give Congress the benefit of the doubt. But over the decades, as his confidence made his judging more self-assured, he pressed ever more vigorously on firm enforcement of the provisions of the Bill of Rights. In the present context (Article III and the Seventh Amendment), he was throughout the last ten years of his tenure on the Court at the far pole of the Court pushing for an aggressive and puristically historical interpretation of Article III and the Seventh Amendment, deeply skeptical of congressional authority to limit the role of Article III or the jury trial in any way. In all of the cases in this period in which the Court was divided, Justice Brennan voted for a broader interpretation of the Constitution and a correspondingly narrow scope of congressional authority.

The final example is Justice Scalia. As his opinions in *Granfinanciera* and *Stern* make clear, he saw these cases through the heavily textualist lens he has applied throughout the Bill of Rights.[57] From his perspective, the entirety of the public rights doctrine is an atextual exception to the plain language of Article III and the Seventh Amendment. For him, the only

56 Hutchinson (1998), Justice White's most careful reader, treats the link between Justice White's experience in the Justice Department and his deference to Congress as central to Justice White's constitutional perspective.

57 The Confrontation Clause and Second Amendment cases are typical.

justifications for tolerating that exception would be stare decisis and specific historical evidence.[58] Hence his view in both cases that prior cases compelling what they might, for him the public rights doctrine should be confined as narrowly as possible to disputes to which the Government is a party.

[58] To be sure, Justice Scalia does leave open the possibility that historical evidence would justify moving bankruptcy judges into the category of military and territorial courts for which Article III jurisdiction is not required. Intriguingly, he says only that "the subject has not been briefed, and so I state no position on the matter" (131 S. Ct. at 2621). Justice Thomas included a similar qualification at the end of his opinion in *Wellness*.

6

Sovereign Immunity and the Bankruptcy Power: From *Hoffman* to *Katz*

6.1 INTRODUCTION

The murky boundary of Article III's limits on Congress's authority is not the only area in which the Court has considered the Bankruptcy Power. The Court also has repeatedly considered the interplay between bankruptcy adjudication and the intertwined topics of sovereign immunity and the Eleventh Amendment. The specific question is whether a bankruptcy court has the authority to order monetary relief against a State. It is here that Congress has spoken most clearly in favor of a broad exercise of the Bankruptcy Power. The end result, much as it was in the preceding chapter, was a congressional amendment intended to overturn the Court's narrow interpretation of the Bankruptcy Code, followed by a decision by the Court giving ground, finding room in the Constitution for Congress's vision of an effective bankruptcy process.

The story proceeds in three parts: a brief introduction to the Court's troubled and highly contested jurisprudence on the relation between the Eleventh Amendment and congressional power; the story of the Court's decisions in *Hoffman* and *Nordic Village* concluding that the Bankruptcy Code did not abrogate the sovereign immunity of the States or the Federal Government, respectively; and the final episode – the Court's acknowledgment in *Katz* that Congress not only had the power to abrogate sovereign immunity, but unquestionably had exercised it in the Bankruptcy Code.

6.2 SETTING THE STAGE: FROM *FITZPATRICK* TO *UNION GAS*

Like *Marathon*, *Granfinanciera*, and *Stern*, the Court's decisions in *Hoffman* and *Nordic Village* appear primarily as pawns in an extended conflict – in this case a heated debate that the Justices have carried on for decades about the proper relation between federal legislative power under Article I of the Constitution and the federal judicial power under Article III of the Constitution, as mediated by the Eleventh Amendment.

Because the Court's Eleventh Amendment jurisprudence has been so controversial (Young 1999, 7–12), a brief summary should be adequate. All would agree that Congress's proposal and the States' prompt ratification of the Eleventh Amendment in 1795 reflected a direct rejection of the Court's 1793 decision in *Chisholm v. Georgia*[1] affirming a money judgment entered directly against a State. But the Court has had a much harder time defining the boundaries of the sovereign immunity flowing from the Amendment's ratification. Despite a good deal of contrary history, the Court by the 1930s settled on the idea, never yet rejected by the Court, that the Eleventh Amendment's ratification reflected a broader underlying principle of sovereign immunity "inherent in the plan of the Convention." Thus, it has become well settled that after adoption of the Eleventh Amendment the federal judicial power does not extend to suits against the States, whether the suits arise under state law or federal law.

The Justices have not, however, been able to settle a closely related question: the extent to which Congress can enact legislation that abrogates the sovereign immunity of the States in private litigation (as opposed to suits by other States or the United States itself). There is of course no question that Congress can enact legislation abrogating the sovereign immunity of the United States itself (otherwise the United States would be entirely immune from suit). It is not nearly so clear, however, that the Constitution permits suits against the States for money damages, as opposed to injunctive relief against State officers.[2] The Court first addressed that question definitively in its 1976 holding in *Fitzpatrick v. Bitzer*, permitting the recovery of money judgments against the States in statutes enacted to enforce the Fourteenth Amendment. The premise of *Fitzpatrick* was that because the Fourteenth Amendment was adopted after the Eleventh Amendment, it made sense to interpret it as a limitation of the sovereign immunity principles reflected in the

[1] 2 Dall. 419.

[2] Suits for injunctive relief always have been available, under the fiction of *Ex parte* Young, 209 U.S. 123 (1908), that a suit for injunctive relief against a state officer is not in fact a suit against the State; that fiction rests on an irrebuttable presumption that the State has not commanded the officer to violate federal law. Mashaw 2012, 306-07 (discussing injunction against public official affirmed in Union Pacific R.R. v. Hall, 91 U.S. 343 (1875)). The Eleventh Amendment bars suits for injunctive relief brought against the State itself. Alabama v. Pugh, 438 U.S. 781 (1978).

Eleventh Amendment.[3] Given the broad enforcement powers that Section 5 of the Fourteenth Amendment granted Congress, the Court readily recognized congressional power in that context to abrogate the sovereign immunity of the States.

That answer was not particularly satisfying from a federal regulatory perspective. Federal regulatory legislation traditionally has been adopted under the authority of the Commerce Clause (Article I, § 8, cl. 3) or (more recently) the Spending Power (Article I, § 8, cl. 1). Because the original Constitution granted those powers before the ratification of the Eleventh Amendment, it remained an open question whether the Court would extend the holding of *Fitzpatrick* to permit the enforcement of monetary damage remedies against the States under Article I legislation, or whether the Court instead would conclude that the Eleventh Amendment reflected (or effected) a categorical removal of such authority.

The issue began to reach the Court a decade after *Fitzpatrick*, with a series of cases presenting broadly worded private causes of action, included in federal regulatory statutes, which would extend to the States if enforced in accordance with their natural meaning. Starting in 1985, the Court decided a series of those cases.[4] In each case, the Court declined to address the question of Congressional power, holding instead that the language of the statute in question would need to be incontrovertibly clear to persuade the Court that Congress intended to take a step so remarkable as to impose a private right of action for damages on the States, and concluding in each case that the language was insufficiently clear.

It was plain, however, that the issue would not go away. The positions of the Justices seemed firmly settled. In each case, Justice (and then Chief Justice) Rehnquist, Justice White, and Justice O'Connor voted in favor of state immunity. A fourth vote came from Chief Justice Burger, followed by his successor, Justice Scalia. A fifth vote came from Justice Powell, followed by his successor, Justice Kennedy. At the same time, the dissenters were equally inveterate in their views. In each case Justice Brennan dissented, joined by Justices Marshall, Blackmun, and Stevens. In each case, Justice Brennan argued that neither the Eleventh Amendment nor any principle of sovereign immunity implicit in the Constitution justified a bar on federal enforcement of money judgments against the States. In the view of the

3 This "later amendment trumps earlier" idea should be familiar from the idea discussed in the preceding chapter that the Seventh Amendment might be regarded as a later limitation on the power originally granted to Congress in the Bankruptcy Clause.

4 Atascadero State Hosp. v Scanlon, 473 U.S. 234 (1985); Welch v. Texas Dep't of Highways & Pub. Transp., 483 U.S. 468 (1987); Dellmuth v. Muth, 491 U.S. 223 (1989).

dissenters, the Court's doctrine reflected such a departure from the proper understanding of the doctrine of sovereign immunity that the Court's continued line of decisions should be considered open for reexamination at any time.

The matter finally came to a head in the Court's October 1988 Term, when the Court confronted three separate cases raising this problem. The first of the cases, argued in October, was *Pennsylvania v. Union Gas Co.*, considering liability under the Comprehensive Environmental Response, Compensation, and Liability Act (CERCLA). The second, argued in February, was *Dellmuth v. Muth*, arising under the Education for All Handicapped Children Act (EAHCA). The third, argued the last month of the Term (in April), was *Hoffman v. Connecticut Department of Income Maintenance*, arising under the Bankruptcy Code.

Because *Muth* and *Union Gas* had been argued (and tentatively decided) before the Court began to consider *Hoffman*, the views of the Justices in those cases are central to understanding *Hoffman*. *Muth* is easy enough to understand. The Justices divided along their normal grounds: a majority (the Chief Justice and Justices White, O'Connor, Scalia, and Kennedy) held that the statute (the EAHCA) did not have the "unmistakable clarity" needed to abrogate State sovereign immunity. Justices Brennan, Marshall, Blackmun, and Stevens dissented.

Union Gas, however, was a much more challenging case. The problem there was that Congress had amended CERCLA after the Court's earlier Eleventh Amendment decisions to explicitly include "States" in the category of "persons" on whom liability could be imposed. Faced with that statute, Justice Scalia joined the traditional dissenters (Justices Brennan, Marshall, Blackmun, and Stevens), agreeing that Congress had exercised any power it possessed to impose liability on the States under that statute. The other four Justices who had been in the majority in the earlier cases (the Chief Justice and Justices White, O'Connor, and Kennedy) concluded that the statute was not "unmistakably" clear, and thus could not be held to impose liability on the States.

As Justice Scalia's prior opinions had made clear, he felt no compulsion to read CERCLA narrowly to avoid state liability. He repeatedly had taken the view that Congress had no authority to impose liability on the States under the Commerce Clause. Accordingly, it did not matter to him at all whether the statute was clear or not, because it would be ineffective in any case. Predictably enough, he wrote separately to emphasize his continued view, concluding that CERCLA did not impose liability on the States because that would violate the Constitution.

Ordinarily, with four Justices holding that the statute *did* not grant immunity, and one Justice holding that the statute *could* not grant immunity, the case would have come down as yet another decision limiting the federal power. But Justice White, oddly, added a section to the end of his opinion, noting that the majority of the Court had concluded that CERCLA exercised Congress's power to impose liability on the States. Although he disagreed with that reading of the statute, he decided to defer to it for purposes of resolution of the case. Accordingly, he went on to address the question of congressional power. There, he delphically voted in favor of congressional power: "I agree with the conclusion reached by Justice Brennan in Part III of his opinion, that Congress has the authority under Article I to abrogate the Eleventh Amendment immunity of the States, although I do not agree with much of his reasoning" (491 U.S. at 43–44). Accordingly, he voted to affirm the court of appeals' decision imposing CERCLA liability on Pennsylvania, leaving a precedent, of a sort, in favor of congressional power.

6.3 APPLYING THE RULES: *HOFFMAN*

6.3.1 *Background*

It was against that backdrop that the Court came, in *Hoffman*, to consider whether the Bankruptcy Code imposed monetary liability on the States. The statute plainly intended to impose liability on States in some circumstances, but some sloppy last-minute drafting left Congress's precise purpose unclear. The original Commission bill had included a broad abrogation of all sovereign immunity at the state or federal level (Commission Bill § 1–104). Concerned about the constitutionality of that provision, Congress early on limited the abrogation of immunity to two limited areas: when the Government makes a claim against the bankrupt; and when the debtor wishes to offset its liability to the Government against the Government's claim against the bankrupt (House Committee on the Judiciary 1977; Senate Committee on the Judiciary 1978, 29–30; H.R. 8200, 95th Cong., 2nd Sess. § 106). Later in the process, after both the House and Senate Committees had reported a bill, negotiators added a provision that included a relatively broad abrogation of sovereign immunity. The earlier limited provisions are now subsections (a) and (b) of Section 106 of the Code; the later broad abrogation is subsection (c). That provision, the subject of *Hoffman*, states that "[e]xcept as provided in subsections (a) and (b) of this section and notwithstanding any assertion of sovereign immunity ... a provision of this title that contains 'creditor' ... applies to governmental units" (H.R. Doc. 93–137 Pt. II).

Hoffman itself arose out of the financial disarray of a seedy Connecticut nursing home operator. When Connecticut authorities determined that the nursing home (Willington) had overcharged the State for Medicaid reimbursements, the State began recouping the alleged past overpayments by withholding funds from payments currently due to Willington. The resulting cash flow crunch drove Willington directly into bankruptcy. At the time of the bankruptcy, Willington had about $64,000 in pending Medicaid claims, against almost $200,000 that the State alleged Willington still owed it. Connecticut did not file a claim for the balance of the alleged overpayments, but it did decide to withhold the entirety of the $64,000 of pending claims. Hoffman (the case's namesake) was appointed as a trustee in the bankruptcy court to pursue the State of Connecticut for the $64,000.

To make matters more complicated, the bankruptcy court considered the Willington matter in conjunction with a separate adversary proceeding, also instituted by Hoffman, and also seeking recovery from Connecticut. The second proceeding arose out of the personal bankruptcy of Edward Zera. In that case, claiming that Zera owed the State back taxes, Connecticut garnished a company (apparently one of Zera's customers) to collect $2100 in back taxes. Shortly thereafter, Zera filed for bankruptcy; Hoffman sued to recover the $2100 as a preference (under Section 547 of the Bankruptcy Code).

After the bankruptcy court rejected the State's claim of immunity under the Eleventh Amendment, the State appealed to the district court. At that point, the United States intervened to defend the constitutionality of the Bankruptcy Code provisions in question. The district court ruled that Connecticut was immune and the Second Circuit affirmed, reasoning that Section 106(c) did not provide the "unmistakable clarity" required to abrogate immunity under the Court's then-extant Eleventh Amendment cases.

6.3.2 *Argument and Decision*

As noted above, the case reached the Supreme Court for argument in April of 1989 – after the argument and voting in *Union Gas* and *Muth*, but before those decisions were announced. The pool memo (HOFF001, authored by a law clerk from Justice Kennedy's chambers) took the straightforward view that the petition was plainly certworthy, based on a conflict (not seriously disputed) with decisions of the Third and Seventh Circuits. Indeed, the Solicitor General urged that the Court grant review even though it had prevailed in the court of appeals.

For the pool memo writer, the principal question of interest was whether the case should be held for *Union Gas* or immediately considered. The pool memo proceeded from the premise that the Court in *Union Gas* would hold that CERCLA did not abrogate Pennsylvania's sovereign immunity. Interestingly, the record suggests that the basis for the Court's decision would be that the Constitution did not permit abrogation of those powers (suggesting that Justice White changed his view on that question quite late in the proceedings).[5] Accordingly, the decision would shed no light on the conflict at issue in *Hoffman* – whether Section 106(c) should be read to abrogate the immunity of Connecticut. Although no record survives of the deliberations among the Justices on the question of whether to grant review, the copy of the pool memorandum in Justice Blackmun's files includes a comment by Justice Blackmun's clerk that "the SG's position appears sound" (HOFF001:11) and a notation in Justice Blackmun's handwriting that he planned to vote in favor of review (HOFF001:1).

The case was set for the last session of the Term, in April, to be argued under the shadow of the still-pending decisions in *Muth* and *Union Gas*. It seems plain that the Justices viewed the case as yet another case in the line of strict-statutory-construction Eleventh Amendment cases. Justice Blackmun's pre-argument notes suggest, for example, that he readily would support enforcement against the State, indicating that "[there] is suff[icient] clarity here if one wishes to see it" (HOFF003). As for the constitutional question, he viewed the question as whether he should "[e]quate power [under] Art. I § 8 to XIV [amendment]," and indicated that "[s]urely t[he] policy arguments look this way: Why favor t[he] St[ate]s this way?" (HOFF003).

The statutory question preoccupied the Justices at the oral argument (HOFF087) – which involved a rare instance of an argument by the party (Hoffman as trustee). Specifically, the problem that concerned them (and especially Justice Scalia) was how to give any meaning to Sections 106(a) and 106(b) if Section 106(c) worked a broad abrogation of sovereign immunity. Because the first two subsections abrogate sovereign immunity in specific situations, why would Congress include those narrower provisions if (c) provided a broad and all-encompassing waiver? Hoffman's answer, which is consistent with the historical record summarized above, is that early drafts of the statute included only the narrow abrogations (in (a) and (b)), that the broad abrogation in (c) was added at the last moment to broaden immunity, and that Congress simply failed to consider the propriety of revising (or removing) (a) and (b).

5 An April 5, 1989, note from Blackmun's clerk regarding the relation between *Union Gas* and *Hoffman* reports the understanding (as of April 5) that *Union Gas* would "hold that Article I powers cannot abrogate [the] Eleventh Amendment" (HOFF002).

Justice Scalia emphasized the opening of subsection (c), which indicates that the abrogation of immunity under subsection (c) operates "notwithstanding" the narrower provisions in subsections (a) and (b). In his view, the language "can't be unmistakably clear, if only because of the first phrase [of Section 106(c)], which, as far as I can ascertain, is utterly meaningless [under your reading of the statute.] That is really, truly gobbledygook" (HOFF087:10). He emphasized an alternative reading, under which the statute didn't abrogate immunity, but simply bound the State to particular determinations (such as amounts of taxes owed and the like).

To be sure, Justice Scalia was just as critical of the opposite interpretation, pressed by the Federal Government, which supported Connecticut based on its interest in a broad understanding of sovereign immunity. Under the Government's view, subsections (a) and (b) grant narrow abrogations related to monetary relief; subsection (c) does not deal with monetary relief at all, but simply binds the States to adjudications bankruptcy courts make with regard to the title of particular assets. Justice Scalia found it mystifying that Congress would write Section 106(c) the way it did if it intended such a narrow interpretation, which he regarded as "not ... very plausible" (HOFF087:25).

To make matters worse, under close questioning from Justices Stevens and Scalia, counsel for the Government readily admitted that there did not appear to have been "a careful review of [the provisions for which a binding effect] would be triggered [under his reading]," and that as a policy matter the statute did not "make a lot of sense" under the Government's reading (HOFF087:26–27). He also had to concede that his reading did not have "a great explanation" for what Congress intended by providing that subsection (c)'s broad grant of immunity would apply "except as provided in" the narrow provisions in subsections (a) and (b) (HOFF087:32).

Interestingly, the Justices appeared completely uninterested in the State of Connecticut's argument that the Constitution did not permit Congress to abrogate the State's sovereign immunity, presumably because all of them by that point had joined opinions in *Union Gas* reflecting a position on that topic. Counsel for the State received only a single question, whether in her view the immunity question was the same for Article I courts and Article III courts (HOFF087:35).[6]

6 Although the transcript does not identify the questioner, it well might have been a rare question from Justice Brennan; his law clerk had suggested to him that immunity should be even narrower in Article I courts than in Article III courts (HOFF035:2).

A memorandum written by a clerk for Justice Blackmun after the argument, but before the Justices met to vote on the matter, provides a strictly legal analysis of the case, summarizing the consensus of the law clerks for the various Justices (HOFF005). The consensus among the clerks seemed to be that the case followed directly from *Muth* (then still in circulation), which was expected to reinforce the almost insuperably high "plain-meaning" requirement for abrogating sovereign immunity. Thus, although all agreed that the Government's reading of Section 106(c) was weak, all seemed to accept that it introduced enough doubt to defeat an argument for abrogating sovereign immunity. Interestingly, Justice Blackmun's clerk recommended that Justice Blackmun vote that the statute did not abrogate immunity, despite Justice Blackmun's vote to dissent in *Muth* and in all of the earlier Eleventh Amendment cases (HOFF005). And Justice Blackmun's personal notes suggest a similar diffidence. For one thing, he worried that the statute "gives me diffi[culty] wi[th] its lack [of] clarity as to many points," for another he recognized that he "could n[ot] command a majority" for a determination that the statute abrogated the State's immunity (HOFF006).

And so it should be no surprise – if even Justice Blackmun thought it hard to find abrogation of immunity – that the Justices would find the statute inadequate to abrogate sovereign immunity. What was most surprising (in light of the long string of 5–4 decisions in the area) was the 7–2 vote to reverse, with all except Justices Brennan and Marshall reading the statute as inadequate to abrogate sovereign immunity. So far as the available notes suggest (HOFF007, from the files of Justice Blackmun), none of the Justices mentioned the Bankruptcy Clause or addressed the possibility that its relation to the Eleventh Amendment might differ in any way from that of the Commerce Clause. The only dispute apparent from the Conference was the view apparently expressed by Justices Stevens and Blackmun that it was unnecessary to rely on the higher standard of "unmistakable" clarity to reject Hoffman's claim of abrogation. In their view, at least at the time of the Conference, the language of the statute itself seemed inadequate to support a claim of abrogation (HOFF015).

6.3.3 *The Opinions*

Given the strong vote and the tenor of the questioning at argument, it was easy to predict what sort of opinion would emerge. So presumably no one was surprised when Justice White circulated a terse (only seven pages) draft just three weeks later (HOFF026, 037, 082). The opinion made three brief points. First, it emphasized the requirement of "unmistakable clarity" that the Court soon would reaffirm in *Muth* (HOFF026:4). Second, the poorly crafted statute did not approach that level of clarity (HOFF026:4–6).[7] Finally, anticipating the arguments of Justice Brennan in dissent and reaffirming a point to be made in *Muth*, legislative history could play no role in determining whether Congress abrogated immunity under the Eleventh Amendment (HOFF026:6–7). Chief Justice Rehnquist (HOFF011, 40, 083) and Justices O'Connor (HOFF009, 039, 081) and Kennedy (HOFF14, 042, 060) joined the first draft of Justice White's opinion in short order. Getting a fifth vote, however, turned out to be considerably more difficult than it would have appeared from the 7–2 Conference vote.

First, to the surprise of no one, Justices Brennan (HOFF013, 041, 084) and Marshall (HOFF010, 038, 080) indicated that they would be dissenting.[8] A bit more surprising, given his comments at the argument and at the Conference (where he found the statute "n[ot] suff[iciently] clear" (HOFF007)), Justice Scalia in early June circulated an opinion concurring in the judgment, relying entirely on his opinion in *Union Gas* (apparently a dissent by that point) to the effect that Congress had no power under the Commerce Clause to abrogate immunity (HOFF027, 043, 061).[9] Stating that "there is no basis for treating its powers under the Bankruptcy Clause any differently," he voted to affirm the court of appeals, but declined to take a position on the question of statutory interpretation (HOFF027:1).[10] Even worse for Justice White, though perhaps not apparent at the time, internal correspondence shows that Justices Stevens and Blackmun refrained from joining Justice White's opinion because of its direct reliance on

7 The opinion incorporated almost word for word the point made by the Government in oral argument, that Section 106(c) would under a broad reading "apply to over 100 Code provisions." Compare HOFF026:4 (first draft of Justice White's opinion) with HOFF085:25–28 (argument of Deputy Solicitor General Thomas Merrill).

8 Departing from his regular practice of writing the principal dissents in this line of Eleventh Amendment cases, Justice Brennan assigned the dissent in *Hoffman* to Justice Marshall (008, 036).

9 Justice Scalia's unwillingness to join Justice White's opinion likely reflected dissatisfaction with Justice White's reasoning, rather than a simple jurisprudential preference for the constitutional analysis. That is at least a reasonable inference from Justice Scalia's then-circulating opinion in *Union Gas*, in which he vociferously criticized Justice White's opinion concluding that CERCLA was not specific enough to abrogate state sovereign immunity (491 U.S. at 29–30).

10 Although she already had joined Justice White's opinion, Justice O'Connor eventually offered a brief concurrence indicating that she shared Justice Scalia's view of the constitutional question, but joined Justice White's opinion because a majority of the Court chose to address the question whether Congress clearly intended to abrogate that immunity. HOFF020, 069.

the "clarity" requirement, from which they both were dissenting in *Muth* (HOFF012).

At that point, with five Justices favoring immunity splitting 4–1 on the reason, Justice Marshall circulated his dissent (HOFF029, 045, 063), which argued straightforwardly that the simplest interpretation of the statute abrogated sovereign immunity even under the "unmistakable clarity" standard (HOFF029:1–6). Because this required him to address the constitutional question, he concluded that the statute was constitutional. His reasoning, however, was parallel to Justice Scalia's. He noted the Court's soon-to-be-issued ruling in *Union Gas* that Congress had such power under the Commerce Clause and stated simply: "I see no reason to treat Congress' power under the Bankruptcy Clause any differently, for both constitutional provisions give Congress plenary power over national economic activity" (HOFF029:6). Thus, like Justice Scalia, it did not occur to him to consider the possibility that the Clause might relate specifically to congressional authority over judicial administration.

With the circulation of Justice Marshall's opinion, however, the votes quickly shifted away from Justice White's position. It was no surprise that Justice Brennan joined Justice Marshall's opinion the same day (HOFF017, 047, 065). But it was a surprise that Justice Stevens quickly sent a note offering to join the opinion as well (HOFF018, 030). Justice Stevens explained that "[a]fter wrestling with the case" he ultimately had decided to come down in favor of immunity, notwithstanding his contrary vote at the post-argument Conference (HOFF018:1).[11]

Justice Stevens's note to Justice Marshall expressed an intent to "add a few paragraphs of my own" (HOFF018:1). The "few paragraphs" turned out to be a four-page dissent, circulated the next day (HOFF048, 067). Justice Stevens emphasized the clarity with which the legislative history indicated congressional intent to abrogate the State's immunity. Reiterating the argument Hoffman had emphasized, Justice Stevens explained that the tension between the limited abrogations of immunity in subsections (a) and (b) and the broader abrogation in subsection (c) was an artifact of the statute's drafting history.

Specifically, he argued that Congress added subsection (c) because of a developing understanding of what it would take for Congress to abrogate the

[11] Justice Stevens requested two minor changes – one asking Justice Marshall to state that the statute satisfies "even" the unmistakeable clarity standard – but described them as "suggestions" and indicated that he was "going to join yo[u] regardless." Justice Marshall promptly circulated a second draft accommodating those requests (HOFF023, 052, 070), and Justice Stevens immediately joined (HOFF050, 068).

State's immunity. In his view, the intent of Congress was quite clear; the joint floor statements at the time of the change explain: "The provision is intended to comply with the requirement in case law that an express [abrogation] of sovereign immunity is required in order to be effective" (HOFF048:2 (quoting 124 Cong. Rec. 32394) (1978)). The statements also specifically addressed the possibility of recovering a money judgment against a governmental entity: "As provided, section 106(c) overrides [an earlier version] with the result that the government is subject to avoidance of preferential transfers" (HOFF048:2 (quoting 124 Cong. Rec. 32394 (1978)).

Justices Brennan and Marshall immediately joined Justice Stevens's dissent, and Justice Blackmun joined the dissents of Justice Stevens (HOFF024, 075) and Marshall (HOFF053, 074). At that point, the original group of seven Justices for Justice White's position had diminished to four. As a result, Justice White recast his opinion later that day to shift it to a plurality opinion for four Justices (HOFF032). The decision was handed down later that day as a 4–1–4 split, with Justice Scalia's concurrence based on the constitutional issue providing the balance of decision.

It is fair to wonder whether Justice White could have avoided that outcome had he written with more care. Justice Scalia had joined opinions of this sort frequently; he joined Justice Kennedy's majority opinion in *Muth* just a week earlier. And Justices Stevens and Blackmun, so far as the record reflects, apparently did not even consider dissenting until they read Justice White's proposed majority opinion; they seem to have been repulsed by Justice White's opinion, not persuaded by Justice Marshall's.

However interesting that hypothetical inquiry might be, two points are important. The first is the treatment of the constitutional premise. None of the Justices considered whether there might be any relevant difference between Congress's authority "To regulate Commerce . . . among the several States" and its authority "To establish . . . uniform Laws on the subject of Bankruptcies." The plurality relied on a presumption that Congress had not intended to abrogate immunity, Justice Scalia on the view that Congress never could abrogate immunity, and the dissenters on the view that abrogations of immunity should readily be recognized, even if they were clear only from legislative history.

The second is the Court's use of such a narrow lens to read the statutory language. To be sure, if the rule by the time of *Muth* is that the language must be unmistakably clear, the Court's decision is a fair application of that rule. But within the domain of bankruptcy cases, it is not hard to share Bob Rasmussen's view that this is a case in which "the Court overrode a relatively clear text to further the judicially created policy of immunizing the government from suit" (Rasmussen 1993, 553 n.85).

6.4 AN INTERPRETIVE INTERLUDE: *NORDIC VILLAGE*

6.4.1 *Background*

The Justices confronted another case under section 106(c) just two years later, this time in a dispute involving the immunity of the United States rather than one of the States. The facts are similar to, though perhaps even more flagrant than, those in the dispute that the Court addressed in Hoffman. Specifically, several months after Nordic Village, Inc. had sought relief under Chapter 11, an officer of Nordic Village made a $20,000 tax payment to the IRS, defraying a small share of outstanding delinquent employment taxes, penalties, and interest.[12]

Recognizing the plain impropriety of the post-petition preferential payment, the bankruptcy trustee sought to recover the payment from the Government. With no substantial defense on the merits, the Government argued that it could interpose the defense of sovereign immunity, relying on *Hoffman*. The court of appeals rejected that argument, noting that the Court was evenly divided on the proper interpretation of Section 106 in *Hoffman*, and taking the plurality at their word that the claim of immunity depended on the all-but-insuperable presumption against abrogation. Because that presumption did not apply to federal legislation abrogating the Federal Government's immunity, the court of appeals ruled for the trustee, rejecting the claim of immunity.

At the Court, the case was teed up for immediate review. The pool memo (from a law clerk working for Chief Justice Rehnquist) argued that the case readily warranted review, emphasizing both the conflicting views of the lower courts and the challenge of transferring the analysis of the fractured *Hoffman* Court to the context of federal (as opposed to state) immunity (USNV004). At the same time, because of Justice Brennan's retirement (and replacement by Justice Souter), there was some reason to think the Court might be more likely to find a majority to read the statute in a decisive way.[13]

12 Although the record does not make it clear why this was done, it likely reflects the risk that the officers of Nordic Village would bear personal responsibility and criminal liability (under 26 U.S.C. § 6672) for unpaid withholding taxes.

13 Justice Blackmun's clerk commented on the pool memo that "DHS's [i.e, David Souter] addition to the Court will resolve this issue contrary to [the court of appeals]. The confusion below warrants a Grant" (USNV004:14).

Thus, it was no surprise that the Court agreed to review the case. Two weeks later, the retirement of Justice Marshall (to be replaced by Justice Thomas) left only Justices Stevens and Blackmun of the Justices who had read Section 106(c) as abrogating immunity in *Hoffman* just twenty-four months earlier.

Against that background, Justices Blackmun and Stevens could be expected to line up against the Government. Thus, Justice Blackmun's clerk thought the case would be "very easy" for him (USNV008:18). Because Justice Blackmun had joined Justice Marshall's opinion in *Hoffman* that found Section 106(c) to include an "unmistakably clear" abrogation of sovereign immunity, as well as Justice Stevens's opinion recounting the compelling legislative history, she thought it obvious that Justice Blackmun would vote to affirm (abrogating immunity) even if the United States was entitled to the same protection as the States. Justice Blackmun's own pre-argument notes suggest that he planned to vote to affirm based on his position in *Hoffman*, but expected that the Court would reverse (USNV005). Justice Blackmun's clerk had the same expectation, explaining that he was "not overly optimistic that [the newly appointed Justices Souter and Thomas] will join the waiver bandwagon" (USNV008:20).

6.4.2 *Argument and Decision*

In the end, the Justices seem to have found little need for the idea that the presence of the Eleventh Amendment makes it easier for Congress to abrogate federal sovereign immunity than to displace State sovereign immunity. The Justices were well aware of the outrageousness of the IRS's behavior in this case. At the argument, for example, the Justices questioned the Government's representative at length about the willful violation of the Bankruptcy Code in the IRS's receipt of the payment (Tr. 8–9). But the particular facts of the case had no apparent effect on the decision. Justice Blackmun's notes from the Conference (USNV009) suggest that the discussion was desultory. The Justices from the *Hoffman* majority joined the two new Justices with votes to reverse, finding that Section 106(c) did not abrogate the sovereign immunity of the Federal Government. Interestingly, apparently reflective of what happened when he assigned the 7–2 majority in *Hoffman* to Justice White, Chief Justice Rehnquist assigned the opinion in *Nordic Village* to Justice Scalia. On the other side, Justice Blackmun (the senior dissenter after the retirement of Justices Brennan and Marshall) assigned the dissent to Justice Stevens, presumably expecting him to hew closely to the reasoning of his *Hoffman* dissent (USNV010).

6.4.3 *The Opinions*

The only substantial question of doubt was what Scalia would say about the statute now that he could not use the Eleventh Amendment to avoid discussing it. When he circulated his proposed opinion less than a month after the argument (USNV002, USNV027), the answer was clear. He started by candidly agreeing that the decision in *Hoffman* had "no binding force here," because the eight Justices that considered the question were "evenly divided over" the meaning of Section 106 (USNV002:3). But before turning to the language of Section 106 (which he had found so troubling in the *Hoffman* deliberations), he paused to articulate another clear-statement rule – that abrogations of sovereign immunity must be "unequivocally expressed" (USNV002:3) and "construed strictly in favor of the sovereign" (USNV002:4). Against that interpretive background (which would have called for a contrary analysis in *Hoffman*), he readily demonstrated that Section 106(c) was ambiguous. Because of its poor drafting it plausibly could be read to abrogate immunity and with equal plausibility could be read not to abrogate immunity (USNV002:5–7). Abjuring any obligation to select the most sensible reading of the statute, he let the case fall entirely on the interpretive canon. This time, all six of the other Justices supporting immunity promptly joined.[14]

For the dissenters, all that was left for Justice Stevens was to remind the majority of the undeniably clear legislative history showing that Congress had written Section 106(c) with the decided intention of imposing liability on the United States in cases such as this. He was particularly critical of the Court's refusal even to attempt to understand Section 106. In words that would soon seem prescient, he complained:

> Surely the interest in requiring the Congress to draft its legislature with greater clarity or precision does not justify a refusal to make a good faith effort to ascertain the actual meaning of the message it tried to convey in a statutory provision that is already on the books. The Court's stubborn insistence on "clear statements" burdens Congress with unnecessary reenactment of provisions that were already plain enough when read literally. . . . The fact

14 The Chief Justice (USNV014, 031) and Justices White (USNV011, 029), Thomas (USNV013, 030), Souter (USNV015, 032), and Kennedy (USNV016) all joined without comment within ten days. Justice O'Connor waited until after circulation of the dissent but then also joined without comment (USNV018, 023).

> that Congress has ample power to correct the Court's unfortunate error does not justify this refusal to obey its command.[15] (USNV003:7–8)

His spirited dissent (USNV003, 021), however, could get only Justice Blackmun's joinder (USNV019, 022, complimenting Justice Stevens on a "strong" opinion), and only the most cursory response from Justice Scalia.[16]

6.5 CONGRESS TALKS BACK: *KATZ*

This time, the unwillingness of the Court to take Congress at its word bore fruit quickly. As part of the Bankruptcy Reform Act of 1994, Congress explicitly overruled both *Hoffman* and *Nordic Village*. Recognizing that the Court had held the previous statute insufficiently explicit, the revised statute indicated directly that "sovereign immunity is abrogated as to a governmental unit" with respect to specified sections of the Bankruptcy Code. The legislative history refers directly to *Hoffman* and *Nordic Village*; the revised text was based directly on language proposed by the National Bankruptcy Conference.[17]

Given the voting breakdown in *Hoffman* (and *Union Gas*) – in which four Justices took the position that the Constitution prohibited Congress from abrogating state sovereign immunity under its Article I powers – it should be no surprise that the constitutionality of the revised provision should return to the Court. What is most surprising is that it took until October Term 2005, more than a decade after Congress enacted the revised statute. The dispute that finally brought the issue to the Court was in every way pedestrian. A local bookstore (Wallace's Bookstore) sought relief in bankruptcy, having done business with a Virginia community college. Because the bookstore had made payments to the college shortly before filing for bankruptcy, the bankruptcy court appointed a trustee, Katz, who like Hoffman before him gave his name to the Supreme Court's decision. In due course, Katz instituted an adversary proceeding against the college. Because the college was an entity of the State of Virginia, it interposed a defense of sovereign immunity, which was accepted by the bankruptcy court, district court, and court of appeals.

By the time *Central Virginia Community College v. Katz* reached the Court, the retirements of Justices White and Blackmun had left Justice Stevens as the lone Justice remaining from the *Union Gas* majority that

15 To provide some objective perspective, Bob Rasmussen characterizes *Nordic Village* as a case in which the Court "overrode a relatively clear text" (Rasmussen 1993, 553 n.85).

16 Justice Scalia's second (and final) draft (USNV025) made only a slight revision to a single sentence (USNV025:7).

17 Gibson (1995) provides a compelling discussion of the amendment process.

had upheld Congressional authority to abrogate state sovereign immunity. Moreover, the Court already had overruled *Union Gas* in *Seminole Tribe of Florida v. Florida*, holding that Congress did *not* have power under the Indian Commerce Clause to abrogate state sovereign immunity.[18] Moreover, as in *Nordic Village*, contemporaneous personnel shifts suggested a strong likelihood that the Justices would uphold the claim of immunity. To be sure, there were four likely votes against immunity: Justices Stevens, Souter, Ginsburg, and Breyer all had voted to uphold abrogation of state immunity under the Commerce Clause (and the Indian Commerce Clause) in *Union Gas* and *Seminole Tribe*. On the other hand, the Court still had four committed skeptics of congressional power to abrogate state immunity: Justices O'Connor, Scalia, Kennedy, and Thomas remained from the group holding abrogation impermissible in *Union Gas* and *Seminole Tribe*. The only Justice with no prior votes in the area was Chief Justice Roberts, who had replaced Chief Justice Rehnquist since the Court last addressed the question.

Against that backdrop, the natural expectation would have been that the Chief Justice (a former law clerk for Chief Justice Rehnquist) would follow the views of Chief Justice Rehnquist, joining the remainder of the *Seminole Tribe* majority to invalidate the revisions to Section 106. That is what Chief Justice Roberts did, but the rest of the Court did not so readily fall in line. Rather, Justice O'Connor, despite her concurring opinion in *Hoffman* explicitly joining Justice Scalia's views about abrogation under the Commerce Clause, switched sides to join Justice Stevens in affirming Congressional power to abrogate state sovereign immunity.

The course of the decision in Katz differed from the earlier cases even in the briefing. Where the briefs in *Hoffman* did not even mention the Bankruptcy Clause, the briefs in *Katz* directly present an argument that the grant of power to establish "Uniformity" gives Congress a special power to create uniform results, which necessarily would bind all involved parties. Indeed, that argument is the centerpiece of respondent's argument on the merits. Parallel arguments of bankruptcy uniqueness were presented in amicus briefs filed by the National Association of Bankruptcy Trustees, by a noted group of law professors, and by the renowned historian Bruce Mann.[19] Perhaps most interestingly, the United States (which had argued against abrogation of immunity, on statutory grounds, in *Hoffman* and *Nordic Village*) did not appear as an amicus to support the claim of immunity.

18 517 U.S. 44 (1996).

19 Those briefs are available online at the same web site at which I have posted the Justices' papers, www.bksct.net.

Against that backdrop, the opinion of the Court is remarkable, with an ode to the importance of the Bankruptcy Power unlike anything to grace the United States Reports before (or since). Drawing heavily from the amicus briefs, the Court emphasized the clarity with which bankruptcy law intruded on state sovereignty when the Constitution was adopted. Taking an approach quite different from the analysis in *Hoffman* and *Nordic Village*, the Court concluded, whatever the case might be with respect to the Commerce Clause, that the Bankruptcy Clause was understood at the time as an exception to any principles of sovereign immunity the States retained "in the plan of the convention": The ineluctable conclusion, then, was that the States agreed in the plan of the Convention not to assert any sovereign immunity defense they might have had in proceedings brought pursuant to "Laws on the subject of Bankruptcies." Accordingly, the Court concluded, the Bankruptcy Code was not at all subject to the Eleventh Amendment constraints that the Court found binding in *Hoffman*.[20]

The analytical contrast to the earlier cases could hardly be starker. The Court in *Katz* included a detailed discussion of cross-jurisdictional insolvency conflicts during the Revolutionary Era, emphasizing the point that those who wrote the Constitution surely would have wanted a single tribunal to have complete coercive authority to administer the entire proceeding. Even more telling, faced with a technical distinction between "in rem" and "in personam" powers (with the in rem powers on a much more solid historical footing), the Court dismissed the power of the historical labels to constrain: "Whatever the appropriate appellation, those who crafted the Bankruptcy Clause would have understood it to give Congress the power to authorize courts to avoid preferential transfers and to recover the transferred property" (546 U.S. at 372). More attention to that perspective could have avoided not only the confrontation with Congress brought about by *Hoffman* and *Nordic Village*, but also the continuing disarray of judicial administration attributable to the detour of *Marathon*, *Granfinanciera*, and *Stern*.

6.6 THE UNFORTUNATE IRRELEVANCE OF BANKRUPTCY TO CONSTITUTIONAL DOCTRINE

So where does that leave us? The operating thesis of the book is that the Court's blind spot about the importance of bankruptcy in the Constitution's

[20] It is surely no coincidence that Justice Stevens wrote for the Court here. As he made clear after leaving the bench, he for many years regarded the Court's hostility to enforcement of federal statutes against the States as entirely misguided (Stevens 2011). More recently, he included a specific constitutional amendment reversing those decisions in his list of six favored constitutional amendments (Stevens 2014).

scheme of regulation causes the Court systematically to underweight that interest when it confronts other interests of weight. As with the other chapters in the book, the evidence falls far short of proof. Here, for once, though, the Court did find distinct value in the Bankruptcy Clause, in a context in which it has rejected congressional authority under several parallel clauses. For that reason, it would be possible to view *Katz* as a marker of the breadth of the Bankruptcy Clause – the only plainly extant decision upholding congressional authority to abrogate state immunity. It well might be, though, that the Court after *Seminole Tribe* lost the appetite for fighting these battles with Congress. In the decade since *Katz*, the Court has not had a major decision extending (or limiting) its application to other bases of congressional authority. Under that reading, it is just a coincidence that *Katz* happened to bring the Bankruptcy Clause before the Court as it turned away from the immunity area that had been a staple of its docket for three decades.

The question for me is whether this is an exception that supports my thesis or an exception that undermines my premise. What I can say on that subject is that the Court found this value only after repeated and strongly worded input from Congress, and only in a case in which the Government stood by and allowed a redoubtable collection of amici to present more or less undisputed historical evidence about the relevance of the Clause. In that context at least, the Court read the Clause literally and allowed it to prevail over an ahistorical and wholly unanchored implied constitutional doctrine. Whatever it is, it is not a strong statement for the Court's predisposition to interpret the Bankruptcy Power broadly. To me, it says more about the Court's unwillingness to provoke a constitutional confrontation over minor provisions in the Bankruptcy Code than it does about a predilection for broad implementation of the Bankruptcy Power.

Section B – Interpretive Strategy: The Court, the Solicitor General, and the Code

Turning from the constitutionality of the Code to its interpretation, we consider five statutory cases that divided the Court in the early days after the Code's enactment. The most pervasive theme, evident in the earliest of these cases to reach the Court, is the tension between a narrow interpretation of the Bankruptcy Power and a narrow interpretation of the Code. The cases display the Court's erection and ever more vigorous application of a rule of construction presuming that Congress did not intend to change prior law. Despite more than a decade of congressional effort, this premised on the assumption that economic growth demanded a more vigorous system. Thus, the only one of those cases that upholds a broad bankruptcy power (*Bildisco*) does so on the premise that the Court should not interpret the Code as making major changes in prior law. Not coincidentally, the lens of history suggests that this has turned out to be by far the most important case – making the system an effective tool for reorganizing large businesses (airlines in particular) that could not practically be resolved outside the courts.

The narrow interpretation of the Code reaches its zenith in *Kelly* and *BFP*. Where early cases like *Bildisco* and *Midlantic* had balanced bankruptcy interests against other federal statutory regimes, *Kelly* and *BFP* presented direct conflicts between clear text implementing the interests of the bankruptcy system and the relatively unanchored interests of the States. The conspicuous undervaluation of the bankruptcy system against uncodified State policies provides an important corollary to *Bildisco*, *Midlantic*, and *Ron Pair*, where the Bankruptcy Code collides with the interests of statutory schemes supported by federal agencies.

7

Bankruptcy versus Labor Law: *Bildisco*

With Loring Veenstra

The Supreme Court got its first chance to interpret the Bankruptcy Code quickly – *NLRB v. Bildisco* reached the Court less than six months after the decision in *Marathon*. The case is interesting not only because it gave the Court its first look at the substance of the new Code, but because the divided opinions in that case sowed the seeds of what would ripen over time into a consistent practice in the statutory context that parallels what we have discussed above in the constitutional context: at every opportunity for reasonable disagreement, subordinating the interests of the bankruptcy process to competing state and federal interests.

The case is a good one for our analysis, because it presents a direct conflict between the new Bankruptcy Code and another of the major loci of federal policy – labor law. Looking ahead to the features of the cases considered in the chapters to come, it also is fair to say that several overlapping characteristics made *Bildisco* the hardest case for ruling against the bankruptcy interest. First, the relevant bankruptcy power (limiting collective bargaining agreements) was well established under the Act (something that will not be true in the later chapters). Second, the framework under the Code if anything broadened the bankruptcy court's power as compared to the Act. Third, the Solicitor General's ability to make a strong presentation against the bankruptcy interest was hampered by the Solicitor General's obvious bias toward its client, the NLRB. Finally, and perhaps most importantly, the case arose at a time when a large group of the Justices, for reasons wholly unrelated to the bankruptcy process, were concerned about excessive overbreadth of the labor power.

So how does it turn out? With all of those features weighing in favor of the bankruptcy side, the Court elevated the bankruptcy interest over the labor interest, albeit only by a 5–4 vote, and only after last-minute negotiations that came close to gutting the Court's stance on the case's most important issue.[1]

7.1 INTRODUCTION

During the height of the 1980s recession, a small New Jersey partnership filed for bankruptcy and sought to set aside a labor agreement with its employees. The company, Bildisco, was in the business of distributing building supplies; it employed eighteen workers.[2] By most measures, the bankruptcy was unremarkable – the case involved neither millions of dollars nor the prospect of economy-wrenching unemployment. In fact, according to the company's own estimates, setting aside the labor agreement would have saved the company a mere $100,000. As it happens, however, the bankruptcy became embroiled in extended litigation over the extent to which the Teamsters could force the company to comply with federal labor law while in Chapter 11.

The case squarely presents a conflict between two distinct federal legal systems. Federal labor law prohibited Bildisco from terminating its labor agreements without following specific bargaining procedures.[3] At the same time, collective bargaining agreements, such as the labor agreement in *Bildisco*, are executory contracts. The Bankruptcy Code granted explicit authority to terminate an executory contract of a debtor whenever termination would further the debtor's reorganization.[4] The facial conflict between the Bankruptcy Code and the National Labor Relations Act set the stage for a Supreme Court decision reconciling the two statutes. Because neither statute mentioned the other, the case presented the Justices with a simple and direct question: Do the bankruptcy interests in terminating executory contracts warrant an exception to the labor policies protecting collective bargaining agreements?

A bit of background is necessary to set the stage for *Bildisco*. Sections 7.2 and 7.3 examine the political and legal context of *Bildisco*, focusing primarily on organized labor's decline in the 1980s and lower court treatment of the issues. Section 7.4 discusses the Court's process, including the shift during the

1 Dembart and Markell (2004, 392) conclude bluntly that *Bildisco* was a case in which "[p]olicy was a determining factor." Tabb (1987, 521-22) takes a similar view, suggesting that Chief Justice Rehnquist's opinion was grounded in "the 'practical effect' of * * * circumventing bankruptcy law limitations on the enforceability of unassumed executory contracts," and that the principal bases for Justice Brennan's opinion were "the labor law policies of encouraging collective bargaining and preventing economic warfare."

2 The factual background comes from the *Bildisco* Petition Appendix at 69.

3 29 U.S.C. § 158(d) (1984).

4 11 U.S.C. § 365(a) (1984)

course of deliberations to give considerably more credence to the concerns of labor policy. Sections 7.5 and 7.6 discuss *Bildisco*'s aftermath and examine the congressional response to the case, closing with a brief postscript regarding *Bildisco*'s effect on the G.M. and Chrysler bankruptcies of this century.

7.2 LABOR POLITICS IN THE 1980S

Bildisco was decided as organized labor was enduring a long decline in political power from the heights of the 1940s and 1950s. In 1964, 29.3% of non-agricultural wage and salary workers were members of a union.[5] In New Jersey, where Bildisco was operated, 39.4% of non-agricultural wage and salary workers were union members in 1964.[6] By 1984, when *Bildisco* was announced, union membership, both nationally and in New Jersey, had declined by about 35% (to 19.1% nationally and 25.0% in New Jersey). In addition to declining membership, labor's power was weakened by a hostile atmosphere in Washington, D.C. due to Republican control of both the Presidency and the Senate. President Reagan's decision in 1981 to fire striking air traffic controllers, coupled with the lowest incidence of labor strikes since the Bureau of Labor Statistics began keeping records in 1947, emboldened employers to take harsh lines with their unions (West 1986, 67).

In the bankruptcy arena, organized labor was fighting mostly losing battles against companies looking for relief from high-cost employment agreements. Of those bankruptcies, those in the airline industry were the most visible. The deregulation of the airline industry in the late 1970s and the advent of small low-cost carriers put severe economic pressure on the large established airlines. CEOs such as Continental's Frank Lorenzo realized that the Bankruptcy Code was a potent weapon against unions and labor contracts. Continental filed for bankruptcy in September of 1983. Lorenzo immediately repudiated the union contracts and rehired back a portion of Continental's workers, most at about half pay. The pay cuts persisted through a series of strikes by three of the company's unions and remained in place as the company moved out of bankruptcy in June of 1986.

Those bankruptcies were devastating to labor, not only because of what local unions individually lost, but also because of the developing perception that many of the bankruptcies terminating labor agreements had been

5 Georgia State University Union Membership Database, available at http://unionstats.gsu.edu (last visited May 3, 2010)

6 Georgia State University Union Membership Database, available at http://unionstats.gsu.edu (last visited May 3, 2010).

successful. The *New York Times* noted, for example, that Continental's repudiation of its union contracts had allowed it to reduce labor costs from 36% of overall costs to 22%. The newspaper reported that, as a result of repudiation, Continental was able to turn a profit within a year of entering into bankruptcy. Public perception of the severity of the 1980s recession, coupled with a sense that cutting labor costs in bankruptcy "worked" to resuscitate profits, was a dangerous and often fatal combination for organized labor's interests (Salpukas 1985).

7.3 THE LEGAL CONTEXT OF *BILDISCO*

The conflict between the National Labor Relations Act ("NLRA") and the Bankruptcy Code was not new. Rather, it was simply another phase of a conflict between labor law and bankruptcy policy that had played out under the old Bankruptcy Act. Given the importance of labor cases under the old Act to the Court's resolution of *Bildisco*, some prefatory discussion of the Act's provisions and the cases applying it is necessary.

7.3.1 *The Code and the NLRA*

In the bankruptcy context, an executory contract is a contract in which continuing material obligations burden both sides. All would agree that the term includes collective bargaining agreements – the agreements between employers and union employees regarding salary, benefits, seniority, etc.: employers have ongoing obligations to pay for wages and employees have similarly protracted obligations to work. The relevant provision of the old Act, Section 313(1), provided (much like Section 365 of the Code) that the debtor could apply to the bankruptcy court to reject its executory contracts. Conversely, the NLRA explicitly subjects an employer to liability if it terminates or modifies an unexpired collective bargaining agreement. For example, Section 8(a)(5) of the NLRA (29 U.S.C. § 158(a)(5)) makes it an unfair labor practice for an employer to "refuse to bargain collectively with the representatives of his employees."

An employer's duty to bargain collectively is quite explicit and unambiguously includes, among other things, a prohibition on unilateral modification of a contract. Rather, NLRA Section 8(d) contemplates an extended negotiating process over any change in the terms and conditions of employment. Specifically, it provides "that no party to [a collective bargaining agreement] shall terminate or modify such contract unless" it (1) provides the other party to the contract with timely written notice of the proposed modification, (2) "offers to meet and confer with the other party," (3) provides timely notice to the Federal Mediation and Conciliation Service and any similar state agencies, and (4) "continues in full force and effect . . . all the terms and conditions of the existing contract for a period of sixty days after such notice is given or until the expiration date of such contract, whatever occurs later."[7] The apparent tension between Section 313(1) of the Bankruptcy Act and Section 8(a) of the NLRA produced two highly visible appellate decisions. Oddly enough, although they took quite different approaches to resolving that tension, both cases were decided by the Second Circuit in 1975, shortly before enactment of the Code.

7.3.2 Kevin Steel

The first case, *Kevin Steel*, concerned a steel fabricator and erector located in West Haverstraw, New York. Kevin Steel filed for bankruptcy in September of 1973 and sought leave of the court to reject its labor contract with the local branch of the AFL-CIO. When the bankruptcy judge allowed Kevin Steel to reject the contract, the union appealed. The district court reversed, concluding that the bankruptcy court did not have the power to allow the debtor to reject the contract.[8]

On appeal, the questions before the Second Circuit were whether the bankruptcy court (as opposed to the NLRB) had the authority to reject a collective bargaining agreement, and if so, what standard should govern rejection. On the first point, the Second Circuit concluded that the language in Section 313(1) allowing rejection of executory contracts contained no exceptions for labor agreements. Rather, the court of appeals reasoned that because a debtor-in-possession was a different legal entity than the pre-bankruptcy corporation, it was not subject to labor contracts entered into by the pre-bankruptcy Kevin Steel.[9] The court analogized a debtor-in-possession to a company's purchaser. A purchaser is generally not bound by pre-existing labor agreements and is free to renegotiate such agreements with the union; the

7 At least for purposes of labor law, it would have seemed difficult to dispute the application of those provisions to a debtor in bankruptcy. 29 U.S.C. § 152(2) defines the term "employer" to include "any person acting as an agent of an employer, indirectly or directly." A trustee or debtor-in-possession seems likely to be either the employer itself or a person acting as the employer's agent, and so readily within the meaning of that provision.

8 Shopmen's Local Union No. 455 v. Kevin Steel Products, Inc., 519 F.2d 698, 700 (2d Cir. 1975) [hereinafter *Kevin Steel*].

9 *Kevin Steel, supra*, 519 F.2d at 704.

court applied the same reasoning to the bankruptcy context.[10] This "new entity" reconciliation between the Bankruptcy Act and the NLRA is problematic for several reasons. Not only does it more or less ignore the NLRA's broad definition of "employer," it renders the "rejection" mechanism of the Bankruptcy Act largely superfluous. If the debtor were not bound by pre-bankruptcy contracts, there would be no reason for the Act to have prescribed a process for rejecting them.

Even though the Second Circuit concluded that a debtor-in-possession was not subject to a collective bargaining agreement for the purposes of determining whether it should comply with § 8(d), the court took two steps to accommodate that conclusion to labor law interests. First, the court (which had just held that the debtor was not a party to the collective bargaining agreement for purposes of labor law) nevertheless concluded that a bankruptcy court should go through the motions of rejecting the collective bargaining agreement for purposes of the Bankruptcy Act. Second, the *Kevin Steel* court articulated a heightened standard for rejection of a collective bargaining agreement. Although the traditional standard under Section 313 required the debtor only to show that rejection would improve the debtor's financial status, the *Kevin Steel* court found that a slightly more stringent standard was necessary because of the "importance of the policies behind the Labor Act."[11] Thus, the court held that the bankruptcy judge should permit rejection of a collective bargaining agreement only "after thorough scrutiny, and a careful balancing of the equities on both sides."[12]

7.3.3 REA Express

Thirty-four days after *Kevin Steel* was decided, a different panel of Second Circuit judges issued a ruling in a similar case involving REA Express.[13] REA Express was in the business of transporting shipments by air and rail. It was party to two collective bargaining agreements, covering approximately 6,600 of its employees. REA filed for bankruptcy in February of 1975 and sought to reject its labor agreements. The bankruptcy judge denied REA's petition to reject the agreements, finding that he did not have power under Chapter 11

[10] *Kevin Steel, supra,* 519 F.2d at 704 ("Until the debtor . . . assumes the old agreement or makes a new one, it is not a 'party' under section 8(d) to any labor agreement with the union and is simply not subject to the termination restrictions of the section.").

[11] *Kevin Steel, supra,* 519 F.2d at 706.

[12] *Kevin Steel, supra,* 519 F.2d at 707.

[13] *Brotherhood of Railway, Airline and Steamship Clerks, Freight Handlers, Express and Station Employees,* AFL-CIO v. REA Express, Inc., 523 F.2d 164 (2d Cir. 1975) [hereinafter *REA Express*].

to allow the rejection.[14] REA appealed, and the district court reversed the bankruptcy judge, approving rejection. Predictably enough, the unions then appealed to the Second Circuit.

One possible difference between *REA Express* and *Kevin Steel* is that the labor agreements in *REA Express* were governed by the Railway Labor Act rather than the NLRA. The court thought that unimportant though, reasoning that the two statutes provide similar protections to workers and mandate, with some differences, particular procedures an employer must follow to terminate or modify a collective bargaining agreement.[15]

On the merits, the *REA Express* court agreed with *Kevin Steel*'s holding that a debtor-in-possession is a new entity, distinct from the employer, and thus relieved of its bargaining obligations under the Railway Labor Act. The *REA Express* court did not agree, however, with the *Kevin Steel* standard for rejection of a collective-bargaining agreement under Bankruptcy Act Section 313. Rejecting *Kevin Steel*'s "balancing of the equities" approach, the *REA Express* court concluded that rejection of a collective bargaining agreement should be authorized only where "it clearly appears to be the lesser of two evils, and that, unless the agreement is rejected, the carrier will collapse, and the employees will no longer have their jobs."[16] The difference between the two standards was not a mere technicality. On the contrary, the *REA Express* standard put employees last in line to feel the hurt of reorganization, fearing loss of benefits only if they were the straw that would break the debtor's back. Under *Kevin Steel*, by contrast, rejection of collective bargaining agreements was not markedly more unlikely than the rejection of other contracts.

7.3.4 *The* Bildisco *Bankruptcy*

Bildisco filed for bankruptcy on April 14, 1980. After filing for bankruptcy, the company's compliance with its labor contracts became sporadic. The union complained to the National Labor Relations Board (the "Board") that Bildisco had refused to grant wage increases, pay pension and welfare contributions, and turn over union dues – all in violation of the collective bargaining agreement. On July 31, 1980, the Board issued a complaint, alleging that Bildisco had engaged in unfair labor practices under the NLRA by unilaterally modifying its collective bargaining agreement. Bildisco did not respond to the

[14] *Railway Express, supra,* 523 F.2d at 167.

[15] *Railway Express, supra,* 523 F.2d at 168–169.

[16] *Railway Express, supra,* 523 F.2d at 172.

Board's complaint until after the bankruptcy court approved rejection of its labor contract on January 15, 1981.

By that time, more than five months after the Board had issued its complaint, the Board's general counsel had moved for summary judgment based on Bildisco's failure to respond. Bildisco then argued that the rejection of the collective bargaining agreement by the bankruptcy court related back to the date of bankruptcy, so it could not be liable for refusing to comply with the agreement in the post-petition/pre-rejection period. The Board disagreed, and on April 23, 1981, granted the motion for summary judgment – noting that Bildisco had not shown good cause for its failure to respond to the complaint in a timely manner. When both proceedings produced appeals, the Third Circuit consolidated them for joint consideration. In one, the Board sought enforcement of its order against Bildisco for violation of the NLRA. In the other, the union appealed the district court's affirmance of the bankruptcy court's rejection of the collective bargaining agreement.

The Third Circuit's opinion mirrored that of *Kevin Steel*. The court used the "new entity" approach to conclude that the bargaining requirements of NLRA Section 8(d) did not apply to a debtor in bankruptcy.[17] The Third Circuit had a harsh assessment of *REA Express*, accusing that Second Circuit panel of "trampling upon the grave" of *Kevin Steel*.[18] Turning to policy, the Third Circuit reasoned that *REA Express*'s more stringent standard for rejection (the "likely to fail" standard) would "exalt the perpetuation of the collective bargaining agreement over the more pragmatic consideration of whether the employees [would] continue to have jobs at all."[19] Ultimately, the Third Circuit concluded (1) that it would adopt the *Kevin Steel* standard, and (2) that Bildisco was not liable for committing an unfair labor practice in the post-petition/pre-rejection period.

Although the Third Circuit's doctrinal approach mirrored that of *Kevin Steel*, the two courts' sense of the broader economic implications of their respective decisions diverged sharply. The *Kevin Steel* court thought that business use of bankruptcy laws to void union contracts would be infrequent, suggesting that only a "foolhardy employer would provoke a strike by trying

[17] In re Bildisco, 682 F.2d 72, 78-79 (1982) [hereinafter In re *Bildisco*] ("[A] debtor-in-possession is a new entity, separate and apart from the pre-bankruptcy company, and does not become a party to an executory contract unless it assumes the contract. Bildisco, as a debtor-in-possession was not a party to the collective bargaining agreement, and therefore not bound by § 8(d)").

[18] Waxing indignant, the court characterized the *REA Express* panel as "adding a substantial gloss to a previously stated holding but improperly citing the former case as the authority for the new formulation" and "disguis[ing] an expansion of the law by pretending that the court is simply applying a previously stated rule of law." In re *Bildisco, supra*, 682 F.2d at 79 n.11.

[19] In re *Bildisco, supra*, 682 F.2d at 80.

to terminate an existing labor contract."[20] Indeed, that court doubted that its approach would encourage businesses to swarm into bankruptcy proceedings: "we doubt many will attempt to do so."[21] By 1982, when the Third Circuit considered the Bildisco bankruptcy, the judicial rhetoric had changed. The Third Circuit offered no conciliatory references to "foolhardy" employers or the likely limited effect of the decision. Rather, it noted the severe recession and proposed that in a period of economic distress, the choice between the *REA Express* approach and the *Kevin Steel* approach was between choosing to lose one's job because of a union's intransigence or choosing to keep it, albeit at a lower wage, by succumbing to an employer's demands.[22]

7.4 THE COURT'S DECISION

7.4.1 *Before the Argument*

7.4.1.1 To Hear or Not to Hear?

Unlike most of the cases that we examine, the Court's decision to consider *Bildisco* was a close one. The Court faced twin petitions, one from the NLRB (represented by the Solicitor General) and one from the Teamsters (representing the Bildisco employees). To the author of the pool memo (from Justice Blackmun's chambers), the conflict between *REA Express* and *Bildisco* was easily a sufficient reason for review; he was wholly persuaded by the argument of the Solicitor General that the difference between the Act and the Code was unimportant (BILD001:8–9). Not all of the Justices agreed, however. In particular, Justice Powell's handwritten pre-Conference notes display the view (evidently crediting the change from the Act to the Code) that there was "No conflict" and that the issues "could benefit from further consideration by C[ourts of] A[ppeals]" (BILD001:1). At the Conference, three Justices (Brennan, Blackmun, and Marshall) voted to grant and five voted to deny (Chief Justice Burger, and Justices Powell, Rehnquist, Stevens, and O'Connor); Justice White asked for a week to "take a second look" (BILD036). A week later, after further deliberation, Justice White voted to grant, bringing the two cases before the Court for plenary consideration (BILD037).

20 *Kevin Steel, supra*, 519 F.2d at 703.
21 *Kevin Steel, supra*, 519 F.2d at 705–706.
22 In re *Bildisco, supra*, 682 F.2d at 81 n.3.

7.4.1.2 The Disparate Views of the Clerks

It is clear from the initial views of the law clerks that the legal questions were debatable; the bench memoranda from the chambers of Justices White, Powell, and Blackmun all display divergent views. Justice White's clerk thought the fiction that the debtor was a "new entity" not bound by the collective bargaining agreement wholly untenable, but reasoned that the bankruptcy court should have power to reject those agreements to prevent "frustrat[ion of] bankruptcy goals" (BILD046:19). To deal with the labor policy issues, he thought that the Justices reasonably could "cabin" the district court's discretion to reject by requiring the employer to give reasonable notice and bargain in good faith before rejection (BILD046:23–25). As for the standard of rejection, he preferred the much more lenient *Kevin Steel* standard, reasoning that the *REA Express* standard amounted to discrimination in favor of employees; he doubted that the status of employees could "justify immunizing [them] from all sacrifices until all other parties have given up as much as possible" (BILD046:27–28).

Justice Powell's clerk, by contrast, saw the case almost entirely through the lens of the Court's labor law cases considering when successor employers are bound by preexisting collective bargaining agreements. Most importantly, Justice Powell in his first term on the Court had joined a heated dissent by Justice Rehnquist from the decision in *NLRB v. Burns Internal Security Services*; the dissent argued that the Court had extended successorship obligations far too broadly.[23] As applied to *Bildisco*, that suggested a predisposition against binding the debtor in bankruptcy to the pre-bankruptcy collective bargaining agreement.

Moreover, because it was established that a company that buys a business is not directly bound by the seller's collective bargaining agreement, it seemed odd to her that the same rule would not apply when the company's business was transferred to a debtor in bankruptcy. She found particularly compelling the special rule in Bankruptcy Code Section 1167, which restricts the debtor's right to reject a Railway Labor Act agreement; the absence of a similar provision protecting NLRA agreements suggested a free hand for rejection. Justice Powell's marginal notes show that he found those points telling (BILD038:19–23). Still, like Justice White's clerk, she saw no reason why the debtor should not be obligated to bargain with the union, and Justice Powell noted that he was "inclined to agree" (BILD038:24–29). Justice Powell's clerk was particularly concerned that the union would not bargain realistically with the

[23] 406 U.S. 272, 296–310 (1972).

employer unless a credible threat of rejection brought it to the table. Agreeing, Justice Powell's marginal comment asked: "What incentives are there for Union to bargain seriously rather than 'put-off' rejection by delaying tactics?" (BILD038:37).

For yet another take on the case, Justice Blackmun's clerk would have given the NLRB much more credence. Like Justice White's clerk, she focused on the incongruity of holding the debtor free of the collective bargaining agreement as a "new entity," though bound under Section 365 to pay damages for the breach of contracts that it rejects (BILD002:25–31). But she drew a different conclusion from that point. She found the plight of employees unacceptable: "If the employees have to stand in line with other creditors for their damages, they will recover little and it will be late" (BILD002:34). Accordingly, she concluded that the contracts remained fully binding after the bankruptcy filing and that the employer's failure to comply amounted to an unfair labor practice, sanctionable by the NLRB (BILD002:35–40).

7.4.2 *Argument*

If the argument revealed anything, it was that several of the Justices were firmly set against giving the NLRA a broad hand in this context. To be sure, criticism of the labor position was facilitated by misstatements from both of the attorneys arguing on that side of the case. First, the attorney for the Solicitor General (representing the NLRB) faced withering criticism (apparently from Justice Rehnquist) when he argued that Congress had adopted the "likely to fail" standard from *REA Express*. When he misspoke and suggested that "Congress did indicate some awareness" of the Second Circuit decisions, he was asked "How did Congress indicate that awareness?" When he admitted that the only evidence related to amendments to the Bankruptcy Act, that there was no reference to those cases in the Code's legislative history, he retreated to the "general principle that Congress is presumed to be aware of how the law has developed." And even there he was pressed: "Is there any general principle that Congress is presumed to be aware of every district court, every court of appeals decision, or every decision of this Court, however episodic it may be?" (Transcript at 3–4).

Similarly, when counsel for the Teamsters argued that full compliance with NLRA procedures "should be a condition precedent to rejection," a position much more extreme than the Teamsters had taken in their brief, Justice White asked, incredulously, whether "they must comply literally with all the requirements of 8(d)?" (Transcript at 10–11). At that point, the Teamsters representative readily agreed that "in terms of the policy considerations here, ... I don't think so" (Transcript at 11).

The Section 8(d) problem was compounded in an interchange with Justice Stevens. First, Justice Stevens asked whether the debtor should be obligated to provide the sixty-day notice of an intention to modify a collective bargaining agreement that subsection 8(d)(1) requires. Apparently attempting to waffle, the attorney explained "I think that literally it all should apply, but I think ... since we are seeking an accommodation of the two statutes ... I think both statutes have to bend to meet that public interest" (Transcript at 17). When Justice Stevens suggested that "in other words, I think what you are saying is no, it doesn't apply," the attorney acknowledged that "the public interest would tolerate something less than total compliance" (Transcript at 17–18).

At that point, Justice Stevens suggested that the attorney essentially had abandoned his whole argument: "It seems to me, then, that you are really not arguing that 8(d) applies, but rather, that you are arguing that the extent to which there has been pretermination negotiation and notice and bargaining is part of a standard that should be applied by the bankruptcy judge in deciding whether or not to approve rejection." When the attorney insisted "[r]espectfully" that he was "not arguing that," but rather urging a "per se requirement in accordance with Section 8(d) to get the parties together," Justice Stevens responded that this was "a per se requirement that requires a modest rewriting of the statute" (Transcript at 18).

By contrast, the argument for the company was relatively uneventful. The most important event probably was his revelation that the facts on the ground had changed significantly. When Bildisco filed for bankruptcy it had eighteen employees; when the bankruptcy court allowed rejection of the collective bargaining agreement nine months later, it had only three. When the case reached the Supreme Court, Bildisco had ten employees, but only one was performing a job that previously would have been performed by a union member (Transcript at 37). That certainly underscored a fact setting in which protracted compliance with the traditional labor process would seem a dubious use of resources.

7.4.3 *The Initial Decision*

Most of the Justices said relatively little during the argument. So the questions expressing skepticism about the labor position said little about how the votes actually would line up. That question was resolved, at least tentatively, a few days later at the Conference. The notes from the files of Justices Blackmun and Powell suggest an unusually tentative and far-ranging discussion, motivated both by uncertainty about the outcome and by the multiple overlapping issues the case presented.

What seems to have emerged from the discussion was that the Justices were unanimous in the view that the bankruptcy court could reject a collective bargaining agreement, a holding with which not even the NLRB could quarrel. They were, though, closely divided on the central practical question: whether a company's obligation to comply with a collective bargaining agreement remained in force after a bankruptcy filing, so that it would be a sanctionable unfair labor practice to act unilaterally upon filing for relief in bankruptcy. The Chief Justice and Justices Powell, Rehnquist, Stevens, and O'Connor thought that the bankruptcy filing made the agreement unenforceable; Justices Brennan, Marshall, Blackmun, and White thought that the agreement should remain in force (BILD007, 041). Although this is an important tempering of labor law in bankruptcy, what is important is the closeness of the question: Four Justices supported the NLRA on that point, one that had seemed unthinkable to the courts of appeals (all of which had thought the bankruptcy filing absolved the company from any further obligation of compliance).

Justice Stevens provided the most detailed reasoning for the majority position (and Justices Powell and O'Connor noted their agreement with his explanation).[24] At the time of the Conference, Justice Stevens took the view that "a CBA must be treated just as any ex[ecutory] c[on]t[rac]ts," but at the same time "an unfair labor practice could be committed by the Debtor such as failing to bargain for a new CBA" (BILD041:2). Conversely, Justice Brennan characterized the case as "difficult"; he rejected the idea that the debtor was a "new entity," reasoned that "[u]ntil rejection the cba remains in effect," and accordingly "would enforce the B[oar]d's order" that Bildisco's unilateral actions amounted to an unfair labor practice (BILD041:1). Justice White found the case "Imp[ortant]" and "tough" (BILD007:1), agreeing that "CBAs are rejectable," but thinking that the contract "[i]n the interim . . . is binding" (BILD041:1).

Although less clear, there also seemed (at least at that time) to be a consensus that the appropriate standard for rejection was far closer to the lenient *Kevin Steel* standard than it was to the more onerous *REA Express* standard. The Chief Justice thought the more onerous standard was "unrealistic" and

24 Justice O'Connor went so far as to say that Justice Stevens's comments struck her as "absolutely * * * correct and crystal clear to me" (BILD007:3). As we will see below, her views diverged from his upon more detailed consideration.

would "go too far" (BILD007:1). Justices Brennan and White both expressed support for the Chief Justice's summary on that point, despite their stark rejection of his views on the pre-rejection treatment of the collective bargaining agreement (BILD041:1).

7.4.4 *The Opinions*

The Chief Justice assigned the opinion to Justice Rehnquist. His first draft, circulated less than a month later (BILD009, 042, 049, 080, 123), was uncompromising in its elevation of bankruptcy policy over labor-law interests. He organized the case around two problems: when a bankruptcy court could reject a collective bargaining agreement and whether the collective bargaining agreement remained in force until any rejection. On the first point, he emphasized the unqualified grant of authority to reject executory contracts in Section 365 and the explicit exception for Railway Labor Act contracts in Section 1167; together those seemed to compel the conclusion that rejection is permitted. That section of the opinion does not so much as mention Section 8 of the NLRA (BILD009:6–8).

As for the appropriate standard, he rejected the *REA Express* "likely to fail" standard with a paean to bankruptcy policy perhaps as broad as anything ever to appear in the *United States Reports*. The basic problem was that he found the "likely to fail" standard "fundamentally at odds with the policies of flexibility and equity built into Chapter 11 of the Bankruptcy Code" (BILD009:10). He agreed that the "rights of workers under collective bargaining agreements are important," but criticized the "likely to fail" standard as "subordinat[ing] the multiple, competing considerations underlying a Chapter 11 reorganization to one issue: whether rejection of the collective bargaining agreements is necessary to prevent the debtor from going into liquidation" (BILD009:10). The draft even repackaged the resolution of the labor law issue (enforcing the results of collective bargaining) as a choice between competing creditors of the bankrupt:

> by elevating one group of creditors over another, the *REA Express* standard is at odds with two fundamental premises of reorganization under the Bankruptcy Code–that all classes of creditors are treated fairly and equitably . . . and all creditors within a class equally. . . . [C]onditioning rejection of collective-bargaining agreements on the risk of liquidation would exalt the rights of organized workers over those of other employees. (BILD009:11)

Against that policy backdrop, the opinion adopted a test for rejection almost identical to that of *Kevin Steel* and the Third Circuit in *Bildisco*, allowing rejection when the collective bargaining agreement "burdens the estate" and "after careful scrutiny, the equities balance in favor of rejecting the labor contract" (BILD009:11). He did not even mandate bargaining by the debtor; he merely stated that "the basic interests of the parties might well be served by reaching a private solution" and that the court "may inquire into what measures have been taken to negotiate a private settlement, and when appropriate, [may] encourage the parties to do so" (BILD009:11).

Turning to Section 8(d), the opinion dismissed the idea that the debtor must comply with Section 8(d) before rejection, emphasizing "detailed and immutable requirements" that "fail to reflect the exigencies of a party in bankruptcy" (BILD009:12). From that point, the draft turned to the NLRB's argument that the debtor would be guilty of an unfair labor practice if it ceased compliance with a collective bargaining agreement before obtaining formal rejection. The draft sidestepped the idea that the debtor is a "new entity" not bound by the pre-petition agreement at all. Rather, he reasoned that bankruptcy provides the exclusive process for challenging a breach of contract by a bankrupt, and thus precludes the NLRB from forcing the debtor to comply. That point leads in turn to the view that the collective bargaining agreement "is no longer immediately enforceable" from the moment of filing, and thus no longer "an enforceable contract within the meaning of NLRA §8(d)" (BILD009:18).

As with the prior section of the opinion, Justice Rehnquist rested his analysis directly on the view that labor law could not properly impede bankruptcy policy:

> The fundamental purpose of reorganization is to prevent a debtor from going into liquidation, with an attendant loss of jobs and possible misuse of economic resources. . . . [T]he authority to reject an executory contract is vital to the basic purpose [of] a Chapter 11 reorganization, because rejection can release the debtor's estate from burdensome obligations that can impede a successful reorganization. (BILD009:14)

If the opinion had survived unamended it would have marked a truly remarkable acceptance of the importance of bankruptcy in mitigating the costs to the economy of financial distress, in the Court's first assessment of the substance of the Code. And it did gain prompt and unconditional joinder from the Chief Justice (BILD016, 056) and Justices Powell (BILD043, 052) and O'Connor (BILD012, 053). But it was clear just a week after he circulated the opinion that Justice Rehnquist would be hard-pressed to find a fifth vote for the broad reasoning of the first draft. Rather than joining the opinion, Justice

Stevens circulated a detailed[25] memorandum identifying problems going to the core of Justice Rehnquist's draft (BILD017, 044, 057, 079, 112).

Most importantly, the focus of Justice Stevens's concerns was on Justice Rehnquist's articulation of bankruptcy policy. He started by rejecting the first point Justice Rehnquist made, that special treatment for collective bargaining agreements would violate a policy of treating similarly situated creditors equally. In his view, "a collective bargaining agreement is not substantially similar to any other type of executory contract, in light of the unique function of collective bargaining agreements, and their unique value as tools of national labor policy" (BILD017:1–2). Moreover, he noted, the opinion is inconsistent in pressing the idea that employees must be treated the same as other creditors, because it later agrees to a special standard for rejecting collective bargaining agreements (albeit a relatively lenient one) (BILD017:3–4).

He also objected to the policy discussion that supported the ability to unilaterally modify a collective bargaining agreement, noting that the opinion explains that requiring compliance with the NLRA "would be inconsistent with the policies underlying chapter 11." Rejecting Justice Rehnquist's analysis of the case through the lens of bankruptcy policy, Justice Stevens complained that

> [t]he opinion does not ... explain why the policies of the Bankruptcy Code should prevail over the policies of the Labor Act. This is understandable, since it would be difficult (and unwise) for a court to attempt to weigh competing policies and make an essentially legislative choice between them unless absolutely necessary. Instead of permitting a party to violate one statute in order to serve the policies of another, the starting point for statutory construction in a case such as this should be, if possible, to find a construction that renders both statutes consistent. (BILD017:5)

Happily for Justice Rehnquist, Justice Stevens agreed with Justice Rehnquist's statutory analysis – that the filing of a bankruptcy petition renders the contract unenforceable, under the NLRA or otherwise. Thus, he would prefer that the opinion state that "§ 8(d) does not apply to rejection of a collective bargaining agreement, rather than to assume it does apply but can be ignored" (BILD017:6).

Finally, Justice Stevens challenged the lenient "balance of the equities" test Justice Rehnquist had proposed for rejecting collective bargaining agreements. Again challenging what he regarded as an arbitrary elevation of

[25] Justice Powell remarked, "Wow! Eleven pages" on his copy of the memorandum (BILD044:1).

bankruptcy interests over labor interests, he asked that the opinion explain "that, at a minimum, the Labor Act requires the parties to have made reasonable efforts to reach an agreement ... prior to ... rejection of the contract" (BILD017:7). As he put it, "requiring the parties to seek an agreement on the future of their collective bargaining agreement ... would serve ... labor policies and minimize the likelihood of labor strife through precipitous rejection of the agreement" (BILD017:8). Thus, he recommended, rejection should be permitted only when "the parties' inability to reach agreement threatens the success of the debtor's reorganization" (BILD017:8).

Justice Rehnquist wrote back the next day, explaining (BILD018, 045, 059, 076, 110) that he "ha[d] read, but not yet fully digested, your 11-page tome of [yesterday]" (BILD018:1).[26] Rather than revising his draft to align itself with Justice Stevens's concerns, he responded that "my purposes would be better served, and yours would be too, if you could translate the three criticisms ... of the presently circulating draft into concrete suggestions." He went on to express the view that he expected he could accommodate any suggestions Justice Stevens might make, though he had the impression that the memorandum was recommending language quite similar to the "*REA Express* standard which I thought was unanimously rejected by the Conference discussion of this case" (BILD018:2).

On the same day, Justice O'Connor weighed in with her views, generally urging Justice Rehnquist, if possible, to retain his original draft. She found it appropriate that bankruptcy policies should be "taken into account in deciding which of several higher-than-normal standards for rejection should be adopted" and doubted whether it was useful to require district courts to intervene in the bargaining process (BILD019, 058, 077, 111).

After taking a few weeks to craft specific suggestions, Justice Stevens returned with another detailed submission (BILD020, 060, 075, 109), requesting three specific revisions. The first two requests would change the tone of the opinion – moving away from the emphasis of the first draft on the needs of bankruptcy as driving the decision toward the view that the language of the statutes, read together, drove the result. Thus, his first request asked Justice Rehnquist to delete the two sentences explaining how bankruptcy policy supported a right of rejection (BILD020:1). His second request asked for deletion of section II(B) of the first draft, the section that had relied on

[26] He explained, "At this point I think I know how Francis Scott Key must have felt on that early morning in Baltimore Harbor when he wrote the second verse of *The Star-Spangled Banner*" – and proceeded to quote the entire verse (which describes the "foe's haughty host," "dimly seen through the mists of the deep," and the "breeze ... that fitfully blows, half conceals, half discloses") (BILD018:1).

Supreme Court of the United States
Washington, D. C. 20543

CHAMBERS OF
JUSTICE WILLIAM H. REHNQUIST

November 17, 1983

Re: Nos. 82-818 & 82-852 NLRB v. Bildisco & Bildisco

Dear John:

I have read, but not yet fully digested, your 11-page tome of November 16th. At this point I think I know how Francis Scott Key must have felt on that early morning in Baltimore Harbor when he wrote the second verse of The Star-Spangled Banner:

"On the shore, dimly seen through the mists of the deep,
Where the foe's haughty host in dread silence reposes,
What is that which the breeze, o'er the towering steep,
As it fitfully blows, half conceals, half discloses?"

I think that my purposes would be better served, and perhaps yours would be too, if you could translate the three criticisms of Part II of the presently circulating draft into concrete suggestions. For what it is worth, and based on my present understanding of the contents of your letter, I have the following reactions:

(1) I was very leery in my draft of saying anything more about the Bankruptcy Code in general than I thought was absolutely necessary to decide this case. I do not feel that I am qualified to make any sort of an exegesis on the meaning of the Bankruptcy Code, and I didn't think that the briefs afforded us all that much help if we were inclined to make the effort. If you could make specific suggestions in connection with your first point, I think I would be better able to deal with them.

FIGURE 7.1 Justice Rehnquist's Memorandum in *NLRB v. Bildisco* (excerpt). (BILD018)

bankruptcy policy to support the view that compliance with Section 8(d) was not a condition precedent for rejection. In place of that section, Justice Stevens submitted a three-paragraph insert, summarizing his early memorandum, omitting the paean to bankruptcy policy and explaining that Section 8(d) was wholly inapplicable after bankruptcy filings (BILD020:1–3).

The third request was considerably more substantive. There, Justice Stevens asked for deletion of the paragraph from the original draft (quoted above) that had extolled the virtues of private bargaining but stopped short of requiring the parties to bargain. In its place, Justice Stevens submitted a five-paragraph insert, also drawing directly on his earlier memorandum, which raised the standard for rejection much higher. Specifically, it permitted the court to consider rejection "only if the parties' inability to reach an agreement threatens the success of the debtor's reorganization," and conditioned rejection on a "finding of fact that an affirmance of the contract would prevent the successful rehabilitation of the debtor" (BILD020:3–6).

Because Justice Rehnquist needed the vote of Justice Stevens to retain a majority, he could not ignore the suggestions. But neither did he accept them entirely. Rather, it appears, he spent another week discussing the matter directly with Justice Stevens, leading to yet another memorandum, this one from Justice Rehnquist to the other members of the majority, summarizing the changes to which he and Justice Stevens had agreed (BILD023). As a result of that discussion, he generally accepted the first two (arguably stylistic) suggestions. With regard to the rejection standard, however, the resolution was much more of a compromise. As discussed above, Justice Rehnquist's first draft in practice (the "burdens the estate" standard) probably would have routinized elimination of collective bargaining agreements in the early stages of most reorganizations. By contrast, the revision proposed by Justice Stevens (the "prevent ... successful rehabilitation" standard) would have centered reorganization on the question of the collective bargaining agreement, deferring the possibility of any global solution until it could be determined whether it was feasible to preserve the preexisting labor arrangement on any terms.

Ultimately, the two seem to have agreed on a compromise standard, with some language from each of the proposals, but sufficiently lacking in specificity to preclude the polar results of either of the original proposals. Specifically, the compromise language required a finding that rejection would "serv[e]" the policy of "permit[ting] successful rehabilitation of debtors" (BILD023:4). By linking rejection to "successful rehabilitation," the standard went much farther than the original requirement that the contract merely "burden" the estate. Conversely, by eliminating the specific requirement of a finding that rejection would "prevent ... successful rehabilitation," the compromise made it feasible for a debtor to resolve labor issues as part of a general solution to the company's financial problems. When all of the affected parties agreed to the revisions (BILD022, 024, 061, 090, 108), the result was an opinion for a full majority.

Remarkably, those negotiations proceeded with no activity from the four dissenting Justices. Justice Brennan had assigned the dissent to himself shortly after the Conference (BILD008, 047, 078, 121), but he did not circulate a draft until February, almost two months after the majority Justices had resolved their disagreements. At that point, Justice Brennan's opinion (BILD027, 064, 091, 105), giving an even freer rein to labor policy than Justice Stevens had requested, was almost entirely beside the point. With only minor revisions (BILD033, 071, 096, 099), the opinion for the Court was final.

Looking back, the most obvious puzzle about the case is why Justice Stevens compromised so much to reach agreement with Justice Rehnquist. Through the course of his career, he obviously was quite willing to write separately to express his distinct views. Against that habit, his acceptance of the marked shift from his detailed early analysis to the agreed-upon compromise is noteworthy. More broadly, we can only wonder whether an earlier and more aggressive approach from Justice Brennan and the dissenters could have produced a different outcome. The clarity and steadfastness of Justice Stevens's writing on the unfair labor practice question makes it unlikely that Justice Brennan could have said anything to sway Justice Stevens's views on that question.

But it does seem at least plausible that an early effort by Justice Brennan might have led to the formulation of a standard for rejection that would be more favorable to labor and less favorable to the debtor. Justice Stevens had to move far from his original position to reach an agreement with Justice Rehnquist. His position on that question might have been closer to the position of the dissenters; if so, it might have been possible to persuade Justice Stevens that it made more sense for him to split the narrower difference between himself and the dissenters instead of the broader distance between himself and the majority. The parallels to the process that led to *Midlantic* (discussed in the next chapter) are apparent.

7.5 *BILDISCO'S* AFTERMATH

7.5.1 *The Continental Bankruptcy*

The Continental Airlines bankruptcy was front page news as the Justices were considering *Bildisco*. Continental entered into bankruptcy on September 24, 1983 (the clerks submitted their bench memoranda the following week), immediately and unilaterally cancelled its union contracts, laid off more than half of its workforce, and imposed a 50 percent pay cut on its remaining employees (Washington Post 1984). The bankruptcy was like *Bildisco,* multiplied by thousands more jobs and millions more dollars. One week after the company filed for bankruptcy, the pilots' union and the flight attendants' union went on strike in protest of the wage cuts (Salpukas 1984). Unions in the case charged (with considerable justification) that Continental filed for bankruptcy with the "sole and exclusive purpose of abrogating its contractual obligations [under the collective bargaining agreements]" (Townsend 1984a, 3). On January 31, 1984, Continental sought bankruptcy court permission to reject the union contracts (Washington Post 1984). The Court issued its decision in *Bildisco* just a few weeks later, on February 22, 1984.

The bankruptcy broke the airline's unions. Continental's CEO, Frank Lorenzo, waged and won a public relations battle against the national pilots' union (the Airline Pilots Association), and hundreds of unionized pilots crossed picket lines to return to work. Union-member anger mounted during the bankruptcy at the union's inability to force Continental to adhere to previously bargained-for agreements. Continental's hard line with the unions provoked violence: Two striking pilots were convicted on charges of conspiracy to plant pipe bombs in the homes of working pilots who had crossed picket lines. By September of 1985, two years after Continental filed for bankruptcy, six hundred pilots remained on strike but the union was no longer recognized as the pilots' majority representative. Continental's employees reported feeling intimidated and powerless to protest working conditions or dismissal (Salpukas 1985).

The Justices were aware of the developing situation at Continental as they considered *Bildisco*. Justice Powell's handwritten notes before the argument noted the concern that "E[astern] A[ir] L[ines] [*sic*] says it must cut labor costs to survive" (BILD038:45).[27] And Justice White noted at the decisive Conference that *Bildisco* would "affect Continental" (BILD041:2). At about the same time, a note from Justice Blackmun's clerk shows that at least one of the Justices was directly aware of a supplemental brief from the AFL-CIO alerting the Justices to Continental's unilateral rejection of its collective bargaining agreements (BILD003). Five days after receiving that brief, the same clerk sent Blackmun a detailed memo arguing that employees would have to strike to protect themselves if an employer was able to set terms unilaterally immediately after filing for bankruptcy, lest they lose their status as the majority representative of the employees (BILD005). Nor did the Justices lose sight of that issue. When he circulated his dissent, Justice Brennan included a detailed footnote emphasizing the deep "unilateral" wage cuts Continental imposed days after its bankruptcy filing (BILD034:15 n.16).

From a longer perspective, we can observe in hindsight that the violence that revolved around the Continental proceeding was precisely the kind of "strife" about which Justice Stevens was concerned and which dominated Justice Brennan's dissent. At the same time, there is little in the subsequent

[27] The comment suggests considerable prescience, as Eastern would file for bankruptcy in 1989.

history of the airline industry to undermine the view that rejection of the collective bargaining agreements in fact was necessary for Continental to survive.

7.5.2 Congressional Reaction

The decision also had an immediate impact in the press and on Capitol Hill. Although the discussion above emphasizes how much worse the decision could have been for labor, major newspapers characterized the decision as a significant defeat. The *Washington Post* described the decision as "another blow to unions" (Behr 1984), the *Christian Science Monitor* reported that the decision gave employers "an edge in labor bargaining" (Townsend 1984b), and Linda Greenhouse at the *New York Times* called the decision a "sharp setback for organized labor" (Greenhouse 1984). Business groups downplayed the decision, arguing that it would merely give businesses "flexibility," downplaying bankruptcy as a "shield, not a sword" (Lewin 1984).

The reaction on Capitol Hill from the Democratically controlled House was immediate and negative. Representative Peter W. Rodino Jr., head of the Judiciary Committee, introduced a bill on the day after the decision intended to overturn both parts of the ruling. The Rodino bill, closely tracking the *REA Express* standard, conditioned rejection of a bargaining agreement on a showing that absent the rejection "the jobs covered by such agreement [would] be lost and any financial reorganization of the debtor [would] fail."[28] Representative Paul Simon proposed an even broader response that would have given the National Labor Relations Act explicit priority over the Bankruptcy Code (Greenhouse 1984).

In news coverage on the day following the decision, the *New York Times* assessed the chances of early action by Congress on these bills as slight – noting that Congress had already been struggling for the past two years to respond to the Court's ruling in *Marathon*.[29] But *Bildisco* appears to have galvanized Labor's political machine to make a major legislative push.[30] According to Keller (1984), the principal lobbying battle was waged between a Labor alliance of the AFL-CIO and the Teamsters and a business alliance

[28] 130 Cong. Rec. H1942 (daily ed. March 26, 1984) (remarks of Rep. Rodino).

[29] Because the Court stayed the effect of its decision in *Marathon* to allow Congress an opportunity to remedy the constitutional problems that case identified, the Court decided *Bildisco* before Congress had adopted a legislative response to *Marathon*.

[30] For a more comprehensive discussion of the politics surrounding the statute's passage, see Gibson (1984); Rosenberg (1984).

of the Chamber of Commerce and the National Association of Manufacturers. In any event, by March 21, 1984 (less than a month after the decision), Democrats and Labor groups had pushed legislation through the House purporting to overrule *Bildisco* and require court approval before a labor contract could be abrogated. In a tactical move, Democrats attached the *Bildisco* bill to *Marathon* legislation already in progress.

After quick passage by the House, the bill predictably stalled in the Republican-controlled Senate. Senator Strom Thurmond offered an amendment preserving the *Bildisco* approach.[31] Senator Robert Packwood offered yet another substitute amendment that would have required the trustee's proposal to make the "minimum modifications in [the] employees' benefits and protections that would permit the reorganization."[32] Both amendments provoked strong controversy and threats of filibuster (Keller 1984). Because of the controversy over the competing *Bildisco* amendments, the bill went to the Conference Committee without any collective bargaining provision. It then emerged from the Committee blackbox with the provision now embodied in Code Section 1113.[33] Contrary to the *New York Times*' prediction of delay, a version of the House bill passed the Senate and was signed into law by President Reagan on July 10, 1984, as part of the Bankruptcy Amendments and Federal Judgeship Act of 1984. The *Washington Post* reported that the bill was "a defeat for labor, but a far cry from [*Bildisco*], which allowed companies to abrogate contracts without the permission of a judge" (Barbash 1984).

7.6 A POSTSCRIPT ON GM AND CHRYSLER

The upheavals of the Great Recession refocused attention on the interface between labor contracts and bankruptcy, especially with the landmark filings of General Motors and Chrysler. These bankruptcies demonstrate how the *Bildisco* Court's preference for business flexibility over employee contract security has changed bargaining incentives for labor groups and shaped national sentiment toward the bankruptcy process. General Motors and Chrysler were brought down by a confluence of diminished demand for new cars, high legacy costs, and soaring debt loads. By the end of 2008 it became clear that neither car company would survive without government assistance. The public narrative proceeded from the premise that bankruptcy for these

31 130 Cong. Rec. S6082 (daily ed. May 21, 1984).

32 130 Cong. Rec. S6181-82 (daily ed. May 22, 1984).

33 Interpretation of the legislative history and the intent of Section 1113 has been complicated by the fact that the bill passed by the Senate and considered by the Conference Committee included neither Senator Packwood's nor Senator Thurmond's amendments.

companies was unthinkable, because consumers would not buy from companies that might not remain in existence long enough to meet obligations under service and warranty contracts. The spillover effects from a possible liquidation were seen as especially dangerous because of the devastation it would wreak on the companies' large supplier networks.

As it happens, the Federal Government stepped in with loans that kept both companies afloat. The default provisions of these loans were strict; most notably, the companies were required to extract sweeping concessions from their labor unions (Hyde and Higgins 2009). The loans put labor groups in a difficult position. The terms of the government loans meant that unions commanded extraordinary leverage over the car companies, because a strike would put the company into default. At the same time, if organized labor pushed the automakers into default, the companies would almost certainly be forced into bankruptcy, where a judge would allow the automakers to make unilateral modifications to union contracts.

The negotiations between the automakers and their unions reflected the extraordinary pressure created by the government loan conditions, but also showcase how the post-*Bildisco* bankruptcy mechanism has shaped unions' bargaining strategies. Both firms faced potential liquidation if they could not extract concessions from the UAW. There is little doubt that the automakers would have been able to reject and modify their union contracts in bankruptcy. *Bildisco* and Section 1113 guaranteed them this flexibility under any reading of the matter, because modification of the contracts in those cases indeed would have been "necessary to the reorganization." Therefore, the choice facing the UAW in the post-*Bildisco*, post-Section 1113 world was between negotiating a pre-bankruptcy settlement, on the one hand, or waiting for the bankruptcy filing and then proceeding under the Section 1113 framework, on the other. Both firms and unions decided to negotiate pre-bankruptcy settlements with the automakers.

This is all precisely in accord with the incentives created by *Bildisco* and Section 1113. From the employer's perspective, a pre-bankruptcy settlement is preferable because (1) the employer avoids having to pay employees at the prior contract's rate during the post-petition/pre-rejection period (as Section 1113 requires), (2) the employer avoids the possibility of a strike during bankruptcy, and (3) it may put the employer in a stronger position vis-à-vis other creditors demanding that the debtor cut labor costs. The incentives for unions are even stronger. A pre-bankruptcy settlement is likely to survive bankruptcy because (1) the employer will likely agree not to seek rejection of the contract in bankruptcy, and (2) even if an employer seeks rejection, a judge would be unlikely to allow rejection since the equities would favor maintaining a contract that was entered into just before a bankruptcy filing.

Commentary surrounding the automaker bankruptcies show that unions were cognizant of the incentive structures created by *Bildisco* and Section 1113. Indeed, experts attributed the unions' willingness to negotiate with the companies, in part, to the likelihood that such negotiated contracts would survive bankruptcy (Higgins 2009; Glynn 2009). The unions gambled correctly. In the end, the pre-bankruptcy settlements survived both automakers' bankruptcies. Neither firm sought rejection of their collective bargaining agreements. These two bankruptcies may not be prototypical of the situation facing most unions in bankruptcy – the General Motors and Chrysler proceedings were dominated by the Federal Government. But the timing of the unions' choice to settle with the automakers is characteristic of the post-*Bildisco*, post-Section 1113 landscape.

7.7 CONCLUSION

Bildisco shows a Court unanimous in holding that the statutory framework of the Bankruptcy Code must supersede the framework of the NLRA. This stemmed from the Justices' concern that application of the National Labor Relations Act could interfere with the proper administration of bankruptcy. Until the writing of the opinions, there appears to have been very little concern about the reverse: that the elevation of bankruptcy law could interfere with labor law. In part, labor law was given short shrift because this so plainly had been the rule before adoption of the Code. It was not even on the table to suggest that adoption of the Code should have contracted the Bankruptcy Power in the labor context. In that setting, the Court's choices in the case were primarily about policy tradeoffs between the various proposed approaches. The split in the case boiled down to the weight the Justices gave to labor policy. To Justices Rehnquist, O'Connor, and Powell, labor policy was of little value, if not an active hindrance to economic activity. Because the dissenters, joined by Justice Stevens, saw an affirmative and positive role in bankruptcy for labor law, the Court did not, in the end, give employers the free hand with collective bargaining agreements that bankruptcy law gives them with other contracts. So labor policy might not have swept the table, but it did win quite a bit.

We are left to wonder if the sweeping rhetoric that was Justice Rehnquist's first response to the dispute would have played a substantial role in shaping future perspectives on the Code more broadly. The circulation of his draft in *Bildisco* turns out in hindsight to be the high-water mark of the Court's deference to Congress's vision of a Code that fundamentally altered the bankruptcy process. Starting with Justice Stevens's rejection of Justice Rehnquist's policy analysis, never again would the Justices suggest that the broad goals that motivated adoption of the Code should be used as a lens to justify a broad reading of the text Congress adopted. At most, as the subsequent chapters illustrate, Justices would argue – often in futility – that the Court should give the Code at least a literal interpretation, applying it as broadly as the words suggested on their face.

8

Bankruptcy versus Environmental Law: *MidLantic*

With Loring Veenstra

Two years after *Bildisco*, *Midlantic National Bank v. New Jersey Department of Environmental Protection* presented another closely contested bankruptcy case. Where *Bildisco* pitted the new Bankruptcy Code against labor law, *Midlantic* juxtaposed the Code with environmental law. More fundamentally, *Midlantic* produced the Court's first interpretation of Congress's broadened bankruptcy regime: Case law under the old Act limited the bankrupt's ability to ignore environmental law, but language in the Code suggested that Congress contemplated a much broader freedom of action going forward.

The Court did not, however, credit the broader language of the Code. Rather, the Court adopted a clear-statement rule under which it would *presume* that provisions of the Bankruptcy Code have the same meaning as predecessor provisions of the Bankruptcy Act. As in *Hoffman* and *Nordic Village* (discussed in Chapter 6), the Court applied a presumption *against* the intention to reform the bankruptcy system. Application of the clear-statement rule in *Hoffman* and *Nordic Village* reflected the Court's unwillingness to treat bankruptcy differently in a context of long-standing constitutional concern. But the *Midlantic* Court wrote on a clean slate, and on that slate inscribed an interpretive rule premised on a counterfactual intention of Congress that the new Bankruptcy Code should preserve rather than modernize the old regime.

The vigor of that new rule is apparent from its application here, in the face of substantial broadening of the relevant provisions of the Code from the predecessor provisions of the Act. Paralleling *Marathon* in the constitutional domain, this is the case where the Court most firmly set itself on a course to downplay the major changes Congress provided in the Code. To make the matter even more intriguing, the unpublished papers document a contingency of the result unknown in the existing literature – that Justice Powell "stole" a Court in this case. The decision at Conference favored the bankrupt; it was only a changed vote in the opinion writing that led to the Court's adoption of Midlantic's bankruptcy-narrowing analysis.

Section 8.1 situates the *Midlantic* decision within the broader state and federal environmental movements of the 1980s, which sought to regulate polluting industries that had caused a series of environmental disasters in the 1970s. Section 8.2 examines the history of Section 554 and the emergence of the abandonment exception in pre-Bankruptcy Code common law. Section 8.3 sets the stage for the case that reached the Court, which grew out of the activities of the notorious polluter Russell Mahler, the principal behind the *Midlantic* debtor. Section 8.4 details the Supreme Court's consideration of the decision (relying on the case files of Justices Brennan, White, Marshall, Blackmun, and Powell). Section 8.5 investigates the Solicitor General's amicus brief and considers why the Solicitor General might have succeeded in *Midlantic* despite his failure in *Bildisco*. Section 8.6 concludes with a brief canvas of *Midlantic*'s legal aftermath.

8.1 POLITICAL BACKGROUND

Midlantic was decided as state and federal efforts to curtail pollution reached their zenith in the mid-1980s. Environmental disasters in the post–World War II era, including the Cuyahoga River fire in 1969 and Three Mile Island in 1979, convinced much of the public that stricter measures were necessary to control industrial pollution (Adler 2004, 101). State pollution programs began in earnest in the 1960s, but the Federal Government became involved in the 1970s with the creation of the Environmental Protection Agency, major amendments to the Clean Air Act, and the passage of the Clean Water Act.[1] Most important was the 1980 adoption of the Comprehensive Environmental Response, Compensation, and Liability Act (CERCLA).

The rise of federal activity in this period led to an uneasy tension with state efforts to combat environmental pollution. Although the premise of federal environmental intervention was that the federal government would complement state laws,[2] federal programs often preempted more aggressive state programs. Scholars routinely explain that the passage of federal environmental laws reflected rent-seeking by polluters that sought lax federal regulations to preempt the increasingly effective regulation at state and local levels (Adler

[1] The E.P.A. was organized under President Nixon in 1970, the major amendments to the Clean Air Act granting it authority in that area followed later that year, and the Clean Water Act followed in 1972.

[2] *Midlantic* Brief for the United States at 1.

2004, 102). Those critics often point to the 1965 enactment of the Motor Vehicle Pollution Control Act, which stymied state efforts to place harsh limits on automobile exhaust emissions. It surprised no one that major economic interests, sensing that some form of environmental regulation was inevitable, sought (often successfully) standardized (lower) federal pollution limits (Adler 2004, 103).

That left significant uncertainty about how state pollution laws would coexist with their federal counterparts. For example, the New York and New Jersey statutes at issue in *Midlantic* dated to the 1970s.[3] New York's statute explicitly attempted to integrate state law with federal environmental protection efforts; the statute's stated purpose was to "regulate the management of hazardous waste ... in this state and to do so in a manner consistent with the Federal Solid Waste Disposal Act [and other federal laws]."[4] New York required the owners and operators of waste processing facilities to go through a permitting process and prohibited the "disposal of hazardous waste without authorization."[5] Disposal under that statute included "the abandonment, discharge, deposit, injection ... or placing of any substance so that such substance or any related constituent thereof may enter the environment."[6] New Jersey's pollution control laws were similar, explicitly prohibiting the unauthorized disposal of hazardous waste.[7]

Widespread public concern about the environment drove the regulatory efforts. For example, polls showed a public anxious about the effects of pollution throughout the 1970s and early 1980s. A 1982 Roper survey showed that 37% of Americans still thought that government environmental protection laws and regulations had not gone "far enough" (Bowman and Ladd 1995, 22). Similarly, 44% of Americans told pollsters in 1984 that they thought environmental pollution was a "very serious threat" to citizens like themselves and 56% thought there was "too little involvement by the government in the environment" (Bowman and Ladd 1995, 20–23).

3 New York passed a set of comprehensive environmental regulations in 1978, and New Jersey passed an environmental package in 1970.

4 N.Y. Envtl. Conserv. § 27–0900 (McKinney 1980).

5 N.Y. Envtl. Conserv. § 27–0914 (McKinney 1980).

6 N.Y. Envtl. Conserv. § 71–2702 (McKinney 1980) ("[N]o solid waste facility shall accept or receive for disposal, any hazardous waste [or] chemical waste, ... unless such facility has installed a system for the interception, collection and treatment of any and all leachate generated at the facility, and has obtained approval from the department for the entire system.").

7 N.J. Stat. Ann. § 13:1E-42 (West 1980).

8.2 BANKRUPTCY ABANDONMENT UNDER THE ACT AND THE CODE

Midlantic would turn on the long-recognized power of the bankruptcy trustee to "abandon" property. Within bankruptcy law, abandonment is a technical term, which entails the relinquishment of title or control of property by the bankruptcy trustee. A trustee typically abandons property when it is burdensome to the estate, in the sense that there is little reason to expect that continued exploitation of the property will produce a return for creditors of the estate. Once the trustee has abandoned the property, lien holders on the property have the opportunity to foreclose and take title. If lien holders do not choose to foreclose and if the debtor has no interest in continued use of the property, the state takes over responsibility for the abandoned property.

As it happens, the Act had not codified the trustee's power to abandon. Rather, trustees abandoned burdensome property through the exercise of their larger power to dispose of the estate's assets. In discerning a right to abandon as part of the right to dispose, case law under the Act limited the abandonment power in important ways. Specifically, with some variation, the leading cases generally prohibited abandonment that would violate a statute or endanger public health and safety. For example, a leading Fourth Circuit decision under the Act (*Ottenheimer v. Whitaker*) considered the power of a trustee to abandon the debtor's floating barges. The Fourth Circuit found abandonment impermissible, based on the conclusion that abandonment of the barges would have resulted in their eventual sinking, which would have violated a federal statute forbidding the obstruction of navigable waterways. That decision (like others), rested on the uncodified status of the abandonment power: "[T]the judge-made rule [of abandonment] must give way when it comes into conflict with a statute enacted to ensure the safety of navigation."[8] Another example comes from the oft-cited Pennsylvania bankruptcy court decision in *Lewis Jones*. The court there refused to permit three public utilities to abandon underground steam lines because the trustee's plan did not provide for the sealing of the abandoned lines. The bankruptcy court found that there were no applicable local health and safety laws forbidding abandonment, but nevertheless found that the court's equitable power to "safeguard the public interest" was broad enough to obligate the trustee to seal the steam lines.[9]

In the Code, however, Congress explicitly codified the abandonment power. Specifically, Section 554(a) provides broadly, with no exceptions, that

8 Ottenheimer v. Whitaker, 198 F.2d 289, 297–298 (4th Cir. 1952).

9 *In re* Lewis Jones, 1 Bankr. Ct. Dec. 277, 280 (Bankr. E.D. Pa. 1974).

"the trustee may abandon any property of the estate that is burdensome to the estate or that is of inconsequential value to the estate." That set the stage for the obvious question: whether the unqualified codification should be read literally (permitting abandonment of property merely because it is burdensome) or more narrowly, implicitly adopting the qualifications developed in case law under the old Act.

8.3 THE FACTUAL SETTING

8.3.1 *Quanta Resources Corporation*

If the plight of a small and inconsequential labor force in *Bildisco* presented a weak setting for labor policy, the facts of *Midlantic* presented serious environmental issues directly. The debtor in *Midlantic*, Quanta Resources Corp., was the latest corporate incarnation of a waste processing business owned and operated by notorious polluter Russell W. Mahler. Mahler had operated Quanta under a variety of names during the 1970s and early 1980s and had been at the center of several high profile dumping scandals. Mahler, dubbed a "toxic waste entrepreneur" by the *New York Times*, was in the business of oil reclamation. His companies collected waste oil from large industrial firms such as Ford and Alcan Aluminum and treated the waste to separate out and then resell reusable oil; the byproducts of the waste-oil reclamation process were highly toxic.

Mahler operated three terminals for processing waste oil; two in New York (in Syracuse and Long Island City) and one in Edgewater, New Jersey. He owned more than two dozen trucks that transported the waste oil. As it happens, instead of dumping the byproducts in state designated and authorized areas, Mahler directed his employees to dump the waste into New York sewers, landfills, and, in one case, an abandoned mine shaft. Contemporary observers concluded that Mahler saved millions of dollars by dumping carcinogen- and mutagen-contaminated oil byproducts in unlawful locations in New York and New Jersey (Chavez 1982).

He was finally caught in 1978 after he began directing his truck drivers to an auto service garage near Wilkes-Barre, Pennsylvania. His drivers would hook their trucks to a hose outside the garage that led through a bore hole down into an abandoned coal mine. An anonymous tip led investigators to the garage and the bore hole. Unfortunately, the mine overflowed before state officials were able to act, dumping hundreds of gallons of toxic waste oil into the Susquehanna River (among other things, a source of drinking water for the nearby city of Danville). When Pennsylvania authorities investigated, they readily discovered many other instances of Mahler's illegal dumping. At that point, with the discovery of his activities in New York and New Jersey, the entire scheme unravelled (Chavez 1982).

Subsequent investigations by New York and New Jersey officials revealed Mahler's deft maneuverings through state and city political circles. In one instance, Mahler was able (apparently through the payment of kickbacks to state officials) to secure a contract for the cleanup of a lagoon that Mahler's own illegal dumping had contaminated. Then, instead of transporting the lagoon's waste to an authorized dump site, Mahler simply piped some of the waste across the road and dumped the rest into a New York landfill (Blumenthal 1982). Mahler's activities eventually resulted in large fines, though not a great deal of jail time. Remarkably, his total sentences amounted to only four years – one year from a Pennsylvania conviction for illegal dumping and three years from a federal conviction for conspiracy to bribe city officials (Chavez 1982; New York Times 1984).

In 1980, after the Pennsylvania criminal investigation was underway, Mahler sold his waste processing company to a Wall Street investment firm, Warburg Paribas Becker Inc. The investors renamed the business "Quanta," presumably hoping to obscure the Mahler connection. The new owners of Quanta were able to borrow $600,000 from Midlantic National Bank for working capital, in return for which they granted Midlantic a security interest in a variety of things, including Quanta's inventory (waste oil); apparently Mahler's continuing participation as vice president of sales did not trouble Midlantic.[10] Quanta also successfully obtained a temporary operating permit from New Jersey environmental regulators. Unfortunately, less than a month later New Jersey regulators found PCB-contaminated oil during an inspection of Quanta's Edgewater facility. New Jersey authorities directed that Quanta promptly cease operations. In the fall of 1981, when negotiations between New Jersey regulators and Quanta officials about cleanup of the site proved unproductive, the company entered bankruptcy (Chavez 1982; Barbanel 1984).

8.3.2 Midlantic *in the Lower Courts*

Quanta's waste-oil storage containers and its processing facilities were in poor physical condition when the company entered bankruptcy. PCBs contaminated 400,000 gallons of waste oil at the Edgewater facility and 70,000 gallons

10 *Midlantic* Petitioner's Brief at 12. From the vantage point of the present era, the bank's casual approach to "know your customer" considerations is jarring.

at the Long Island City facility. To make matters worse, the storage tanks at both facilities had begun to leak; substantial PCB contamination extended beneath the surface of the soil at both sites. Still, because a portion of Quanta's waste oil inventory was not contaminated with PCBs, the estate was able to sell some of Quanta's waste oil for $288,000. It was the view of the bankruptcy trustee that the properties, in their contaminated state, factoring in their mortgages, had no value to the estate. Thus, because cleaning up the toxic contamination would have resulted in a net loss to the estate, the trustee sought to abandon both the New York and New Jersey properties.[11] If he was successful, the $288,000 would be distributed to Midlantic as proceeds of the inventory in which it had held a security interest. If not, the trustee would expend those funds to clean up the properties and Midlantic would take little or nothing.

Relying on the newly enacted Section 554, the trustee petitioned the bankruptcy court to allow abandonment of both sites. The provision of Section 554(a) that permits the trustee to abandon property only "[a]fter notice and a hearing" is a substantial limitation on the trustee's freedom to act quickly.[12] At the bankruptcy court hearing on the question, regulators from New York and New Jersey argued that the trustee should not be allowed to abandon the properties in their present state because they presented a danger to the environment and the general public. New York also argued that it should have a first lien on the Long Island City property to the extent of any monies that New York might expend to bring the abandoned property into compliance with state law. The bankruptcy judge rejected those arguments, refusing to grant New York priority and permitting abandonment of the New York and New Jersey properties. When the district court agreed with the bankruptcy court's decision, the case came to the Third Circuit.[13]

[11] *Midlantic* Brief for Petitioner at 12–13; *Midlantic* Brief for the United States at 9.

[12] The notice and hearing requirement was added to the draft Bankruptcy Code quite late in the process, with no explanation. Compare Section 554(a) with the parallel provisions in S. 2266 and H.R. 8200, the bills sent to the Conference Committee by the Senate and House, respectively.

[13] The text simplifies the procedural path considerably. The bankruptcy court decided the New York and New Jersey questions separately. When it decided the New York issues, the City appealed the decision to authorize abandonment, but the State (which had sought priority over Midlantic) did not appeal. After the district court affirmed, the case went to the Third Circuit, because the bankruptcy was in New Jersey, even though the relevant property was in New York, in the territory of the Second Circuit. When the bankruptcy judge later authorized abandonment of the New Jersey property, the parties consented to a direct appeal from the bankruptcy court to the Third Circuit, which consolidated the two cases for consideration. *In re* Quanta Res. Corp., 739 F.2d 927, 928 (3d Cir. 1984).

At the Third Circuit, in addition to arguing that Congress had meant to incorporate pre-Code practices into Section 554(a), New York argued that 28 U.S.C. § 959(b) independently barred the trustee from abandoning property in contravention of State law. That statute provides that

> a trustee . . . shall manage and operate the property in his possession as such trustee, receiver, or manager according to the requirements of the valid laws of the State in which such property is situated, in the same manner that the owner or possessor thereof would be bound to do if in possession thereof.

New York contended that the trustee's decision to abandon fell within his "management" and "operation" of the property and therefore had to be conducted in compliance with state law. The trustee disagreed, arguing that "management" and "operation" referred only to the trustee's responsibilities in a Chapter 11 bankruptcy where the trustee administers the estate as an ongoing concern. The Third Circuit devoted significant coverage to the Section 959(b) issue, but ultimately concluded that the provision was not an independent prohibition on the trustee's abandonment power – but rather a clear indication that "the congressional scheme was not intended to subjugate state and local regulatory laws."[14]

On the bankruptcy question, the Third Circuit panel voted 2–1 to reverse the district court, holding that the Bankruptcy Code did not authorize the Quanta trustee to abandon the properties in contravention of state environmental law. The Third Circuit acknowledged the wide leeway that Section 554(a) granted trustees to abandon burdensome property, but contended that Congress had intended to incorporate pre-Code judicial exceptions into the law. The circuit judges explained that "where it is argued that Congress intended to withdraw police power from a state, that intention must be unmistakable."[15] Because Congress had not explicitly overruled pre-Code exceptions to the abandonment power, the court concluded that Section 554 implicitly incorporated those exceptions. In dissent, Judge Gibbons harshly criticized the majority's use of an interpretive principle to overcome the unequivocal language of Section 554(a). The dissent also argued that putting the financial cost of cleanup on the estate raised the specter of an unconstitutional taking by forcing the estate's secured creditors to bear the price of cleanup in the form of reduced payouts.[16]

14 *In re* Quanta Res. Corp., 739 F.2d 912, 919 (3d Cir. 1984) [hereinafter In re *Quanta Res. Corp.*].

15 In re *Quanta Res. Corp.*, *supra*, 739 F.2d at 916.

16 In re *Quanta Res. Corp.*, *supra*, 739 F.2d at 925 (Gibbons, Circuit Judge, dissenting).

8.4 *MIDLANTIC* AT THE SUPREME COURT

As in *Bildisco*, the facts on the ground changed substantially before the case reached the Supreme Court. State regulators had stepped into the void left by the bankruptcy trustee and had secured both sites. New York cleanup efforts were complete; remediation in New Jersey was well under way. Thus, by the time the Justices considered the case, it was clear that no environmental catastrophe would flow from the trustee's unilateral abandonment of the contaminated sites.

That circumstance left the States in a less than ideal position. They had argued in the bankruptcy court that abandonment should not be permitted because of the environmental havoc that would result. But by stepping into the gap left by the trustee and eliminating that threat to public health and safety, the States refocused the Court's attention, away from the public risk of a contaminated water supply and back to the private "who pays?" aspect of the case. Because the States had covered, or were preparing to cover, the costs of cleanup, the only real live issue left in the case was whether the estate could be forced to reimburse the state treasuries for cleanup. The States argued that because the trustee should not have been allowed to abandon the sites, it was reasonable to force the estate to pay for cleanup that the estate should have conducted itself.

The resulting conflict between the environmental and bankruptcy laws split the Justices down the middle. For one group of Justices (a majority at the Conference), using restrictions on the trustee's power to abandon as a way to shift the cost of clean-up to the bankruptcy estate was an impermissible interference with the bankruptcy priority rules – elevating the otherwise unsecured claims of environmental regulators above the secured claims of Midlantic. The remaining Justices, a minority at Conference but ultimately the prevailing group, could not tolerate the potential harm from unilateral abandonment, with the attendant removal of all oversight of dangerous public hazards.

8.4.1 *The Views of the Clerks*

When the case came to the Court, the law clerks from all sides of the Court, so far as the record appears, regarded the case as unexceptional. The pool memo from a clerk of Chief Justice Burger recommended that the Court deny review, emphasizing that the Third Circuit had decided a question of first impression (MIDL004:9–11). Justice Powell's clerk agreed, commenting that "CA3's holding appears to be reasonable" and that "I think that this Court should wait for other CA's to consider the question" (MIDL003:1). Justice

Blackmun's clerk thought that "CA3 certainly seems to have reached the sound result – I do not see why the private interests of creditors who dealt with the bankrupt sh[ould] prevail over the public interest in enforcement of its environmental laws" (MIDL045:11). He agreed that he was "less prepared to say how firmly grounded in the statute is the result," but concluded that "given the . . . absence of other case law on the matter, the Court should probably hold off" (MIDL045:11). No record of the Justices' discussions survive, but plainly at least four of the Justices took a contrary view; the Court granted review in February of 1985.

The bench memoranda from the Blackmun and Powell clerks (the only ones available to us) displayed similar views of the case. Both clerks found the pre-Code case law much more compelling than the language of the Code. Blackmun's clerk emphasized the pre-Code common law restrictions on bankruptcy courts' abandonment powers and argued that "nothing in the legislative history of the 1978 Act or § 554(a) suggests that Congress meant to disturb this traditional notion of the abandonment power" (MIDL047:26). Foreshadowing the discussion of Justice Powell's majority opinion, she argued that "[t]he normal rule of statutory construction is that when Congress intends for legislation to make an important change in the way a judicially created concept should be interpreted it says so" (MIDL047:28). Reducing the trustee's unqualified reading of Section 554(a) to absurdity, she argued that no court would permit a trustee to abandon a contaminated truck in the middle of a busy tunnel or abandon a stick of dynamite on a company furnace. Because these "abandonments" could not be acceptable, she concluded that the statutory abandonment power could not be unequivocal. For her, the question was one of the reasonableness of particular limits on the abandonment power (MIDL047:28). Following a similar line of reasoning, Justice Powell's clerk argued that the Court should affirm the Third Circuit decision, applying the same general interpretive principle to conclude that Congress's adoption of Section 544 implicitly recognized the judicially created limitations on the trustee's abandonment power (MIDL005:3).

Oddly inattentive to the operative language of the statute, the clerks found the policy arguments for the environmental side of the case powerful. The clerks pointed out that there were good reasons to impose the costs of cleanup on Quanta's creditors rather than on the public at large. Specifically, the clerks concluded that the creditors, unlike the general public, had assumed the risk that Quanta's violation of environmental statutes would adversely affect their economic fortunes (MIDL005:6, MIDL047:32). Similarly, both clerks argued that allowing the trustee to abandon environmentally contaminated properties would risk allowing firms involved in toxic waste industries to transfer their liabilities for environmental cleanup to the State while distributing still-valuable property among the creditors (MIDL005:6–7, MIDL047:33). The clerks were particularly critical of Midlantic's argument that forcing the trustee to clean up a property amounted to an unconstitutional taking of Midlantic's security interest. Because Quanta had been subject to environmental laws before it declared bankruptcy, neither clerk could see why the continuing application of those laws in bankruptcy would amount to an impermissible or unforeseeable change in the creditors' ability to recoup their investment (MIDL005:7, MIDL047:31–32).

8.4.2 *Oral Argument*

It was clear from the argument that the views of the Justices would be more disparate. The harshest questioning about the environmental hazards came from Chief Justice Burger, who seemed incredulous that the trustee could insist on an unqualified power of abandonment. For those Justices, the actual facts of the case were almost wholly irrelevant. What mattered was the implications for future scenarios: "Do you mean that the trustee could abandon a burning building . . .? . . . [The court] cannot say, well, wait a minute, you can't abandon it without taking some precautions against having this property be a public danger?" (MIDL090:7–8).

For his part, Justice Stevens seemed concerned that a vote for the creditors would send the wrong message: "Couldn't one argue . . . that the signal ought to be that you should not be lending money to these companies unless you are satisfied they will be able to comply with the environmental laws? That that is just another precaution that the business community ought to take before financing a venture like this . . . ?" (MIDL090:24).

On the other side, equally skeptical questioning challenged lawyers for New Jersey and New York about whether conditioning abandonment of a property on the trustee's cleanup efforts was akin to creating a priority claim for the State. For example, Justice O'Connor pressed New York's Solicitor General for much of his time on the priority problem: "[I]sn't this really a question of priority of claims? It seems to me the abandonment question in this context is pretty much of a red herring" (MIDL090:29).

The state lawyers also were challenged as to why they should have a right of reimbursement after Quanta's bankruptcy filing that they would not have had under ordinary state law. Justice Rehnquist, for example, wanted to know, if the property had been abandoned from the bankrupt's estate, "how are you any worse off than before Quanta's bankruptcy?" When the

New York Solicitor General responded that the debtor "was completely without assets to do anything about the situation," Justice Rehnquist retorted: "But I presume that was the case on the day it filed for bankruptcy" (MIDL090:28). In a similar vein, Justice O'Connor was concerned that under state law the State "would have to come in and take whatever measures it wanted to take, and by its own law try to get priority to be recouped," and wondered "why should the filing of a bankruptcy change that outcome?" (MIDL090:30). For Justice Powell, at least, these interchanges seemed to present the strongest claims for affirmance, as he underscored his assessment that "WHR agrees with SOC that problem here is priority of claims, not abandonment" (MIDL006:3).

8.4.3 *Conference*

At Conference, the Justices voted to reverse the Third Circuit by a narrow vote of 5–4. The Chief Justice and Justices White, Rehnquist, Stevens, and O'Connor favored the unqualified right to abandon urged by the trustee and the bank; Justices Brennan, Marshall, Blackmun, and Powell favored the regulators' concerns about public safety. Justice Powell's notes suggest that the Justices favoring the trustee stressed the language of the Code. The Chief Justice, for example, argued that the "[p]lain language of [the] statute permits abandonment. Here the CA created priority of claims not authorized by Act [*sic*]" (MIDL007:1). Similarly, Justice White commented that the "statute rewrites the Bankruptcy Act" and asked "Why should unsecured creditors be required to bear this burden?" (MIDL007:1). In the same vein, Justice Rehnquist thought that the trustee had a "clear right to abandonment" and that the question was one "of priority" (MIDL007:3). Most importantly in light of what was to come, Justice Stevens qualified his vote for reversal by characterizing the case as "close," and commenting that there "must be some discretion [to limit abandonment] if abandonment itself increases the hazard," offering the example of a "bomb [that] may explode" (MIDL007:3).

For his part, Justice Powell's initial view of the case was quite conflicted. His preliminary memorandum (written after reading the briefs but before receiving anything from his clerk) suggested that he was "inclined to agree" with the court of appeals "[d]espite the unequivocal language of § 554(a)" (MIDL004:4). He was particularly impressed with the argument, which he attributed to the Solicitor General, that "§ 554 is a codification of a judge-made rule that ... had recognized that the trustee's abandonment authority was subject ... to general police powers of the states" (MIDL004:5–6). At the Conference, he professed that his vote in favor of the State regulators was "tentative," indicating the he would "want to re-read Gibbon[s'] dissent" (MIDL007:2).

8.4.4 *The Opinions*

8.4.4.1 The Draft Majority Opinion of Justice Rehnquist

The Chief Justice assigned the majority opinion to Justice Rehnquist, who quickly circulated a draft (MIDL059, 083, 116) that closely tracked the position he had taken at the Conference. He noted that the "Bankruptcy Code expressly authorizes abandonment for the first time in the history of bankruptcy legislation," and that the language, "absolute in its terms, … makes no mention of other factors to be balanced or weighed and permits no easy inference that Congress was concerned about state environmental regulations" (MIDL059:6–7). In his view, the legislative history suggesting ratification[17] of case law under the Act fell "far short of" the "extraordinary clarity" necessary to "read into unqualified statutory language exceptions or limitations based upon legislative history" (MIDL059:8). In sum, Justice Rehnquist offered a pedestrian resolution, implementing the language of the Code as best as its text could be understood, buttressed by the same sense he had shown in his *Bildisco* draft of Congress's intent in the Code to make the bankruptcy process more comprehensively effective.

Justice Rehnquist did not, though, limit his discussion entirely to the text. Rather, reflecting the discussion at the argument and at the Conference, he closed his proposed opinion by repeating the point he made at the Conference, in language quite similar to the early draft of *Bildisco* discussed in the previous chapter, arguing that the regulators'

> interest in these cases lies not just in protecting public health and safety but also in protecting the public fisc. … Barring abandonment and forcing

[17] The legislative history was quite weak, even by the standards of the 1980s. It amounted to a citation to the *Collier* treatise in a document prepared not in support of the Bankruptcy Code itself, but rather in support of a predecessor statute, the proposed Bankruptcy Act of 1973. The *Collier* treatise, in turn, though not quoted itself in the legislative history, stated that "recent cases illustrate … that the trustee in the exercise of the power to abandon is subject to the application of general regulations of a police nature" (Collier 1967, § 70.42(3)). Justice Rehnquist noted with considerable justification: "A Senator or Congressman seeking to familiarize himself with the statutory provision for abandonment in the Code, therefore, in order to divine that the statutory power to abandon was to be conditioned on compliance with state police power regulations, would not merely have had to look at the legislative history of the precursor to the Code, but also would have had to read the several-page treatise section cited in that earlier legislative history" (MIDL059:10).

> a cleanup, however, would effectively place [the regulators'] interest in protecting the public fisc ahead of the claims of other creditors. Congress simply did not intend that § 554 abandonment hearings would be used to establish the priority of particular claims in bankruptcy. (MIDL059:13–14)

Justice Rehnquist's draft also included a paragraph softening the statutory analysis, apparently in an effort to respond to the concerns of Justice Stevens, the fifth vote for his majority. The draft emphasized that the holding did "not exclude the possibility that there may be a far narrower condition on the abandonment power than that advanced by [the regulators] here, such as where abandonment by the trustee might itself create a general emergency that the trustee would be uniquely able to guard against" (MIDL059:13). Referring to an example from the Solicitor General's brief, abandonment of "dynamite sitting on a furnace in the basement of a schoolhouse," and commenting that he "kn[e]w of no cases in which trustees have sought to abandon dynamite under such circumstances," he suggested that "the existence of the narrow exception which we reserve would surely embrace that situation" (MIDL059:13). Justices White (MIDL051, 084, 114) and O'Connor (MIDL010, 082, 120) promptly agreed without qualification, followed a few weeks later by the Chief Justice (MIDL020, 075, 112), but Justice Stevens did not respond. Thus, Rehnquist had four votes, but as in *Bildisco* he still needed Justice Stevens to provide the fifth vote needed for his opinion to gain majority support.

Justice Rehnquist circulated a second draft (MIDL013, 086, 113), which included only a single substantive revision, a footnote related to the question whether it was important that "abandonment itself violates state law" (MIDL013:11 n.4); that discussion (footnote 4 of the draft majority opinion) would turn out to be the focal point of subsequent discussions. In the second draft, Justice Rehnquist broadened his discussion of that problem to emphasize the importance of bankruptcy policy, contending that allowing state law to trump the right of abandonment would "plainly frustrate the federal bankruptcy policy of expeditiously reducing the assets of the estate to money for distribution to creditors" (MIDL013:11 n.4), and thus that the Bankruptcy Code should preempt any laws purporting to restrict abandonment.

8.4.4.2 The Draft Dissent of Justice Powell

Justice Brennan assigned the dissent to Justice Powell (MIDL009, 119), perhaps hoping to ensure that his hesitant vote did not shift to support for the majority. Noting that his "vote to affirm was quite tentative," and that he "f[ou]nd the case troubling," Justice Powell nevertheless responded that he would "be glad to try [his] hand at a dissent" (MIDL008, 118). Moving much more quickly than Justice Brennan had in his response to Justice Rehnquist's *Bildisco* draft, Justice Powell circulated his draft dissent (MIDL052, 060, 088, 121) less than two weeks after Justice Rehnquist circulated his draft majority opinion.

The draft dissent could not have taken a methodological tack more different from that of the majority draft. Frankly acknowledging the limited importance of the statutory text to his position, Justice Powell rested directly on the scope of the abandonment power under the Act. Part I of the draft detailed the "judicially-developed doctrine designed to protect legitimate state or federal interests" (MIDL052:2). Justice Powell emphasized a "rule of statutory construction" requiring "specific intent" to recognize legislation as shifting the meaning of a statute that courts previously had interpreted (MIDL052:3). Indeed, though he offered no citations to support the claim, he went so far as to assert that "[t]he Court has followed this rule with particular care in construing the scope of bankruptcy codifications" (MIDL052:3). Part II emphasized that the all-but unqualified abandonment power recognized by Justice Rehnquist's draft was unprecedented, an easy point given the paucity of prior judicial or legislative attention (MIDL052:3–7). Finally, Part III emphasized Congress's undisputed concerns about "protecting the environment against toxic pollution" (MIDL052:7), as support for Justice Powell's "unwilling[ness] to presume that ... § 554(a) ... implicitly overturned long-standing restrictions on the common-law abandonment power" (MIDL052:8).[18]

Justice Rehnquist responded with a third draft of his proposed opinion (MIDL021, 076, 108); the most important change was a revision trying to downplay Justice Powell's health and safety concerns by emphasizing that a requirement that the trustee provide notice before abandoning hazardous property would "[i]n almost all cases ... give the State adequate opportunity to step in and provide needed security" (MIDL021:13). But Justices

[18] The records include two drafts of Justice Powell's dissent that precede the first circulated draft. The main substantive revision softened the "verbal bomb shell" (Justice Powell's words, MIDL014:1) with which his clerk began the draft for a dissent. Justice Powell worried that the rhetorical flourish might be "injudicious" unless it were "accurate in every respect" (MIDL016:1). As discussed in detail in Chapter 13, where I quote the relevant passage, the draft began with a hypothetical about the abandonment of dynamite on a stove in the basement of a school, followed by a caustic description of the environmental contamination at issue in *Midlantic*, both drawn almost word for word from the brief of the Solicitor General.

Brennan (MIDL017, 087, 109), Marshall (MIDL019, 074, 111), and Blackmun (MIDL018, 089, 110) promptly agreed to Justice Powell's dissent without requesting any changes in the draft.

8.4.4.3 The Switched Vote of Justice Stevens

At that point, four Justices had agreed to each of the opinions, but there had been no word from Justice Stevens. Finally, ten days after the circulation of Justice Powell's dissent, Justice Stevens weighed in with a detailed memorandum explaining that he had decided to switch his vote (MIDL022, 077, 107). He noted that the original draft majority opinion had troubled him in several ways, and that he had started by trying "to formulate some suggested editorial changes that would clarify the scope of the holding" (MIDL022:1). He went on to say, however, that "further study of the case has undermined my confidence in my Conference vote" (MIDL022:1).

As in *Bildisco*, Justice Stevens was much more concerned with Justice Rehnquist's policy views than his statutory analysis. Specifically, he questioned Rehnquist's characterization of the issues in the case as solely about "who pays." He maintained that if the case had been about the simple shifting of financial responsibility for cleanup

> from one party to another – if abandonment did nothing more than . . . make an adjustment in the rights of various creditors – state law could be ignored in deciding whether or not to approve abandonment. But if the abandonment has health as well as financial consequences, and if it is prohibited by state law because of the health consequences, I think the trustee has some duty to comply with state law. (MIDL022:3)

Because the case as presented to the bankruptcy court in fact involved allegations of health hazards related to the abandonment, he thought it improper to dispose of the case solely as a financial matter.

Once he had reached that conclusion, he had become "persuaded that the key to the case is the discussion in your [i.e., Justice Rehnquist's] footnote 4" (MIDL022:3), discussed above. On that point, he could not conclude "[u]nder our normal preemption analysis" that Congress intended to preempt state laws about abandonment. Accordingly, "[w]ith some embarrassment, I have therefore concluded that I must change my vote" (MIDL022:4).

Because Stevens's change of heart meant that Powell was now writing for the majority, Powell promptly circulated an opinion with the necessary revisions to serve as an opinion for the Court rather than a dissent (MIDL027, 061, 078, 106). Again, Justices Brennan (MIDL029, 079, 103) and Blackmun

(MIDL030, 080, 102) promptly joined, followed later by Justice Marshall (MIDL055, 069, 098); none requested substantive changes.[19]

Justice Powell's draft majority opinion, however, did not immediately satisfy Justice Stevens. Just as Justice Stevens had found that Justice Rehquist's opinion made the abandonment power too broad, he thought Justice Powell's made it too narrow (MIDL032). He agreed abandonment in *Midlantic* "was clearly improper" because the trustee took no steps to reduce danger related to abandonment.[20] But again Justice Stevens was much less worried about the correct resolution of *Midlantic* than he was about problems that had not yet arisen. For example, he worried about what should happen in cases in which the trustee (or the judge) acted more cautiously: "[W]hat if the bankruptcy judge had imposed conditions that required the trustee to ... forestall any imminent danger of a serious tragedy? The last paragraph of your opinion seems to state that such an abandonment would also be impermissible" (MIDL032:1). Justice Stevens made his problem quite clear:

> I found that I could not subscribe to Bill Rehnquist's proposed disposition because it seemed to authorize the trustee to abandon without any constraint whatsoever imposed by State law. You have convinced me that position is untenable. I am also inclined to believe that the opposite extreme would be equally unsatisfactory. Specifically, I could not subscribe to a holding that the State could veto any abandonment, no matter how many safety precautions were taken and no matter how much money the estate had spent in an effort to rectify the problem. (MIDL032:1–2)

Justice Stevens closed with a gentle suggestion that "it might be wise to narrow our holding" (MIDL032:2).

Anxious to gain a majority for his opinion, Justice Powell sent back revised pages of his opinion privately to Justice Stevens, indicating that he "believ[ed that] these meet your concerns," but that he would "of course, consider any language changes you may suggest" (MIDL034). Justice Stevens responded with a request for yet another round of clarifying revisions (MIDL035), focusing on the possibility that a State might seek to bar abandonment for reasons unrelated to public health and safety. Justice Powell (with little other choice) agreed to those revisions as well. Papering over the leverage Justice Stevens

19 Justice Blackmun sent a separate note mentioning two minor typographical errors (MIDL053).

20 MIDL032:1. Justice Powell's draft dissent had included a passage noting the trustee's failure to take "even relatively minor" protective steps (MIDL052:3 n.3). Justice Powell lengthened the passage substantially in the proposed majority (MIDL033:4 n.3), presumably in response to the concerns of Justice Stevens.

was exercising, Justice Powell commented with characteristic grace that he was "glad to make the changes suggested" and that he was "assuming that these changes will be satisfactory to [the Justices] who have joined me, as I view your language as a clearer statement of what the opinion already purports to say" (MIDL038). In any event, when Justice Stevens finally agreed to join the opinion (MIDL068), Justice Powell had obtained his hard-fought majority.

It was, in truth, an overstatement to suggest that the changes did not shift the opinion at all. They did, though, leave the core of Justice Powell's reasoning intact, as the final version indicated that the abandonment power was conditioned on the bankruptcy court's "formulat[ion of] conditions that will adequately protect the public's health and safety," and specifically that "a trustee may not abandon property in contravention of a state statute or regulation that is reasonably designed to protect the public health or safety from identified hazards" (MIDL067:12). More importantly, they resulted in a majority opinion justifying a heavily skeptical treatment of the Code's reforms, rather than the "we call them like Congress wrote them" approach Justice Rehnquist had offered.[21]

8.5 THE ROLE OF THE SOLICITOR GENERAL

As in *Bildisco*, the Solicitor General filed an amicus brief urging a narrow construction of the Bankruptcy Code. Although the Solicitor General did not participate in the argument, the record suggests that his brief was far more effective than the States' briefs in persuading the Justices to protect the environmental power. Probably the most successful theme of the Solicitor General's presentation was situating the position of the United States between radical outcomes advocated by the States on one side and the trustee on the other. The Solicitor General argued that because the United States had interests both as a trustee, via the Office of the United States Trustee (the OUST), and as an environmental regulator, it was ideally situated to identify and promote a fair medium between the two competing approaches to the case.[22]

In truth, though, the case raised issues of little or no concern to the OUST. As Chapter 12 explains in detail, the primary mission of the OUST is to limit the disharge available to debtors; its principal activity in the Supreme Court

[21] In the vein of providing an objective assessment, Charles Tabb concludes that Justice Rehnquist has much the better of the argument, characterizing Justice Powell's opinion as "arguably at odds with the Code's distribution scheme" (Tabb 1987, 540).

[22] *Midlantic* Brief for the United States at 1.

has been to press the interests of creditors seeking to retain claims against arguably miscreant debtors. The combination of the remoteness of the issues in *Midlantic* from the mission of the OUST and the absence of any OUST signatory on the brief suggests that the OUST took no substantial role in the formulation of the position of the Solicitor General's position in *Midlantic*. In sum, beneath the cloak of evenhandedness, what the Solicitor General actually filed was a brief advancing the regulatory interests of the EPA.

We have noted above that the perspective of the Solicitor General shaped Justice Powell's earliest views of the case. The effectiveness of the Solicitor General's presentation continued in the drafting of the opinions, as evidenced by the close parallels between early drafts of Justice Powell's opinion and the Solicitor General's amicus brief. For example, the discussion of Section 959(b) in the earliest drafts of the opinion imported quotes and significant analysis from the Solicitor General's discussion. Thus, both the Solicitor General and Justice Powell concluded that Section 959(b) applied to abandonment, in part because Section 959 addresses both "management" and "operation" of property and courts are "obliged to give effect, if possible, to every word Congress used."[23] Justice Powell also borrowed the Solicitor General's analysis of the origins of Section 959[24] and accepted the Solicitor General's dismissive take on Midlantic's Takings Clause arguments by not addressing them. The central standard of the decision – the requirements for abandonment – is closely rooted in the same nuisance principles that the Solicitor General recommended to the Court.[25] But most importantly of all, Justice Powell found his core interpretive link – infusing the language of the Code with Bankruptcy Act jurisprudence – in the brief of the Solicitor General.[26] As we will see in the chapters to come, this is the true jurisprudential legacy of *Midlantic*, and it comes directly from the Solicitor General. We can only wonder whether the case – as close as it was – might have been decided differently had the Solicitor General perceived its institutional interests less single-mindedly.

The force of the Solicitor General's presentation in this case contrasts notably with the ineffectiveness in *Bildisco*. Four distinct points are apparent. First, in *Bildisco* the Solicitor General effectively had to argue that Congress's

23 Compare *Midlantic* Brief for the United States at 18 (quoting Reiter v. Sonotone Corp., 442 U.S. 330, 339 (1979)), with Justice Powell's printed Chambers Draft (MIDL015:6) (same).

24 Compare *Midlantic* Brief for the United States 20, with Justice Powell's printed Chambers Draft (MIDL015:7).

25 Compare *Midlantic* Brief for the United States 39 with Third Draft (MIDL067:12).

26 Compare *Midlantic* Brief for the United States 25-26 with Justice Powell's printed Chambers Draft (MIDL015:2–3).

enactment of the Code was designed to narrow the power of bankruptcy courts, a difficult argument to make given the similarity of the relevant sections of the Code to the parallel language in the Act. In *Midlantic*, by contrast, the Solicitor General did not have to argue for the narrowing of bankruptcy courts' power; it only had to argue for maintaining the status quo.

Second, requiring union and NLRB consent to bankruptcy contract modification would have intruded much farther into the central bankruptcy function than conditioning abandonment on reasonable compliance with environmental law. The Justices seemed firmly convinced – and the adverse facts of *Bildisco* (with only a single union employee at the time the Court considered the case) doubtless contributed to that view – that the refusal of union holdouts to give ground could destroy a bankrupt's ability to successfully emerge from Chapter 11. In *Midlantic*, by contrast, the Justices could defer to environmental law with no effect other than having the trustee write a check out of available funds; the only losers were other creditors. Again, the specific facts of *Midlantic* – the fortuitous post-bankruptcy sale producing a large cash payment for the estate – doubtless had something to do with this.

Third, the Court might have expected that the population of bankruptcies affected by *Bildisco* (bankruptcies involving collective bargaining agreements) would be much larger than the population of bankruptcies that was affected by *Midlantic* (bankruptcies involving companies in environmentally sensitive industries). Would the Court have been so cavalier in limiting the trustee's authority over something more central to run-of-the-mill business reorganizations?

Finally, the Solicitor General was probably less effective in *Bildisco* because it represented one of the parties to the case (the National Labor Relations Board). Involving state environmental law rather than federal, *Midlantic* allowed the Solicitor General to position himself as analyzing two legal regimes to which the Solicitor General did not have any particular institutional allegiance. Therefore, it was able to play (or at least don) the role of a neutral arbiter between the positions of the parties. In *Bildisco*, by contrast, the Solicitor General was institutionally obligated to represent the views of the National Labor Relations Board, views so extreme (from the perspective of the Justices) that not a single Justice accepted them. The free hand of the Solicitor General to craft his own position in *Midlantic* is doubtless a major part of the reason for the Solicitor General's success there. But as it turns out, the position the Solicitor General chose to take – elevating the interests of creditors over the interests of bankruptcy administration – would turn out to be the norm, rather than the exception.

8.6 THE LEGACY OF *MIDLANTIC*

It is easy to wonder how things might have changed if just one vote was different, if Justice Stevens had been slightly less engaged in the case, perhaps, and maintained the view he expressed at the Conference. If Justice Powell's dissent had been slower to appear, would Justice Stevens have tried harder (as he did in *Bildisco*) to reach an accommodation with Justice Rehnquist? More broadly, if Justice Powell's draft dissent had remained just that – the comments of four dissenters – would the Court ever have moved so far down the path it has chosen, in which the Bankruptcy Code so regularly gives way to the interests of other federal and state regulatory schemes? If *Midlantic* is the turning point from which the thesis of this book has arisen, the interactions among Justices Rehnquist, Powell, and Stevens over the decision of that case are the crux of the entire subject.

Perhaps it is relevant that *Midlantic*, unlike *Bildisco*, did not prompt Congressional intervention. And moving forward, the Court has cited the decision with some frequency, more than a dozen times. Its exclusive use by the Court, however, has been for its strong presumption against derogation from prior statutory interpretation. The strength of that principle is apparent from the pattern of its use. In all but one case the principle has been cited in a majority opinion. The only contrary example, *United States v. Ron Pair Enterprises, Inc.*, is the subject of Chapter 10.

9

Bankruptcy versus Criminal Law: *Kelly*

The rather tortuous journey of Carolyn Robinson to vindication in the Supreme Court has a seedy beginning, with her 1980 conviction arising out of the fraudulent receipt of Connecticut public assistance benefits while receiving social security benefits at the same time. The timing of her conviction coincided with the early years of the victims' rights movement, which gave increased significance to the condition of her probation that obligated her to make restitution to her victim. The burden of that financial obligation, in turn, led to a bankruptcy filing, which led in due course to the Supreme Court. Her tale warrants discussion here because the Supreme Court's rejection of her claim in *Kelly v. Robinson*[1] has become the paradigmatic example of the Court's persistent elevation of other systemic values over a "close analysis of the statutory text" (Rasmussen 1993, 554 n.85).

9.1 CRIMINAL RESTITUTION AND VICTIMS' RIGHTS

Much of *Kelly*'s significance comes from its juxtaposition with the rise of the victims' rights movement. The rapid rise of the movement during the late 1970s often is attributed to the Supreme Court's 1973 decision in *Linda R.S. v. Richard D.*[2] The Court in that case held that the mother of an illegitimate child had no standing to challenge a prosecutor's refusal to prosecute the alleged father of the child for failure to pay child support. The opinion was widely noted both for the Court's statement that a crime victim seeking to compel prosecution is no more than "a private citizen [without any] judicially cognizable interest in the prosecution or

[1] 479 U.S. 36 (1986).
[2] 410 U.S. 614.

non-prosecution of another," and for its suggestion that legislatures could "enact statutes creating victims' rights, the invasion of which [would] creat[e] standing."[3]

By the time President Reagan took office, the subject had sufficient popular traction to justify a national Task Force on Victims of Crime, which went so far as to recommend a victims' rights amendment to the United States Constitution.[4] Although Congress did not go that far, it did enact in rapid sequence the Victim and Witness Protection Act (1982) and the Victims of Crime Act (1984). Parallel legislative activity at the state level has been pervasive: every State now has adopted some form of victims' rights legislation, and most have amended their constitutions (National Crime Victim Law Institute 2011.)

The most well-known result of the victims' rights movement was the introduction of the "victim impact statement," which ensured that the victim had an opportunity to explain the impact of the defendant's crime to the sentencer at a criminal trial.[5] That practice generated considerable controversy at the Supreme Court, with a 1987 decision in *Booth v. Maryland*[6] holding that the Eighth Amendment prohibited the use of such information at the sentencing phase of a capital trial followed just four years later by the decision in *Payne v. Tennessee*[7] overruling *Booth* and permitting the use of victim impact statements in capital sentencing.[8]

Kelly involves the other major policy tool of the victims' rights movement, compensation of victims. Traditionally, restitution had been available only as a condition of probation. But with the adoption of the Victim Witness Protection Act of 1982 (the "VWPA"), restitution became available as a

3 410 U.S. at 617 n.3, 619.

4 President's Task Force on Victims of Crime (1982, 114–115). The report proposed an additional clause at the end of the Sixth Amendment: "Likewise, the victim, in every criminal prosecution shall have the right to be present and to be heard at all critical stages of judicial proceedings." The report, along with a wealth of related information, is available at the web site of the Office for Victims of Crime in the Department of Justice (www.ovc.gov), a component that traces its existence to the recommendations of that report.

5 President's Task Force on Victims of Crime (1982, 33) (Executive and Legislative Recommendation 10(a)).

6 482 U.S. 496 (1987).

7 501 U.S. 808 (1991).

8 Justice Powell wrote the opinion for the Court in *Booth* shortly before his 1987 retirement. Between 1987 and the 1991 decision in *Payne*, Justice Kennedy replaced Justice Powell and Justice Souter replaced Justice Brennan (who had joined Justice Powell's opinion in *Booth*). The majority to overrule *Booth* consisted of the four Justices who had dissented from that decision, together with the new Justices Kennedy and Souter.

criminal sentence. During the intervening years, the use of restitution as a criminal sentence has grown rapidly; it is now mandatory for most federal crimes.[9]

9.2 BACKGROUND

9.2.1 *The Factual Setting*

Robinson's malfeasance involved the wrongful receipt of public assistance benefits from 1973 to 1976. Apparently, she failed to advise the Connecticut Department of Income Maintenance (coincidentally enough, also the respondent in *Hoffman*, discussed in detail in Chapter 6) that she was receiving social security benefits at the same time. Before her sharp dealing came to light, she had received almost ten thousand dollars in improper benefits. In the summer of 1980, she pleaded guilty to larceny in the second degree. In November of 1980, a Connecticut Superior Court sentenced her to one to three years' imprisonment, but suspended the prison term, placing her on five years' probation on the condition that she make restitution to Connecticut authorities at the rate of $100 per month.[10] The restitution payments started on January 16, 1981, but Robinson filed a petition for bankruptcy less than a month later, listing the defrauded Connecticut authorities as her only creditors. In the ordinary course, Robinson received a discharge on May 14, 1981.

9.2.2 *Litigation in the Bankruptcy Court*

When Connecticut authorities noticed that Robinson had no intention of making the required restitution payments, they began efforts to collect the funds from her. In 1984, Robinson responded by filing a motion in the bankruptcy court asking for a declaration that the 1981 bankruptcy had discharged her obligation to make those payments. The bankruptcy court denied her request, pointing to two provisions of the 1978 Code. The first, Section 101(11) (now 101(12)) defined the "debt" that is subject to discharge as "liability on a claim." The second, Section 523(a)(7), limited the discharge so that

9 The Task Force in 1982 had recommended a blanket rule that restitution be mandatory for all crimes (President's Task Force on Victims of Crime 1982, 33) (Executive and Legislative Recommendation 10(c)). Congress instead has mandated restitution on a case-by-case basis down through the years.

10 The restitution obligation could have been considerably more onerous. If Robinson had made all sixty of the required payments, she would have repaid only $6,000 of the $10,000 of benefits she wrongfully obtained.

it would not reach criminal sentences. Specifically, it protected any debt "to the extent such debt is a fine, penalty, or forfeiture payable to and for the benefit of a governmental unit, and is not compensation for actual pecuniary loss." The bankruptcy court concluded that the obligation to Connecticut authorities was not a debt because it did not involve "liability on a claim," and alternatively that it was protected as a "fine" or "penalty" under Section 523(a)(7).[11]

9.2.3 *The Court of Appeals*

When the district court simply adopted the opinion of the bankruptcy court, Robinson appealed to the Second Circuit. In a carefully reasoned opinion by the highly regarded Judge Amalya Kearse, the Second Circuit disagreed. On the first point, she easily concluded that Robinson's obligation was a "debt." It was of little relevance, she explained, that the victim could not force Robinson to pay, because the statute focused on Robinson's obligation to pay, not the victim's ability to compel payment. Moreover, it was plain that Congress sought the "broadest possible definition" of a claim (quoting the House Report), "intending that virtually all obligations to pay money be amenable to treatment in bankruptcy proceedings."[12]

On the exemption question, Judge Kearse concluded that the restitution obligation was not protected from the bankruptcy process. To be sure, the restitution obligation was in some sense a "penalty," imposed as it was in the course of criminal sentencing, but it was just as plainly "compensation for actual pecuniary loss." Because the relevant exception explicitly excludes penalties that provide that kind of compensation, it seemed plain that the restitution payments were dischargeable. She noted that the relevant Connecticut statute limited restitution to payments "for the loss or damage caused [by the offender]," and reasoned that "[t]he conclusion is inescapable that Robinson's obligation to make restitution payments to [state authorities] in the exact amount lost by [those authorities], was designed to be, among other things, compensation for [their] actual pecuniary loss."[13]

Judge Walter Mansfield added a short concurrence, praising Judge Kearse's "thorough and carefully considered opinion," but lamenting "the unfortunate

[11] 45 B.R. 423.

[12] Robinson v. McGuigan (*In re* Robinson), 776 F.2d 30, 35–39 (2nd Cir. 1985) [hereinafter In re *Robinson*].

[13] In re *Robinson, supra*, 776 F.2d at 39–41.

result compelled by the language of the relevant provisions of the Bankruptcy Code," which would inevitably "stultify" criminal restitution payments. He concluded that he "hope[d] that Congress will remedy this unfortunate loophole by amending [Section] 523(a)(7) to make criminal restitution non-dischargeable in bankruptcy."[14]

9.3 THE SUPREME COURT'S DECISION

9.3.1 *The Decision to Review*

Connecticut promptly took the case to the Supreme Court. Twenty-six States joined an amicus brief supporting the petition, which underscored the significant intrusion of the decision into the state criminal process. The law clerk from Justice Blackmun's chambers who reviewed the matter for the pool recognized that the case did not squarely conflict with the decision of any other court of appeals, but recommended review, motivated in part by the then-pending decision in *Midlantic*, which in her view indicated that "the Court seems inclined to read the Code to avoid conflict with the States' exercise of their police powers" (KERO022:9). The law clerk who reviewed the pool memo for Justice Powell concluded that *Kelly* was "essentially a statutory construction case, and construing the statute properly seems to lead to a bad policy result" (KERO044:11). In his view, the basic problem was the one that Judge Kearse had identified: that Section 523 explicitly carved out of its protection a category of criminal sentences that provide "compensation for pecuniary loss." If that language was not intended to reach restitution orders, then it was difficult to understand why it appears in the statute at all. The clerk also agreed with Justice Blackmun's clerk that the circuit conflict was oblique, but emphasized a substantial conflict with other bankruptcy courts. More importantly, perhaps recalling the still-pending deliberations in *Midlantic*, he concluded that "I am not sure another circuit case would help this Court analyze the issue" (KERO044:11).

Justice Powell's notes regarding the conference on the petition (KERO046) do not describe the remarks of any of the Justices, but do indicate that seven of the nine Justices voted to grant the petition outright, Chief Justice Burger indicated that he would "join three," and only Justice Stevens voted to deny the petition.

[14] In re *Robinson*, *supra*, 776 F.2d at 41–42.

9.3.2 *Briefing and Argument*

The available files have information about the pre-argument views of Justices Powell and Blackmun. Justice Powell's file memorandum started with a notation of his regard for Judge Kearse.[15] His initial reading led him to "tentatively believe that CA2 is mistaken" (KERO047:3). He thought a "plausible argument can be made" to support the debtor's position, but was quite persuaded that the State's position "is consistent with what clearly must be sound public policy" (KERO047:4).

Like the clerk that had written the pool memo, Justice Powell's clerk took a contrary view (KERO048).[16] Working through the statute and its legislative history, he took the view that "CA2 was substantially correct" (KERO048:8) and that "[b]oth the plain meaning of the statute and the legislative history indicate that the order in this case was dischargeable" (KERO048:1). Justice Powell reacted to his law clerk's analysis as "persuasive," but he did not change his view. His contemporaneous notes state that "I need to consider this more carefully. I see little substantive difference between a penal 'fine' and a restitution order. A fine is not dischargeable" (KERO048:1). A month later, as the argument approached, Justice Powell's clerk wrote another memorandum on the matter, designed to provide the best arguments to support the conclusion that Justice Powell preferred. The law clerk explained that "[t]he general feeling [among the law clerks] is that the result reached by CA2 is so intrusive on the states that it is incumbent on this Court to rewrite the statute to avoid that result" (KERO050:2), and presented what he characterized as "the best of the arguments inventive clerks have designed to reach the result" (KERO050:1).

Justice Blackmun's pre-argument notes indicate a similar predisposition. He agreed with Judge Kearse's view that debt "is broadly defined," but thought that Section 523(a) was "fed[eral] law n[ot] intended to interfere w[i]t[h] St[ate] crim[inal] proc[ee]d[in]gs" (KERO023). He regarded the restitution obligation as a "penal sanction," noting that it could "rehabil[itate] and force offender to confront cons[e]q[uence]s o[f] his conduct" (KERO023).

At the argument, the Justices became preoccupied with the effect of a discharge on the criminal process. The conversation started when one of the Justices suggested to Carl Schuman (from the office of the Connecticut Attorney General) that "there's no suggestion in this case that if

[15] "Judge Kearse is an excellent judge [and] her opinion is carefully written" (KERO047:2).

[16] Although the memorandum from Justice Powell's clerk is dated four days after Justice Powell's file memorandum, the clerk had not seen Justice Powell's memorandum when he wrote. Justice Powell was in Richmond for the summer, and his memorandum had not reached his chambers in Washington by the time his clerk completed his own memorandum.

this restitution order is discharged, that the state could not say this is a breach of probation and put [Robinson] in jail?" (Transcript at 7–8). The double negatives perhaps made the inquiry confusing; Schuman took the Justice to be attempting to clarify what Schuman regarded as obvious – that Connecticut could not use Robinson's decision to discharge her restitution obligation as a reason for returning her to prison. Schuman readily conceded that Connecticut could *not* treat the discharge itself as a violation of her probation.

At that point, the Justice (apparently forgetting Robinson's gender) expressed some surprise: "Well, it was a condition of his probation that he make restitution . . . [a]nd maybe he can avoid some civil action against him in bankruptcy but that's all that the discharge does, isn't it?" When Schuman reiterated the view that the question before the Court was whether the State could punish her for violating her probation, the Justice asked point blank: "Can you put him in jail for claiming his discharge in bankruptcy?" When Schuman said "[w]e can't," the Justice responded with surprise: "You say he's completely free of his criminal sentence?"[17] Plainly troubled by the colloquy, the Justice returned to the same topic during the presentation of Francis Dineen on behalf of Robinson. He started by asking if a victory for Robinson would "mean that the state cannot revoke the probation?" (Transcript at 43). When Dineen insisted that "there's no question," the Justice, plainly discomfited, closed by asking: "Has anybody ever tested that out?"

In retrospect, the most successful point of the argument was Schuman's description of a parallel pending case in which a Connecticut court had imposed a restitution obligation as part of a sentence in a negligent homicide case, obligating the defendant to pay the decedent's funeral expenses (Transcript at 13). The fact pattern plainly stuck with the Justices; during the argument for Robinson one of them asked Dineen how she would analyze an order entered in a negligent homicide case. She conceded that "there are many" orders of that type, adhering to her view that any

[17] Transcript at 8. The State's position on that point is odd. Ordinarily, prosecutors would take the broadest possible view of the criminal power, which would include the idea pressed by the Justices at oral argument, that whatever the bankruptcy might do to Robinson's monetary obligation it could not limit the State's right to revoke Robinson's probation and return her to prison for violation of the terms of her probation. Perhaps the State thought that it would trivialize the State's claim that the financial obligation passed through bankruptcy unaffected if the State argued that it retained the right to return Robinson to prison for nonpayment even if it lost the ability to sue for the money directly. Still, the State's evinced lack of interest at returning Robinson to prison makes the dispute look much more like a dispute about money and much less like a dispute about the integrity of its criminal process.

related restitution obligation would be discharged in bankruptcy (Transcript at 28).[18]

9.3.3 *The Conference*

When the Justices met two days later to consider the matter, seven Justices voted to reverse. The dominant view was that Congress could not reasonably be regarded as having intended a discharge of the criminal restitution obligation. Chief Justice Rehnquist justified his vote by explaining that "Cong[ress] did not intend such a sweeping ch[an]ge" (KERO026:1), because "prior to [the] new act, it would not have been discharged" (KERO052:1). Justice Blackmun explained his vote consistently with his pre-argument notes, stating that the "federal law was not intended to interfere with state criminal process" (KERO052:2). Justice Powell described it as "a close and difficult case," with "statutory language ... not easy to construe," but suggested that "HAB is right that Fed[eral] B[an]kruptcy law could not have intended to interfere with State criminal justice. Congress could not have intended this" (KERO052:2). Justice Scalia, in his first week as a Justice, explained that he "would like to reverse, but plain language is not easy to avoid" (KERO052:3). Only Justice Stevens took a contrary view, voting to affirm based on the "plain language" (KERO052:3). He emphasized that "Cong[ress] knew what it w[as] d[oin]g" and that this "is no homicide restitution order" (KERO052:3).

9.3.4 *The Opinions*

Perhaps sensing a parallelism between *Kelly* and Justice Powell's majority opinion in *Midlantic* the previous Term, Chief Justice Rehnquist assigned *Kelly* to Justice Powell. Moving quickly, Justice Powell circulated a draft of the opinion on October 22 (14 days after the argument). As I noted in the introduction to the book, the draft's atextual approach was unusually frank.[19] A typical opinion in a case like this would have started by analyzing the statutory language, asserting that a plain reading compelled the desired result, and then turned to extraneous concerns as if they were a makeweight or afterthought. Consistent with those expectations, the draft started with the platitude that the "starting point in every case involving construction of a statute is the language

[18] The colloquy arose in response to Dineen's suggestion that separate provisions for debts incurred by fraud or willful malice would protect most criminal restitution orders from discharge, whatever the result in *Kelly*. The point of the Justice's comment was that those exceptions would not protect a debt arising out of a crime based on "mere" negligence.

[19] Tabb (1987, 541–547) provides a more detailed analysis of the opinion as a matter of doctrinal reasoning.

itself" (KERO085:6 (quoting a concurring opinion by Justice Powell in an earlier case)).

But instead of moving on at that point to analyze the text, the draft shifted gears to state: "But the text is only the starting point. As Justice O'Connor explained last Term, 'In expounding a statute, we must not be guided by a single sentence or member of a sentence, but look to the provisions of the whole law, and to its object and policy'" (KERO085:6). The draft then proceeded to offer two sections discussing the "object and policy" of the Bankruptcy Code that should inform the Court's reading of it.

The first argued that courts traditionally had "been reluctant to interpret federal bankruptcy statutes to remit state criminal judgments" (KERO085:6). The draft took the view that the "most natural construction of the [1898 Bankruptcy] Act would have allowed criminal penalties to be discharged in bankruptcy," but noted that "the courts did not interpret the Act in this way" (KERO085:7–8). The draft even quoted a 1901 district court opinion – sounding much like the Justices at conference in *Kelly* – stating that "nothing but a ruling from a higher court would convince me that congress, by any provision of the bankruptcy act, intended to permit the discharge, under its operations, of any judgment entered by a state or federal court imposing a fine in the enforcement of criminal laws" (KERO085:8).[20] The presentation of that interpretive practice under the Act led to an invocation of the decision in *Midlantic*, in which "[j]ust last Term we declined to hold that the Bankruptcy Code silently abrogated another exception created by courts construing the old Act" (KERO085:9).

The draft followed that point with a second pre-textual section. Moving outside the bankruptcy context, that section discussed *Younger v. Harris*[21] as an example of the "fundamental policy against federal interference with state criminal prosecutions" (KERO85:10). As taken with a salient hypothetical as in his *Midlantic* opinion a few months earlier, Justice Powell opened that section of the draft with the "negligent homicide" example from the argument, pointing to the likelihood that a restitution order in such a case was protected only by the language at issue in *Kelly* (KERO085:11).

Against that backdrop, the draft finally turned to the language at issue in the case – quoted for the first time on the thirteenth page of a sixteen-page draft. The draft did not address the question whether a restitution order could

20 Quoting In re *Moore*, 111 F. 145 (W.D. Ky. 1901).

21 401 U.S. 37 (1971) (holding that the non-statutory doctrine of "Our Federalism" deprives federal courts of the power to issue injunctions against state criminal prosecutions).

be characterized as a debt, but instead rested on the conclusion that a criminal restitution order in any event was protected from discharge as a fine or penalty. Even on that point, though, the draft did not directly attempt to explain what Congress could have meant other than restitution when it excluded criminal punishments that "compensat[e] for pecuniary loss." Rather, the draft simply asserted that "[i]f Congress had intended … to discharge state criminal sentences, 'we can be certain that there would have been hearings, testimony, and debate concerning consequences so wasteful, so inimical to purposes previously deemed important, and so likely to arouse public outrage'" (KERO085:14 (quoting Justice Powell's dissent in the notorious "snail-darter" case)).[22] The draft followed with a paragraph suggesting that the language was not so clear as to compel its application to restitution, emphasizing the non-compensatory goals of the criminal justice system, "not operated primarily for the benefit of victims, but for the benefit of society as a whole. Thus, it is concerned not only with punishing the offender, but also with rehabilitating him" (KERO085:15). Those non-compensatory goals, the draft reasoned, were enough to protect the obligation from discharge.

Justices White (KERO029, 070), Blackmun (KERO010, 071, 088, 106), and Scalia (KERO086, 107) joined the opinion on the next day, with Justice Brennan's joinder (KERO012, 032, 110) one day later giving the opinion a majority of the Court. That is not to say that all went according to plan. For one thing, Justice O'Connor wrote promising to join, but asking that the opinion be revised to state expressly that a criminal restitution obligation was not even a debt subject to the bankruptcy process (KERO069). Justice Powell promptly wrote back, stating with an accommodating tone that he thought "some Justices were in doubt as to whether a restitution order is a 'debt,'" and that Justice Blackmun in particular had taken the position at the Conference discussion that a restitution obligation was a debt. Accordingly, Justice Powell "thought it prudent simply to leave the question open." He did, however, offer to revise the draft to state that nothing in the language or legislative history "compels the conclusion" that a restitution order is a debt for purposes of Section 523 (KERO076). Justice O'Connor responded later the same day that she "would appreciate seeing the change you suggest" (KERO077). The revision appeared a few days later in the next draft (KERO091:13 n.12).

[22] The reference is to TVA v. Hill, 437 U.S. 153 (1978), in which the Court affirmed an injunction against the completion of a dam in Tennessee based on the likely harm to the habitat of a small fish (the snail darter). The reference was something of an odd choice – three members of the *TVA* majority (Justices Brennan, White, and Marshall) were in the group from whom Justice Powell was hoping to gain votes in *Kelly*.

The other oddity was a brief note from Justice Marshall indicating that "[i]n due course I expect to file a dissent in this one" (KERO030, 087, 108). Given Justice Marshall's vote with the majority at the Conference, the note came as something of a surprise. But with a solid majority already in hand it suggested no cause for concern. Justice Marshall circulated his dissent (KERO04) just a week later.[23] The draft dissent found "unconvincing the majority's conclusion that the criminal restitution order at issue here is not 'compensation for actual pecuniary loss,'" pointing out that a "purely penal [restitution order] would not connect the amount of restitution to the damage imposed'" (KERO021:2–3). The draft closed by responding to Justice Powell's quotation from his dissent in the snail-darter case with a quote from the majority opinion in the snail-darter case (with which Justice Marshall had agreed) that "the commitment to the separation of powers is too fundamental for us to pre-empt congressional action by judicially decreeing what accords with common sense and the public weal" (KERO021:6).[24] Justice Stevens joined the dissent a few days later (KERO036, 081, 095, 115). The decision was announced on November 12, the first decision of the Term, five weeks to the day after the argument.

9.4 THE AFTERMATH

Later events suggest that Justice Powell's reluctance to address the question whether a criminal restitution obligation could amount to a "debt" at all was as prudent as he suggested in his correspondence with Justice O'Connor. That question came to the Court two Terms later, in *Pennsylvania Department of Public Welfare v. Davenport*.[25] *Davenport* involved a proceeding under Chapter 13; the exception from discharge at issue in *Kelly* does not apply in Chapter 13, so if the obligation was a debt, the Chapter 13 proceeding would discharge it. Writing for a majority of seven, and emphasizing Congress's intention to craft as capacious a definition of "debt" (and "claim") as possible, Justice Marshall concluded that the broadened definition of "debt" in the 1978 Code in fact did reach the restitution obligations in question. Justices

23 By that point, Justice Powell's draft had seven votes, with Chief Justice Rehnquist having joined during the intervening days (KERO014, 034, 092).

24 Given his attention to the snail-darter case in his opinion, it is reasonable to think that Justice Marshall's change of vote might have been motivated by the reliance of Justice Powell's draft on the dissent from that case. If so, the reference did not trouble Justices Brennan and White, who also had joined the majority in the snail-darter case but had signed on to Justice Powell's opinion within a few days after he circulated it.

25 495 U.S. 552 (1990).

Blackmun and O'Connor dissented.[26] The result, then, was that a debtor could discharge a state restitution obligation only if the debtor could succeed in Chapter 13.

As it happened, Justice Marshall still did not have the last word on the matter. It turned out that Justice Powell also was correct when he contended in *Kelly* that any suggestion that a bankruptcy might discharge a criminal sentence would draw immediate legislative activity. Less than six months after the decision in *Davenport*, Congress adopted the Criminal Victims Protection Act of 1990; Section 3 of that statute directly overruled *Davenport*, revising the Code so that the Chapter 13 discharge would not affect any debt "for restitution included in a sentence on the debtor's conviction of a crime."[27]

[26] Justice Marshall's majority included himself and Justice Stevens (the dissenters from *Kelly*), two Justices who had joined the Court after *Kelly* (Justices Kennedy and Souter), and three Justices who had agreed with *Kelly* but would not extend it to Chapter 13 (Chief Justice Rehnquist and Justices Brennan and White).

[27] Pub. L. No. 101–581, 104 Stat. 2865. The related report was explicit about the amendment's purpose: "[T]his amendment will have the effect of overruling the Supreme Court's recent decision in Pennsylvania Department of Public Welfare v. Davenport, 110 S. Ct. 2126 (1990), which held that criminal restitution obligations are dischargeable debts under chapter 13." S. Rep. No. 101–434 (1990).

10

Setting Text against Tradition: *Ron Pair*

With Loring Veenstra

Three years after *Midlantic*, the Court took up another case involving a provision of the Bankruptcy Code that appeared plain on its face but had a conflicting pre-Code common-law history. In *Ron Pair*, for once, the Court reversed interpretive course, finding that the language of the Code was so clear that pre-Code judicial decisions could not limit the statute's meaning.[1] It is not, we think, a coincidence that the Court picked this case to follow that approach, when it had the effect of draining funds from the bankruptcy estate by allowing secured creditors (in this case the Internal Revenue Service) to collect post-filing interest.

10.1 THE FACTUAL SETTING

In the wake of the U.S. recession of the early 1980s, a mid-sized Michigan firm filed for bankruptcy. The bankruptcy involved neither large sums of money nor scandal. Despite its lack of distinction – or perhaps because of it – the bankruptcy produced a legal wrangling that reached the Supreme Court four years later. Although the firm has lost its eponymous name (and now calls itself Midwest International Standard Products), the business survives to this day, at the same location near the north end of Lake Michigan. Ron Pair was, and still is, in the business of industrial air purification. The company manufactures and installs devices that minimize the dust created in the loading of shipping containers. Ron Pair's originally revolutionary devices attach to the end of the tubes which suck material out of storage bins and deposit it into containers. The devices regulate the transfer of substances from bin

[1] Rasmussen views the decision as a straightforward conflict between a textualist approach and a broader consideration of different perspectives on bankruptcy policy, with the majority blindly following the text and the dissent criticizing the failure to consider the policy implications (Rasmussen 1993, 569–571).

to container and reduce the amount of dust generated during the loading process.[2]

The relevant problem was that Ron Pair failed to forward various tax payments to the Federal Government in the years before it entered bankruptcy. As a result, the Internal Revenue Service (IRS) obtained a tax lien on Ron Pair's assets. Then, while the company was in bankruptcy, the IRS sought to recover not only the principal amount of the unpaid taxes, but also interest on its tax claim up to the date it was paid. Ron Pair conceded that it owed the IRS interest that had accrued before the bankruptcy petition was filed. The company contended, however, that the Government was not due interest that had accrued post-petition. The Government's efforts to collect post-petition interest spurred a dispute that eventually reached the Supreme Court.

10.2 THE LEGAL SETTING

Ron Pair was not the first case in which the IRS had sought post-petition interest. In fact, the Government had made the same argument in a series of cases as early as the 1950s.[3] As it happens, however, the Government was uniformly unsuccessful in presenting this argument under the Bankruptcy Act. In that milieu, a creditor's right to accrue interest terminated at the filing of the bankruptcy petition. As Justice Holmes explained, that rule "was laid down not because of the words of the statute but as a matter of fundamental principle."[4] To the extent the Act addressed the question at all, it suggested that the principle was absolute. Most obviously, Section 63 of the Act explicitly permitted interest on judgments and written instruments to the extent it "would have been recoverable at th[e] date [of the filing]."

Cases under the Act generally recognized three non-statutory exceptions to that largely non-statutory bar on post-filing interest, for cases in which (1) the debtor was actually solvent, (2) the property held by the creditor to secure the debt produced income during the course of the bankruptcy proceeding, or (3) the value of the creditor's collateral was sufficient to cover both the claim and post-petition interest (i.e. the claim was oversecured).[5] The exception for oversecured creditors was attractive to the Government. Tax liens generally covered all of a debtor's property and thus in many cases left the Government

2 About Midwest International, http://www.midwestmagic.com/about/ (last visited October 15, 2013).

3 *In re* Kerber Packing Co., 276 F.2d 245 (7th Cir. 1960); United States v. Bass, 271 F.2d 129 (9th Cir. 1959); United States v. Harrington, 269 F.2d 719 (4th Cir. 1959).

4 Sexton v. Dreyfus, 219 U.S. 339, 344 (1911).

5 *In re* Kerber Packing Co., 276 F.2d 245 (7th Cir. 1960).

oversecured. Hence, the IRS argued that it should be allowed post-petition interest as an oversecured creditor under the third exception.

Interestingly enough, the courts in that pre-statutory age uniformly rejected the IRS's argument. For the most part, the courts regarded the question as foreclosed by an older Supreme Court decision, *City of New York v. Saper*, which had rejected a claim for interest on tax claims in a case in which the Government did not have a lien.[6] The courts also relied heavily on the idea that it was inappropriate to allow the Government to collect post-petition interest, to the detriment of other involuntary creditors, when it had not bargained with the debtor for its right to interest. As the Fourth Circuit put it,

> when the creditor extended credit, he relied upon the particular security given as collateral to secure both the principal of the debt and interest until payment and, if the collateral is sufficient to pay him, the contract between the parties ought not be abrogated by bankruptcy. This rationale has no application to tax liens.[7]

Thus, by 1978, there were three exceptions to the general prohibition against post-petition interest accrual and a fourth "exception to an exception" denying oversecured nonconsensual creditors (namely the Government) post-petition interest.

The Code responded to that problem by codifying the treatment of post-filing interest in the provisions of Section 506. At the highest level of

6 336 U.S. 328 (1949).

7 United States v. Harrington, 269 F.2d 719, 721 (1959). For similar discussion by the Seventh Circuit, see *In re* Kerber Packing Co., 276 F.2d 245, 246-47 (7th Cir. 1960):

> This exception has been recognized by the courts to the extent of allowing post-bankruptcy interest to creditors who are deemed to have bargained for collateral to secure not only the principal obligation but the interest thereon as well. ... The specific security involved in cases where the third exception has been applied resulted from a voluntary transaction between the debtor and creditor and the payment of interest was contemplated by the parties. There is a very clear distinction between those liens where exceptions have been provided and the [tax] lien here asserted by the government.

The Ninth Circuit had much the same thing to say in U.S. v. Bass, 271 F.2d 129, 131 (9th Cir. 1959):

> The government submits that the asserted distinction between contractual and statutory liens is without merit and does not support disallowance of post-bankruptcy interest on a liened tax claim. ... We think these and similar considerations advanced by the government are overborne by what we regard as a meaningful distinction, as far as the question is concerned here, between statutory and contractual liens.

generality, the basic treatment of post-petition interest remained the same under the Code: in general, creditors were not entitled to it. The Code did, however, codify some of the judicially created exceptions. Of relevance to *Ron Pair*, Section 506(b) codified the exception for oversecured creditors, providing,

> [t]o the extent that an allowed secured claim is secured by property the value of which, after any recovery under subsection (c) of this section, is greater than the amount of such claim, there shall be allowed to the holder of such claim, interest on such claim, and any reasonable fees, costs, or charges provided under the agreement under which such claim arose.

Because the codification did not confirm the continuation of the tax-lien exception, the Government saw an opportunity to relitigate the issue on a new statutory slate. The Ron Pair bankruptcy became the IRS's legal vehicle. Because the debtor had stipulated that the Government's claim was oversecured and agreed that the Government was owed pre-petition interest, the case was ideal for the Solicitor General to take to the Supreme Court. The facts of the case were also favorable to the Government; the small size of the Government's claim (about $50,000) made it unlikely that other creditors would be completely pushed out by any interest the Government collected, and resolution of the small company's bankruptcy seemed insignificant to the State and local economies.[8]

10.3 *RON PAIR* IN THE LOWER COURTS

The issue came to a head in the bankruptcy court when the debtor proposed a plan that did not provide for post-petition interest on the tax claims. The Government objected, claiming that it was entitled to post-petition interest on its claim under Section 506 because its claim was oversecured. The bankruptcy judge denied the Government's objection, concluding that Section 506 did not authorize the payment of post-petition interest.

On appeal, the district court reversed, agreeing with the IRS that the plain language of Section 506 entitled the Government to post-petition interest. The court explained that Section 506(b) has three components. The subsection first defines what constitutes an oversecured claim. A claim

8 The Government's pre-petition claim totaled $53,278 (Ron Pair Brief for the United States 9).

is oversecured to "the extent that an allowed claim is secured by property the value of which ... is greater than the amount of such claim." That means that a creditor is oversecured on its claim to the extent that the claim is secured by property with value greater than that of the claim.

The district court read the second and third components of Section 506(b) to separately grant the oversecured creditor interest and reasonable fees or charges. The subsection reads: "[T]here shall be allowed to the holder of such claim, interest on such claim, and any reasonable fees, costs, or charges provided under the agreement under which such claim arose." The grammatical structure of the subsection and the placement of commas suggests that the provision for "interest on such claim" is separate from "any reasonable fees, costs, or charges provide under the agreement." If provision for interest were separate from the existence of an agreement between the parties, interest would be allowed on all oversecured claims, even where there was no contract between the parties. If, however, the phrase "interest on such claim" were connected to "under the agreement under which the claim arose," then post-petition interest would be available only to those creditors enforcing an agreement with the debtor. Concluding that the punctuation compelled the former reading, the district court ruled for the Government, reversing the bankruptcy court.

The debtor appealed to the Sixth Circuit, which reinstated the judgment of the bankruptcy court. The Sixth Circuit doubted that Congress's enactment of the Code was intended to change the pre-Code common law on post-petition interest. The appellate judges were of the opinion "that the language of section 506(b), when read in light of the pre-Code judicially created doctrine, codifies pre-Code law on the issue of allowable post-petition interest."[9] *Midlantic* seemed to provide a firm foundation for the court of appeals' rejection of the IRS argument.

10.4 *RON PAIR* IN THE SUPREME COURT

10.4.1 *Certiorari*

The Sixth Circuit's decision in *Ron Pair* was not the first post-Code court of appeals decision on the availability of post-petition interest to an oversecured

9 *In re* Ron Pair, 828 F.2d 367, 372 (6th Cir. 1987).

creditor. A year earlier, the Fourth Circuit had ruled, on nearly identical facts, that Section 506(b) *did* permit an oversecured nonconsensual creditor to collect post-petition interest.[10] The conflict seemed plain, because the Sixth Circuit noted the Fourth Circuit's decision, but explicitly disagreed, emphasizing that court's failure to follow *Midlantic* and pre-Code case law.[11] The Blackmun clerk that wrote the pool memo noted the split and recommended that the Court review the case, emphasizing her view of bankruptcy law as "an area in which uniformity is particularly desirable" (RPEI001:6). No record of the Justices' deliberations on the question survives, but it is apparent that they promptly agreed to hear the case.

10.4.2 *Oral Argument*

At oral argument, the Solicitor General's task was to convince the Court that Congress intended to change the pre-Code practice of denying the Government post-petition interest on tax liens. The government representative again was Larry Wallace, who had appeared for the NLRB in *Bildisco*. He emphasized his view that the plain language and grammatical structure of Section 506(b) distinguished the provision of interest from the collection of fees due under an agreement.

Understandably given *Midlantic*, some of the Justices were skeptical that Congress would have changed pre-Code law without any indication in the legislative history. For example, Justice O'Connor thought "it a little odd that there [was] nothing in the legislative history and nothing more explicit than the placement of commas" to change the pre-Code rule (RPEI070:6). The Solicitor General's representative admitted that "it [was] a little odd" but argued that there were other signals, "more explicit than the changing of commas," demonstrating that Congress intended to change pre-Code law (RPEI070:6).

Justices also asked about the repetitive use of the phrase "such claim," which appears four times in subsection 506(b):

> To the extent that an allowed secured claim is secured by property the value of which, after any recovery under subsection (c) of this section, is greater than the amount of **such claim**, there shall be allowed to the holder of **such claim**, interest on **such claim**, and any reasonable fees, costs, or charges provided under the agreement under which **such claim** arose [our emphasis].

10 *In re* Best Repair, 789 F.2d 1080, 1082 (4th Cir. 1986).
11 *In re* Ron Pair, 828 F.2d at 372–73.

The fourth time the phrase is used, "such claim" appears to refer to a consensual claim, because it is a claim arising under an agreement between the parties ("the agreement under which such claim arose"). Some of the Justices suggested that because the fourth usage of "such claim" referred to a consensual claim arising from an agreement between the parties, the earlier references to "such claim" also might be limited to consensual claims. If that were true, the clause providing for "interest on such claim" would grant interest only on consensual claims, and would not reach the Government's nonconsensual tax lien (RPEI070:14–15).

Predictably enough, the Solicitor General's representative disagreed, arguing that it was contrary to standard rules of statutory construction to infer the meaning of words used at one point in a passage from their usage later in the same passage. Rather, he argued, the first three usages of "such claim" referred to a general oversecured claim, while the last usage referred separately to a consensual claim. As he put it: "One would have to read . . . from the back to front. It's a strained reading of the text that would not occur in the absence of an effort to preserve prior law beyond what would seem to be justified by the text" (RPEI070:15).

The debtor's lawyer did not present well. At times he sounded confused; he often was unable to respond to the questions posed by the Justices. At one notable point, he regrettably fell into the trap of arguing that the language of Section 506(b) was ambiguous because it differed from pre-Code law rather than because the words of the statute were themselves ambiguous (RPEI070:30–31). By conceding, in effect, that the Government had the better "plain language" interpretation of Section 506(b), Cohen locked himself into arguing that (1) Section 506(b) was ambiguous because it departed from pre-Code judge-made law; and (2) therefore, because section 506(b) was ambiguous, the Court should use pre-Code law to determine its meaning (RPEI070:31–33). The Justices were not receptive to that essentially circular reasoning, as Justice Scalia emphasized that "at the outset we looked to the words of the statute," as opposed to prior judicial practice under a different law (RPEI070:34).

Justice Scalia was particularly hostile to the debtor's reliance on the *absence* of legislative history indicating an intention to depart from pre-Code law: "[W]hy do you need legislative history to show that a change is made? Congress can surely make a change in a statute without ever having a committee meeting, can't it?" (RPEI070:34). That particular interchange left the door open for the Solicitor General's representative on rebuttal to offer the rhetorical flourish that the debtor's interpretation disregarded the law-making procedures of Article I of the Constitution, "which does not require legislative history in order for Congress to make a change in the law" (RPEI070:43).

The debtor waited until the final minutes of argument to turn to what seems to have been the strongest argument – that the interpretive principle announced in *Midlantic* required Congress to have specific intent to change pre-Code law. It led directly into a plainly canned response from the Solicitor General's representative, attempting to distinguish *Midlantic* (and *Kelly v. Robinson*) as cases in which the Court "properly w[as] cautious about affecting areas other than bankruptcy, important areas such as abandonment of property to the detriment of health and safety or obligations to make restitutions to victims of crime" (RPEI070:43). *Ron Pair*, by contrast, he argued, involved a "core bankruptcy matter," where no such concern was present (RPEI070:43).

10.4.3 *The Conference*

The vote at Conference was 5–4 to reverse the Sixth Circuit and allow the Government to collect post-petition interest. As far as Justice Blackmun's notes reflect, the discussion was perfunctory; the Justices seemed well settled into their positions before the Conference met. Chief Justice Rehnquist and Justices White, Blackmun, Scalia, and Kennedy formed a solid majority for reversal, favoring the IRS. Justices O'Connor, Stevens, Brennan, and Marshall would have affirmed, favoring the debtor. Those favoring reversal questioned the applicability of the pre-Code case law. For example, Justice Rehnquist asked why the "pre-Code cases [were] critical" in light of the "sweeping ch[an]ges [made] by t[he] Code" (RPEI005:1). Justice Blackmun's personal notes suggest that he found the case "close, but [the] SG has t[he] slightly better argum[en]t" (RPEI003). The Justices in the majority were also harshly critical of the debtor's presentation in its briefs and at oral argument. In particular, Justice White thought that the debtor's position "makes no sense" (RPEI005:1). Predictably, the Justices favoring the debtor emphasized the language and the desirability of continuing pre-Code practices. On the first point, Justice Stevens emphasized that the "[p]lain language favors US" (RPEI005:2). On the second, Justice Brennan commented that "Cong[ress] need[ed] to s[ay] so if it intended t[o] change" (RPEI005:1); Justice O'Connor, characterized the "old law" as "good and reasoned" (RPEI005:2).

10.4.4 *The Majority Opinion*

The Chief Justice assigned the majority opinion to Justice Blackmun. Consistent with the apparently desultory discussion of the case at the Conference (and quite differently from all the other cases we discuss), the opinions in this case were published largely in the form in which they were originally circulated. Justice Blackmun circulated a first draft of his opinion in late December 1988 (RPEI008, 034, 069); he gained a majority bloc by mid-January 1989 without any requests for changes by the other Justices. Blackmun and his clerks specifically declined to respond to Justice O'Connor's dissent – his papers show that both Justice Blackmun and his chamber thought the "SOC dissent [was] lukewarm" and a rebuttal to her position unnecessary (RPEI018).

Blackmun's principal task was to explain why the Court could ignore the judge-made rule, which pre-dated the Code, in deciding the meaning of the new bankruptcy statute. The opinion set the stage by arguing that, as a general matter, Congress intended that the Bankruptcy Code modernize bankruptcy law, and "as a result made significant changes in both the substantive and procedural laws of bankruptcy" (RPEI008:4–5). Because the overhaul of the bankruptcy system was so substantial, argued Blackmun, "it [was] not appropriate or realistic to expect Congress to have explained with particularity each step it took" (RPEI008:5). Therefore, because the renovations to the bankruptcy system were so extensive, the only appropriate touchstone of statutory construction was the plain language of the statute (RPEI008:5).

Unlike the Sixth Circuit (but mirroring the analysis of the district court), Justice Blackmun found the meaning of Section 506(b) clear from the grammatical structure of the subsection and the location of the commas. For the majority, it was crucial that the clause "interest on such claim" in Section 506(b) was set apart by commas, and separated from the reference to "fees, costs, or charges" by the conjunctive phrase "and any" (RPEI008:6). Hence, the majority reasoned, the phrase "interest on such claim" could not be part of the list of items modified by "provided for under the agreement." Therefore, interest was available as a matter of bankruptcy law, without regard to any agreement between the parties.

To be sure, *Midlantic* complicated the majority's interpretive task. There, the Court had avowedly disregarded the plain language of the bankruptcy statute and interpreted the Code to implicitly incorporate case law under the old Act. As we discuss in detail in Chapter 8, *Midlantic* articulated the view that "if Congress intends for legislation to change the interpretation of a judicially created concept, it makes that intent specific."[12]

[12] Midlantic Nat'l Bank v. New Jersey Dep't of Envtl. Prot., 474 U.S. 494, 501 (1986).

With considerable disingenuity, Justice Blackmun explained *Midlantic* as "not rest[ing] solely, or even primarily, on a presumption of continuity with pre-Code practice" (RPEI008:8). Rather, he urged, *Midlantic* was appropriate in that case because "a contrary result would [have rendered] abandonment doctrine inconsistent with other provisions of the Code itself" (RPEI008:8). Observing no clear conflict between granting the Government post-petition interest and other provisions of the Code, Blackmun reasoned that the principle in *Midlantic* was inapplicable. In closing, Justice Blackmun characterized *Midlantic* and *Kelly* as cases in which a literal reading of the Code "was in clear conflict with state or federal laws of great importance" (RPEI008:10). For Blackmun, at least, the lower stakes of *Ron Pair* justified a departure from *Midlantic*.

10.4.5 *The Dissent*

On the other side, Justice Brennan assigned the dissent (RPEI025, 033) to Justice O'Connor, who had spoken strongly at oral argument about the "odd[ity]" of the Government's position. She agreed to "tackle the dissent," though she emphasized that her vote at Conference was "tentative" (RPEI026, 032). Like the majority, her proposed dissent (RPEI016, 042, 054) attracted votes from the others who had agreed with her at the Conference, with neither discussion nor requests for substantive changes.[13]

She launched a two-pronged attack on the majority's position. First, she criticized the majority's view of the plain meaning of Section 506. She ridiculed the majority's willingness to ground the decision on something as "exceedingly arbitrary and indefinite" as the placement of a comma (RPEI016:1). Having emphasized the relatively weak basis of the majority's statutory reading, she turned to her affirmative point: the settled course of decisions under the Act, left unaddressed in the language of the Code. She emphasized the holding in *Midlantic* that bankruptcy statutes, "regardless of how clear their language may appear, will not be deemed to have changed pre-Code law unless there is some indication that Congress thought it was effecting such a change" (RPEI016:4). Applying *Midlantic*, it was easy for her to reason that (1) disallowing post-petition interest on tax liens was an established pre-Code bankruptcy practice, (2) there was no indication that Congress intended to

[13] The files do not include a request for changes from Justice Brennan, though they include a note from Justice O'Connor thanking him for his "suggested changes" and agreeing to insert them in the next draft of her dissent. Comparison of that draft (RPEI020, 047, 058) to the first draft indicates that the changes were not substantial.

change pre-Code law, and (3) therefore it could not be presumed that the drafters of Section 506 silently abrogated pre-Code law (RPEI016:5–7).

10.5 EXPLAINING *RON PAIR*

10.5.1 *The Division of the Justices*

Of all the statutory cases we consider in the book, this is the only one in which the Court concluded that the Code overturned case law under the old Bankruptcy Act. And, at least as far as the case files available to us indicate, this is the only one of our cases in which the Justices seriously debated anything about how the scope of reforms in the Code might relate to its interpretation. The case files do not show that the Justices were overly concerned about the policy aspects of the case. Rather, for once they actively debated the relevance of pre-Code judge-made law in interpreting the Code.

But the pattern of votes suggests that the decisions of the individual Justices were not entirely dependent on the interpretive debate the opinions suggest on their face: a 5–4 vote in favor of preserving Bankruptcy Act case law in *Midlantic* followed by a 5–4 vote in the opposite direction in *Ron Pair*. If that interpretive debate had been the ultimate issue at stake, we would expect the shift of one or perhaps two votes in the center of the Court, with most Justices standing with their *Midlantic* votes. But that is not what we see. Five of the Justices voted the same way in both cases: Justices Brennan, Marshall, and Stevens voted to preserve pre-Code case law; Justices Rehnquist and White to abandon it. A sixth vote that was stable was the vote of Justice Scalia,[14] replacing Chief Justice Burger's vote to abandon pre-Code case law.

The other three votes, however, shifted. The first is easy to explain: Justice Kennedy joined the opinion in *Ron Pair* rejecting pre-Code law shortly after he replaced Justice Powell, who had written the opinion in *Midlantic* preserving pre-Code law. What is not so easy to explain is the dual switch of positions by Justices Blackmun and O'Connor; both of the Justices that wrote about the relevance of pre-Code law did so in opinions that took the opposite position from their vote in *Midlantic*. Justice Blackmun's willingness to join Justice Powell's opinion in *Midlantic* was followed by his sharp limitation of

14 Justice Scalia's view on that question would seem to be overdetermined: If any Justice would emphasize plain language over broader systemic concerns, we would expect it to be Justice Scalia. For his later praise of *Ron Pair* on this point, see Scalia and Garner (2012, 141). As we will see in the next chapter, however, even Justice Scalia was unable to maintain purity on that point.

that decision in *Ron Pair*; Justice O'Connor followed her joinder of the dissent from *Midlantic* with her *Ron Pair* dissent decrying the Court's failure to adhere to *Midlantic*.[15]

But turning the discussion back to the major theme of this book helps us to situate *Ron Pair* more comprehensibly. The principal argument of this book is that the Court systematically has underweighed the interest in reading the Bankruptcy Code and Bankruptcy Clause broadly, and that it has given inadequate weight to the major expansions wrought by the Code. In most cases, the Code unambiguously broadened the powers and reach of the bankruptcy court, its ability to interfere in legal and institutional regimes previously irrelevant to it. Thus, in most cases a vote to say the Bankruptcy Code has changed nothing is a vote to limit the reach of the Bankruptcy Power.

But *Ron Pair* is the case that distinguishes between the two theories, because *Ron Pair* is the rare case (the only one of which I am aware) coming to the Supreme Court in which the Bankruptcy Code, fairly read, narrowed the powers bankruptcy courts held under the Act. By omitting from its codification the well-settled exception denying interest payments to the Government, the statute seemed (at least on its face) to limit the intrusion of the bankruptcy process on affected creditors. The decision of the Justices to ignore that limitation confirmed the IRS's ability to continue collecting interest after bankruptcy.

Another useful way to compare *Midlantic* and *Ron Pair* is to look at the vote shifts that support the analytically disparate results. Of the seven Justices who voted in both cases, Justice O'Connor voted to limit the Bankruptcy Power in both cases; Justice Blackmun voted to broaden it; Justices Brennan, Marshall, and Stevens voted to limit that power in *Midlantic* but broaden it in *Ron Pair*; and Justices Rehnquist and White voted to broaden that power in *Midlantic* but limit it in *Ron Pair*. But the lack of any strong commitment in favor of (or opposed to) a strong Bankruptcy Power should come as no surprise. As we explained with a broader dataset in Chapter 4, none of the Justices display notedly strong (or weak) tendencies on the question we explore.

Although that scattershot pattern of votes at first glance might seem debilitating to our thesis, we do not see it that way. We are not arguing that particular Justices are for (or against) bankruptcy. Rather, we argue that the Justices decide these cases hampered by a significant policy lacuna. Thus, operating without advice from a strong institutional voice articulating the importance of the Bankruptcy Power, the Justices in close cases (like the ones we examine in detail) naturally turn to the non-bankruptcy policies that the

15 We are not the first to note that switch; Heidt (1991, 369) noted it shortly after *Ron Pair*.

case affect most directly. We submit that the votes in these cases reflect predispositions on *those* policies – the policies with which the Bankruptcy Power threatens interference. Thus, in our view the *Midlantic* Court divided largely along lines of the Justices' level of concern about environmental policy: the majority of Justices more concerned and the dissent of Justices less concerned. Conversely, the *Ron Pair* Court considered a case blending considerations of creditors' rights and protection of the federal fisc, and divided on that question, with a majority of the Justices seeing fit to limit the interference of the bankruptcy proceeding with the ordinary course of the business of collecting debts.

10.5.2 *The Solicitor General, Creditors, and the Public Fisc*

Another obvious parallel between *Midlantic* and *Ron Pair* is that the Solicitor General prevailed in both cases. To be sure, the weakness of opposing counsel aided the Solicitor General substantially in *Ron Pair*.[16] But we also want to introduce another feature to the mix. We suggested in *Bildisco* (which the Government lost) that the Solicitor General is most hampered in presenting a powerful argument when the Solicitor General appears in support of an agency directly affected in the case. This seems to be much less true in cases involving the IRS, perhaps because the Justices take much more seriously the importance of protecting the federal fisc. From that view, *Ron Pair* likely seems a case in which the amount at stake for the bankruptcy estate in any particular case is small – the interest on $54,000 during the term of the proceeding, almost certainly amounting to no more than $10,000.

The fiscal interests at stake for the Government, however, were substantial. In 1988, the year that *Ron Pair* reached the Supreme Court, the Government filed 838,000 notices of tax liens and made 14,000 seizures of property (Internal Revenue Service 1988, 54). In 1986 and 1987, the Government filed 837,000 and 767,000 notices of tax liens, respectively (Internal Revenue Service 1988, 58). IRS reports to Congress for these years do not include estimates as to the total dollar amounts of the tax liens, but statistics from more recent years that do include that information (National Taxpayer Advocate 2009, 10) suggest that federal tax-lien collections exceeded hundreds of millions of dollars a year even thirty years ago at the time of *Ron Pair*. To be sure, the Solicitor General did not emphasize those statistics in his brief, but it is apparent that the Court's willingness to grant government creditors post-petition

[16] We will see the same problem in the next chapter.

interest involved more than just a minor displacement to consensual creditors; it did provide substantial support for government revenue collection efforts.

10.6 THE AFTERMATH: *RAKE V. WADE* AND ITS REJECTION

The media's coverage of *Ron Pair* was disproportionately small given the attention the decision received in the legal community. The only major newspaper to devote an article to the decision was the Los Angeles Times, which had little to say beyond characterizing it as a "victory for the federal government" (Los Angeles Times 1989). Other publications mentioned the ruling only as part of general discussions of the Court's term (Washington Post 1988; Fanning 1988; Oregonian 1988).

By contrast (as illustrated in Appendix C), the Court has cited *Ron Pair* on more than thirty occasions, more than *Bildisco* and *Midlantic* combined and more than twice as frequently as *Kelly*. The references to *Ron Pair* invariably support a plain-meaning approach to interpretation[17] or a particular reading of a comma-laden phrase.[18]

Perhaps of more interest, *Ron Pair* has a substantial follow-on decision, *Rake v. Wade*,[19] itself sufficiently controversial to warrant Congressional overruling.[20] The controversy that grew into *Rake v. Wade* developed out of the clause in Section 506(b) (so central to the textual analysis in *Ron Pair*) that protected fees due under an agreement between the parties. It seemed plain after *Ron Pair* that interest was available to oversecured creditors even in the absence of an agreement providing for it. Subsequent lower courts then held, where there was an agreement, that the applicable interest rate should be the rate provided in the parties' contract. There was an obvious disconnect between those two analyses: making interest available whether or not there is an agreement, but drawing the rate of interest from the agreement between the parties. That disconnect resulted in several cases in which a creditor with a consensual claim sought post-petition interest even though the agreement between the parties did not provide for any interest. The cases arose in the home

[17] See, e.g., Lamie v. United States, 540 U.S. 526, 534 (2004).

[18] See, e.g., Smith v. City of Jackson, 544 U.S. 228, 250 (2005); Int'l Primate Prot. League v. Administrators of Tulane Educ. Fund, 500 U.S. 72, 80 (1991).

[19] 508 U.S. 464 (1993).

[20] Bankruptcy Amendments Act of 1994, §305, Pub. L. No. 109–108, 119 Stat. 99.

mortgage context, where state law often prohibited interest on arrearages.[21]

When the lower courts fell into disarray, the Court granted review. Again, as in *Ron Pair*, the Court eschewed pre-Code practice, holding in *Rake* that the plain language of Section 506, as interpreted in *Ron Pair*, clearly required interest in such cases. Because back mortgage payments typically are themselves mostly unpaid interest, the payment of interest on those arrearages amounts as a practical matter to the payment of interest on interest. That circumstance, coupled with the frequent state prohibition of such interest, motivated Congress promptly to overrule *Rake* by amending Section 1322 to bar the payment of interest on mortgage arrearages cured in a Chapter 13 plan (the specific facts of *Rake*). The legislative history documents Congress's rejection of the Court's analysis:

> [Section 1322(e)] will have the effect of overruling the decision of the Supreme Court in *Rake v. Wade* ... In that case, the Court held that the Bankruptcy Code required that interest be paid on mortgage arrearages paid by debtors curing defaults on their mortgages. Notwithstanding State law, this case has had the effect of providing a windfall to secured creditors at the expense of unsecured creditors by forcing debtors to pay the bulk of their income to satisfy the secured creditors' claims. This had the effect of giving secured creditors interest on interest payments, and interest on the late charges and other fees, even where applicable law prohibits such interest and even when it was something that was not contemplated by either party in the original transaction. This provision ... will limit the secured creditor to the benefit of the initial bargain with no court contrived windfall. It is the Committee's intention that a cure pursuant to a plan should operate to put the debtor in the same position as if the default had never occurred (House Committee on the Judiciary 1994, 55).

In short, Congress determined that the amount necessary to cure a default should not include interest arising solely under Section 506, but rather should be determined by reference to the agreement between the parties and nonbankruptcy law.

10.7 CONCLUSION

Ron Pair differs from the other cases that we have examined because the dispute between the Justices over the correct interpretive principle in the

[21] See *In re* Laguna, 944 F.2d 542, 545 (9th Cir. 1991); Landmark Fin. Services v. Hall, 918 F.2d 1150, 1153–1155 (4th Cir. 1990); *In re* Capps, 836 F.2d 773, 776 (3d Cir. 1987); *In re* Terry, 780 F.2d 894, 895–896 (11th Cir. 1985).

case more directly considers the issues about which we write than any of the Court's other cases. Thus, the case (so far as the opinions suggest) turns directly on the correct balance between the plain language of a statute and pre-statute common law. That alone would make it a valuable example. But it also provides a useful segue to the next chapter, in which the Solicitor General's arguments on behalf of creditor's rights extend even more overtly into the private realm.

11

Bankruptcy and State Sovereignty: *BFP*

Our last case presents a paradigmatic example of our thesis in action. *BFP v. Resolution Trust Corporation*[1] pitted relatively plain statutory language supporting the debtor-in-possession against policy interests supporting a secured creditor.[2] Following upon *Ron Pair*, an important explanation for the Court's decision to favor policy over the language of the statute was its perception of a need to protect the availability of non-bankruptcy remedies for secured creditors. Parallel to that argument, we see here the Solicitor General appearing (as is so often the case) in support of the secured creditors, successfully arguing to limit the effects of bankruptcy on the rights of secured creditors.

11.1 INTRODUCTION

Speculators borrow money to purchase a house in Newport Beach, California. They make no down payment and fail to make any of the mortgage payments. After a few months, the lender, a local savings and loan association, forecloses, selling the house at auction for well under the purchase price (though more than the mortgage). The borrowers then file for bankruptcy, and, in the bankruptcy proceeding, try to invalidate the foreclosure sale as a fraudulent transfer, arguing that the house was worth substantially more than the sales price. A typical enough story, though perhaps a surprise that it occurred more than twenty years ago.

After the lower courts dismissed the borrowers' claim, the Supreme Court granted certiorari to resolve a circuit conflict. Following full briefing and argument, the Court held that a bankruptcy court does *not* have the power

[1] 511 U.S. 531 (1994).

[2] For a different reading, consider Dembart and Markell (2004, 391), who take at face value the claim of Justice Scalia that his majority opinion was driven by the plain meaning of the statute. I believe that the discussion below suggests that perspective is insupportable.

to overturn a real property foreclosure that is properly conducted under state law. The case involved interpretation of Section 548 of the Bankruptcy Code, which permits a bankruptcy trustee (or debtor-in-possession) to avoid certain transfers of property if the debtor "received less than a reasonably equivalent value in exchange for such transfer." Thus, the legal question in *BFP* was whether the consideration received in a foreclosure sale constitutes "reasonably equivalent value" as a matter of law, without respect to the relation between that amount and the ordinary fair market value. I represented the Resolution Trust Corporation in the Supreme Court, arguing that bankruptcy courts should not have the power to second guess the bidding that takes place at regularly conducted and non-collusive foreclosure sales without clearer language to that effect in the Bankruptcy Code.[3] Yet even I readily acknowledge that the most natural reading of the statute would support some assessment of the price received at the sale. Thus, from my perspective, *BFP* presents a conflict between policy and the result that follows most naturally from the statute.

Considering the nature of that conflict, it might come as a surprise that Justice Scalia is the author of the more holistic opinion, which gives priority to institutional concerns. In this case, it is Justice Souter who provides the strongly worded dissent peppered with a biting reliance on the plain language of the statute. Before I discuss the opinions in detail, I provide some background on the history of the legal issue. Then I turn back to the case itself, emphasizing the facts of the underlying transactions, the lower court decisions, and the process by which the Justices shaped those opinions.

11.2 FORECLOSURE AS A FRAUDULENT CONVEYANCE

Like many bankruptcy cases, *BFP* presents a conflict between the powers of a bankruptcy court and rights under a separate legal regime. On the one hand, bankruptcy law generally requires that creditors suffer equally from a debtor's financial distress. Among other things, that means that one creditor should not profit to the detriment of other creditors through transactions with a distressed debtor before formal bankruptcy proceedings begin (Baird 2010; Warren and Westbrook 2005). Thus, the Bankruptcy Code prohibits both transfers that the debtor makes fraudulently or for inadequate consideration (both are called fraudulent transfers, Section 548), and payments that the debtor makes to creditors shortly before bankruptcy (labeled preferences,

3 That participation inevitably influences my account. For more objective accounts, see Lawless (1996); Warren and Westbrook (2005, 571).

Section 547). On the other hand, real property law provides rules that specify when, and under what circumstances, conveyances become final. Even though foreclosure prices often are just a fraction of the sales prices achieved through other types of market transactions, real estate rules generally prohibit challenges to foreclosure sales based solely on price (Nelson and Whitman 2007; American Law Institute 1997, § 8.3).

Given the reality of low-price foreclosure sales, the debtor's recourse is to protect itself either by bidding the property up to a fair value at the foreclosure sale or by selling the property in a consensual transaction before the foreclosure and applying the proceeds against the debt (Mann 1997). The rationale is that rules interfering with the finality of foreclosure sales depress the prices received at those sales by making it riskier for third parties to bid. At a policy level, the concern is that the market for distressed real property could suffer if the purchaser's title depends upon a judge's after-the-fact determination of a "fair" valuation of the property as of the date of foreclosure.

The bankruptcy and real property regimes potentially conflict when a distressed borrower files for bankruptcy shortly after its property has been sold at a foreclosure sale for substantially less than its fair market value. Invalidating such a sale would further the interests of non-foreclosing creditors in maximizing the value of the bankruptcy estate, at least in a case in which the property was worth more than the total amount due to the foreclosing creditor. At the same time, invalidating such a sale would interfere with the ability of the secured-credit system to redeploy collateral to a solvent owner in an expeditious manner. Rules that lengthen the period when collateral remains in the hands of the distressed borrower impose costs by interfering with the effective rehabilitation and use of land and improvements. The question is whether fraudulent transfer rules under the bankruptcy regime apply to foreclosure sales that the real property regime validates.

The problem is complicated somewhat by the long history of rules banning and invalidating fraudulent transfers, which predate the first bankruptcy statute by centuries. Those rules have been, and remain, a common feature of state law, parallel to the applicable provisions of the Bankruptcy Code. Most famously, Britain's 1571 Statute of Elizabeth invalidated any conveyance made with the intention to hinder, delay, or defraud creditors.[4] Many states adopted similar statutes, long before the adoption of a general federal bankruptcy law in 1898 (National Conference of Commissioners on Uniform State Laws 2013). Even after the adoption of the Bankruptcy Act of 1898, this continued

4 Act Against Fraudulent Deeds, 13 Eliz., c. 5.

to be a fertile field for state legislative activity (Reilly 2005). Thus, NCCUSL[5] in 1918 promulgated the Uniform Fraudulent Conveyance Act (the UFCA). The UFCA provided a uniform template for harmonizing the preexisting body of state fraudulent conveyance law, which had consisted of a patchwork of specific statutes modeled on the Statute of Elizabeth. Twenty-six States eventually adopted the UFCA (National Conference of Commissioners on Uniform State Laws 2013). However, most state law now tracks the 1984 Uniform Fraudulent Transfer Act (the UFTA), which has been adopted in 43 States (National Conference of Commissioners on Uniform State Laws 2013).

Of importance to this discussion, both the UFTA and the UFCA permit a court to invalidate a transfer not only because of a showing of actual or intentional fraud by the debtor/transferor, but also upon a showing of constructive fraud – generally some showing that the debtor received an inadequate consideration for the transferred assets.[6] Although the 1984 UFTA for the most part harmonized state fraudulent transfer law with the federal fraudulent transfer provisions enacted in the Bankruptcy Act of 1978 (National Conference of Commissioners on Uniform State Laws 2013), the problem in *BFP* reflects a slight difference between the federal and state definitions. The question is how to deal with involuntary transfers (such as foreclosure sales). One possibility would be that involuntary transfers are not covered. The debtor hardly can be said to defraud its creditors when one of its creditors compels the conveyance. Still, if the goal is to prevent one creditor from getting an unfair share of the borrower's property, then a case can be made for examining involuntary transfers. On that point, the definition of conveyance in UFCA § 1 did not refer specifically to involuntary transfers, but a few cases applying it had concluded that it nevertheless extended to foreclosure and execution of sales, at least in cases where the sales or underlying loans were alleged to be collusive.[7]

Responding to those rulings, both the UFTA and the Bankruptcy Code make it plain that their avoidance powers would extend to involuntary transfers. Thus, the definition of "transfer" in UFTA § 1(12) refers explicitly to

5 The National Conference of Commissioners on Uniform State Laws (NCCUSL), now known as the Uniform Law Commission, for more than a century has been the dominant trade group promulgating uniform statutes for adoption by state legislatures.

6 Specifically, UFCA § 4 addresses transfers without "fair consideration"; UFTA § 3 addresses transfers without "reasonably equivalent value."

7 Hearn 45 St. Corp. v. Jano, 27 N.E.2d 814 (N.Y. 1940) (overturning foreclosure sale based on fictitious judgment and gratuitous mortgage); Lefkowitz v. Finkelstein Trading Corp., 14 F. Supp. 898, 899 (S.D.N.Y. 1936) (overturning collusive foreclosure sale where purchaser immediately conveyed the assets to the children of the defaulting borrower); Catabene v. Wallner, 85 A.3d 300, 302 (N.J. 1951) (permitting attack on foreclosure sale based on gratuitous mortgage); *see also* UFCA § 1 comment 12.

"involuntary" transfers. And in 1984, Congress added a parallel reference to "involuntary" transfers in Section 101 in 1984.[8] As discussed below, the *BFP* Court held in substance that those amendments had no purpose other than to ensure that bankruptcy courts could invalidate collusive foreclosure sales.[9]

Because foreclosure sales typically do not bring high prices, the natural question arises whether a court can overturn such a sale as a fraudulent conveyance in the more common situation of when the sale is not collusive. In the language of both the UFTA and the Bankruptcy Code, the issue is whether the sale returns a "reasonably equivalent value" for the transferred asset. The term, which is not used elsewhere in the Bankruptcy Code, appears to derive from the references to "fair equivalent" value in Bankruptcy Act § 67d, 11 U.S.C. § 107(d). It appeared first in the bill proposed by the Bankruptcy Commission.[10] From there, it found its way into the Bankruptcy Code as adopted by Congress in 1978 and then into the Uniform Fraudulent Transfer Act promulgated by NCCUSL in 1984.

To its credit, the UFTA addresses the problem directly: Section 3(b) of the UFTA states specifically that a person that buys at "a regularly conducted, non-collusive foreclosure sale" gives reasonably equivalent value. Conversely, despite repeated and pervasive amendments of the Bankruptcy Code, Congress to this day has not spoken directly to the question. All that can be discerned from the Code (Section 548) is that a bankruptcy court is authorized to invalidate a sale for less than "reasonably equivalent value."

Because the UFCA and the parallel language in the old Bankruptcy Act (Section 67d) extended to constructive fraud (transfers for which the debtor does not receive a "fair equivalent"), it is difficult in hindsight to understand why it was not until 1980 that a federal court first squarely faced the question whether the fraudulent transfer provisions of federal bankruptcy law could overturn a foreclosure sale validly conducted under state law. When it did arise, the Fifth Circuit in *Durrett v. Washington National Insurance Co.*[11] considered a Texas foreclosure in which an unrelated third party purchased real estate for the amount of the outstanding debt. Responding to evidence

8 Bankruptcy Amendments and Federal Judgeship Act of 1984, Pub. L. No. 98–353, § 463(a), 98 Stat. 333, 378–79.

9 As Justice Souter pointed out in his dissent from *BFP*, that reading closely resembles a bill that Congress considered, but did not enact. S. 445, 98th Cong., 1st Sess. § 360 (1983) (protecting non-collusive foreclosure sales) (discussed in 511 U.S. at 554 n.6 (Souter, J., dissenting)). Thus, Congress arguably rejected the position espoused by the *BFP* majority and codified in the UFTA.

10 Commission Bill § 4–08, Report of the Commission on the Bankruptcy Laws of the United States, Part II, H.R. Doc. No. 137, 93rd Cong., 1st Sess. 175–176 (1973).

11 621 F.2d 201 (1980).

supporting a finding that the debt was only 57 percent of the hypothetical fair market value of the property, the Fifth Circuit invalidated the sale. Despite the imprecision of the statute, the Fifth Circuit seemed to adopt an almost absolute rule requiring invalidation of foreclosure sales returning less than 70 percent of fair market value.

At the time, the result in *Durrett* shocked real estate professionals and had a destabilizing effect on the industry, at least in Texas (Sweat 1984; Warren and Westbrook 2005). The Supreme Court in *BFP* characterized *Durrett* as "unprecedented," explaining that "[t]o our knowledge no prior decision had ever applied the 'grossly inadequate price' badge of fraud under fraudulent transfer law to set aside a foreclosure sale."[12] Many institutional lenders at that time did adopt policies of bidding 70 percent of the appraised value in foreclosure sales, but the limited ex ante likelihood that a loan would lead to a foreclosure sale that would be followed by a bankruptcy with a colorable *Durrett* claim makes it difficult to believe that those lenders raised interest rates or otherwise limited the extension of credit. For example, promptly after *Durrett*, title insurance regulators responded by requiring insurers to include an exception to title insurance policies that left foreclosure purchasers exposed to the risk of *Durrett* litigation (Texas Department of Insurance 1993; Stark 1995, 610).

The title insurance question was a major topic in the Supreme Court's deliberations. First, it was raised in the briefs of the RTC and the Federal Home Loan Mortgage Corporation (supporting the RTC as an amicus).[13] It also was a topic of interest to Justice O'Connor at the oral argument (Transcript at 25–26), was emphasized in the Court's opinion,[14] and dismissed as insignificant in Justice Souter's dissent.[15]

More seriously, the publicity surrounding the decision spawned similar challenges around the country. For the most part, however, other courts were not as receptive to those challenges. First, *In re Madrid* produced a contrary view from the Ninth Circuit's Bankruptcy Appellate Panel, which held that the price received at a non-collusive foreclosure sale is by definition reasonably equivalent value under Section 548.[16] The *Madrid* court explained: "We

[12] 511 U.S. at 542.

[13] BFP RTC Brief 28 n.21; BFP Freddie Mac Brief 13 & n. 10 (discussing similar forms promulgated by the American Land Title Association).

[14] 511 U.S. at 544.

[15] 511 U.S. at 568 n.20 (Souter, J., dissenting)

[16] Lawyers Title Ins. Corp. v. Madrid (*In re* Madrid), 21 B.R. 424 (B.A.P. 9th Cir.), *aff'd on other grounds*, 725 F.2d 1197 (9th Cir. 1982).

decline to follow *Durrett*'s 70% fair market value rule for the reason that a regularly conducted sale, open to all bidders and all creditors, is itself a safeguard against the evils of private transfers to relatives and favorites."[17] After the Sixth Circuit took a view similar to the view of the Ninth Circuit,[18] the Seventh Circuit responded with *In re Bundles*, offering yet another answer: a vague test under which courts should consider "all the facts and circumstances" in deciding whether to invalidate a sale.[19] To sum up, when the *BFP* case began in California, three of the courts of appeals (the Fifth, Sixth, and Seventh) had considered the question directly, with each taking a distinctly different view of the protection a foreclosure sale should receive in bankruptcy.[20]

11.3 *BFP* IN THE LOWER COURTS

11.3.1 The Dispute

The facts of *BFP* play out like a law school hypothetical, with a strong scent of misconduct by the defaulting borrowers and of carelessness by the foreclosing lender. In the underlying purchase and loan transactions, Wayne and Marlene Pedersen borrowed about $350,000 from Imperial Savings Association to purchase a home in Newport Beach, California, from Sheldon and Ann Foreman. Originally, the purchase price was $350,000 plus certain rare coins. Before the sale closed in the fall of 1987, however, press reports indicating that Wayne Pedersen had been involved in the fraudulent sale of rare coins made the Foremans understandably reluctant to accept the coins. Accordingly, the sale was restructured so that the consideration would be $350,000 in cash (the proceeds of the Imperial loan) plus a $200,000 promissory note from a newly formed partnership ironically named BFP (composed of the Pedersens and another individual named Russell Barton), which ultimately took title to the property.[21] To complicate matters further, only Wayne Pedersen executed the deed from the Pedersens to BFP; he signed Marlene's name to the BFP deed

[17] 21 B.R. at 426-27.

[18] *In re* Winshall Settlor's Trust, 758 F.2d 1136 (6th Cir. 1985).

[19] 856 F.2d 815 (1988).

[20] The circuit conflict deepened considerably during the course of litigation in *BFP*, as three additional courts of appeals adopted the Seventh Circuit's multi-factor *Bundles* approach: Barrett v. Commonwealth Federal Savings & Loan Ass'n, 939 F.2d 20 (3rd Cir. 1991); Cooper v. Ashley Communications, Inc. (*In re* Morris Communications NC, Inc.), 914 F.3d 458 (4th Cir. 1990); Grissom v. Johnson (*In re* Grissom), 955 F.2d 1440 (11th Cir. 1992).

[21] BFP v. Imperial Savings & Loan Ass'n (*In re* BFP), 974 F.2d 1144, 1145 (9th Cir. 1991) [hereinafter In re *BFP*]; J.A. 45–47 (reprinting allegations regarding the fraudulent coin incident in adversary complaint filed in the bankruptcy court).

without her permission.[22] The Foremans retained a second lien on the house to secure the obligation of BFP to repay the note that they accepted in place of the coins.

In any event, neither BFP nor the Pedersens made any payments on the Imperial loan. When the Foremans stopped making those payments after a few months,[23] Imperial commenced foreclosure proceedings.[24] In another semi-comic interlude, the foreclosure sale was delayed by an involuntary bankruptcy proceeding filed by Off Road Vehicles – Recreation and Family Campground, Inc. (ORV). ORV claimed title to the property based on a separate deed from the Pedersens (both signed this instrument – apparently designed to defraud their partner Russell Barton). Because the Pedersens executed the ORV deed after the BFP deed, and without the consent of Barton, the bankruptcy court held the ORV deed invalid and dismissed the ORV bankruptcy proceeding.[25] At that point, the Imperial foreclosure proceeded, producing a July 1989 sale of the property for about $430,000 to a stranger to the earlier transactions, Russell Osborne. That price was about 125 percent of the Imperial debt, but only about 75–80 percent of the Pedersens' original purchase price.[26] Then, shortly after the foreclosure sale, a state court, responding to a complaint from the Foremans based on the fraudulent behavior of the Pedersens, rescinded the sale from the Foremans to the Pedersens.[27] But because Osborne already had purchased at the foreclosure sale, without knowledge of the malfeasance of the Pedersens, the decree invalidating the initial conveyance came too late to affect Osborne's status as a bona fide purchaser for value. Osborne resold the property five months later for about $660,000.[28] Shortly thereafter, Wayne Pedersen pleaded guilty to federal charges of mail fraud (based on a nationwide telemarketing operation associated with his coin business) and then went into hiding. He remained

[22] The courts eventually concluded that the deed was valid despite the forgery. In re *BFP*, *supra*, 974 F.2d at 1147–48.

[23] Because the Foremans' lien was inferior to the Imperial lien, it would not survive the Imperial foreclosure sale, at which the Foremans apparently did not bid. When the Pedersens and BFP made no payments on the Imperial loan, the Foremans presumably continued payments for a time on the hope that the value of the property eventually could support repaying both the Imperial loan and the money due to them.

[24] J.A. 52 (adversary complaint filed in the bankruptcy court).

[25] J.A. 24 (docket entries in ORV bankruptcy).

[26] The parties vigorously contested the validity of the foreclosure sale as a matter of California law, but the Ninth Circuit rejected those claims (In re *BFP*, *supra*, 974 F.2d at 1149 n.7) and the parties did not raise them in the Supreme Court.

[27] J.A. 252–281; In re *BFP*, *supra*, 974 F.2d at 1147 n.3.

[28] In re *BFP*, *supra*, 974 F.2d at 1145–46; Pet. 5–6 & n.2.

a fugitive through the date of the Supreme Court's decision (Granelli 1994).

A cynic might suppose that a loan to a borrower prone to engage in such transactions reflects a failure to consider the "character" of the borrower (Federal Deposit Insurance Corporation 1999; Ruth 1999, 99). Among other things, for example, the record makes it quite clear that the borrowers did not plan to occupy the home, but to flip it. Specifically, the Pedersens transferred the property to BFP as part of the transaction in which they borrowed funds from Imperial to pay to the Foremans. That point warrants emphasis because loans on investment purchases of real estate tend to be riskier than loans on owner-occupied real estate; as a result, savings and loan associations traditionally had been unwilling to make such loans. Also, the record makes it clear that the newspaper reports about Pedersen's fraudulent activity occurred weeks before Imperial made the loan – those reports were serious enough to convince the Foremans to alter the deal but apparently did not concern Imperial's loan officer.[29]

To put the lender's (lack of) diligence in context, it is useful to recite a few facts about what was going on with Imperial during this time. During the early 1980s, Imperial had been one of the nation's largest thrift holding companies. Unfortunately, though predictably, the mismatch between the high rates it paid on deposits and the low rates it earned on mortgages gave it a negative return on equity throughout the early 1980s. All told, it incurred about $140 million in losses between 1981 and 1985 (Tye 1990).

In the mid-1980s, however, a compatriot of the infamous Michael Milken named Victor Goulet acquired a controlling share of Imperial (Stein 1989). Goulet promptly installed Kenneth Thygerson as CEO. Thygerson was an evangelical Midwesterner who led Imperial rapidly into the realm of higher-risk junk bonds and collateralized debt obligations,[30] purchased from Milken's firm Drexel Burnham Lambert (Stein 1989). The higher income from those investments kept Imperial afloat for several years, but when Milken's empire unraveled in the early 1990s, those investments went bad and Imperial became insolvent. Eventually, the RTC spent about $400 million to resolve claims arising out of Imperial's failure (Barth et al. 2004, 265–270).

[29] In re *BFP*, *supra*, 974 F.2d at 1145–1146 (reporting the sequence of events leading up to the sale from the Foremans to the Pedersens).

[30] Imperial apparently had the dubious distinction of being the purchaser of the first collateralized debt obligations ever syndicated (Cresci 2005).

11.3.2 *The Bankruptcy*

After the failure of their efforts to exclude Barton from a share of the profits and to prevent the foreclosure by Imperial, the Pedersens took BFP into Chapter 11, hoping to recapture the profits that Osborne made when he resold after the foreclosure.[31] In the bankruptcy court, BFP promptly filed an adversary proceeding, arguing that the foreclosure sale was a fraudulent conveyance under Section 548 of the Bankruptcy Code. BFP contended that the property was worth about $750,000. For what it is worth, the historical analysis at zillow.com suggests that the property (225 Via Genoa in Newport Beach) did not reach a persistent valuation above $600,000 until about 1999; zillow.com estimates the property's current value (as of 2016) at about $2.2 million.

The bankruptcy court concluded that the sale was properly conducted and not collusive and accordingly granted separate motions to dismiss BFP's complaint.[32] BFP appealed separately from the bankruptcy court's rulings on motions by Osborne (the purchaser) and Imperial (the lender). The Osborne appeal went to the district court, which summarily rejected BFP's claims, relying on *Madrid*.[33] The Imperial appeal went to the Bankruptcy Appellate Panel, which also rejected BFP's claims.[34] Bankruptcy Judge Volinn dissented from the B.A.P. decision, arguing that the panel should adopt the *Bundles* approach, which by that time had become the majority rule in the courts of appeals.[35]

11.3.3 *The Ninth Circuit*

After consolidating separate appeals from the decisions of the district court and bankruptcy appellate panel, the Ninth Circuit affirmed. By the time the issue came to a head, Imperial had failed and come under the control of the Resolution Trust Corporation. The court of appeals recognized the disarray in the existing circuit court decisions. Following the lead of its bankruptcy appellate panel, the court, in an opinion written by Judge Sneed, chose to adopt the Sixth Circuit's approach, holding that the price at a non-collusive, regularly conducted foreclosure sale is by definition reasonably equivalent value under

31 It would seem rational that the Pedersens would not have wanted BFP to enter bankruptcy *before* the *ORV* ruling, but it is not clear why BFP did not file *after* the *ORV* ruling but before the foreclosure sale occurred. Perhaps the Pedersens waited until Osborne had sold the property, at which point they could be sure it was worth more than the debt.

32 Pet. App. 28–32 (granting Osborne motion to dismiss); Pet. App. 33–40 (granting Imperial motion to dismiss).

33 Pet. App. 41–48.

34 132 B.R. 748 (1991).

35 132 B.R. at 751–752.

Section 548. The opinion acknowledged that the Seventh Circuit's approach presented a "persuasive" "plain-language interpretation" of the statute, but rejected that approach based on the conclusion that "broader considerations require a different result."[36] Specifically, the court explained, a rule leaving foreclosure sales subject to post-hoc price assessments would "undermin[e] the price maximizing objectives of [the statute] because potential buyers will discount their assessment of the true market value of the property to reflect this uncertainty. . . . It makes little sense to interpret [the statute] in a way that will discourage healthy foreclosure bidding."[37]

11.4 *BFP* IN THE SUPREME COURT

11.4.1 *Granting Review*

BFP's counsel (a solo practitioner in Newport Beach) promptly filed a petition for a writ of certiorari, bringing the case to the Supreme Court. The respondents were the purchaser at the sale (Osborne) and the RTC, acting as receiver for Imperial. Osborne, predictably enough, filed a brief in opposition to the petition. The RTC, however, filed a brief recommending that the Court grant the petition, noting the stark conflict in the courts of appeals and suggesting that the recurrence of the question demonstrated its importance.[38]

In hindsight, reasonable minds can differ about the importance of the question. In truth, the problem arises only in a reasonably unusual situation marked by considerable volatility in real-estate prices. First, the property has to be sold at foreclosure at a time when the property's value is relatively low. If the property were known to be valuable at the time of foreclosure, the debtor typically could prevent the foreclosure by filing for bankruptcy before the sale rather than afterwards. Then, the property would have to appreciate substantially and rapidly. The increase has to be large enough to produce a value that would repay the loan of the foreclosing lender and produce a surplus sufficient to justify the litigation costs; the increase has to be rapid enough to support a bankruptcy filing sufficiently soon after the foreclosure sale to

[36] In re *BFP*, *supra*, 974 F.2d at 1148.

[37] In re *BFP*, *supra*, 974 F.2d at 1148–1149 (relying on Ehrlich (1985)).

[38] The FDIC and RTC were two of the largest creditors in foreclosure proceedings in Texas, one of the locations hit hardest by the S&L crisis. The application of the *Durrett* rule in the Fifth Circuit (which includes Texas) motivated the RTC and the FDIC to take advantage of the opportunity to get a case before the Court that might overturn *Durrett*.

permit a challenge in the bankruptcy court. The existence of the circuit conflict shows that the scenario is not wholly unrealistic, but at the same time, it is fair to say that the facts are atypical.

Despite the RTC's concession and the disarray in the courts of appeals, the pool memorandum (prepared by one of Justice White's clerks) recommended that the Court deny review (BFPR001). The concern of the law clerks was that the case might be moot. Even if the Court did overturn the decision of the Ninth Circuit, it is not clear that the bankruptcy court could provide meaningful relief to BFP. The concern was that Osborne (the purchaser at the foreclosure sale) already had sold the property. Worried that the Bankruptcy Code might not permit the bankruptcy court to enter a monetary judgment against Osborne if (as seemed likely) the property itself had passed into the hands of a good-faith purchaser, the author of the pool memo recommended denial (BFPR001:8). A reply brief arguing that the case was not moot persuaded neither the White Clerk nor the clerk responsible for the matter in Justice Blackmun's chambers (BFPR002).

Notwithstanding the views of the law clerks, the Justices decided the case warranted their attention. Justice Kennedy (formerly a colleague of Judge Sneed's on the Ninth Circuit) pressed the view that the case was not moot, but asked that it be relisted to consider reformulating the questions presented for decision (BFPR003). Justices O'Connor (BFPR004), Blackmun (BFPR005), and Thomas (BFPR006), however, preferred to grant review without changing the questions, and the Court proceeded on that basis.

11.4.2 *Argument and Decision*

The most active questioners at the argument were Justices Scalia, O'Connor, and Souter. Interrupting petitioner's counsel at the beginning of the argument, Justice Scalia suggested that it was senseless to place a value on foreclosed property that ignored that the property would be sold at foreclosure. Justice Scalia commented:

> If you're willing to individualize [at all], why not go all the way and say, this is not only property of a sort that's being sold at a foreclosure sale, but is property that's being sold on a rainy Tuesday when some of the best buyers in town are on summer vacation? ... It is property that is subject to foreclosure under certain State rules ... and whatever it fetches under those rules has to be the fair value of that particularly individuated property. (Transcript 5, 7)

For his part, Justice Souter pressed both respondents on his view that the statutory reference to "value" could not be read to support an inquiry limited solely to compliance with state procedures. Speaking to counsel for the RTC, he asked: "I have difficulty squaring your argument . . . with the language of the statute . . . It seems to me that if all that Congress wanted [was to require compliance with state law] they took a very obtuse way to require that" (Transcript 25, 31). Speaking to counsel for Osborne, he explained:

> [T]he trouble, it seems to me, with your argument is that if the phrase in question . . . means nothing more than you say it does . . . it would have been infinitely simpler for Congress simply to say that a bona fide sale conducted in accordance with the requirements of State statutory or common law will be conclusively presumed to realize a fair or sufficient value. (Transcript 38–39)

Justice O'Connor was primarily concerned about the potential adverse effects of the decision on foreclosure bidding. Speaking to petitioner's counsel, she asked: "[I]f we accept your . . . position, wouldn't one of the practical effects be . . . that . . . a seller could get still less at a foreclosure sale because it would be relatively more easy to upset the result of a foreclosure sale?" (Transcript 16). Speaking to counsel for the RTC, she sought a detailed explanation of ways in which foreclosure sales differed from voluntary sales (Transcript 20–21).

When the Justices met to consider the case on the Friday after the argument, they found themselves closely divided. Five Justices voted to affirm (the Chief Justice and Justices O'Connor, Kennedy, Scalia, and Thomas); four Justices were set on reversal (Justices Blackmun, Stevens, Souter, and Ginsburg[39]) (BFPR010). But among the Justices voting to affirm, there was considerable doubt about how to explain the decision. The Chief Justice, for example, would have accepted a rebuttable presumption that the sale was valid, apparently one that would extend to all sales that could not be overturned under state law (BFPR010:1). Justices Thomas (BFPR010:2) and O'Connor aligned themselves with the Chief Justice, though Justice O'Connor suggested (in Justice Blackmun's report) that she "would like to adopt C9 rule but [the] stat[ute] [provides] no support" (BFPR010:1). Justice Scalia pressed the view he had articulated at oral argument, arguing that overturning a foreclosure sale was "extraordinary," and that "noone w[oul]d b[e] safe for several years, even with a rebuttable presumption" (BFPR010:1).[40] Justice Kennedy aligned himself with Justice Scalia, commenting, "we s[hould] n[ot] get into this" (BFPR010:2).

39 Justice Ginsburg had replaced Justice White in the summer of 1993, after the Court granted review but before the oral argument.

40 Justice Blackmun's notes describe Justice Scalia as promoting a "rigid categorical rule" supported by "illusory logic" (BFPR010:1).

Interestingly, Justice Stevens on the other side also suggested a rebuttable presumption. Apparently he had something less lenient in mind than the Chief Justice, "like *Bundles*," because he viewed that perspective as a basis for reversal (BFPR010:1). The two junior Justices, Justices Souter and Ginsburg, aligned themselves readily with Justice Stevens (BFPR010:1–2).

11.4.3 *The Opinions*

11.4.3.1 The Majority

Although the Chief Justice did not seem to share Justice Scalia's initial conception of the matter, he did assign the majority opinion to Justice Scalia. Justice Scalia's draft opinion, implementing the analysis he offered at the conference, quickly gained five votes, though three of his colleagues requested a variety of revisions. First, the Chief Justice sought clarification (BFPR016) that the opinion would offer broad protection for properly conducted foreclosure sales. The original draft had suggested loosely that a bankruptcy court could overturn any sale that suffered from "[a]ny irregularity"; the Chief Justice asked that the draft specify that the bankruptcy court could overturn a foreclosure sale only for a "material irregularity" or perhaps one that "would invalidate the sale under state law."[41] Justice Scalia quickly accepted the second option (BFPR015), and the Chief Justice then sent a note joining the opinion unconditionally (BFPR018).

Justice Scalia then was caught in a debate between Justices O'Connor and Kennedy on the appropriate justification for a plain-statement rule to justify avoiding the statute's plain language. Justice Kennedy seemed to think that the federalism concerns raised by *BFP* were inadequate to justify application of a strong plain-statement rule, and that the language of Section 548 was vague enough for him to support the result without discussion of that topic. Specifically, Justice Kennedy found the extended discussion of Justice O'Connor's opinion in *Gregory v. Ashcroft*[42] (in which Justice Kennedy had joined) inappropriate, because that case "applies to the more touchy situation when a federal law impinges upon a 'most fundamental' aspect of state sovereignty" (BFPR021).

[41] The files in *BFP* are evidently quite incomplete. They do not contain copies of the first or second drafts of Justice Scalia's opinions (the drafts that motivated the requests for revisions). Nor do they contain all of the Chief Justice's correspondence with Justice Scalia. His note requesting revision apologizes for failing to ask for the revision in an "earlier join letter" that does not appear in the file.

[42] 501 U.S. 452 (1991).

Justice Scalia wrote back to Justice Kennedy the same day, suggesting a compromise: "If no one else objects, I would be willing to drop the paragraph on *Gregory v. Ashcroft*. I would want, however, to strengthen the previous paragraph by bringing forward some of the deleted material. Absent objection, I will recirculate with that change" (BFPR024). As it happens, Justice O'Connor, who had joined Justice Scalia's draft in its original form (BFPR015), did object. Apparently fond of her opinion in *Ashcroft*, she wrote the same day to Justice Scalia, advising him that she "hope[d] you will not drop the citation and reference to *Gregory v. Ashcroft*. It has relevance to the issue in this case in my view" (BFPR022). Attempting to resolve the dispute, Justice Scalia in turn wrote back to Justice O'Connor explaining frankly: "I need Tony's vote. Would it be acceptable to you and him if I included a '*cf.*' citation to *Gregory v. Ashcroft*?" (BFPR023). Grudgingly, Justice O'Connor acquiesced: "Yes, a '*cf.*' cite is better than nothing" (BFPR024). Justice Kennedy at that point also acquiesced: "A '*cf.*' cite to *Gregory v. Ashcroft* would suit me fine" (BFPR025). Apparently trying to assuage Justice O'Connor's displeasure, he explained: "My primary concern was to preserve the importance of *Gregory* by not trivializing it through overuse" (BFPR025).

Putting the interpretive debate to the side, Justice Scalia's draft relied heavily on the point he pressed at oral argument. He reasoned: "An appraiser's reconstruction of 'fair market value' could show what similar property would be worth if it did not have to be sold within the time and manner strictures of state-prescribed foreclosures. But property that *must* be sold within those strictures is simply *worth less*" (BFPR026:7) (emphasis of Justice Scalia). He continued: "No one would pay as much to own such property as he would pay to own real estate that could be sold at leisure and pursuant to normal marketing techniques" (BFPR026:7). Most strikingly, he offered a bold analogy to the effect of zoning laws and other general property regulations: "And it is no more realistic to ignore that characteristic of the property (the fact that state foreclosure law permits the mortgagee to sell it at forced sale) than it is to ignore other price-affecting characteristics (such as the fact that state zoning law permits the owner of the neighboring lot to open a gas station)" (BFPR026:7–8).[43]

[43] Justice Scalia's basic argument is something of a tangent. The question is not whether a foreclosure sale produces "fair market value," but whether it produces "reasonably equivalent value." As emphasized in the RTC's brief, the term "reasonably equivalent" value is a unique term in the Bankruptcy Code. Although the Court recognized that "reasonably equivalent" value is not the same thing as "fair market value," nothing in the statute compelled the Court to infer that any objective post hoc assessment of "value" was irrelevant.

Justice Scalia's opinion also noted that a federal rule invalidating these sales would extend fraudulent transfer law far beyond its traditional boundaries. He made that point in two distinct ways. First, he argued with considerable vigor that a broad federal rule would be so inconsistent with the centuries-long tradition of fraudulent transfer law that the Court could not plausibly infer congressional intent adequate to justify such an intrusive result (BFPR026:9–12). Writing with evident enjoyment, he started the discussion by commenting that "[s]ome sense of history is needed to appreciate this" (BFPR026:7) and went on to demonstrate that "[f]raudulent transfer law and foreclosure law enjoyed over 400 years of peaceful coexistence in Anglo-American jurisprudence until the Fifth Circuit's unprecedented 1980 decision in *Durrett*" (BFPR026:11). Against that backdrop, he could rely on the requirement from *Midlantic* of "clea[r] textual guidance" to justify "such a radical departure" from prior practice (BFPR026:11). Only at that point, in a section rendered largely desultory by the deletions made to accommodate Justice Kennedy, did the opinion turn to an alternative federalist justification for the decision, that federal invalidation of foreclosure sales would entrench on areas traditionally reserved to the states (BFPR026:12–13).

The historical discussion was by far the most persuasive part of the Court's opinion. If the rules against fraudulent transfers are designed to deter fraudulent transactions by overturning them, it is odd to say that a transaction conducted under the auspices of the State is fraudulent. It makes sense to use a nebulous concept like "reasonably equivalent value" to justify a flexible examination of transactions that an insolvent conducts with another private party. But it is hard to accept such a vague formulation as directing an indeterminate scrutiny of transactions that are conducted under mandatory rules of state law. It should be clear, however, that there is little of "plain language" interpretation either in that analysis or in the more extended *Ashcroft* analysis of his first draft. Whatever the justification, the plain structure of the decision is to explain why the Court should not be willing to implement the most natural reading of the words Congress chose in the Code.

11.4.3.2 The Dissent

That point did not escape the attention of Justice Souter, to whom Justice Blackmun assigned the dissent (BFPR011). Justice Souter's scorching draft for a dissent called the Court to account for "derogation" from "the straightforward language used by Congress" (BFPR030:1). He started by characterizing the decision as "hold[ing] that ... a peppercorn paid at a non-collusive and procedurally regular foreclosure sale [is] to be treated as the 'reasonable equivalent' of the value of a California beachfront estate" (BFPR030:1). He directly confronted the central point of Justice Scalia's opinion: the argument that a property subject to foreclosure is simply "worth less," and thus that fair market value cannot be relevant in determining reasonably equivalent value for such a property. Justice Souter retorted aptly that this is "neither a plausible interpretation of the statute," "nor [the] only ... alternative" to "equating 'reasonably equivalent value' at a foreclosure sale with 'fair market value'" (BFPR030:3).

Having rejected Justice Scalia's reading, Justice Souter took a much broader view of a bankruptcy court's power to pursue such core bankruptcy policies as obtaining a maximum and equitable distribution for creditors and ensuring a "fresh start" for individual debtors by avoiding foreclosure sales, "policies ... at the core of federal bankruptcy law" (BFPR030:13). Although Justice Souter's discussion of the language of the statute is compelling, his discussion of bankruptcy policy is less impressive, primarily because it does not match the facts of the case. First, the idea that reversal of the Ninth Circuit would further a fresh start is a considerable stretch, given the likelihood in most cases that any value recovered would go to unsecured creditors and attorney's fees. That is particularly true in *BFP*, where Wayne Pedersen was a fugitive from justice throughout the bankruptcy proceeding and the Supreme Court's process. Similarly, because no creditors appeared to complain about unfavorable treatment, Justice Souter's concern about equitable distribution among creditors seems off point.

Justice Souter explained that in his view the statute's reference to "reasonably equivalent" value plainly indicates that the "fair" market value is relevant to the bankruptcy determination. Recommending something closely akin to the *Bundles* approach adopted by the Seventh Circuit, Justice Souter contended that "the bankruptcy court must compare the price received by the insolvent debtor and the worth of the item when sold and set aside the transfer if the former was substantially 'less than' the latter" (BFPR030:3). He remarked: "Nor would any ordinary English speaker, concerned to determine whether a foreclosure sale was collusive or procedurally irregular ... direct an adjudicator ... to ascertain whether the sale had realized 'less than a reasonably equivalent value'" (BFPR030:4).

The most interesting part of Justice Souter's approach is his response to the plain-statement rule that Justice Scalia rests on *Midlantic*. Justice Souter took the view that the "words and meaning of [the Code] are clear," and offered a citation suggesting that a "party seeking to defeat [the] plain meaning of

Bankruptcy Code text bears an 'exceptionally heavy burden.'"[44] In his view, no reasonable application of a plain meaning rule could overcome the clarity of the text at issue in *BFP*:

> What plain meaning provides and courts can provide, the policies underlying a national bankruptcy law fully support. This case is a far cry from the rare one where the effect of implementing the ordinary meaning of the statutory text would be patent absurdity or demonstrably at odds with the intention of the drafters (BFPR030:13).

Finally, he downplayed the significance of *Midlantic*, suggesting that "[o]nly over vigorous dissent did the Court read the ... generally-worded abandonment power as not authorizing abandonment 'in contravention of a state statute or regulation that is reasonably designed to protect the public health or safety from identified hazards'" (BFPR030:17 n.******). Justice Souter pointedly referenced the dissent of then-Justice Rehnquist in that case, joined by Justice O'Connor, two of the five Justices forming the majority in *BFP*.

Justice Souter had a much easier time getting votes for his opinion than Justice Scalia did. Justices Ginsburg (BFPR031) and Stevens (BFPR032) joined without qualification. Justice Blackmun, oddly enough, asked that Justice Souter delete a reference to a dissenting opinion Justice Blackmun had written in *Perez v. Campbell*.[45] Justice Blackmun explained that his dissent was "based more on respect for precedent than disagreement with the majority's general approach in determining the reach of the Bankruptcy Code" (BFPR035). Justice Souter asked if he could retain the citation to *Perez*, but drop a parenthetical quoting from Justice Blackmun's dissent (BFPR033). When Justice Blackmun agreed (BFPR037), the opinions were complete, with Justice Scalia retaining a majority in support of his strongly atextual opinion. As persuasive as Justice Souter's arguments were on a wholly textual basis, their inability to persuade forms a suitable ending to our discussion of the Court's statutory cases.

11.5 CONCLUSION

BFP completes the pattern of the Court's underenforcement of the Bankruptcy Code. Of the cases studied here, it probably has the strongest language in favor of a broad reading of the Code, balanced against the weakest competing interest. The case involves no contrary federal statutory regime (as in *Bildisco* and *Midlantic*), no core sovereign interest at stake (as in *Kelly*),

[44] BFPR030:3 (quoting Patterson v. Shumate, 504 U.S. 753, 760 (1992)).
[45] 402 U.S. 637 (1991).

and not even the interest of the federal tax regime (as in *Ron Pair*). There is only a general state tradition of establishing the rules for buying and selling land, a tradition that federal law routinely preempts and revises both inside and outside of bankruptcy. Yet even in that context, the result is a profoundly policy-driven, atextual rejection of the idea that broad application of the Bankruptcy Code has any apparent support.

PART III

AMICI AND THE COURT

The secondary thesis of the book is that the absence of a major administrative presence in the Executive Branch has hindered the development of a broad and coherent bankruptcy system. Specifically, the administrative vacuum has left the Supreme Court adrift, underinformed about the importance of a robust bankruptcy system to a modern capitalist economy. Lacking the support of agency-based institutional knowledge and expertise, the Solicitor General has not been an effective proponent of Congress's broad vision of the Bankruptcy Code.

To examine that question directly, this part of the book turns from the case studies to a broader analysis of the role that amici have played in the Court's bankruptcy cases. To organize that presentation, I categorize the various ways in which amici might provide information that influences the Court. As Chapter 1 explains, this is a departure from the existing literature on amici. Scholars commonly consider the contribution of the parties and amici from a strategic perspective – analyzing the likelihood that the contribution of amici will alter the Court's judgment to favor the amici, with the purpose of the brief being to "provide information about the preferences of other actors ... relevant to the ability of the justices to attain their [presumably policy-oriented] goals" (Epstein and Knight 1999, 215). That the amici regard the matter as important is information that might affect the Court's ruling, but its relation to the legal issues that the Court confronts in most cases is indirect at best.

This project employs a much more legalist conception of decisionmaking, within which the central question is how the information the amici provide might be relevant to the legal and policy questions that the Justices confront. Recognizing the fluidity of any particular categorization, my reading of the briefs, argument transcripts, opinions, and other materials about these cases suggests three distinct ways in which amici provide information that contributes to the Court's analysis, which I summarize briefly in the paragraphs that follow.

The first, expert knowledge, is the most readily justified. A conspicuous example is the Court's common references to amicus briefs from the American Psychiatric Association as authoritative guides regarding issues like volitional capacity that relate to criminal responsibility.[1] In the same way, the Court often acknowledges (and defers to) the work of academic historians, occasionally with strikingly laudatory descriptions.[2] Here, it is important to distinguish between the Court's use of historical information it locates through its own research and the information that amici bring to it. The former situation is only indirectly relevant, because it suggests a vacuum in which neither the parties nor the amici have provided information the Court requires for resolution of the dispute. The latter situation, by contrast, is directly relevant, because it involves the transmission of relevant information into the decision-making process from entities (or individuals) that are not parties to the dispute at hand.

Expert knowledge also comes to the Court in the form of data; quantitative information that amici provide to the Court. Given the Court's limited access to relevant data and relatively poor track record at identifying and selecting data without the assistance of others (Larsen 2012; Silver 2013), that type of information can play a major role in the decisionmaking process. One prominent example involves data about the effect on insurance premiums of requiring universal coverage that Justice Ginsburg used in her opinion upholding the Affordable Health Care Act.[3] A similar example (also from Justice Ginsburg) involves data about the frequency of errors in blood-alcohol tests, relevant to the defendant's right to confront the scientist that performed a laboratory test introduced into evidence against the defendant. She credited the conclusion that the "risk of

1 *E.g.*, Clark v. Arizona, 548 U.S. 735, 777 (2006); Kansas v. Crane, 534 U.S. 407, 411 (2002); Riggins v. Nevada, 504 U.S. 127, 137 (1992).

2 *E.g.*, Boumediene v. Bush, 553 U.S. 723, 746 (2008) (describing "amici whose expertise in legal history the Court has relied upon in the past"); INS v. St. Cyr, 533 U.S. 289, 302 n.16 (2001). Indeed, on occasion the Court is almost apologetic about its lack of deference to historical expertise. See New Jersey v. New York, 523 U.S. 767 n.3 (1998) (noting arguments of amici New York Historical Society and New York Landmarks Conservancy, which the State of New York disclaimed, and emphasizing that "nothing in this opinion is meant to disparage the scholarship those briefs embody").

3 National Federation of Independent Business v. Sebelius, 132 S. Ct. 2566, 2614 (2012) (crediting that information to briefs filed by the American Association of People with Disabilities and by the State Governor of Washington).

human error [is not] so remote as to be negligible" to evidence submitted in an amicus brief for the National Association of Criminal Defense Lawyers.[4]

A second category provides a uniquely valuable perspective on a question of import, a filing in which the identify of the amicus itself is a large part of the relevant information. The best example here is the brief of military leaders filed in *Grutter v. Bollinger*,[5] documenting their firm conviction that affirmative action plays an important role in military preparedness. Justice O'Connor's opinion upholding the Michigan Law School's affirmative action program quoted directly that brief's assertions that "based on their decades of experience, a highly qualified, racially diverse officer corps is essential to the military's ability to fulfill its principle mission to provide national security," and that "the military cannot achieve an officer corps that is *both* highly qualified *and* racially diverse unless the service academies and the ROTC used limited race-conscious recruiting and admissions policies."[6] Signed by a broad spectrum of high-ranking officers and civilian military leaders, the brief's effectiveness was bolstered by its impartial – purely output-oriented – perspective on the utility of affirmative action. In the same vein, a group of accomplished female attorneys recently filed a brief in *Whole Women's Health v. Hellerstedt* emphasizing the important role that access to abortion had played in their ability to pursue a legal career; the goal of the brief was to persuade the Court of the practical significance of restrictions on abortion access implemented by the State of Texas. Similarly, few would doubt that the Executive Branch's decision to support one side or the other in important cases can influence the Court's decision-making process. For example, it is commonly asserted (Elman 1986) that the willingness of the Solicitor General to press for the rejection of the "separate but equal" standard was important in the path of the Court to its unanimous decision in *Brown v. Board of Education*.[7]

The final possibility is a residual one, that attorneys writing briefs for amici will influence the Court's decisions solely because of their exercise of legal skills superior to those of the parties' attorneys. As Richard Lazarus has demonstrated (2007), regular litigants before the Court have come to use a relatively small cadre of highly experienced (and presumably capable) advocates. Similarly, the Solicitor General's participation in criminal cases that involve state

4 Bullcoming v. New Mexico, 131 S. Ct. 2705, 2711 n. 1 (2011).
5 539 U.S. 306 (2003)
6 *Grutter*, 539 U.S. at 331.
7 347 U.S. 483 (1954).

authorities rests, at least in part, on the view that the Solicitor General will provide the Court with more persuasive legal arguments than the state criminal authorities. That perspective is heightened when a local criminal authority appears before the Court without the aid of the state attorney general. But the Solicitor General is not the only amicus that can aspire to such influence. For example, Hirshman (2015, 69–114) provides a carefully researched account documenting the effectiveness of the ACLU's Women's Rights Project (led by Ruth Bader Ginsburg) at moving the Court toward greater protection for women under the Equal Protection Clause, overcoming frequently inept representation by counsel for the affected parties. I view this category as residual because legal argumentation is a dominant feature of almost all of the amicus briefs that the Court receives. Although many briefs doubtless aspire to provide information in the earlier categories, in most cases the brief's contribution, if any, is to provide arguments or authorities that contribute to resolution of the legal issues before the Court.

With that framework as a guide for assessing effectiveness, I turn now to the role that amici have played in the Supreme Court's bankruptcy cases, broadening the analysis from the specific case studies to all eighty-two of the Court's decisions about the Code (summarized in Appendix A). My discussion falls into two parts. The first considers the role of the Solicitor General, by far the most important "institutional" or "strategic" amicus for the Court in this context. The case studies in the preceding chapters document the importance of the Solicitor General in several of the Court's most challenging bankruptcy decisions; Chapter 12 summarizes and extends that discussion by providing a general overview of the Solicitor General's influence and effectiveness. Finally, Chapter 13 looks more generally at the universe of all amici, analyzing the role that amici of all kinds have played in the Court's bankruptcy decisions.

12

The Supreme Court, the Solicitor General, and Statutory Interpretation

The case studies in the preceding part of the book frequently touched on the role of the Solicitor General in bankruptcy cases. If the principal thesis of the book is that the Court has underenforced the Bankruptcy Power, the principal explanation is that the Code's failure to create an agency with responsibility for administering the Code has led to a vacuum of expertise that has left the Court lacking the kind of information it needs to apprehend the importance of the Bankruptcy Power to the modern economy. The obvious question, though, is why the Solicitor General has not played that role. After all, with the sole exception of *Granfinanciera*, the Solicitor General did participate in each of the cases that the case studies examine in detail.

As I illustrate below, the Solicitor General's role has been almost diametrically opposed to the system-buttressing role that an agency would produce. In every one of those cases except *Marathon*, where it appeared (unsuccessfully) to defend the constitutionality of the Code, the Solicitor General has opposed a broad interpretation of bankruptcy power. Moreover, the evidence indicates that the hostile posture of the Solicitor General has had a cognizable effect on the decisions that the Court in fact has rendered.[1] The Court does not always defer to the Executive. Still, when the Solicitor General can convince the Court that its position is reasonable and that a contrary outcome would harm important interests, the Court has given the benefit of the doubt to the Solicitor General's narrower interpretation. This is true even when (as in *BFP*) that result does considerable injury to the language of the statute. Indeed, I think that is more likely to be true in bankruptcy cases than in other private law cases, because the Solicitor General's view is less likely to reflect the agency bias apparent in cases in which an agency defends its own programs.

[1] Black and Owens (2014) provide empirical analysis that quantifies the substantial influence of the Solicitor General on the Court's decisions.

Other writers have noticed that the Supreme Court often defers to the government in bankruptcy cases in which the Government is a party (Rasmussen 1993; Lawless 1996, 114–115), but what they have not noticed is the pervasiveness of the Solicitor General's role as a party and as an amicus in bankruptcy cases. For those who regard bankruptcy law as a "private law" topic of little general interest, it may be interesting that the Solicitor General has appeared in about 70% of the Court's bankruptcy cases (57 of 82).[2] Of those cases, the Government was a party in 22 and appeared as an amicus in the other 35. The Government advocated a narrow construction of the Bankruptcy Power in more than 80% of the cases (47 out of 57 cases), and was quite successful in those cases (winning 36 out of 47 (77%)); the Government's views prevailed in all five of the cases in which it appeared as an amicus to advocate a broad construction of the Bankruptcy Power and in three out of five of the cases when it took that view as a party. In the aggregate, that works out to a broad application of the Code in 33% (19/57) of the cases in which the Solicitor General appeared, but a much more substantial 56% (14/25) of those in which the Solicitor General did not appear.

To understand why the Solicitor General has appeared in such a large share of these cases, it is useful to analyze the varied interests that the Federal Government might have in bankruptcy. Recognizing that any categorization is arbitrary and subjective, I have broken the cases down into the six general categories summarized in the sections that follow.

12.1 AGENCY CASES

In agency cases, the Solicitor General typically appears when a bankruptcy stay or discharge threatens the interests of a federal regulatory agency. These are cases like *Ohio v. Kovacs*, which involved the ability of a debtor to discharge an environmental obligation in bankruptcy,[3] or *Patterson v. Shumate*, which involved the ability of a bankrupt debtor to protect an ERISA retirement plan.[4] It is easy to see why the Solicitor General would appear in such cases and easy to understand why the Court would be interested in the views of the Federal Government. The Solicitor General has appeared in ten agency

2 I omit cases like U.S. Bancorp Mortgage Co. v. Bonner Mall Partnership, 513 U.S. 18 (1994), involving questions about mootness. Appendix B provides a list of the cases and the categorization of them that I discuss in this chapter.

3 469 U.S. 274 (1985).

4 504 U.S. 753 (1992).

cases: four times as a party (once each on behalf of the NLRB, CFTC, ICC, and FCC),[5] and six times as an amicus (twice in environmental cases on behalf of the EPA, three times in ERISA cases on behalf of the Department of Labor or the PBGC, and once in a case involving an order of the ICC).[6]

The only cases of this type in which the Solicitor General did *not* appear are two ERISA cases about the exempt status of IRAs.[7] I can speculate that the Department of Labor institutionally might prefer a broad exemption, while the Office of the United States Trustee (for the reasons discussed below) might prefer a narrower exemption; the crosscutting institutional incentives might justify a decision not to participate. Given the concern about agency bias expressed above, it should be no surprise that the Solicitor General has prevailed in only two of the four cases in which it appeared as a party, but five of the six cases in which it appeared as an amicus.[8]

By far the most interesting of the agency cases is *Midlantic*, in which the Solicitor General's position did prevail, even though he did not present oral argument. As discussed above, the Solicitor General apparently benefited because it was arguing for the continuation, and not the narrowing, of pre-Code law. From the more overarching perspective of this closing part of the book, though, it is noteworthy that the Solicitor General did not directly represent a particular government agency and was not a party in the case. The consideration that Justice Powell gave to the Solicitor General's brief (emphasized in detail in Chapter 8) shows the Solicitor General at the peak of effectiveness as an arguably neutral arbiter between competing positions. As Chapter 8 points out, the effective presentation in *Midlantic* provides a pointed contrast to *Bildisco*, where the need to defend the view of the NLRB markedly weakened the Solicitor General's influence.

5 NLRB v. Bildisco & Bildisco, 465 U.S. 513 (1984); CFTC v. Weintraub, 471 U.S. 343 (1985); ICC v. Transcon Lines, 513 U.S. 138 (1995); FCC v. NextWave Personal Communications, Inc., 537 U.S. 293 (2003).

6 Ohio v. Kovacs, 469 U.S. 274 (1985) (EPA); Midlantic Nat'l Bank v. New Jersey Dep't of Environmental Protection, 474 U.S. 494 (1986) (EPA); PBGC v. LTV Corp., 496 U.S. 633 (1990) (ERISA); Patterson v. Shumate, 504 U.S. 753 (1992) (ERISA); Raymond B. Yates, M.D., P.C. Profit Sharing Plan v. Hendon, 541 U.S. 1 (2004) (ERISA); Security Services v. KMart Corp., 511 U.S. 431 (1994) (ICC).

7 Clark v. Rameker, 134 S. Ct. 2242 (2014); Rousey v. Jacoway, 544 U.S. 320 (2005).

8 The Solicitor General's view did not prevail when it appeared as a party in *NextWave* and *Bildisco*, or when it appeared as an amicus in *Kovacs*.

12.2 TAX CASES

Insolvent businesses and individuals often owe money to taxing authorities, and taxing authorities typically have special rights in bankruptcy. Thus, it is not surprising that the Solicitor General frequently appears in tax cases. By my count, the Solicitor General has appeared in nine of the eleven tax cases: eight in which the IRS was a party[9] and one in which the Solicitor General appeared as an amicus in support of a state tax-lien claimant.[10] Interestingly, after losing its first two cases in this category, the views of the Solicitor General have prevailed in all but one of those cases in the last twenty-five years.[11]

Although some of that success might reflect selection bias (the Solicitor General might be doing a good job of selecting cases for litigation in the Supreme Court), I also think, as the discussion of *Ron Pair* in Chapter 10 emphasizes, that the Court has shown special solicitude for the Government's interest in protecting the fisc. This view of the IRS as a different kind of agency goes far to explain the differential rate of success in those cases as opposed to the agency cases discussed above.

12.3 UNITED STATES TRUSTEE CASES

The third category implicates interests of the Office of United States Trustee (the OUST). I include in this category seventeen cases involving the various statutory responsibilities of the OUST. By far the most important of those is the breadth of the bankruptcy discharge and related sanctions for misconduct. On that point, the OUST typically has an interest in urging that the discharge not be available to wrongdoers; Section 727 of the Bankruptcy Code gives it

9 United States v. Whiting Pools, 462 U.S. 198 (1983); United States v. Energy Resources Co., 495 U.S. 545 (1990); Begier v. IRS, 496 U.S. 53 (1990); Holywell Corp. v. Smith, 503 U.S. 47 (1992); United States v. Noland, 517 U.S. 535 (1996); United States v. Reorganized CF&I Fabricators, 518 U.S. 213 (1996); Young v. United States, 535 U.S. 435 (2002); Hall v. United States, 132 S. Ct. 1882 (2012). I do not include United States v. Nordic Village, 503 U.S. 30 (1992), treating that case instead as a sovereign immunity case, or United States v. Ron Pair Enterprises, 489 U.S. 235 (1989), which I treat in the secured credit category below. It is somewhat arbitrary to put *Nordic Village* in the sovereign immunity category, but leave *Whiting Pools* in the tax category. In my view, though, the tax-law context heavily influenced the sovereign immunity issues in *Whiting Pools*, while the Court's treatment of *Nordic Village* took little account of the tax-law context.

10 Raleigh v. Illinois Dep't of Revenue, 530 U.S. 15 (2000). In two other cases involving state taxing authorities, the Solicitor General chose not to appear: Florida Dep't of Revenue v. Picadilly Cafeterias, Inc., 554 U.S. 33 (2007); California State Board v. Sierra Summit, 490 U.S. 844 (1988). Neither involved a point of significance to the IRS.

11 The views of the IRS did not prevail in *Whiting Pools* or in *Energy Resources*, but they did prevail in *Begier*, *Holywell Corp.*, *Noland*, *Raleigh*, *Young*, and *Hall*.

the authority in all cases to object to a discharge or seek revocation of a discharge. Under Section 330, the OUST also participates in the determination of the proper fees for attorneys (and other professionals), a role of considerable importance in Chapter 11 cases. Third, the OUST plays a role in administering the means test used since BAPCPA to assess eligibility for relief under Chapter 7.

The Solicitor General has appeared as a party in one of those cases[12] and as an amicus in thirteen of them.[13] In each of the ten appearances involving the discharge or exemptions, the Solicitor General, furthering the institutional interests of the OUST, argued in favor of a narrow discharge or exemptions.[14] Again, as with the tax cases, this is an area in which the Court appeared, at least for a time, to have given considerable credence to the institutional position of the OUST; the Solicitor General prevailed in the first seven discharge and exemption cases. That pattern may have shifted in recent years, as the Solicitor General has lost all three of the cases in that area in which it has participated during this decade.[15]

In the four remaining cases, the Court ruled against the availability of fees (which I code as narrow) in both of the fee cases[16] and for a narrow application of the means test in both of the means test cases.[17] The Solicitor General urged a broad application in only one of those cases – *Baker Botts*; interestingly, the Solicitor General's position in that case was a shift from the opposite position that the OUST had taken in the lower courts. The Supreme

12 Lamie v. United States Trustee, 540 U.S. 526 (2004).

13 Grogan v. Garner, 498 U.S. 279 (1991); Field v. Mans, 516 U.S. 59 (1995); Cohen v. De la Cruz, 523 U.S. 213 (1998); Archer v. Warner, 538 U.S. 314 (2003); Kontrick v. Ryan, 540 U.S. 443 (2004); Marrama v. Citizens Bank of Massachusetts, 549 U.S. 326 (2007); United Student Aid Funds v. Espinosa, 559 U.S. 260 (2010); Hamilton v. Lanning, 560 U.S. 505 (2010); Schwab v. Reilly, 560 U.S. 770 (2010); Ransom v. FIA Card Services, 562 U.S. 61 (2011); Bullock v. BankChampaign, N.A., 133 S. Ct. 1754 (2013); Law v. Siegel, 134 S. Ct. 1188 (2014); Baker Botts v. ASARCO, LLC, 135 S. Ct. 2158 (2015).

14 Perhaps it is not a coincidence that the Court ruled in favor of the debtor in all three of the cases in that area in which the Solicitor General did not participate: Taylor v. Freeland & Kronz, 503 U.S. 638 (1992), Kawaauhau v. Geiger, 523 U.S. 57 (1998), and Harris v. Viegelahn, 135 S. Ct. 1829 (2015). The Solicitor General well might have refrained from appearing faced with a choice of opposing the interest of the OUST or presenting a losing argument that supported the OUST's interests.

15 United Student Aid Funds, Inc. v. Espinosa, 559 U.S. 260 (2010); Bullock v. BankChampaign, N.A., 133 S. Ct. 1754 (2013); Law v. Siegel, 134 S. Ct. 1188 (2014).

16 Lamie v. United States Trustee, 540 U.S. 526 (2004); Baker Botts v. ASARCO, LLC., 135 S. Ct. 2158 (2015).

17 Schwab v. Reilly, 560 U.S. 770 (2010); Ransom v. FIA Card Services, 562 U.S. 61 (2011).

Court noted the shift in its opinion rejecting the argument of the Solicitor General.[18]

12.4 SOVEREIGNTY CASES

A fourth category involves conflicts between the broad powers of bankruptcy courts and the sovereign powers of state and federal governments. There are six sovereignty cases; four involve sovereign immunity and two involve efforts to discharge criminal penalties. The Solicitor General has appeared in three of them, twice as an amicus[19] and once on its own behalf.[20] Again, it is easy to understand why the Solicitor General would wish to appear in those cases.

As previous commentators have noted, the decisions in those cases are notorious for their atextual approaches (Rasmussen 1993; Bussel 2000; Lawless 1996, 27–33). Interestingly, those cases appear to reflect a shift over time in the Court's concerns for the intrusion of bankruptcy into sovereign interests; in both areas, the sovereign interest prevailed in the early cases, but not in the later ones.[21] The Solicitor General's participation here is not particularly noteworthy; it prevailed in the two sovereign immunity cases in which it appeared (*Hoffman* and *Nordic Village*), but lost in the criminal fine case in which it appeared (*Davenport*). As Chapter 6 suggests, those cases seem to turn in large part on the Justices' predispositions about the role of courts in protecting sovereigns.

12.5 SECURED CREDIT CASES

The largest category (which includes *BFP*) involves conflicts between secured creditors and other claimants on the bankruptcy estate. At first glance, the eighteen cases in that group present a conundrum: Why would the Federal Government have a strong interest in the way bankruptcy courts distribute assets among distinct groups of creditors? To understand the

[18] 135 S. Ct. at 2168.

[19] Hoffman v. Connecticut Dep't of Income Maintenance, 492 U.S. 96 (1989) (sovereign immunity); Pennsylvania Dep't of Public Welfare v. Davenport, 495 U.S. 552 (1989) (criminal fine).

[20] United States v. Nordic Village, 503 U.S. 30 (1992). I could also include here United States v. Whiting Pools, 462 U.S. 198 (1983), but I have included that case as a tax case. The Solicitor General did not appear in *Kelly v. Robinson*, Tennessee Student Assistance Corp. v. Hood, 541 U.S. 440 (2003), or Centennial Virginia Community College v. Katz, 546 U.S. 356 (2005).

[21] In the immunity area, the Government prevailed in *Hoffman* and *Nordic Village*, but not in *Hood* or *Katz*. In the criminal fine area, the Government prevailed in *Kelly*, but not in *Davenport*.

Government's interest, it is necessary to look to the banking and savings and loan crises of the 1980s and 1990s. By the conclusion of those crises, more than 1600 banks and 1000 thrifts were closed, and the federal taxpayers had contributed hundreds of billions of dollars to ensure the adequacy of the FDIC and FSLIC deposit insurance funds (Federal Deposit Insurance Corporation 1999; Curry and Shibut 2000; Barth et al. 2008).

Those crises are complex historical events. For example, the ill-handled deregulation of S&L interest rates was a major contributor to the depth of the S&L crisis, with excessive levels of deposit insurance and an undue reluctance to close large institutions being other significant factors (Federal Deposit Insurance Corporation 1999; Barth et al. 2008; Stern and Feldman 2004). Ultimately, for whatever reason, the Government bore the great majority of the losses related to those crises. Among other things, this meant that by the mid-1980s the Government found itself one of the largest holders of distressed debt in this country.[22]

At that point, the perspective of the Federal Government, as a participant in bankruptcy policy debates, shifted sharply. Until then, the principal interest that the Federal Government had in bankruptcy was in the first class of cases presented above (agency cases). Thus, aside from cases assessing the constitutionality of the Code and transition to it,[23] four of the first five cases that received plenary decisions from the Supreme Court under the Bankruptcy Code (a group that brings us up through October Term 1985) were agency cases, and the last one was a case to which the IRS was a party.[24] When secured credit cases first began to appear on the Court's argument calendar in the mid-1980s, the Solicitor General did not appear regularly. Of the first six of those cases that reached the Supreme Court, the Government was a

[22] I cannot adduce data to support this statement, but rely on the collective portfolios of the FDIC, FSLIC, RTC, FmHA, and the SBA at the time. The first three entities held distressed debt that they acquired when they closed failed private institutions. The last two entities, by contrast, had (and have) an institutional mission that obligates them to make risky loans. A quip common to the Executive Branch during that era suggested that the SBA and the FmHA "were obligated to make bad loans and very good at it."

[23] Central Trust Co. v. Official Creditors' Committee of Geiger Enters., 454 U.S. 354 (1982); Northern Pipeline Constr. Co. v. Marathon Pipe Line Co., 458 U.S. 50 (1982); United States v. Security Industrial Bank, 459 U.S. 70 (1982).

[24] United States v. Whiting Pools, 462 U.S. 198 (1983) (IRS); NLRB v. Bildisco & Bildisco, 465 U.S. 513 (1984); Ohio v. Kovacs, 469 U.S. 274 (1985) (amicus on behalf of EPA); CFTC v. Weintraub, 471 U.S. 343 (1985); Midlantic Nat'l Bank v. New Jersey Dep't of Environmental Protection, 474 U.S. 494 (1986) (amicus on behalf of EPA).

party in two (one as a secured creditor,[25] one as an unsecured creditor).[26] The Solicitor General filed amicus briefs in support of secured creditors in two (but did not present oral argument)[27] and did not appear at all in two cases.[28]

By the early 1990s, however, the Solicitor General began to participate regularly in cases presenting conflicts between the interests of secured creditors and other claimants on the estate. Thus, starting in 1991, for a five-year period running through 1997, the Solicitor General appeared in all of these cases except one (five out of six),[29] presenting argument on behalf of the secured creditors in each of the five, once as a party (*BFP*), but four times as an amicus.[30] Of import here, the Solicitor General's stated justification for appearing in those cases as an amicus was its oft-repeated explanation that the financial crises of the 1980s had left the Federal Government (through the FDIC, FSLIC, and RTC) as one of the largest secured creditors in bankruptcy proceedings.[31]

The Solicitor General's practices have changed in recent years, as those crises have faded from memory and other relevant interests (such as the role of the PBGC as a large unsecured creditor) have come to the fore. As the importance of the Government's role as a secured creditor has diminished, the Solicitor General has participated less regularly on behalf of secured creditors. Thus, it has argued on behalf of secured creditors only twice in the six cases

25 United States v. Ron Pair Enters., 489 U.S. 235 (1989).

26 United States v. Security Industrial Bank, 459 U.S. 70 (1982). That case does not, strictly speaking, interpret the Bankruptcy Code, because it involves the constitutionality of Section 522(f). Nevertheless, it does present a square conflict between the interests of secured and unsecured creditors. Accordingly, I include it in that category.

27 United Savings Ass'n v. Timbers of Inwood Forest Associates, Ltd., 484 U.S. 365 (1988); Norwest Bank Worthington v. Ahlers, 485 U.S. 197 (1998).

28 Johnson v. Home State Bank, 501 U.S. 78 (1991); Union Bank v. Wolas, 502 U.S. 151 (1991).

29 The Solicitor General did not appear in Nobelman v. American Savings Bank, 508 U.S. 324 (1993).

30 The Solicitor General argued as an amicus in Dewsnup v. Timm, 502 U.S. 410 (1992); Rake v. Wade, 508 U.S. 464 (1993); Citizens Bank v. Strumpf, 516 U.S. 16 (1995); and Associates Commercial Corp. v. Rash, 520 U.S. 953 (1997). I omit from this list U.S. Bancorp Mortgage Co. v. Bonner Mall Partnership, 513 U.S. 18 (1994). Although the lower-court decision involved the new-value rule (an issue ultimately resolved in Bank of America Nat'l Trust & Savings Ass'n v. 203 N. LaSalle Street Partnership, 526 U.S. 34 (1999)), the Supreme Court's argument and decision involved the propriety of vacating an appellate court decision when the parties settle after the decision. The Solicitor General appeared, arguing that it was appropriate to vacate the decision (an outcome that would have furthered the interests of the secured creditors in that case).

31 See, for example, the motions seeking divided argument in *Dewsnup*, *Rake*, and *BFP*.

TABLE 12.1 *SG Participation and Outcomes in Secured Creditor Cases.*

	1982–1991	1992–1997	1998–2015
Secured Creditor Victories	5/6	5/6	4/6
SC Victories (SG Argued)	1/1	4/5	2/2
SG Participation (for SC)	3/6	5/6	2/6

decided after 1997.[32] Indeed, the increasing difficulties of the PBGC presage a period in the not-too-distant future in which the Solicitor General might become a leading advocate for unsecured creditors. The effectiveness of the SG's participation in those cases is noteworthy; secured creditors have won seven of the eight cases in which the Solicitor General has argued on their side.

My discussion is of course speculative and not readily susceptible of proof. And it certainly is true that secured creditors win most of the time in the Supreme Court even when the Solicitor General does not argue on their side (five out of eight cases).[33] Certainly many factors influence Supreme Court decisions other than the views of the Solicitor General. There plainly is a selection bias – the Solicitor General has considerable control over the cases that come before the Court when the United States is a party, and in other cases the Solicitor General need not participate if the arguments on the "Government" side are unappealing. In addition, the question of "deference" is tied up with the merits of the cases that come before the Court. Those who think the analysis in *BFP* and *Dewsnup* is transparently correct[34] will see no reason to credit the Solicitor General's appearance in those cases as promoting positions to which the Court might have wished to defer. I do think, however, that

32 Bank of America v. Caulkett, 135 S. Ct. 1995 (2015) (no participation); RadLAX Gateway Hotel, LLC v. Amalgamated Bank, 132 S. Ct. 2065 (2012) (arguing for secured creditors); Till v. SCS Credit Corp., 541 U.S. 465 (2004) (arguing for unsecured creditors); Hartford Underwriters Ins. Co. v. Union Planters Bank, N.A. 531 U.S. 1 (2000) (no participation); Bank of America Nat'l Trust & Savings Ass'n v. 203 N. LaSalle Street Partnership, 526 U.S. 434 (1999) (arguing for secured creditors); Fidelity Financial Services v. Fink, 522 U.S. 211 (1998) (no participation). *Till* is particularly interesting because the Government's brief in that case relied explicitly on the interest of the IRS in limiting the rights of secured creditors, almost directly opposed to the interest that it pressed on behalf of the IRS in *Ron Pair*.

33 By my reckoning, the only losses for secured creditors occurred in *Timbers* (the Solicitor General filed a brief but did not argue), *Fink* (the Solicitor General did not participate), and *Till* (the Solicitor General argued for the unsecured creditor).

34 Most observers take the opposing view. Lawless (1996, 20–27), for example, characterizes Dewsnup as "nontextualist" and "result-oriented."

the discussion above offers good reason to think that in close cases – and *BFP* certainly was a close case – the views of the Solicitor General were important to the Court's final decision. Most importantly, in both of those cases the position articulated by the Solicitor General was one that would play to the Court's general skepticism about bankruptcy powers – an argument that the Bankruptcy Code should be interpreted to permit as little interference as possible with the ordinary course of a secured creditor's enforcement of its security interest.

12.6 BANKRUPTCY INTERESTS

I close with a final category, nine cases in which the Solicitor General appears despite the absence of any of the concrete institutional interests summarized above. In those cases, participation appears to be justified solely by the interests of the Solicitor General in the bankruptcy system as a federal statutory enactment, apart from any particular effect a decision would have on any specific component of the Executive Branch. I include here five cases in which the Supreme Court considered the constitutionality of provisions of the Bankruptcy Code. Four of those cases involved the Code's jurisdictional provisions (*Marathon*, *Stern*, *Arkison*, and *Wellness*, all discussed in Chapter 5);[35] the other considered whether attorneys are "debt relief agencies" for purposes of BAPCPA.[36] In *Toibb v. Radloff*, the Court itself asked for the Solicitor General's participation when the party declined to participate.[37] In yet another, the Government happened to be a party (as a creditor) in a case raising the general problem of whether enactment of the Code justified dismissal of cases pending at that time under the old Act.[38] In the other two cases, the Solicitor General appeared to present opinions on the general questions of whether a "probate exception" prevents bankruptcy courts from resolving issues related to the disposition of estates[39] and whether an order denying confirmation of a plan is appealable.[40]

The Solicitor General's position in those cases generally has called for broad application of the Code, in part because of the institutional interest

35 The Solicitor General did not participate in *Granfinanciera*.

36 Milavetz, Gallop & Milavetz v. United States, 559 U.S. 229 (2010).

37 501 U.S. 157 (1991) (holding that individuals are eligible for relief under Chapter 11). The Court asked the Solicitor General to respond to the debtor's petition when the Chapter 7 trustee declined to participate in the Court. When the Solicitor General indicated that the case warranted review, but that it agreed with the debtor's position, the Court appointed a member of the Bar to defend the judgment of the court of appeals.

38 Central Trust Co. v. Official Creditors' Committee, 454 U.S. 354 (1982).

39 Marshall v. Marshall, 547 U.S. 293 (2006).

40 Bullard v. Blue Hills Bank, 135 S. Ct. 1686 (2015).

in defending the constitutionality of the United States Code.[41] The Solicitor General urged the constitutionality of the Code as applied in four of those five cases (all but *Stern*). In the other cases, I find it harder to identify an institutional basis for the Solicitor General's position. It well might be explained as purely a doctrinal prediction based on the desire of the Solicitor General to provide accurate advice. The Solicitor General's influence is heightened if its advice tends to conform with the Court's assessment of the legal problems that it confronts. When no institutional interest interferes, the Solicitor General accordingly has a strong incentive to provide advice as accurately as possible. In this group of cases, the Solicitor General recommended a broad application of the Code in only two of the four cases,[42] but prevailed in all of them.

12.7 SUMMARY

The discussion above is intentionally loose and hypothetical. I do not offer a theory to explain all of the Solicitor General's bankruptcy cases. Nor would I suggest that the Solicitor General is the central element of Supreme Court decisionmaking in bankruptcy cases. For example, some of the cases discussed above (like *BFP*, *Ahlers*, *LaSalle*, and *RadLAX*) might be viewed more generally as illustrating the doubt that Justices have about the capacity of bankruptcy courts to value property. But in the context of the case studies of the preceding chapters, the hesitancy of the Court to allow the Bankruptcy Code to interfere with the accepted baselines of other regimes provides a valuable perspective. I read *Ahlers*, *LaSalle*, and *RadLAX* as examples of the Court's reluctance to allow the bankruptcy court to overturn the basic corporate norm that creditors must be paid before shareholders.

Other cases seem at first glance to display a rigidly textualist interpretive stance, *Ron Pair* being the most commonly noted example here. But that argument cannot take us too far in a domain in which all of the cases must, of necessity, start from statutory language. If the Court's bankruptcy jurisprudence was unusually or inordinately textualist, we would find cases where the Court applied statutory language literally to give

41 28 U.S.C. § 2403 requires notice and an opportunity for the Attorney General to intervene in any case involving the constitutionality of an Act of Congress. The Attorney General is obligated to provide Congress formal notice of any case in which it determines an Act of Congress to be unconstitutional. 28 U.S.C. § 530D.

42 *Toibb v. Radloff* and *Marshall v. Marshall.*

TABLE 12.2 *Pro-Bankruptcy Outcomes, by Federal Interest in Case.*

Type of Case	Pro-Bankruptcy Outcome	%
Agency	5/12	42%
Tax	3/11	27%
Trustee	6/17	35%
Sovereignty	3/6	50%
Secured Credit	5/18	28%
Quasi-Institutional	5/9	56%
"Federal" Cases	27/73	37%
Non-"Federal" Cases	5/9	56%
SG Participation	19/57	33%
No SG Participation	14/25	56%
All Cases	33/82	39%

the Code a broad reading, in the face of persuasive policy norms and commonsense justifications for a contrary result. Yet there are few such cases in the bankruptcy canon – and *Ron Pair* certainly is not one of them.

To summarize, I view the Bankruptcy Code as a relatively unusual type of legislation – a broad and intentionally transformative piece of legislation without any dominant agency support in the Executive Branch (Dembart and Markell 2004). The lack of a strong agency to enforce and interpret the Code has had two related effects on the jurisprudence under the Code. First, and most obvious from Table 12.2, is the likely effect of government participation. In the cases that involve strong Executive Branch interests ("federal" cases for purposes of the Table), those interests have most often weighed *against* the Bankruptcy Power. As I mentioned at the beginning of the chapter, the Court has interpreted the Bankruptcy Power expansively in about a third of those cases, as compared to broad rulings in more than half of the cases in which the Solicitor General did not appear. The numbers are small, but the disparity is stark.

The second effect is more pervasive. Routinely counseled by the Executive Branch to discount the importance of an effective bankruptcy system, the Court has developed a much less forceful sense of the Code's importance than it has for parallel legislation in fields like environmental law, labor law, and pension regulation. Most commonly, the lack of an agency focused on the Code has meant that the federal interest in bankruptcy cases has come from some other legal regime colliding with the bankruptcy system. It is thus only to be expected that this would lead to a relatively unobtrusive interpretation of the Code rather than the kind of broad and comprehensive interpretation that administering agencies typically foster.

13

Learning from Amici

The previous chapter suggests that it is not merely an institutional vacuum that plagues the bankruptcy system. Rather, the Solicitor General is an affirmatively adversarial institution, more likely to identify with the creditors seeking to narrow the relief that the system can provide than with the debtors for the relief of whom the system is designed. As a result, the Solicitor General is not providing the system-justifying information that the Court typically receives from administrative agencies. The natural question is whether other amici fill that gap, a question to which this chapter turns.

In an effort to shed some light on that question, I have examined the opinions, briefs, and transcripts in all of the Supreme Court's bankruptcy cases. The goal is to understand how often, from whom, and for what purpose the Court uses information from the briefs that amici file and the arguments that they present. Recognizing the roughness of the proxy, I decided to use the Court's citations as a gauge of where it gets the inputs that it uses to decide the cases before it. I have examined each of the citations that appear in the Court's opinions in the bankruptcy cases (about 3500 in all) and then allocated those citations into three groups. The first are sources that appear in the briefs of the parties to the case. For my purposes, those sources are of relatively little interest. When the Court refers to sources that the parties cite, it is as likely as not (or at least difficult to rebut) that the sources define a baseline of relatively obvious information available without any special contribution or expertise. The second are sources that do not appear in the briefs of the parties, but do appear in the briefs of amici; it is reasonable to think, for the most part, that the Court found those sources in the briefs of the amici. Those citations are evidence, albeit imperfect, that the amici have provided information that the Court has used, in the form of references to sources that are instructive to at least some of the Justices in resolving the questions before the Court. The third and final group are sources that appear neither in the briefs of the parties nor in the briefs of amici, but rather are added by the Justices themselves. Examination of those sources provides some idea of what the Court is missing – what the parties and amici have not done that might have been useful to the Justices.[1]

13.1 THE CONTRIBUTIONS OF AMICI

13.1.1 *The Raw Numbers*

Before addressing the contributions qualitatively, it is useful first to quantify the role that amici play in bankruptcy cases. Amici filed 287 briefs in the eighty bankruptcy cases in which the Court received briefs and arguments,[2] for an average number of 3.6 briefs per case. There of course was considerable variation in the number of briefs filed per case. Sixteen amici filed briefs in *Arkison* (discussed in Chapter 5). There were twelve cases in which no amicus briefs were filed (with the Solicitor General appearing as a party in seven of those cases), and in three cases the Solicitor General filed the only amicus brief.

The Supreme Court opinions refer explicitly to briefs filed by amici in thirty-one of the sixty-seven cases in which amici filed. Twenty-three of those cases included references to briefs filed by the Solicitor General; thirteen cases included references to amici other than the Solicitor General. Five of those cases included a reference to an oral argument by the Solicitor General as well as the brief; the rarity of oral arguments by other amici explains the absence of references of that sort.[3]

Table C summarizes the sources of all of the citations in the Court's bankruptcy opinions.[4] As the bottom row of that Table shows, about 62% of all citations in the opinions refer to sources that appeared in the briefs of the

1 The research design resembles Larsen (2012), though my data collection is more extensive, as my primary interest extends to all contributions of amici, while her study analyzes only the Court's "legislative factfinding."

2 The Court resolved two of the eighty-two cases (*Langenkamp* and *Central Trust*) summarily, without briefing and argument on the merits.

3 The only oral argument in my data by an amicus other than the Solicitor General was the argument that the State of New Mexico presented in Raleigh v. Illinois Department of Revenue, 530 U.S. 1 (2000).

4 I recognize that the division into categories of sources is arbitrary and that the nature of the sources themselves shifts over time, but nevertheless I think that even the rough categories I use here provide considerable information. See Wilkerson (2006) (discussing the rise of Internet citations in the Court's opinions).

parties, 9% to sources that appeared in the briefs of amici but not in the briefs of the parties, and 29% to sources that did not appear in the briefs. Again, there was considerable variation. For example, the share of citations coming from the parties (arguably a metric of the quality of the party's briefing) ranged from 11% (9 of the 83 sources in *Field v. Mans*) to five cases with over 90% of the sources coming from the briefs of the parties.

More to the point, it is interesting to identify cases in which amici made particularly noteworthy contributions to the body of sources before the Court. To pick a few of the most noteworthy, 49% (18 of 37) of the sources cited in *Norwest Bank Worthington v. Ahlers* appeared in the briefs of the amici but not in the briefs of the parties; Justice White's opinion referred to sources from six different amici that did not appear in the briefs of the parties. The most notable contributions come from the Solicitor General's brief in *Grogan v. Garner*; 46% (25 of 54) of the sources cited in the opinion of Justice Stevens appeared in the brief of the Solicitor General but not in the briefs of the parties.

Trying to generalize from such a broad range of data necessarily is imprecise, but several points warrant attention. The first is the most conspicuous, that almost 30% of the sources to which the Court referred in these cases did not appear in any of the briefs that the Justices received. I discuss the Court's internal generation of information in more detail in the closing section of this chapter. Suffice it to say that it does not suggest a bench going through the motions, issuing opinions that simply summarize and apply the arguments of the parties before them. Another notable finding is the relative balance between citations from the briefs of the Solicitor General and citations from the briefs of other amici. I had expected that the citations from the Solicitor General's briefs would dwarf those from the briefs of other amici. But that is not what the data indicate. As Table D illustrates, the Court cites sources that first appear in the briefs of external amici 40% more often than it does sources from the briefs of the Solicitor General (188 as compared to 134).[5]

The amici that contribute citations to the Court's opinions display remarkable variety – far beyond the small group of "top-shelf" amici (the Chamber of Commerce, AFL-CIO, Washington Legal Foundation, and the like)

5 One question that arises in making those calculations is how to treat sources from the Court's opinions that do not appear in the briefs of the parties, but appear in the briefs of multiple amici. I treated those sources as coming equally from each of the amicus briefs in which the sources appeared (resulting in cases in which the Solicitor General is credited for 2.33 or 0.75 of the sources in the Court's opinions).

well known to regular observers of the Court. The list includes not only bankruptcy-specific trade groups (the National Association of Bankruptcy Trustees (NABT), National Association of Chapter 13 Trustees (NAC13T), and National Association of Consumer Bankruptcy Attorneys (NACBA)), but also the Consumer Education and Protection Association, industry-specific groups (American Institute of Architects, American Automobile Manufacturers Association, and the National Coordinating Committee for Multi-Employer Plans), briefs filed by a group of States and a group of professors, and a variety of specific entities interested in a particular case (American Home Assurance, Inslaw, Overland Express, and the United Mine Workers).

A glance at the briefs that contribute sources cited by the Court underscores that pattern. The Court draws sources from briefs filed by dozens of different groups. By far the most common category is briefs filed by groups of professors (providing sources in eleven cases) or individual professors (providing sources in six cases). The bankruptcy trade groups also are prominent here, with sources coming from the NACBA in seven cases,[6] NABT in five, and NAC13T in one. Briefs displaying the institutional interests of States also are prominent, with briefs from groups of States providing sources in eight cases and from the National Governors Association and related trade groups in six cases; within the framework introduced above, the common use of those briefs suggests that the concerns of the States are themselves relevant to the Justices here as they so obviously are in other contexts. Also, interestingly, one of the most common contributors is the prominent bankruptcy attorney Eric Brunstad, whose briefs have provided sources in five different cases.[7]

The breadth and variety of those sources is more than an interesting observation. It tends to support the concern that the lack of an institutional presence has left a void in the sources of information that normally would be available to the Court. To explore that question with more care I first show that a qualitative assessment of the role of amici can buttress and enrich the implications of the data summarized above. With that point

6 The contribution of the NACBA briefs is not surprising. Aside from the Solicitor General, the NACBA is the most common single amicus to appear in these cases, filing in seventeen of the cases.

7 Brunstad's participation is remarkable. He has filed briefs in ten of the twenty-nine cases argued since 2004 and presented oral argument in eight of the thirty-four cases argued since 2000. No other advocate has argued more than five of the eighty bankruptcy cases in the dataset, and no other attorney outside the Solicitor General's office has argued more than three.

established, I close by looking directly at the types of information that the Court finds neither in the contributions of the parties nor in those of the amici.

13.1.2 *Uses of Information from Amici*

Given the imprecision of the citation data discussed in the previous section as a proxy for the actual process by which the Court acquires information, a threshold question is how certain we can be that the Court in fact is using information that comes from amici. The short answer, albeit anecdotal, is that, for such a small dataset, there are a remarkable number of instances in which the Court's direct use of information from the briefs is so explicit as to be apparent.

The *Midlantic* opinions provide an excellent example. As explained in Chapter 8, the opinion of Justice Powell (drafted first as a dissent) borrows extensively from the brief of the Solicitor General, at the level of concept and at the level of detail. Conceptually, the idea that the Court should presume that Congress intended for the Code to leave jurisprudence under the Act undisturbed – probably the single most important point of doctrine for this entire project – closely parallels the argument of the Solicitor General. At the level of detail, I discuss above several passages that either in their language or in their selection of sources appear to be taken directly from the Solicitor General.

The final point is a rhetorical one not mentioned above, largely because it is obscured in the final opinions. The Solicitor General's brief (at 20) criticizes the decision of the court of appeals as adopting a rule that would permit a trustee to abandon a "case of dynamite sit[ting] on a furnace in the basement of a schoolhouse." The point informed the reactions of the Justices so much that the early drafts of Justice Rehnquist's opinion (drafted as an opinion for the Court) referred directly to that hypothetical and disclaimed any intention to affirm a rule so broad as to permit such an outrage (MIDL013:13). The early drafts of Justice Powell's opinion (still in the form of a dissent) responded fervidly to Rehnquist's portrayal of the Court's holding as prudently narrow:

> Under the Court's holding, although a trustee may not "abandon dynamite on a stove in the basement of a school," [quoting Rehnquist's draft opinion] he may abandon 470,000 gallons of highly toxic and carcinog[en]ic waste in unguarded, deteriorating containers where they present risks of explosion, fire, contamination of water supplies, destruction of natural resources, and injury, genetic damage, or death through personal contact. (MIDL015:1)

If the prose seems excessive, it is taken almost word for word from the brief of the Solicitor General.[8] The passage was largely removed when Justice Powell converted his opinion from a dissent to an opinion for the Court, but that does not undermine the role that the hypothetical played in the process leading up to the Court's decision.

The Court's opinion in *Dewsnup v. Timm*[9] affords another overt example of the use of material from an amicus (again, the Solicitor General). The *Dewsnup* Court considered whether a debtor in a Chapter 7 bankruptcy, owning property subject to a lien for a debt that far exceeded the value of the property, could "strip down" the lien to the value of the property as of the time of the proceeding. The question had plagued the lower courts, with dozens of decisions on either side of the question. When the case came to the Supreme Court, the Solicitor General's brief suggested a novel reading of the relevant statute (Section 506), contending that the most natural reading was one that had not been suggested in the briefing or in the dozens of preceding opinions.

Recognizing the attractiveness of the reading, counsel for the lender embraced the interpretation at the oral argument. The opinion of the Court, in turn, adopted that same reading, crediting it directly to the brief of the Solicitor General.[10] Lest this be written off as a simple case of an attorney in the Solicitor General's office solving a problem for the Court that the parties could not themselves resolve, it bears noting that the Supreme Court's reaffirmance of *Dewsnup* this last Term came in an opinion strongly suggesting that a majority of the Court now is convinced that *Dewsnup* was wrongly decided in the first instance.[11] That suggests a characterization of the situation as much more in line with the thesis of this book, a case in which the Government's

8 "Hazardous wastes, by their very nature, present risks of explosion, fire, contamination of water supplies, destruction of natural resources, and injury, genetic damage, or death through personal contact" (Brief for the Solicitor General 23).

9 502 U.S. 410 (1992).

10 502 U.S. at 415–418; Transcript at 14-15 (argument of Richard Taranto).

11 The Court's opinion in Bank of America v. Caulkett, 135 S. Ct. 1995 (2015), starts by describing a "straightforward reading of the statute" (contrary to *Dewsnup*) under which the debtor would prevail, but rejects that result, commenting that "[u]nfortunately for the debtors, this Court has already adopted a construction of [Section 506] that forecloses this textual analysis" (131 S. Ct. at 1999). Six of the Justices joined a footnote that added: "From its inception, [*Dewsnup*] has been the target of criticism," with supporting references to several sources, buttressed by a quotation of an opinion from Justice Thomas decrying the "methodological confusion created by *Dewsnup*" (131 S. Ct. at 2000 n.†). The only Justices remaining from the *Dewsnup* Court at the time of *Caulkett* were Justice Thomas (who did not participate in *Dewsnup*), Justice Scalia (who dissented in *Dewsnup*), and Justice Kennedy (who did not join the critical footnote). Although he was not on the Court, Chief Justice Roberts participated in *Dewsnup* as the Deputy Solicitor General responsible for that case.

narrow perspective on the bankruptcy system contributed to a decision that the Court has come to regret, which easily could have gone the other way.[12]

Hoffman provides another example of the Court's use of information taken directly from an amicus. As discussed in detail in Chapter 6, the *Hoffman* Court considered whether a poorly written portion of Section 106 of the Bankruptcy Code abrogated sovereign immunity. In an effort to counter that reading, counsel arguing on behalf of the Solicitor General argued that the words in Section 106 alleged to have abrogated immunity were spread so widely through the Bankruptcy Code as to undermine any suggestion that Congress could have intended them to serve as triggers for the waiver of immunity: "We did a computer check preparing for this argument and discovered that over 100 provisions of the Code use the word 'creditor.' So, subsection (1) is very sweeping" (Transcript at 26).

Although that point was not in the Solicitor General's brief, it resonated with the Court sufficiently to become a topic of debate. The first draft of Justice White's opinion stated: "Under petitioner's interpretation of §106(c), however, the only limit is the number of provisions of the Bankruptcy Code containing one of the trigger words. With this 'limit,' §106(c) would apply to over 100 Code provisions" (HOFF037:4). The point did not go unnoticed. Quoting Justice White's draft, Justice Marshall's draft dissent responded: "[T]he Court's conclusion … rests on the mistaken assumption that … 'the *only* limit is the number of provisions in the Bankruptcy Code containing one of the trigger words' [and] raises the specter that '§106(c) would apply to over 100 Code provisions,' offering virtually endless opportunities for money judgments against the States" (HOFF066:3). Responding in his turn, the next draft of Justice White's draft only sharpened the point: "With this 'limit,' §106(c) would apply *in a scattershot fashion* to over 100 Code provisions" (HOFF069:4 (my emphasis added to indicate the inserted phrase)).[13]

The natural question is whether the Court's use of the information it gleans from the Solicitor General's briefs improves the quality of its decisionmaking. The subjectivity of the inquiry may make generalizations uncertain, but a few things are evident. The first is that these cases, like the Court's opinions in general, display a welcome use (with or without acknowledgment) of recognizable expertise. *Katz* (discussed in detail in Chapter 6) offers a ready example. As discussed in Chapter 6, the Court in *Katz* reversed the course it had staked out in *Hoffman* and *Nordic Village*, deferring at last to

[12] The ambivalence of my perspective on *Dewsnup* doubtless reflects my role as the principal drafter of the brief for the Solicitor General in that case.

[13] The passage appears in that form in Justice White's final opinion (492 U.S. at 101).

Congress's ever more explicit directions that the Bankruptcy Code should be applied to abrogate State sovereign immunity. The opinion Justice Stevens authored for the Court included an extended analysis (three separate parts, extending for more than fifteen pages) of the history of the Bankruptcy Clause and Congress's early understanding of it (546 U.S. at 363–379). The dissent of Justice Thomas included a detailed assessment of the same subject (albeit reaching a different conclusion (546 U.S. at 1008–1013)). What is relevant is that between those two passages I count fourteen sources that appeared in the briefs of amici but not the briefs of the parties. Five of the sources came from two briefs of amici with no particular historical expertise (the National Association of Bankruptcy Trustees and a group of State organizations led by the National Governors Association), but nine came from the briefs of Harvard history scholar Bruce Mann and a group of law professors.[14]

It seems equally benign that the Court commonly relies on (or seeks out) the expertise of the agencies on whose behalf the Solicitor General appears. This practice is apparent both at the level of the overall data and also at the anecdotal level. On the global scale, looking to legislative materials (about 12% of all amicus sources), the Solicitor General provided about 64% of sources of that type gleaned from amici. Conversely, the Court relied much more heavily on other amici for more accessible information, such as the two most common categories of amicus sources, Supreme Court decisions (25% of all amici sources, provided 70% by other amici) and bankruptcy statutes (13% of all amici sources, provided 65% by other amici).

Yates v. Hendon is illustrative here. The *Yates* Court considered whether the sole owner of a professional corporation qualified as a participant covered by ERISA, which would shelter certain payments from creditors in a bankruptcy of the owner.[15] The Court cited the Solicitor General's brief ten times, relying on it overtly not only for an understanding of the history of the relevant statutory frameworks, but also for an understanding of such less objective matters as whether a proposed interpretation would (541 U.S. at 11 n.2, 16) afford an "acceptable solution" or "further ERISA's purpose" and "Congress' aim" in enacting the statute.[16] After considerable analysis,

[14] It is interesting to observe that the Court's citation of the major work of Bruce Mann (no relation to the author) on the history of bankruptcy in the colonial era (Mann (2003)) apparently comes from the brief of the professors; Professor Mann's brief did not refer to his own work.

[15] Raymond B. Yates, M.D., P.C. Profit Sharing Plan v. Hendon, 541 U.S. 1 (2004).

[16] Justice Ginsburg's opinion for the Court also relied heavily on sources identified in the brief of the Solicitor General but not the parties: nine of the forty-three sources in her opinion, including among other things three provisions of ERISA, a House Conference Report, and a regulatory proposal not found in the briefs of the parties.

the Court ultimately accepted the position urged by the Solicitor General. Justice Scalia would have gone even further. Noting that "the Solicitor General, in a brief signed by the Acting Solicitor of Labor, has put forward ... the considered view of the agency charged by Congress with the administration and enforcement of [ERISA]," and that "this position is the official view of the Department of Labor, ... not contrived for this litigation," he would have ruled for the Government "on that basis" (541 U.S. at 24–25).

Examples of less pervasive reliance abound. For example, the Court in *Schwab v. Reilly*[17] considered the rather technical question of when creditors should be prejudiced by their failure to object to a debtor's claim that a particular asset is exempt. The question turned for the most part on the structure and purpose of the form on which debtors claim those exemptions. The Solicitor General insisted that the disclosure on the form had a limited purpose, which did not justify a requirement that creditors object. The Court ultimately accepted that argument, noting that "[w]e simply confine the estimate to its proper role: aiding the trustee in administering the asset by helping him identify [valuable] assets" (560 U.S. at 785). Along the way, the Court relied on the Solicitor General's explanation of the form's history (560 U.S. at 787–788) and of common practice with respect to exemptions in small-dollar cases (560 U.S. at 770 n.20).

One particularly intriguing use that the Court makes of amici is the practice of sheltering – in which the Court justifies a step that it has taken by reference to the position of an amicus. This might sound odd in the abstract, but it is surprisingly common. The most prominent example comes in the Court's opinion in *Stern v. Marshall.* In the course of a response to the principal arguments in support of jurisdiction, the Court acknowledged the argument that a ruling restricting the bankruptcy court's jurisdiction would "create significant delays and impose additional costs on the bankruptcy process" (131 S. Ct. at 2619). The Court's rebuttal emphasized, among other things, that the United States viewed the question as a "narrow" one, suggesting that it gave substantial weight to the Solicitor General's assessment of the practical impact. It is surprising for the Court to give open credence to the Solicitor General's view on a question so far removed from its responsibilities or those of any agency on whose behalf it was appearing.

A similar example appears in the Court's opinion in *Till v. SCS Credit Corp.*[18] The issue in *Till* was the interest rate that a bankruptcy court should use to calculate the required payments on a plan. To clarify, the

[17] 560 U.S. 770 (2010).
[18] 541 U.S. 465 (2004).

Bankruptcy Code frequently requires that payments made over time under a plan have a present value at least as great as some specified threshold (often the value of the creditor's collateral). Especially in long-term plans, the selection of the interest rate used to calculate the present value of a stream of future payments can be crucial to the economics of the plan. In *Till*, the Court approved the use of a baseline drawn from the prime rate, adjusted upward to account for the risk of nonpayment. Apparently somewhat defensive about its position, the Court stated at one point: "It is perhaps also relevant that our conclusion is endorsed by the Executive Branch of the Government and the National Association of Chapter Thirteen Trustees" (541 U.S. at 480 n.19 (citing the amicus briefs of the Solicitor General and the trustee group)). Again, as with the previous example, neither the Solicitor General nor the Office of the United States Trustee is in a position to provide insightful expertise about the economics of present value.

Hartford Underwriters Insurance v. Union Planters Bank[19] provides yet another example. In that case, the Court rejected the argument that administrative claimants have an independent right to seek recovery of unpaid priority claims from secured creditors. In a footnote deprecating the practical harm to administrative claimants, the Court noted that the amicus brief of a pair of insurance companies had "draw[n] our attention to the practice of some courts of allowing creditors or creditors' committees a derivative right" to bring such suits when the trustee refuses to bring them (530 U.S. at 13 n.5). The Court did not approve those decisions, but their availability would significantly mitigate any harm administrative claimants might suffer from the Court's holding.

Although much of the discussion above emphasizes references to the briefs filed by the Solicitor General, the Court's direct references to the briefs of other amici are also frequent, often demonstrating that they received considerable attention in the process of the Court's decisionmaking. So, for example, in some cases the opinions rely on amici for empirical information. A notable example appears in *Associates Commercial Corp. v. Rash*[20] (considering the appropriate valuation standard for collateral in bankruptcy). The Court's opinion at one point considered the question of how well secured creditors are protected by the payments made to justify retention of collateral during a bankruptcy (so-called "adequate protection" payments). On that point, the

19 530 U.S. 1 (2000).

20 520 U.S. 953 (1997).

Court accepted – and quoted – the assertion of amicus American Automobile Manufacturers Association that "such payments . . . frequently fail to compensate adequately for the usually more rapid depreciation of assets retained by the debtor" (520 U.S. at 963 n.3). To repeat the obvious point, that is just the type of question on which an expert agency might provide much more informed (and less obviously biased) input.

To be sure, in some cases, the references indicate that the efforts of the amici were unsuccessful. The most notable example is the dissent's reliance in *Hall v. United States*[21] on data provided by the amicus brief of a group of professors regarding the typical duration of bankruptcies under the special procedures in Chapter 12 for family farmers. The Court in that case rejected the effectiveness of a congressional amendment to the Code designed to limit the adverse tax consequences of sales of farms during those bankruptcies. To rebut the Court's suggestion that the unusual length of Chapter 12 proceedings justified the rule adverse to the bankrupt, Justice Breyer's dissent presented data, attributed to the amici, suggesting that Chapter 12 cases typically are quite short (132 S. Ct. at 1890 n.6). A less substantive example is the ringing acknowledgment in *Norwest Bank Worthington v. Ahlers* that "amici paint a grim picture of the problems facing farm families today, and present an eloquent appeal for action on their behalf," set against the conclusion that "relief from current farm woes cannot come from a misconstruction of the applicable bankruptcy laws."[22]

The most common recognition of the role of amici in the Court's opinions is more pedestrian: acknowledgment of and attention to the legal arguments that amici raise in their briefs. Justice White's plurality opinion in *Hoffman* (the topic of Chapter 6) provides a salient example. The Court in that case considered whether the Bankruptcy Code could, or does, abrogate the sovereign immunity of the States; the plurality concluded that the statute was not sufficiently specific to abrogate state immunity. In the course of his opinion, Justice White devoted a remarkably detailed passage (two substantial paragraphs) to a rebuttal of the argument of amicus Inslaw that the Code's grant of authority to "determine" proceedings implicitly waived immunity (492 U.S. at 103). *Milavetz*[23] offers a similar example. The Court in that case held that attorneys are "debt relief agencies" for purposes of provisions of

21 132 S. Ct. 1882 (2012).

22 485 U.S. 197, 209 (1988). The discussion is not purely incidental. Commenting on Justice White's draft opinion, Justice O'Connor stated that she "particularly appreciate[d] your inclusion [of] a recognition of the plight and worth of the family farm. While we can't help solve the problem, at least we acknowledge it" (NBWA021).

23 Milavetz, Gallop & Milavetz v. United States, 559 U.S. 299 (2010).

BAPCPA[24] that impose a variety of notice and disclosure requirements on "debt relief agencies." In the course of its opinion, the Court noticed, and provided a detailed rebuttal of, the argument that another provision (Section 527) undermined the Government's argument that attorneys fall within the definition of debt relief agencies. The Court commented that it was addressing an argument "that Milavetz abandoned," which the Court attributed to the amicus brief of the NACBA (559 U.S. at 238 n.4). Again, in *Howard Delivery*,[25] the Court framed its discussion of the problem before it (the priority status of insurance premia that a bankrupt employer owes to its workers compensation carrier) with parallel citations to competing amicus briefs arguing that the legislative history could be read to favor either side of the question.[26] The opinions suggest, at a minimum, that the Court on occasion takes seriously nonduplicative arguments that amici provide, even when they appear in briefs of less-established amici.

13.2 THE COURT'S OWN CONTRIBUTION

Once we account for the relatively obvious information that parties provide and the more specialized information that amici provide, the residual category is information that the Court locates for itself. This is a subject about which Larsen (2012) has written, emphasizing the relative weakness of the Court's capability when it relies on its own resources as a finder of facts not in the record. For my purposes, however, a somewhat different question is relevant. Looking at the broad spectrum of sources on which the Court relies, an understanding of the kinds of sources that the Court locates for itself provides yet another window on what the Court might have learned from a robust institutional partner in the Executive Branch.

I start with a simple numerical description: If the Court is locating about 30% of its sources for itself, what can I observe about the topics on which it does, and does not, need to rely on its own resources? On the latter point, the parties and their amici provide an overwhelming share of several of the most important types of sources that appear in the Court's opinions. Parallel to the material discussed above, those tend to be the most readily accessible and objectively bounded categories. Bankruptcy statutes provide a good example. Though the Court often goes beyond the briefing to refer by analogy to provisions of the Code or for historical context to preceding versions, in most cases

24 The Bankruptcy Abuse Prevention and Consumer Protection Act of 2005.

25 Howard Delivery Service v. Zurich American Insurance Co., 547 U.S. 651 (2006).

26 547 U.S. at 661 (citing briefs of American Home Assurance Company and National Coordinating Committee for ERISA Plans).

the universe of relevant bankruptcy statutes is apparent; the Court adds only about 12% of those citations to its opinions (77/626, less than one per case); it is no surprise that this also is the single category that is provided most commonly by the parties themselves (81%). Among the other major categories, the Court's contribution to the body of non-bankruptcy statutes and legislative materials is similarly limited, standing at 15% (53/359) and 14% (29/212), respectively.

Conversely, the Court is much more likely to rely on its own efforts to locate secondary sources. So, for example, the Court identifies 64% (146/227) of the citations to books, treatises, *Restatements*, and the like that appear in its opinions.[27] The Court's self-reliance in identifying scholarly periodicals is similar (44% (47/107)), though not quite so marked.

Another area in which the Justices show a considerable amount of self-reliance involves constitutional law. Four of the six cases with the largest number of sources that do not appear in the briefs were the Court's four highly disputed constitutional cases: *Wellness* (74), *Granfinanciera* (47), *Northern Pipeline* (39), and *Katz* (36).[28] On reflection, that does not seem surprising. Constitutional law is an area in which the Justices are most likely to bring their own perspectives, background, and knowledge to the issue. Moreover, because of the greater institutional significance of the decisions, it could be expected that the Justices would invest more effort and attention to their opinions.

The limited size of the dataset makes generalizations difficult. So, for example, at first glance a similar pattern is apparent for state materials (decisions of state courts, as well as state statutes, rules, and constitutions), where the Court identifies 67% (84/124) of those materials itself. On closer examination, though, it appears that more than half of the Court's self-located state citations (46) appear in a single opinion – a fifty-state survey in Justice Souter's opinion for the Court in *Field v. Mans*.[29] The Court's location of bankruptcy court decisions is similarly unbalanced. Overall, the Court locates 47% of those decisions itself (93/200), but 23 of those citations appear in Justice Scalia's opinion for the Court in *Timbers of Inwood Forest*.[30]

27 A substantial share of those citations involve a single treatise, *Norton's Bankruptcy Law and Practice*, cited sixteen times by the Court, with none of those citations appearing in the briefs. Another marked pattern involves the ALI's various *Restatements*. Of the Court's dozen citations to *Restatements*, only three appear in the briefs of the parties and one in the briefs of amici.

28 Aside from *Field* (70), discussed below, the only other non-constitutional decision with so many self-generated sources is the bitterly contested decision in *BFP* (43).

29 516 U.S. 59 (1995).

30 484 U.S. 365 (1988).

Those opinions could be regarded as unrepresentative outliers. In neither case, though, is it apparent why the parties and amici failed to provide the relevant information. In *Field v. Mans*, the issue before the Court was the level of reliance necessary to establish fraud (that would except an obligation from the discharge). At least in hindsight, it does not seem surprising that the Court would look to the well-established common law on that question; yet the briefs provided little guidance on that topic. Nor can this be attributed to a "void" in the briefing; the Court received briefs from its two most ubiquitous amici, the Solicitor General on one side of the case and the NACBA on the other. Perhaps Justice Scalia's citations in *Timbers* are less predictable, amassed to support the point that in practice bankruptcy courts often grant relief from the stay within less than a year. Still, the efficiency of the bankruptcy court is as a practical matter quite relevant to the need for interim compensation for interest-rate losses, and the apparent importance of the case drew an array of high-profile amici.[31] However predictable or unpredictable those topics should have seemed in the briefing, a broader point is apparent: Both of the absent topics involve points on which an institutional perspective would have been useful. The fact-bound question of "reliance" at issue in *Fields* is just the type of topic susceptible to informed regulatory specification; the "on the ground" practical assessment in *Timbers* of the promptitude of bankruptcy judges in business cases is precisely the type of topic on which an involved expert agency would have an informed opinion.

The Justices' frequent inquiries at oral argument about such practical topics provide parallel evidence of the routine lack of desired practical information in this context. In some cases, the questions seem well placed. Two examples from the most recent Term are illustrative. At the oral argument in *Baker Botts v. ASARCO* (considering the availability of fees for the costs of defending challenges to a fee award),[32] Chief Justice Roberts asked counsel: "Do lawyers these days actually charge private clients for fee preparation?" (*Baker Botts* Transcript at 33). That is a question on which any partner in a large law firm probably could provide reasonably accurate information. Similarly, at the oral argument in *Bank of America v. Caulkett* (considering the treatment of bankruptcy of collateral that is worth markedly less than the liens that encumber it),[33] Justice Ginsburg asked counsel for the bank: "What is the value of

31 The Court received seven amicus briefs, including briefs from the Solicitor General, American Bankers Association, then Harvard Professor Tom Jackson, and Kenneth Klee and Ron Levin (prominent bankruptcy experts involved during the 1970s as congressional staffers in the drafting of Chapter 11).

32 135 S. Ct. 2158 (2015).

33 135 S. Ct. 1995 (2015).

a completely underwater second mortgage? How likely is it that the property will ever appreciate to the extent that it will have real value?" (*Caulkett* Transcript at 4). Bank of America is one of the nation's largest residential lenders, and counsel representing the bank in the Supreme Court represent it in a wide variety of appellate matters, including dozens of cases pending on the Court's docket raising the same issue as *Caulkett*. It was not at all surprising that she could provide anecdotal evidence pointing to pending cases as well as statistical evidence presented in the briefs. Justice Kennedy followed up with a similarly practical question: "Do the holders of the second, assuming the second is partially or fully underwater, ever participate in negotiations with the property owner and with the holder of the first lien [offering a reduction of the second lien]," to which counsel offered a similarly informed response.[34]

At other times, though, the Court asks appellate counsel questions about the details of bankruptcy court practice. Often, the questions seem surprisingly ill directed, posed to individuals with little likelihood of any direct experience or knowledge regarding the topic in question. For example, when the Court considered in *Dewsnup v. Timm* whether a bankruptcy court's valuation of collateral should "strip down" a lien to the value of the collateral, Chief Justice Rehnquist asked Tim Dyk (now a judge on the Federal Circuit), arguing for the borrower: "Could you tell us, Mr. Dyk, how does the valuation work? Is the valuation, I take it, at the time of filing? And what happens of the value increases? Is there a hearing on valuation? Can you just tell me how that works?" (*Dewsnup* Transcript at 6). He repeated the same question to counsel for the Solicitor General: "Do you know enough about bankruptcy practice to know what sort of a hearing this initial valuation is? Do the parties call expert appraisal witnesses? Or is it just a seat-of-the-pants type of thing?" (*Dewsnup* Transcript at 33–34). Again, at the argument in *Ron Pair* (considering the need for post-filing interest, considered in detail in Chapter 10), a Justice asked Larry Wallace[35] a question about foreclosure practice: "May I ask, isn't it true that customarily in a mechanic's lien foreclosure that under most state statutes, doesn't the lienor get attorneys' fees and costs?" (*Ron Pair*

[34] Caulkett Transcript at 5. The argument in *Caulkett* was remarkable on the subject at hand, as the Justices peppered counsel for the bank with numerous questions about the practical dynamics of individual bankruptcies. In addition to the two examples in the text, the argument included questions about the role of the trustee in negotiations (Justice Scalia, Transcript at 6), the procedure for a post-bankruptcy foreclosure (Justice Sotomayor, Transcript at 6–7), and the timing of valuation (Justice Kennedy, Transcript at 21).

[35] Lawrence G. Wallace was a long-time Deputy Solicitor General, who presented more oral arguments to the Court (157) than any other advocate since the beginning of the Twentieth Century. Lazarus (2007, 1492 n.28).

Transcript at 7–8). At the oral argument in *Taylor*,[36] considering whether certain litigation proceeds are exempt from the bankruptcy estate, a Justice asked Judge Dyk (appearing again): "Do you have any idea, Mr. Dyk, what percentage of people filing for bankruptcy are represented by attorneys when they file as opposed to, say, people who start civil law suits in the Federal courts?" (*Taylor* Transcript at 13).

With all due respect, Larry Wallace and Judge Dyk are experts about many things, but the details of mechanics lien foreclosures and pro se bankruptcy filers are not among them. It would be easy to continue, but those examples collectively make the point: The Justices are probably not looking in the best place for this kind of information. In most cases, the attorneys that argue cases before the Court, especially when they come from the Office of the Solicitor General, are appellate specialists who have no claim to "hands-on" knowledge about the operation of the bankruptcy system on the ground. The information that such questions solicit, even if counsel answer frankly rather than strategically, is likely to rest on a weak foundation at best. An expert agency would be a much better resource for topics of that sort. And the Solicitor General's representatives would be much more informed if they came to the Court on behalf of such an agency.

The Justices' efforts to situate their cases against current events reflect a similar lack of informed guidance. Chapter 7's discussion of the *Bildisco* decision (assessing the enforceability of collective bargaining agreements in a bankruptcy proceeding) is a good example. *Bildisco* presented a small company with a dozen employees, a context in which the issue is almost trivial. But *Bildisco* came to the Court against the backdrop of the first wave of large airline bankruptcies, and of Continental Airlines in particular, a salient context in which the issue is crucial. As Chapter 7 points out, the Continental bankruptcy was a topic in the Justices' preparations before oral argument, at the Conference at which the case was decided, and in Justice Brennan's dissent. Although several of the Justices seemed to regard the large airline bankruptcies as crucially important, it is easy to criticize the Court's focus on such a case as availability bias – treating the most salient example as representative of routine occurrence. When it comes to sorting out the relative importance of the failure of tiny firms like Bildisco and immense multinational enterprises like Continental, the Court would benefit from the perspective of an institutional player in the Executive Branch with a broad perspective on the system as a whole.

36 Taylor v. Freeland & Kronz, 503 U.S. 638 (1992).

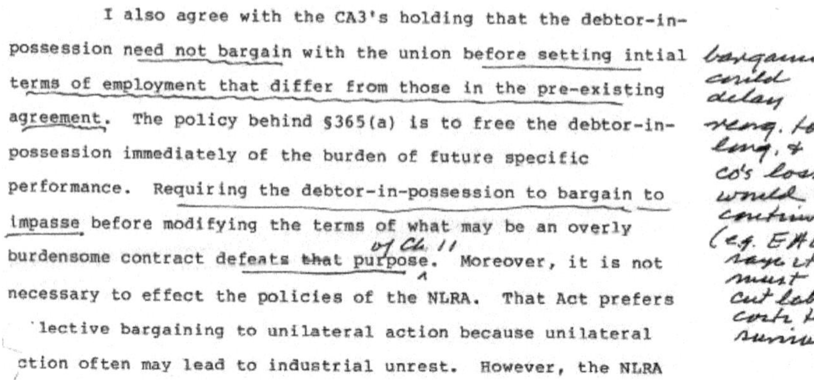

I also agree with the CA3's holding that the debtor-in-possession need not bargain with the union before setting intial terms of employment that differ from those in the pre-existing agreement. The policy behind §365(a) is to free the debtor-in-possession immediately of the burden of future specific performance. Requiring the debtor-in-possession to bargain to impasse before modifying the terms of what may be an overly burdensome contract defeats ~~that~~ purpose of Ch. 11. Moreover, it is not necessary to effect the policies of the NLRA. That Act prefers ·lective bargaining to unilateral action because unilateral ction often may lead to industrial unrest. However, the NLRA

FIGURE 13.1 Justice Powell's Bench Memorandum in NLRB v. Bildisco (excerpt) (BILD038:44). Justice Powell's marginal comments read as follows: "bargaining could delay too long, & co's losses would continue (e.g. EAL says it must cut labor costs to survive)"

The difficulty the Justices confront in assessing the relative importance of competing scenarios appears again in the frequent emphasis on arguably off-point hypotheticals. The use of hypotheticals to explore the boundaries of legal rules is an important and properly valued part of legal reasoning, but at the same time, allowing implausible problems to resolve issues of general application is not always appropriate. The most prominent example here is the preoccupation of the Court in *Midlantic* with implausible horror stories drawn word for word from the brief of the Solicitor General. As discussed in Chapter 8, Justice Rehnquist's draft for a majority opinion found the possibility that a bankruptcy trustee might abandon dynamite on a furnace in the basement of a school sufficiently realistic to warrant a response; the early drafts Justice Powell's clerk wrote for a dissent began with discussion of the same hypothetical (MIDL013:13, MIDL015:1). Nor is that the only successful insertion by the Solicitor General of a remote hypothetical into the Court's deliberations. The Court's opinion in *Cohen*[37] (holding that the Bankruptcy Code does not discharge punitive damage awards awarded as a response to fraud) emphasizes the impropriety of granting a discharge to "a debtor who fraudulently represents to aircraft manufacturers that his steel bolts are aircraft quality [and thus] causes a multi-million dollar airplane to crash" (523 U.S. at 222). Justice O'Connor's opinion for the Court took that far-fetched hypothetical verbatim from the brief of the Solicitor General. Although the parallel hypotheticals that she offers in the same paragraph of the opinion derive from actual discharge cases, the brief of the Solicitor General suggests

37 Cohen v. de la Cruz, 523 U.S. 213 (1998).

no real-world punitive damage award based on fraudulent aircraft parts, much less a discharge of it in bankruptcy (Brief of Solicitor General at 21 & n.11).

The discussion in Chapter 9 of *Kelly v. Robinson* shows a similar preoccupation during the argument and subsequent discussions at Conference with the possibility that a ruling for the bankrupt would allow the discharge of restitution obligations associated with homicide, a topic raised by the State at oral argument. The protestations of Justice Stevens that other provisions in the Code made that result most unlikely seemed to fall on deaf ears. Similarly, the evaluation of governmental sovereign immunity at the oral argument in *Nordic Village* (discussed in detail in Chapter 6) was derailed by an interchange regarding the odd distinction between a rule obligating the Government to return property (a suitcase seized at an airport – subject to turnover to the trustee) and a rule protecting the Government from monetary relief (the money in the same suitcase – which the Government can retain) (*Nordic Village* Transcript at 14–15). The thin distinction between monetary and non-monetary relief was then (and remains to this day) a long-standing oddity of the Court's Eleventh Amendment jurisprudence. The plausibility of the Court's willingness to adhere to that distinction had little to do with the strength or weakness of the Solicitor General's position in *Nordic Village* that the Bankruptcy Code should afford the United States the benefits of those same traditional sovereign immunity protections.

Another routine occurrence that undermines confidence in the Justices' capacity to filter information offered by amici is the Justices' frequent reliance on their own factual preconceptions about situations with which they have relatively little experience. The files display a sustained pattern of comments reflecting little self-awareness about the likelihood that their unrepresentative impressions bias their perspective. The most remarkable example in this context is the routine discussion of what a borrower and lender "bargain for" in a loan transaction. In cases in which the Court holds that the Bankruptcy Code fails to interfere with state-law arrangements for the enforcement of secured loans, Justices frequently explain that the practice in question is something for which the parties "bargained." An early example from the *Dewsnup* argument mentioned above describes the lender's ability to benefit from changes in the valuation of collateral as commonplace: "Of course, that's what the lienholder bargained for" (*Dewsnup* Transcript at 8). That same idea made its way into the Court's opinion, starting with its earliest draft: "We think, however, that the creditor's lien stays with the real property until the foreclosure. That is what was *bargained for* by the mortgagor and the mortgagee" (DNTM042:7; 502 U.S. at 417) (my emphasis). Justice Thomas's opinion for the Court in

Nobelman[38] (extending *Dewsnup* to Chapter 13) made a similar point even more expansively:

> The bank's rights … include the right to repayment of the principal in monthly installments over a fixed term at specified adjustable rates of interest, the right to retain the lien until the debt is paid off, the right to accelerate the loan upon default and to proceed against petitioners' residence by foreclosure and public sale, and the right to bring an action to recover any deficiency remaining after foreclosure. *These are the rights that were "bargained for by the mortgagor and the mortgagee,"* and are rights protected from modification by [Chapter 13]. (508 U.S. at 329–330 (quoting *Dewsnup*) (my emphasis))

Again, consider a comment of Chief Justice Roberts from the argument in *RadLAX*.[39] Counsel for the debtor offered what was intended to be criticism of a lender, claiming that it "simply does not want the asset sold. It would rather take the asset back and hold it for some time period." The Chief Justice retorted, with eery similarity to the *Dewsnup* argument: "Isn't that pretty much what he bargained for when he insisted on security before giving the loan?"[40]

That is not the only subject on which the Justices made such comments; the records of the cases display a variety of similarly self-assured comments. At the oral argument in *BFP*, for example, Justice Scalia asked rhetorically: "Isn't it common knowledge that if you can hold a property on the market for several years and wait for a buyer, you're going to get a much better price than if you have to sell it quite rapidly?" (*BFP* Transcript at 14). Similarly, at the oral argument in *Timbers*,[41] Chief Justice Rehnquist, discussing the importance of the automatic stay, commented: "I had a fair amount of experience representing creditors in bankruptcy under the Act and you just didn't have to put up with all this stuff."[42] The dissent of Justice Stevens in *Barnhill*[43] provides yet another example. The *Barnhill* Court considered the date on which a payment by check is made (for purposes of deciding if the payment is more than ninety days before the bankruptcy). Justice Stevens opened his

38 Nobelman v. American Savings Bank, 508 U.S. 324 (1993).

39 RadLAX Gateway Hotel, LLC v. Amalgamated Bank, 132 S. Ct. 2065 (2012).

40 *RadLAX* transcript at 7. As that comment echoes the preconceptions of the *Dewsnup* deliberations, it might reflect the experience of Chief Justice Roberts mentioned above, appearing as the supervising Deputy Solicitor General on the brief for the Office of the Solicitor General in *Dewsnup*.

41 United Savings Ass'n v. Timbers of Inwood Forest Associates, 484 U.S. 365 (1987).

42 *Timbers* Transcript at 22. The colloquy on that point was noteworthy, because counsel for the lender "beg[ged] to differ with" Rehnquist on that point, resulting in a lengthy and inconclusive interchange.

43 Barnhill v. Johnson, 503 U.S. 393 (1992).

dissent by explaining that the principal problem with the Court's decision (that the payment is made on the date that the check is honored) is that it is not "consistent with the traditional commercial practice of treating the date of delivery as the date of payment when a payment is made by a check that is subsequently honored by the drawee bank."[44] Similarly, just this last Term in *Caulkett* (extending *Dewsnup* to wholly "underwater" second liens), Justice Scalia deprecated any possible application of the ruling to business lending, commenting:

> You know, I'm not familiar with the widespread practice of taking a second mortgage on a business loan unless it's your father-in-law. It's a very common practice for purchases of homes. I'm not aware that it's a common practice in businesses, getting second mortgages. It seems to me quite rare.[45]

I do not suggest that the comments of the Justices on those topics are too often incorrect. Rather, the point is that they reflect little caution about the likelihood that their own experiences provide an imperfect proxy for the information an actual expert might provide on the point in question.

44 BHJN003:1; 503 U.S. at 403. Justice Stevens offered a footnote citing cases that imposed that rule as a matter of law, and he well might have cited U.C.C. §3–310(b), which states that rule explicitly. None of those sources, however, speak to "traditional commercial practice."

45 Caulkett Transcript at 30. The briefing in *Caulkett* provided considerable support for a contrary empirical perspective. *See* Amicus Brief of Loan Syndications and Trading Ass'n at 6 (presenting data indicating about $40 billion of such loans outstanding at the time the Court considered *Caulkett*).

PART IV

CONCLUSION

This book seeks to establish two points: that the Supreme Court's decisions give inadequate weight to the Bankruptcy Clause and Congress's related enactments; and that the absence of an executive branch agency administering the Code has played a substantial role in that outcome. The first point is the simplest, for which I advance both quantitative and qualitative arguments. The raw numbers, summarized in Chapter 4, reveal a narrow interpretation of the bankruptcy process more than 60% of the time. The disparity is even starker in the close cases (those with three or more dissents), in which the Justices presumably have more room to maneuver. In that domain the Court has taken the narrow view almost three-quarters of the time (74%).

With less than a hundred data points, the persuasive force of numbers standing alone is limited. But when we bring to bear the qualitative evidence from the case studies, it is difficult to contest the Court's institutionalization of a routinized pattern of underenforcement. The case studies define a pattern of underenforcement with four prominent attributes. Specifically, responding to Congress's comprehensive overhaul of the Code, the Court

- has never seriously considered the idea that Congress's constitutional authority over bankruptcy supports deference to the choices that the Code implements;
- has adopted a jurisprudential presumption that the overhaul accomplished nothing;
- consistently resolves "conflict" cases (where the Bankruptcy Code collides with some other legal system) through application of the legal framework of the other (non-bankruptcy) system; and
- has narrowed the range and effect of the bankruptcy system at almost every opportunity.

Indeed, I would say that even the occasional "broad" cases turn out to buttress the underenforcement thesis. Consider, for example, the decisions in *Wellness* and *Katz* (discussed in the closing pages of Chapters 5 and 6 respectively). Although those decisions do show a "broad" result as the Court's last word on the constitutional topics, those decisions hardly demonstrate an affirmative shift toward a supportive conception of the Bankruptcy Power. The case studies show a Court that is routinely resolving cases in an area in which it normally acts with no reason to suppose that a broad and effective bankruptcy system serves any cognizable systemic role. Against that broad canvas, what we really learn from *Wellness* and *Katz* is that the routine decisions that happen to limit the Bankruptcy Power do not rest on an affirmatively held perspective that is held so strongly as to justify a protracted constitutional standoff. The same is true in the statutory realm. There, the lone case study in which the Court adopts a broadening rule (*Bildisco*) does so by holding that practice under the Code should track practice under the Act: The result in that particular case broadened the force of the system. But, as the later case studies document, a presumption that the Code changed nothing leads in the great run of cases to a narrow and limited system.

The second of the book's two points – attributing the Court's narrowing perspective to the administrative vacuum in the bankruptcy area – is not so easily established, requiring as it does a comparison of the Court's existing jurisprudence to a counterfactual world in which the Court's activity in the area would reflect pervasive activity and expertise of the United States Bankruptcy Administration proposed by the Commission.[1] Still, the evidence presented here provides four major pieces of evidence to support that point. First, although the quantitative evidence presented in Chapter 4 sheds relatively little light on this question, it does suggest that the Justices are less likely to form pronounced views about the breadth (or narrowness) of the bankruptcy system than they are to form such views in the parallel area of securities law, where the SEC provides a strong executive voice in support of the agency's mission. Second, both the case studies and the numerical analysis (in Chapter 12) show that the Solicitor General's role in bankruptcy cases has been almost diametrically opposed to the role we would have expected from the United States Bankruptcy Administration: We don't have a Court left to its own devices in the bankruptcy realm, we have a Court consistently advised by the executive to downplay the significance of the bankruptcy system. Third, as the preceding paragraph pointed out, on both of the occasions when the Court *has* faced a strong institutional preference for a broad system – the two

[1] Recommended in sections 3–101 through 3–403 of the Commission's proposed bill.

areas of constitutional doctrine discussed in Chapters 5 and 6 – the Court has receded from an initially narrowing view, giving way before Congress's explicit preference for a more capacious system. Fourth and finally, the evidence discussed in Chapter 13 documents a Court that is both persistently at a loss for guidance about the most basic practical attributes of the system and routinely finding information about those topics in the off-the-cuff answers of inexpert appellate advocates or in their own unexamined and anecdotal preconceptions. We cannot delineate the counterfactual world in detail, but it is hard to deny that the Court's perspective on bankruptcy in an agency-focused milieu would have been more generous than it is now.

To be sure, the absence of an agency is not the only possible explanation of the underenforcement. Some readers have suggested, for example, that the "creditor's bargain" justification for bankruptcy (Jackson 2001) supports a system in which the bankruptcy process is limited to activities designed to maximize creditor recoveries. That might explain some of the cases that limit the power of the system to reach out and take assets from creditors (like *BFP*), but it is quite difficult to reconcile with cases like *Midlantic*, which harm creditors by limiting the powers of the trustee, or cases like *Granfinanciera* and *Stern*, which limit the ability of the trustee to coordinate collection activities in one forum. In the end, the creditor's bargain hypothesis is a powerful tool for understanding one of the main things an effective bankruptcy system would do. Taking the hypothesis for that purpose, the Court's frequent choice of paths that limit the system's ability to perform that function is best understood as evidence of the underenforcement I emphasize throughout this work.

I also note the provocative suggestion by Baird and Casey (2013) that the Court's distrust of the Article I bankruptcy judges has led it systematically to lessen the discretion afforded those judges. That resonates with cases like *Marathon*, *Granfinanciera*, and *Stern*. It also justifies the long train of cases limiting the importance of bankruptcy court asset valuations – the most prominent being *BFP*, *203 N. LaSalle*,[2] and *RadLAX*.[3] It also resonates with the widely held perception that the bankruptcy judges resistant to the Court's narrowing decisions commonly develop "workarounds" that mitigate the impracticality of the Court's relatively disengaged perspective. Like the creditor's bargain hypothesis, though, the "don't trust the judges" idea is a poor fit for the broad range of cases. Most obviously, it does not explain why so

2 Bank of America Nat'l Trust & Savings Ass'n v. 203 N. LaSalle Street Partnership, 526 U.S. 434 (1999).

3 RadLAX Gateway Hotel v. Amalgamated Bank, 132 S. Ct. 2065 (2012).

many of the bright-line rules that the Court adopts systematically cut against the debtor. Nor does it explain last Term's decision in *Bullard v. Blue Hills Bank*[4] denying debtors appellate review of bankruptcy court decisions refusing to confirm plans. All of those decisions match my vision of a Court accepting any plausible reason to narrow and hobble the system. In the end, then, I share Baird's view that the Court is acting on a strong preference for bright-line rules in this area. But that preference tells us little about the topic of this project, the location of the boundaries that the rules and standards will define.

Having said that, whether my presentation on those points is convincing or not, it is natural to ask why anybody would care enough to write a book about underenforcement of the Bankruptcy Power. Surely, we know from the press that things are better when there are fewer bankruptcies and things are worse when there are more. If the Court puts a thumb on the scale to make bankruptcy less desirable, then fewer businesses and individuals will use the system and we all will be better off. Right? Shouldn't I be praising a system that has developed to limit the ready availability of bankruptcy relief as support for the indolent and imprudent actors in our economy? If the system makes it harder to file, won't all those potential debtors just work harder to pay off their just debts? My decision to write this book should be proof that I do not see it that way.

That is not to say that it is novel to regard bankruptcy as a starkly moral failure to be stamped out by the harshest of laws. That visceral opposition to the availability of relief from debt has its roots in the earliest stages of industrializing (capitalist) activity in both this country and England (Weiss 1986; Mann 2003). Still, however longstanding the concern, it has been clear from the earliest days of the Industrial Revolution that the pragmatic reality of a capitalist system requires (or at least benefits from) an effective and readily available bankruptcy system. In England, despite strong moralist misgivings, a comprehensive system for relief was in place by the 1860s (Weiss 1986, 38–47). On this side of the Atlantic, Bruce Mann (in the work on which the Court relied in *Katz*) has chronicled the urgent drive that resulted in an effective system for business debtors even before adoption of our Constitution (Mann 2003). By the Revolution, those issues had become, in Madison's words (Federalist 10), a "common and durable source of faction."

The deep-seated resistance to bankruptcy relief reflects a fundamental misapprehension of the role of the bankruptcy system in our society and in our economy. As David Skeel puts it, bankruptcy policymakers are paralyzed by a "phobia" of bankruptcy (Skeel 2009; Skeel and Jackson 2012; Skeel 2012).

4 135 S. Ct. 1686 (2015).

The bankruptcy system does not represent failure; it is the government institution that responds to, and mitigates the costs of, financial failure. A more effective bankruptcy system is not one that is used less, it is one that minimizes the aggregate costs of financial failure, balancing effective relief that promptly redeploys the human capital of individuals and the financial capital of businesses against the losses from the larger body of debts left unpaid. It is especially in times of crisis that bankruptcy relief is important – and that the quality of it is tested. Thus, again and again, with the recurrent financial crises of the nineteenth century, Congress was driven to offer bankruptcy relief (Balleisen 2001; Sandage 2005). But the adoption of a permanent statute in 1898 pushed those concerns to the background. The issue has much more prominence now, amid the lingering aftershocks of the Great Recession.

The recent resolution of Chrysler and General Motors is a telling example of how commonly policymakers underestimate the value an effective bankruptcy system can create. Despite a media consensus that no major car company could survive a bankruptcy filing, at the end of the day the only way that those companies could resolve their financial difficulties was through the bankruptcy system. Critics argue that corners were cut in those proceedings (Roe and Skeel 2009). If true, that only underscores my point: Bankruptcy *can* provide effective relief for the biggest industrial operations, but the system as it currently exists is poorly suited to do so. Comparing the recent successful reorganization of Detroit – using a process that builds directly on the successful auto bankruptcies (Skeel 2015) – to the consequences of Puerto Rico's ineligibility for such relief (Corkery and Walsh 2015) provides a similar example. As Jay Westbrook explained recently (2014), the pattern of those events justifies a rethinking of *all* the major exclusions from the bankruptcy process – for financial institutions, sovereigns, and sophisticated financial instruments.

Perhaps the most pointed illustration of the costs of underenforcement of the Bankruptcy Power comes from the still continuing financial crisis for individual households. Nearly a decade after the crisis broke, individual households remain trapped, stagnant, waiting for an opportunity to move forward. Although there are many reasons for the protraction of the financial crisis, one contributing factor at the household level surely is the impoverished relief available under the Bankruptcy Code. Read by the Supreme Court "in a spirit of mutilating narrowness,"[5] the bankruptcy system has remained largely on the sidelines when the nation needed it most. Figure 13.2 is illustrative: despite foreclosure filings at historic highs, bankruptcy filings

[5] United States v. Hutcheson, 312 U.S. 219, 235 (1941).

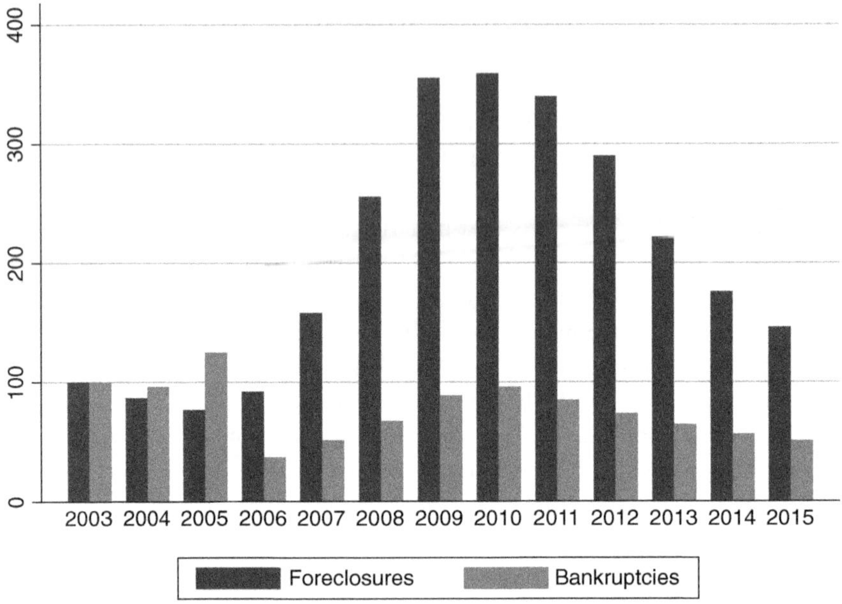

FIGURE 13.2 Bankruptcy and Foreclosure Rates (2003–2015). Author's calculations from foreclosure data provided by Mortgage Bankers Association National Delinquency Survey, Census Bureau Annual Population Estimates, and bankruptcy data from the Administrative Office of United States Courts. The figure shows the share of home mortgage loans in year-end foreclosure inventory and annual bankruptcy filings per capita as a percentage of 2003 data.

remain only slightly higher than normal – and lower than they were during the boom years of the last decade.

A comprehensive and effective bankruptcy system will be a valuable resource when the American economy faces the next big shock, whenever it might come. The discussion above suggests that an expert administrative agency could foster the broad-based support for such a system that would be necessary to sustain it indefinitely. I recognize many of the difficulties that plague any allocation of policy to an agency. The goals of the agency might diverge from the "proper" goals of the bankruptcy system, whatever those might be. The dominant interests of creditors might "capture" the agency. The agency might press a "limited-government" view of the system, attempting to rein in the bankruptcy courts at all points. Or the agency might simply be so underfunded or ineffective as to have little or no effect on the system at all.

But the possible value of such an agency outweighs those concerns. Putting to the side the effects on the Court's jurisprudence that are the focus of this book – presumably not one of the top action items for such an agency – the Bankruptcy Code includes a daunting array of vague concepts, just the sort of thing for an expert agency to flesh out based on practice on the ground. To name just a few from the Court's recent docket, consider the tasks of setting interest rates to convert a stream of payments to present value,[6] assessing when hardship is "undue",[7] calculating disposable income,[8] interpreting the form used to claim exemptions,[9] or defining the types of misconduct that justify denial of a discharge.[10] The list could go on and on. But the point is incontestable: No well-designed system would allocate responsibility for such questions to a group of generalists, insulated by institutional position from any specific knowledge of the relevant system.

The potential benefits are too attractive to resist. An expert administrative actor would bring with it the prospect of a system in which the decisions of specialists have weight in system design. It is hard to doubt that *some* benefits would accrue from a move away from the current system (exacerbated by *Marathon* and *Stern*), which almost ensures that any decisions committed to those with hands-on experience (the bankruptcy courts) will receive scant deference. It is far beyond the scope of this project to *prove* that an agency would foster an "optimal" bankruptcy system. It is enough to show how far-reaching the effects of Congress's choice have been.

6 The problem in Till v. SCS Credit Corp, 541 U.S. 465 (2004).

7 The problem in United Student Aid Funds v Espinosa, 559 U.S. 260 (2010).

8 The problem in Hamilton v. Lanning, 560 U.S. 505 (2010).

9 The problem in Schwab v. Reilly, 560 U.S. 770 (2010).

10 The problem in several of the Court's cases, most recently Bullock v. BankChampaign, N.A., 133 S. Ct. 1754 (2013).

APPENDIX A

The Supreme Court's Bankruptcy Cases

TABLE A.1 *The Supreme Court's Bankruptcy Cases*

Case Name	Broad?	Topic	Vote
Central Trust Co. v. Official Creditors' Committee	N	Code vitiating Act cases	7–2
Northern Pipeline v. Marathon Pipe Line	N	Invalidating judicial appointments	6–3
U.S. v. Sec. Indus. Bank	N	522(f) as a taking	9–0
U.S. v. Whiting Pools	Y	IRS obligation to turn over property	9–0
NLRB v. Bildisco & Bildisco	Y	Rejecting collective bargaining agreement	5–4
Ohio v. Kovacs	Y	Discharging environmental injunction	9–0
CFTC v. Weintraub	Y	Attorney–client privilege	8–0
Midlantic Nat'l Bank v. New Jersey D.E.P.	N	Abandoning contaminated property	5–4
Kelly v. Robinson	N	Discharging criminal penalties	7–2
United Savings v. Timbers of Inwood Forest	Y	Undersecured interest	9–0
Norwest Bank Worthington v. Ahlers	N	New-value rule	8–0
U.S. v. Ron Pair Enters.	N	Oversecured interest	5–4
Cal. State Board v. Sierra Summit	N	Sales tax on bankruptcy sale	6–0
Hoffman v. Connecticut	N	Eleventh Amendment	5–4
Granfinanciera v. Nordberg	N	Seventh Amendment	6–3
U.S. v. Energy Resources	Y	Tax payments in reorganization	8–1
Pa. Dep't of Public Welfare v. Davenport	Y	Discharging criminal penalties	7–2
Begier v. IRS	N	Tax payments as preferences	9–0
PBGC v. LTV	N	Discharging pension obligations	6–3

(*continued*)

TABLE A.1 *(continued)*

Case Name	Broad?	Topic	Vote
Langenkamp v. Culp	Y	Seventh Amendment	8–0
Grogan v. Garner	N	Proving dischargeability	9–0
Owen v. Owen	Y	Judicial liens on exempt property	8–1
Farrey v. Sanderfoot	N	Marital liens on exempt property	9–0
Johnson v. Home State Bank	Y	Chapter 20	9–0
Toibb v. Radloff	Y	Individual Chapter 11	8–1
Union Bank v. Wolas	N	Ordinary-course preference	9–0
Dewsnup v. Timm	N	Lien-stripping in Chapter 7	6–2
Holywell Corp. v. Smith	N	Tax on post-filing income	9–0
United States v. Nordic Village	N	IRS sovereign immunity	7–2
Barnhill v. Johnson	Y	Pay-by-check preference	7–2
Taylor v. Freeland & Kronz	Y	Timeliness of exemption objection	8–1
Patterson v. Shumate	N	Protecting ERISA plan	9–0
Pioneer Investment v. Brunswick Assocs.	N	Late-filed claim	5–4
Nobelman v. American Sav. Bank	N	Lien-stripping in Chapter 13	9–0
Rake v. Wade	N	Interest on arrearages	9–0
Sec. Servs. v. KMart Corp.	N	Filed-rate doctrine	7–2
BFP v. RTC	N	Invalidating foreclosure	5–4
ICC v. Transcon Lines	N	Filed-rate doctrine	9–0
Celotex Corp. v. Edwards	Y	Breadth of stay	7–2
Citizens Bank v. Strumpf	N	Pre-setoff hold and stay	9–0
Field v. Mans	N	Discharging fraud	7–2
US v. Noland	N	Taxes as administrative expenses	9–0
US v. Reorganized CF&I Fabricators	Y	Priority of pension penalties	8–1
Assocs. Comm'l Corp. v. Rash	Y	Replacement value at cramdown	8–1
Fidelity Fin Servs. v. Fink	Y	Invalidating late-perfected lien	9–0
Kawaauhau v. Geiger	Y	Discharging recklessness	9–0
Cohen v. De La Cruz	N	Discharging fraud	9–0
Bank of America v. 203 N. LaSalle	N	New-value rule	8–1
Raleigh v. Ill. Dep't of Revenue	N	Proving tax claims	9–0
Hartford Underwriters v. Union Planters Bank	N	Administrative claims in 506(c)	9–0
Young v. US	N	Discharging taxes	9–0
FCC v. NextWave Pers. Communications	Y	Cancelling FCC license	8–1
Archer v. Warner	N	Discharging fraud	7–2

Case Name	Broad?	Topic	Vote
Kontrick v. Ryan	N	Late discharge objection	9–0
Lamie v. US Trustee	N	Fees for unappointed lawyers	9–0
Yates v. Hendon	N	ERISA-related preference	9–0
Till v. SCS Credit Corporation	Y	Rejecting K rate for Chapter 13 plan	5–4
Tenn. Student Assistance Corp. v. Hood	Y	Eleventh Amendment and student loans	7–2
Rousey v. Jacoway	N	Exempting IRAs	9–0
Centennial Va. Community College v. Katz	Y	Eleventh Amendment	5–4
Marshall v. Marshall	Y	Probate exception	9–0
Howard Delivery Servs. v. Zurich Am. Ins.	Y	Priority of workers' comp premia	6–3
Marrama v. Citizens Bank	N	Bad-faith conversion to Chapter 13	5–4
Travelers Casualty v. PG&E	N	Reimbursing attorney's fees	9–0
Florida Dep't of Revenue v. Piccadilly Cafeteria	N	Transfer-tax exemption for plans	7–2
Milavetz, Gallop & Milavetz v. US	Y	Attorneys covered by BAPCPA	9–0
United Student Aid Funds v. Espinosa	Y	Discharging student loan	9–0
Hamilton v. Lanning	N	Calculating disposable income	8–1
Schwab v. Reilly	N	Borrower misstatements	6–3
Ransom v. FIA Card Services	N	Means-test deductions for car costs	8–1
Stern v. Marshall	N	Seventh Amendment	5–4
Hall v. United States	N	Tax debts in Chapter 12	5–4
RadLAX Gateway Hotel v. Amalg. Bank	N	Credit-bidding in Chapter 11 auctions	8–0
Bullock v. BankChampaign, N.A.	Y	Discharging defalcation	9–0
Law v. Siegel	Y	No surcharge of exemption	9–0
Executive Benefits Ins. Agency v. Arkison	Y	Power to decide Stern claim	9–0
Clark v. Rameker	Y	Inherited IRA not exempt	9–0
Bullard v. Blue Hills Bank	N	Rejection of plan not appealable	9–0
Harris v. Viegelahn	Y	Funds trustee holds at conversion	9–0
Wellness Int'l Network v. Sharif	Y	Power to decide Stern claim	6–3
Bank of America v. Caulkett	N	No stripping of underwater liens	9–0
BakerBotts v. ASARCO, LLC	Y	Fees available for protecting fees	9–0

APPENDIX B

Available Papers of the Justices

TABLE B.1 *Papers of the Justices (By Case)*

Case	Available Papers
Marathon Pipeline	Brennan, White, Marshall, Blackmun, Powell
Bildisco	Brennan, White, Marshall, Blackmun, Powell
Midlantic	Brennan, White, Marshall, Blackmun, Powell
Kelly	Brennan, White, Marshall, Blackmun, Powell
Timbers	Marshall, Blackmun
Ron Pair	Brennan, White, Marshall, Blackmun
Granfinanciera	Brennan, White, Marshall, Blackmun
Hoffman	Brennan, White, Marshall, Blackmun
Sierra Summit	Brennan, White, Marshall, Blackmun
Davenport	Brennan, White, Marshall, Blackmun
Energy Resources	White, Marshall, Blackmun
Owen	White, Marshall, Blackmun
Toibb	White, Marshall, Blackmun
Dewsnup	White, Blackmun
Nordic Village	White, Blackmun
Barnhill	White, Blackmun
Taylor	White, Blackmun
Pioneer	White, Blackmun
BFP	Blackmun
KMart	Blackmun

TABLE B.2 *Papers of the Justices (By Justice)*

Justice	Case	Docket Number	Location
	Marathon Pipeline	81–150	Box 358
	Bildisco	82–818	Box 395
Blackmun	*Midlantic*	84–801	Box 438
	Kelly	85–1033	Box 468
	Timbers	86–1602	Box 499
	Ron Pair	87–1043	Box 517
	Granfinanciera	87–1716	Box 525
	Hoffman	88–412	Box 534
	Sierra Summit	88–681	Box 537
	Davenport	89–156	Box 556
	Energy Resources	89–255	Box 557
	Owen	89–1008	Box 565
Blackmun	*Toibb*	90–368	Box 577
	Dewsnup	90–741	Box 585
	Nordic Village	90–1629	Box 593
	Barnhill	91–159	Box 598
	Taylor	91–571	Box 600
	Pioneer	91–1695	Box 617
	BFP	92–1370	Box 638
	KMart	93–284	Box 644
	Marathon Pipeline	81–150	Box I: 580
	Bildisco	82–818	Box I: 640
	Midlantic	84–801	Box I: 700
	Kelly	85–1033	Box I: 731
Brennan	*Ron Pair*	87–1043	Box I: 804
	Granfinanciera	87–1716	Box I: 810
	Hoffman	88–412	Box I: 815
	Sierra Summit	88–681	Box I: 817
	Davenport	89–156	Box I: 855
	Energy Resources	89–255	Box I: 855
Marshall	*Marathon Pipeline*	81–150	Box 301
	Bildisco	82–818	Box 339
	Midlantic	84–801	Box 383
	Kelly	85–1033	Box 415
	Granfinanciera	87–1716	Box 417
	Ron Pair	87–1043	Box 470
Marshall	*Hoffman*	88–412	Box 479
	Sierra Summit	88–681	Box 480
	Davenport	89–156	Box 507
	Energy Resources	89–255	Box 507
	Owen	89–1008	Box 528
	Toibb	90–368	Box 536

(continued)

TABLE B.2 *(continued)*

Justice	Case	Docket Number	Location
	Marathon Pipeline	81–150	Box 89
	Bildisco	82–818	Box 106
Powell	*Midlantic*	84–801	Box 123
	Kelly	85–1033	Box 146
	Marathon Pipeline	81–150	Box 564
	Bildisco	82–818	Box 629
	Midlantic	84–801	Box II: 39
	Kelly	85–1033	Box II: 65
White	*Ron Pair*	87–1043	Box II: 107
	Granfinanciera	87–1716	Box II: 114
	Hoffman	88–412	Box II: 119
	Sierra Summit	88–681	Box II: 121
	Davenport	89–156	Box II: 140
	Energy Resources	89–255	Box II: 141
	Owen	89–1008	Box II: 154
	Toibb	90–368	Box II: 63
	Dewsnup	90–741	Box II: 175
White	*Nordic Village*	90–1629	Box II: 180
	Barnhill	91–159	Box II: 182
	Taylor	91–571	Box II: 184
	Pioneer	91–1695	Box II: 199

Note: With the exception of the papers of Justice Powell, all of the papers on which this book relies are located at the Library of Congress, in collections identified by the name of the particular Justice. The papers of Justice Powell are at the Washington and Lee University School of Law.

APPENDIX C

References to the Hard Cases

TABLE C.1 *References to the Hard Cases. Table summarizes citations in opinions of federal courts as of May 2015. Columns do not sum because of omitted categories (specialty courts, etc.).*

Case	Total Citations	Supreme Court	Courts of Appeal	District Courts	Bankruptcy Courts
Northern Pipe Line v Marathon Pipeline	2696	33	501	917	1200
Granfinanciera v Nordberg	1424	17	174	634	595
Stern v Marshall	1504	5	74	448	977
Hoffman v Connecticut Dep't	310	7	39	91	172
U.S. v Nordic Village	1517	32	282	840	255
Central Va. Comm'ty College v Katz	262	3	46	74	138
NLRB v Bildisco & Bildisco	950	8	123	198	620
Midlantic Nat'l Bank v New Jersey Dep't	590	13	108	116	351
Kelly v Robinson	870	18	161	294	376
U.S. v. Ron Pair Enters.	3757	37	712	829	2046
BFP v RTC	766	8	115	189	449

APPENDIX D

Sources of the Court's Citations

TABLE D.1 *Sources of the Court's Citations. Table summarizes the share of citations that appear in the briefs of the parties, that appear in the briefs of amici but not the briefs of the parties, and that appear in none of the briefs before the Court. Table omits citations to briefs, argument transcripts, and procedural history.*

Type of Citation	Total Citations	Parties	Amici	Court
Supreme Court Decisions	1053 (29%)	613 (58%)	81 (8%)	359 (34%)
Bankruptcy Statutes	626 (17%)	506 (81%)	43 (7%)	77 (12%)
Lower Court Decisions (Court of Appeals and District Court)	425 (12%)	299 (70%)	32 (7%)	94 (22%)
Federal Statutes (Non-Bankruptcy)	359 (10%)	278 (77%)	28 (8%)	53 (15%)
Books, Treatises, ALI	227 (6%)	58 (26%)	23 (10%)	146 (64%)
Legislative Materials (Reports, Bills, Hearings, Record, CFR)	212 (6%)	143 (67%)	40 (19%)	29 (14%)
Bankruptcy Decisions (Bankruptcy Appellate Panel and Bankruptcy Court)	200 (6%)	86 (43%)	21 (11%)	93 (47%)
State Materials (Cases, Statutes, Rules, Constitutions)	124 (3%)	35 (28%)	5 (4%)	84 (67%)
Law Reviews	107 (3%)	44 (41%)	16 (15%)	47 (44%)
Bankruptcy Rules	77 (2%)	53 (69%)	6 (8%)	18 (23%)
Agency Materials	39 (1%)	30 (77%)	4 (10%)	5 (13%)
Constitutional Provisions	35 (1%)	25 (71%)	3 (9%)	7 (20%)
Dictionaries	36 (1%)	14 (39%)	9 (25%)	13 (36%)
British Cases and Statutes	25 (1%)	14 (56%)	2 (8%)	9 (36%)
"Framing" (Federalist, Farrand, etc.)	24 (1%)	7 (29%)	4 (17%)	13 (54%)
Federal Rules (Non-Bankruptcy)	22 (1%)	11 (50%)	2 (9%)	9 (41%)
Internet, Newspapers	13 (–)	3 (23%)	3 (23%)	7 (54%)
TOTAL	3604	2219 (62%)	322 (9%)	1063 (29%)

APPENDIX E

Sources from the Solicitor General and Other Amici

TABLE E.1 *Sources from the Solicitor General and Other Amici. Table summarizes share of citations that appear in the briefs of the parties, that appear in the briefs of amici but not the briefs of the parties, and that appear in none of the briefs before the Court. Table omits citations to briefs, argument transcripts, and procedural history.*

Type of Citation	Total Amici Citations	Solicitor General	Other Amici
Supreme Court Decisions	81 (25%)	24 (30%)	57 (70%)
Bankruptcy Statutes	43 (13%)	15 (35%)	28 (65%)
Lower Court Decisions (Court of Appeals and District Court)	32 (10%)	14.83 (46%)	17.17 (54%)
Federal Statutes (Non-Bankruptcy)	28 (9%)	15.7 (56%)	12.3 (44%)
Books, Treatises, ALI	23 (7%)	11.3 (49%)	11.7 (51%)
Legislative Materials (Reports, Bills, Hearings, Record)	40 (12%)	24.5 (61%)	15.5 (39%)
Bankruptcy Decisions (Bankruptcy Appellate Panel and Bankruptcy Court)	21 (7%)	6.9 (33%)	14.1 (67%)
State Materials (Cases, Statutes, Rules, Constitutions)	5 (2%)	5 (100%)	0
Law Reviews	16 (5%)	4.5 (28%)	11.5 (72%)
Bankruptcy Rules	6 (2%)	2.3 (38%)	3.7 (62%)
Agency Materials	4 (1%)	1.5 (38%)	2.5 (63%)
Constitutional Provisions	3 (1%)	0.5 (17%)	2.5 (83%)

(continued)

TABLE E.1 *(continued)*

Type of Citation	Total Amici Citations	Solicitor General	Other Amici
Dictionaries	9 (3%)	6.5 (72%)	2.5 (28%)
British Cases and Statutes	2 (1%)	0	2 (100%)
"Framing" (Federalist, Farrand, etc.)	4 (1%)	0	4 (100%)
Federal Rules (Non-Bankruptcy)	2 (1%)	1 (50%)	1 (50%)
Internet, Newspapers	3 (1%)	0	3 (100%)
TOTAL	322	133.53 (41%)	188.47 (59%)

Bibliography

Adler, Jonathan H. 2004. "The Fable of Federal Environmental Regulation: Reconsidering the Federal Role in Environmental Protection." *Case Western Reserve Law Review* 55:93–113.

American Law Institute (Suretyship). 1996. *Restatement of the Law, Third, Suretyship and Guaranty*. St. Paul, Minn.: West Pub. Co.

American Law Institute. 1997. *Restatement of the Law, Third, Property-Mortgages*. West Publishing Company.

Arrington, Theodore S. and Saul Brenner. 2004. "Strategic Voting for Damage Control on the Supreme Court." *Political Research Quarterly* 57:565–573.

Bailey, Michael A., Brian Kamoie, and Forrest Maltzman. 2005. "Signals from the Tenth Justice: The Political Role of the Solicitor General in Supreme Court Decision Making." *American Journal of Political Science* 49:72–85.

Bailey, Michael A. and Forrest Maltzman. 2011. *The Constrained Court: Law, Politics, and the Decisions Justices Make*. Princeton University Press.

Baird, Douglas G. 2010. *The Elements of Bankruptcy*. Foundation Press, 5th edition.

Baird, Douglas G. and Anthony J. Casey. 2013. "Bankruptcy Step Zero." *The Supreme Court Review* 2012:203–231.

Balleisen, Edward J. 2001. *Navigating Failure: Bankruptcy and Commercial Society in Antebellum America*. The University of North Carolina Press.

Barbanel, Josh. 1984. "A Court Bolsters Toxic Waste Law." *New York Times* p. A9.

Barbash, Fred. 1984. "The Judiciary." *Washington Post* p. A17.

Bartels, Brandon L. 2009. "The Constraining Capacity of Legal Doctrine on the U.S. Supreme Court." *The American Political Science Review* 103:474–495.

Barth, James R., Gerard Caprio Jr., and Ross Levine. 2008. *Rethinking Bank Regulation: Till Angels Govern*. Cambridge University Press.

Barth, James R., S. Trimbath, and Glenn Yago (eds.). 2004. *The Savings and Loan Crisis: Lessons from a Regulatory Failure*. Springer, 1st edition.

Behr, Peter. 1984. "Supreme Court Continues Assault; Ruling Another Blow to Unions." *Washington Post* p. D1.

Bergara, Mario, Barak Richman, and Pablo T. Spiller. 2003. "Modeling Supreme Court Strategic Decision Making: The Congressional Constraint." *Legislative Studies Quarterly* 28:247–280.

Black, Ryan C. and Ryan J. Owens. 2014. *The Solicitor General and the United States Supreme Court: Executive Branch Influence and Judicial Decisions*. Cambridge University Press.

Block-Lieb, Susan. 2012. "What Congress Had to Say: Legislative History as a Rehearsal of Congressional Response to Stern v. Marshall." *American Bankruptcy Law Journal* 86:55–119.

Blumenthal, Ralph. 1982. "Accused Polluter Was Paid to Clean up Sites." *New York Times* p. B20.

Bonneau, Chris W., Thomas H. Hammond, Forrest Maltzman, and Paul J. Wahlbeck. 2007. "Agenda Control, the Median Justice, and the Majority Opinion on the U.S. Supreme Court." *American Journal of Political Science* 51:890–905.

Bowman, Karlyn and Everett Carll Ladd. 1995. *Attitudes toward the Environment: Twenty-Five Years after Earth Day*. AEI Press.

Brubaker, Ralph. 2012. "A Summary Statutory and Constitutional Theory of Bankruptcy Judges' Core Jurisdiction after Stern v. Marshall." *American Bankruptcy Law Journal* 86:121–189.

Bussel, Daniel J. 2000. "Textualism's Failures: A Study of Overruled Bankruptcy Decisions." *Vanderbilt Law Review* 53:887–946.

Bussel, Daniel J. 2016. "A Third Way: Examiners as Inquisitors." *American Bankruptcy Law Journal* 90:59–127.

Caldeira, Gregory A. and John R. Wright. 1988. "Organized Interests and Agenda Setting in the U.S. Supreme Court." *The American Political Science Review* 82:1109–1127.

Caporale, Tony and Harold Winter. 2002. "A Positive Political Model of Supreme Court Economic Decisions." *Southern Economic Journal* 68:693–702.

Cardozo, Benjamin N. 1921. *The Nature of the Judicial Process*. Yale University Press.

Carroll, Peter H. III. 1993. "Literalism: The United States Supreme Court's Methodology for Statutory Construction in Bankruptcy Cases." *St. Mary's Law Journal* 25:143–215.

Carruthers, Bruce G. and Terence C. Halliday. 1998. *Rescuing Business: The Making of Corporate Bankruptcy Law in England and the United States*. Clarendon Press; Oxford University Press.

Casey, Anthony J. and Aziz Z. Huq. 2015. "The Article III Problem in Bankruptcy." *University of Chicago Law Review* 82:1155–1234.

Chavez, Lydia. 1982. "Toxic Waste Entrepreneur." *New York Times* p. D1.

Collier. 1967. *Collier on Bankruptcy*, volume 4A. Matthew Bender.

Collins, Jr. Paul M. 2007. "Lobbyists Before the U.S. Supreme Court: Investigating the Influence of Amicus Curiae Briefs." *Political Research Quarterly* 60:55–70.

Collins, Jr. Paul M. 2008. *Friends of the Supreme Court: Interest Groups and Judicial Decision Making*. Oxford University Press, USA.

Collins, Paul M., Pamela C. Corley, and Jesse Hamner. 2015. "The Influence of Amicus Curiae Briefs on U.S. Supreme Court Opinion Content." *Law & Society Review* 49:917–944.

Commission on the Bankruptcy Laws of the United States. 1973. "Report." H.R. Doc. No. 93–137.

Corkery, Michael and Mary Williams Walsh. 2015. "Puerto Rico's Governor Says Island's Debts Are 'Not Payable'." *The New York Times* p. A1.

Corley, Pamela C. 2008. "The Supreme Court and Opinion Content: The Influence of Parties' Briefs." *Political Research Quarterly* 61:468–478.

Countryman, Vern. 1985. "Scrambling to Define Bankruptcy Jurisdiction: The Chief Justice, the Judicial Conference, and the Legislative Process." *Harvard Journal on Legislation* 22:1–45.

Cresci, Gregory. 2005. "Merrill, Citigroup Record CDO Fees Earned in Top Growth Market." *Bloomberg News*.

Cross, Frank B. and Blake J Nelson. 2000. "Strategic Institutional Effects on Supreme Court Decisionmaking." *Northwestern University Law Review* 95:1437–1493.

Cuevas, Carlos J. 1994. "The Rehnquist Court, Strict Statutory Construction and the Bankruptcy Code." *Cleveland State Law Review* 42:435–493.

Curry, Timothy and Lynn Shibut. 2000. "The Cost of the Savings and Loan Crisis: Truth and Consequences." *FDIC Banking Review* 13:26–35.

Daughety, Andrew F. and Jennifer F. Reinganum. 2006. "Speaking Up: A Model of Judicial Dissent and Discretionary Review." *Supreme Court Economic Review* 14:1–41.

Dembart, Lee and Bruce A. Markell. 2004. "Alive at 25 - A Short Review of the Supreme Court's Bankruptcy Jurisprudence, 1979–2004." *American Bankruptcy Law Journal* 78:373–400.

Dunne, Finley Peter. 1901. *Mr. Dooley's Opinions*. University of Michigan Library.

Effross, Walter A. 1992. "Grammarians at the Gate: The Rehnquist Court's Evolving Plain Meaning Approach to Bankruptcy Jurisprudence." *Seton Hall Law Review* 23:1636–1762.

Ehrlich, Scott B. 1985. "Avoidance of Foreclosure Sales as Fraudulent Conveyances: Accommodating State and Federal Objectives." *Virginia Law Review* 71:933–980.

Elman, Philip. 1986. "The Solicitor General's Office, Justice Frankfurter, and Civil Rights Litigation, 1946–1960: An Oral History." *Harvard Law Review* 100:817–852.

Epstein, Lee and Jack Knight. 1999. "Mapping out the Strategic Terrain: The Informational Role of Amici Curiae." In *Supreme Court Decisionmaking: New Institutionalist Approaches*, pp. 215–235. University of Chicago Press.

Epstein, Lee, William M. Landes, and The Honorable Richard A. Posner. 2013. *The Behavior of Federal Judges: A Theoretical and Empirical Study of Rational Choice*. Harvard University Press.

Ernst, Daniel R. 2014. *Tocqueville's Nightmare: The Administrative State Emerges in America, 1900–1940*. Oxford University Press.

Eskridge, William N. and Philip P. Frickey. 1994. "Foreword: Law as Equilibrium." *Harvard Law Review* 108:26–108.

Fanning, Deirdre. 1988. "First Monday Next October." *Forbes* p. 110.

Farnsworth, Ward, Dustin F. Guzior, and Anup Malani. 2010. "Ambiguity about Ambiguity: An Empirical Inquiry into Legal Interpretation." *Journal of Legal Analysis* 2:257–300.

Federal Deposit Insurance Corporation. 1999. "An Examination of the Banking Crises of the 1980s and Early 1990s."

Friedman, Barry. 2006. "Taking Law Seriously." *Perspectives on Politics* 4:261–276.

Gebbia-Pinetti, Karen M. 2000. "Interpreting the Bankruptcy Code: An Empirical Study of the Supreme Court's Bankruptcy Decisions." *Chapman Law Review* 3:173–308.

George, Tracey E. 1997. "Developing a Positive Theory of Decisionmaking on U.S. Courts of Appeals." *Ohio State Law Journal* 58:1635–1696.

Gibson, Richard H. 1984. "The New Law on Rejection of Collective Bargaining Agreements in Chapter 11: An Analysis of 11 U.S.C 1113." *American Bankruptcy Law Journal* 58:325–348.

Gibson, S. Elizabeth. 1995. "Congressional Response to Hoffman and Nordic Village: Amended Section 106 and Sovereign Immunity." *American Bankruptcy Law Journal* 69:311–347.

Gillman, Howard. 2001. "What's Law Got to Do with It? Judicial Behavioralists Test the 'Legal Model' of Judicial Decision Making." *Law & Social Inquiry* 26:465–504.

Glynn, Matt. 2009. "After Bankruptcy, What Next?: Outcome Uncertain as Stakeholders Confront Sweeping Changes That Will Affect How General Motors Does Business in Wake of Biggest Upheaval in Firm's History." *Buffalo News* p. A1.

Graber, Mark A. 1998. "Federalist or Friends of Adams: The Marshall Court and Party Politics." *Studies in American Political Development* 12:229–266.

Granelli, James. 1994. "Partners Take Gamble–And Lose." *Los Angeles Times* p. D1.

Greenhouse, Linda. 1984. "Unions Lose as High Court Backs Companies in Bankruptcy Filings." *New York Times* p. A1.

Greenhouse, Linda. 2006. *Becoming Justice Blackmun: Harry Blackmun's Supreme Court Journey*. Times Books.

Haines, Randolph J. 2003. "The Uniformity Power: Why Bankruptcy Is Different." *American Bankruptcy Law Journal* 77:129–198.

Halliday, Terence C. and Bruce G. Carruthers. 2009. *Bankrupt: Global Lawmaking and Systemic Financial Crisis*. Stanford, Calif.: Stanford University Press.

Hammond, Thomas, Chris Bonneau, and Reginald Sheehan. 2005. *Strategic Behavior and Policy Choice on the U.S. Supreme Court*. Stanford University Press.

Harvey, Anna. 2014. *A Mere Machine: The Supreme Court, Congress, and American Democracy*. Yale University Press.

Harvey, Anna and Michael J. Woodruff. 2013. "Confirmation Bias in the United States Supreme Court Judicial Database." *Journal of Law, Economics, and Organization* 29:414–460.

Heidt, Kathryn R. 1991. "Interest under Section 506(b) of the Bankruptcy Code: The Right, the Rate and the Relationship to Bankruptcy Policy." *Utah Law Review* 1991:361–406.

Higgins, Tim. 2009. "GM, UAW Compromise." *Detroit Free Press* p. 1A.

Hirshman, Linda. 2015. *Sisters in Law: How Sandra Day O'Connor and Ruth Bader Ginsburg Went to the Supreme Court and Changed the World*. Harper.

House Committee on the Judiciary. 1977. "H.R. Rep. No. 95–595, 95th Cong., 1st Sess."

House Committee on the Judiciary. 1994. "H.R. Rep. No. 103–835, 103rd Cong., 2nd Sess."

Hume, Robert J. 2014. "Deciding Not to Decide: The Politics of Recusals on the U.S. Supreme Court." *Law & Society Review* 48:621–655.

Hutchinson, Dennis. 1998. *The Man Who Once Was Whizzer White: A Portrait of Justice Byron R. White*. Free Press.

Hyde, Justin and Tim Higgins. 2009. "UAW Strike Would Kill Loans; Auto Rescue Terms Raise Stakes in Deal Mandating Changes in Pay, Benefits." *Detroit Free Press* p. 1.

Internal Revenue Service. 1988. "Annual Report."

Jackson, Thomas H. 2001. *The Logic and Limits of Bankruptcy Law*. Washington, DC: Beard Books.

Jacobi, Tonja and Matthew Sag. 2009. "Taking the Measure of Ideology: Empirically Measuring Supreme Court Cases." *Georgetown Law Journal* 98:1–75.

Jasanoff, Sheila. 1990. *The Fifth Branch: Science Advisers as Policymakers*. Harvard University Press.

Jeffries, John. 2001. *Justice Lewis F. Powell: A Biography*. Fordham University Press, 2nd edition.

Jensen, Susan. 2005. "A Legislative History of the Bankruptcy Abuse Prevention and Consumer Protection Act of 2005." *American Bankruptcy Law Journal* 79:485–569.

Johnson, Timothy R., Paul J. Wahlbeck, and James F. Spriggs. 2006. "The Influence of Oral Arguments on the U.S. Supreme Court." *The American Political Science Review* 100:99–113.

Johnson, Timothy R., Ryan C. Black, and Justin Wedeking. 2012. *Oral Arguments and Coalition Formation on the U.S. Supreme Court: A Deliberate Dialogue*. University of Michigan Press.

Kahn, Ronald and Ken I. Kersch. 2006. *The Supreme Court and American Political Development*. University Press of Kansas.

Kearney, Joseph D. and Thomas W. Merrill. 1999. "Influence of Amicus Curiae Briefs on the Supreme Court." *University of Pennsylvania Law Review* 148:743–855.

Keck, Thomas M. 2007. "Party, Policy, or Duty: Why Does the Supreme Court Invalidate Federal Statutes?" *The American Political Science Review* 101:321–338.

Keller, Bill. 1984. "Bankruptcy Bill Sparks Business-Labor Dispute." *New York Times* p. D2.

Kennedy, Frank R. 1973. "The Report of the Bankruptcy Commission: The First Five Chapters of the Proposed New Bankruptcy Act." *Indiana Law Journal* 49:422–433.

Klee, Kenneth N. 1980. "Legislative History of the New Bankruptcy Code." *American Bankruptcy Law Journal* 54:275–297.

Knight, Jack and Lee Epstein. 1997. *The Choices Justices Make*. CQ Press.

Landes, William M. and Richard A. Posner. 2009. "Rational Judicial Behavior: A Statistical Study." *Journal of Legal Analysis* 1:775–831.

Larsen, Allison Orr. 2012. "Confronting Supreme Court Fact Finding." *Virginia Law Review* 98:1255–1312.

Larsen, Allison Orr and Neal E. Devins. 2016. "The Amicus Machine." *Virginia Law Review* 102 (forthcoming).

Latour, Bruno. 2010. *The Making of Law: An Ethnography of the Conseil d'Etat*. Polity.

Lawless, Robert M. 1996. "Legisprudence through a Bankruptcy Lens: A Study in the Supreme Court's Bankruptcy Cases." *Syracuse Law Review* 47:1–119.

Lazarus, Richard. 2007. "Advocacy Matters before and within the Supreme Court: Transforming the Court by Transforming the Bar." *Georgetown Law Journal* 96:1487–1564.

Lazarus, Richard. 2011. "The National Environmental Policy Act in the U.S. Supreme Court: A Reappraisal and a Peek behind the Curtains." *Georgetown Law Journal* 100:1507–1586.

Lewin, Tamar. 1984. "Wide Impact Seen in Labor Decision." *New York Times* p. D25.

Lim, Youngsik. 2000. "An Empirical Analysis of Supreme Court Justices' Decision Making." *Journal of Legal Studies* 29:721–752.

Littwin, Angela. 2011. "The Affordability Paradox: How Consumer Bankruptcy's Greatest Weakness May Account for Its Surprising Success." *William and Mary Law Review* 52:1933–2023.

Los Angeles Times. 1989. "High Court Gives Creditors of Bankrupt Firms a Break." p. A3.

Maltzman, Forrest, James F. Spriggs II, and Paul J. Wahlbeck. 2000. *Crafting Law on the Supreme Court: The Collegial Game*. Cambridge University Press.

Maltzman, Forrest and Paul J. Wahlbeck. 1996. "Strategic Policy Considerations and Voting Fluidity on the Burger Court." *The American Political Science Review* 90:581–592.

Mann, Bruce H. 2003. *Republic of Debtors: Bankruptcy in the Age of American Independence*. Harvard University Press.

Mann, Ronald J. 1997. "Strategy and Force in the Liquidation of Secured Debt." *Michigan Law Review* 96:159–244.

Martin, Andrew D., Kevin M. Quinn, and Lee Epstein. 2004. "The Median Justice on the United States Supreme Court." *North Carolina Law Review* 83:1275–1321.

Mashaw, Jerry L. 2012. *Creating the Administrative Constitution: The Lost One Hundred Years of American Administrative Law*. New Haven: Yale University Press.

McKenna, Judith A. and Elizabeth C. Wiggins. 2002. "Alternative Structures for Bankruptcy Appeals." *American Bankruptcy Law Journal* 76:625–710.

McNollgast. 1994. "Politics and the Courts: A Positive Theory of Judicial Doctrine and the Rule of Law." *Southern California Law Review* 68:1631–1683.

Miles, Thomas J. and Cass R. Sunstein. 2006. "Do Judges Make Regulatory Policy – An Empirical Investigation of Chevron." *University of Chicago Law Review* 73:823–881.

Miles, Thomas J. and Cass R. Sunstein. 2008. "The New Legal Realism." *University of Chicago Law Review* 75:831–851.

Mund, Geraldine. 2004. "A Look behind the Ruling: The Supreme Court and the Unconstitutionality of the Bankruptcy Act of 1978." *The American Bankruptcy Law Journal* 78:401–425.

Murphy, Walter F. 1964. *Elements of Judicial Strategy*. University of Chicago Press.

Nadelmann, Kurt H. 1957. "On the Origin of the Bankruptcy Clause." *American Journal of Legal History* 1:215–228.

Nash, Jonathan Remy and Rafael I. Pardo. 2011. "Does Ideology Matter in Bankruptcy – Voting Behavior on the Courts of Appeals." *William and Mary Law Review* 53:919–985.

National Conference of Commissioners on Uniform State Laws. 2013. "Uniform Fraudulent Transfer Act: Summary."

National Crime Victim Law Institute. 2011. "History of Victims' Rights."

National Taxpayer Advocate. 2009. "Annual Report to Congress."

Nelson, Grant S. and Dale A. Whitman. 2007. *Real Estate Finance Law*. Thomson/West.

New York Times. 1984. "1.1 Million Fine in Dumping Case." p. A31.
Oregonian. 1988. "High Court to Hear Business Cases." p. D7.
Owens, Ryan J. 2010. "The Separation of Powers and Supreme Court Agenda Setting." *American Journal of Political Science* 54:412–427.
Owens, Ryan J. and Patrick C. Wohlfarth. 2014. "State Solicitors General, Appellate Expertise, and State Success before the U.S. Supreme Court." *Law & Society Review* 48:657–685.
Pacelle, Richard. 2015. *The Supreme Court in a Separation of Powers System: The Nation's Balance Wheel*. New York, NY: Routledge.
Pardo, Rafael I. and Kathryn A. Watts. 2012. "The Structural Exceptionalism of Bankruptcy Administration." *UCLA Law Review* 60:384–460.
Pildes, Richard H. 2013. "Institutional Formalism and Realism in Constitutional and Public Law." *Supreme Court Review* 2013:1–54.
Plank, Thomas E. 1995. "The Constitutional Limits of Bankruptcy." *Tennessee Law Review* 63:487–584.
Plank, Thomas E. 1998. "Why Bankruptcy Judges Need Not and Should Not Be Article III Judges." *American Bankruptcy Law Journal* 72:567–642.
Posner, The Honorable Richard A. 2010. *How Judges Think*. Harvard University Press.
Powe, Lucas A., Jr. 2009. *The Supreme Court and the American Elite, 1789–2008*. Harvard University Press.
President's Task Force on Victims of Crime. 1982. "Final Report."
Pritchard, A. C. 2002. "Justice Lewis F. Powell, Jr., and the Counterrevolution in the Federal Securities Laws." *Duke Law Journal* 52:841–949.
Pritchard, A. C and Robert B. Thompson. 2009. "Securities Law and the New Deal Justices." *Virginia Law Review* 95:841–926.
Pritchett, C. Herman. 1948. *The Roosevelt Court: A Study in Judicial Politics and Values, 1937–1947*. Macmillan Co.
Provine, Doris Marie. 1980. *Case Selection in the United States Supreme Court*. University of Chicago Press.
Purcell, Edward A., Jr. 2000. *Brandeis and the Progressive Constitution: Erie, the Judicial Power, and the Politics of the Federal Courts in Twentieth-Century America*. Yale University Press, 2nd edition.
Rasmussen, Robert K. 1993. "A Study of the Costs and Benefits of Textualism: The Supreme Court's Bankruptcy Cases." *Washington University Law Quarterly* 71:535–598.
Reilly, Marie T. 2005. "A Search for Reason in Reasonably Equivalent Value after BFP v. Resolution Trust Group." *American Bankruptcy Institute Law Review* 13:261–295.
Richards, Mark J. and Herbert M. Kritzer. 2002. "Jurisprudential Regimes in Supreme Court Decision Making." *The American Political Science Review* 96:305–320.
Roe, Mark J. and David Skeel. 2009. "Assessing the Chrysler Bankruptcy." *Michigan Law Review* 108:727–771.
Rogers, James Steven. 1982. "The Impairment of Secured Creditors' Rights in Reorganization: A Study of the Relationship between the Fifth Amendment and the Bankruptcy Clause." *Harvard Law Review* 96:973–1071.
Rosenberg, Rosalind. 1984. "Bankruptcy and the Collective Bargaining Agreement – A Brief Lesson in the Use of the Constitutional System of Checks and Balances." *American Bankruptcy Law Journal* 58:293–323.

Ruth, George E. 1999. *Commercial Lending*. American Bankers Association.
Salpukas, Agis. 1984. "Continental Air Unions Lose Attack on Pay Cut." *New York Times* p. D1.
Salpukas, Agis. 1985. "Gamble Paying off at Continental Air." *New York Times* p. D1.
Sandage, Scott A. 2005. *Born Losers: A History of Failure in America*. Harvard University Press.
Scalia, Antonin and Bryan A. Garner. 2012. *Reading Law: The Interpretation of Legal Texts*. West, 1st edition.
Schwartz, Alan. 2001. "The New Textualism and the Rule of Law Subtext in the Supreme Court's Bankruptcy Jurisprudence." *New York Law School Law Review* 45:149–197.
Schwartz, Bernard. 1983. *Super Chief: Earl Warren and His Supreme Court – A Judicial Biography*. New York University Press.
Schwartz, Bernard. 1997. *Decision: How the Supreme Court Decides Cases*. Oxford University Press.
Segal, Jeffrey A. and Harold J. Spaeth. 1993. *The Supreme Court and the Attitudinal Model*. Cambridge University Press.
Segal, Jeffrey A., Chad Westerland, and Stefanie A. Lindquist. 2011. "Congress, the Supreme Court, and Judicial Review: Testing a Constitutional Separation of Powers Model." *American Journal of Political Science* 55:89–104.
Segal, Jeffrey A. and Harold J. Spaeth. 2002. *The Supreme Court and the Attitudinal Model Revisited*. Cambridge University Press.
Senate Committee on the Judiciary. 1978. "S. Rep. No. 95-989, 95th Cong., 1st Sess."
Silver, Nate. 2013. "In Supreme Court Debate on Voting Rights Act, a Dubious Use of Statistics." *Five Thirty Eight*.
Skeel, David A. 2003. *Debt's Dominion: A History of Bankruptcy Law in America*. Princeton University Press.
Skeel, David A. Jr. 2009. "Bankruptcy Phobia." *Temple Law Review* 82:333–349.
Skeel, David A. Jr. 2012. "States of Bankruptcy." *University of Chicago Law Review* 79:677–735.
Skeel, David A. Jr. 2015. "From Chrysler and General Motors to Detroit." *Widener Law Review* 24:121–148.
Skeel, David A. Jr. and Thomas H. Jackson. 2012. "Transaction Consistency and the New Finance in Bankruptcy." *Columbia Law Review* 112:152–202.
Spaeth, Harold J. 1979. *Supreme Court Policy Making: Explanation and Prediction*. W.H. Freeman and Co.
Stanley, David T. and Marjorie Girth. 1971. *Bankruptcy: Problem, Process, Reform*. Brookings Institution Press.
Stark, Debra Pogrund. 1995. "The Emperor Still Has Clothes: Fraudulent Conveyance Challenges after the BFP Decision." *South Carolina Law Review* 47:563–613.
Stein, Benjamin. 1989. "On the Junk Heap - The Trashing of a Multi-Billion Dollar California S&L." *Barron's* pp. 6–10.
Stern, Gary H. and Ron J. Feldman. 2004. *Too Big to Fail: The Hazards of Bank Bailouts*. Brookings Institution Press.
Stern, Seth and Stephen Wermiel. 2010. *Justice Brennan: Liberal Champion*. Houghton Mifflin Harcourt.
Stevens, John Paul. 2011. *Five Chiefs: A Supreme Court Memoir*. Little, Brown and Company, 1st edition.

Stevens, John Paul. 2014. *Six Amendments: How and Why We Should Change the Constitution*. Little, Brown and Company.

Sunstein, Cass R., David Schkade, Lisa M. Ellman, and Andres Sawicki. 2006. *Are Judges Political?: An Empirical Analysis of the Federal Judiciary*. Brookings Institution Press.

Sweat, Ray E. 1984. "Title Insurance in 1984: Jurisdiction and the Bankruptcy Amendments and Federal Judgeship Act of 1984." *PLI/Real* 251:327–358.

Tabb, Charles Jordan. 1987. "The Bankruptcy Reform Act in the Supreme Court." *University of Pittsburgh Law Review* 49:477–589.

Tabb, Charles Jordan. 1995. "The History of the Bankruptcy Laws in the United States." *American Bankruptcy Institute Law Review* 3:5–51.

Tabb, Charles Jordan and Robert M. Lawless. 1991. "Of Commas, Gerunds, and Conjunctions: The Bankruptcy Jurisprudence of the Rehnquist Court." *Syracuse Law Review* 42:823–892.

Texas Department of Insurance. 1993. "Form T-1."

Townsend, Ed. 1984a. "As Continental Wins Its Bankruptcy Filing, Unions Seek More Contract Protection." *Christian Science Monitor* p. 3.

Townsend, Ed. 1984b. "Bankruptcy Ruling Gives Employer an Edge in Labor Bargaining." *Christian Science Monitor* p. 5.

Trugman, Wendy Lynn. 1984. "The Bankruptcy Act of 1984: Marathon Revisited." *Yale Law and Policy Review* 3:231–244.

Tye, Larry. 1990. "A Model of S&L Failure: Stumbling on a New Playing Field." *Boston Globe* p. 1.

Wahlbeck, Paul J., James F. Spriggs, and Forrest Maltzman. 1998. "Marshalling the Court: Bargaining and Accommodation on the United States Supreme Court." *American Journal of Political Science* 42:294–315.

Wahlbeck, Paul J., James F. Spriggs, and Forrest Maltzman. 1999. "The Politics of Dissents and Concurrences on the U.S. Supreme Court." *American Politics Quarterly* 27:488–514.

Warner, G. Ray. 1989. "Katchen Up in Bankruptcy: The New Jury Trial Right." *American Bankruptcy Law Journal* 63:1–51.

Warren, Elizabeth and Jay Lawrence Westbrook. 2005. *The Law of Debtors and Creditors: Text, Cases, and Problems*. Aspen Publishers, 5th edition.

Wasby, Stephen L. 1993. *The Supreme Court in the Federal Judicial System*. 4th edition.

Washington Post. 1984. "Continental Asks Judge to Void Contracts." p. F1.

Washington Post. 1988. "Supreme Court Calendar." p. A12.

Weiss, Barbara. 1986. *The Hell of the English: Bankruptcy and the Victorian Novel*. Bucknell University Press.

West, Martha S. 1986. "Life after Bildisco: Section 1113 and the Duty to Bargain in Good Faith." *Ohio State Law Journal* 47:65–161.

Westbrook, Jay Lawrence. 2014. "Sovereign Debt and Exclusions from Insolvency Proceedings." In *A Debt Restructuring Mechanism for Sovereigns: Do We Need a Legal Procedure?*, pp. 251–259. Beck/Hart.

Whiteman, David. 1985. "The Fate of Policy Analysis in Congressional Decision Making: Three Types of Use in Committees." *The Western Political Quarterly* 38:294–311.

Whitford, William C. 2007. "A History of the Automobile Lender Provisions of BAPCPA." *University of Illinois Law Review* 2007:143–193.

Whittington, Keith E. 2001. *Constitutional Construction: Divided Powers and Constitutional Meaning*. Harvard University Press.

Wilkerson, William R. 2006. "The Emergence of Internet Citations in U.S. Supreme Court Opinions." *Justice System Journal* 27:323–338.

Young, Ernest A. 1999. "Sovereign Immunity and the Future of Federalism." *Supreme Court Review* 1999:1–79.

Index

abandonment power
  in bankruptcy proceedings, 128–129
  oral arguments in *Midlantic* concerning, 135–136
  Powell's discussion in *Midlantic* of, 138–142
  Rehnquist's opinion concerning, 137–138
  Solicitor General's discussion of, 142–144
  Supreme Court bench memoranda on, 133–135
abortion rights cases
  amicus briefs in, 195
academic groups
  amici filed by, 212–214, 216–218
"adequate protection" payments, 219–221
administrative law judges
  in Bankruptcy Act of 1898, 44–46
  OSHA enforcement and, 57–59
Affordable Health Care Act, 194–195
AFL-CIO, 120–121
aggrandizement issue
  Wellness case and, 73
airline industry deregulation, 101–102
Airline Pilots Association, 119
Alito, Samuel (Justice)
  opinions in bankruptcy rulings of, 35
  Wellness case and, 73
alter ego claim
  Wellness case and, 75–76
American Automobile Manufacturers Association, 219–221
American Bar Foundation, 25
American Political Development Tradition, 10, 19
amici
  contributions to Supreme Court bankruptcy jurisprudence, 211–221
  failure of, 220
  impact in bankruptcy of, 210–211
  information derived from, 214–221
  information sources for, 247–248
  judicial decisionmaking and influence of, 13–15
  in *Kelly v. Robinson*, 150
  in *Midlantic* case, 214
  quantitative analysis of, 211–214
  sheltering in bankruptcy decisions and, 218–219
  Solicitor General as amicus, 198–199
  Supreme Court and, 193–196
  in *Timbers* case, 222–223
Arkison, see Executive Benefits Insurance Agency v. Arkison
Article I (U.S. Constitution)
  bankruptcy and, 76–78
  federal legislative power under, 79–83
  Granfinanciera case and, 59–61
  Wellness case and, 75
Article III (U.S. Constitution)
  arguments in *Marathon* case and, 52–56

bankruptcy and, 76–78
federal judicial power under, 79–83
Granfinanciera case and, 56–65
jurisdiction in bankruptcy process and, 46–50
Stern v. Marshall case and, 67
Wellness case and, 73
Associates Commercial Corp. v. Rash, 219–221
Atlas Roofing Co. v. Occupational Safety & Health Comm'n, 57–59
Granfinanciera case and, 59–61, 63–65
"attitudinal" decision-making, 8–11, 16–17

Bailey, Michael A., 11, 14, 18
Baird, Douglas G., 233–234
Baker Botts v. ASARCO, 223–225
balance of equities principle
in *Bildisco*, 112–118
in *Kevin Steel* case, 103–104
in REA case, 104–105
Balleisen, Edward J., 39
banking industry
secured credit bankruptcy cases and, 202–206
Bank of America v. Caulkett, 215
Bank of America v. Caulkett, 223–225
Bankruptcy Abuse Prevention and Consumer Protection Act of 2005 (BAPCPA), 29, 200–202, 206–209, 220–221
Bankruptcy Act of 1841, 39–41
Bankruptcy Act of 1898, 25, 44–46
fair equivalent value principle in, 178
fraudulent conveyance and, 176
Internal Revenue petitions involving, 159–161
Midlantic case and language of, 136–137, 143–144
property abandonment in, 128–129
Ron Pair case and, 168–170
Bankruptcy Amendments and Federal Judgeship Act of 1984, 29, 121
Bankruptcy Clause
Congressional power concerning, 39–41
constitutional doctrine and, 76–78
Granfinanciera deliberations and, 59–61
grant of authority in *Marathon* and, 48–56
Hoffman case and, 87–91
Katz case and, 95–96, 216–218
quasi-judicial process in Bankruptcy Code and, 42–43
Ron Pair case and, 168–170
sovereign immunity and, 87, 220–221
Supreme Court indifference to, 231–232
Wellness case and, 76–78
Bankruptcy Code of 1978, *see also* specific chapters, e.g., Chapter 7
abandonment power in, 128–132, 137–138
administrative weaknesses in, 193–198
amendments to, 29
Bankruptcy Power interpretations and, 98
comprehensive vision of, 43–48
Congressional adoption of, 24–30
constitutional doctrine and, 48–56, 206–209
contract termination in, 100–101
criminal restitution payments and, 149–150
EBIA case and, 69–71
fraudulent transfers and, 175–180
Granfinanciera case and, 56–65
Hoffman case and, 83–91
Justices' preconceptions concerning, 227–229
Kelly v. Robinson and, 153–156
labor law and, 99–102
Marathon case and role of, 52–56
Midlantic case and, 133–137, 142–144
National Labor Relations Act and, 100–103, 123
preferential payments as violation of, 92–93
quasi-judicial process in, 42–43
Ron Pair case and changes to, 165–170
Section 106, 91–94, 216
Section 506, 160–165

Section 523, 1, 150
Section 544, 133–135
Section 548, 174–180
Section 1113, 121–123
Section 1167, 108–109
Section 1322, 171–173
secured credit bankruptcy cases and, 202–206
sheltering of payments in, 218–219
sovereign immunity and, 79, 82–83, 216–218
Supreme Court rulings and, 3–4, 12, 16–17, 40–41, 96–97, 191–192
"unmistakable clarity" standard and, 125–126
bankruptcy court
Kelly v. Robinson in, 148–149
in *Kevin Steel* case, 103–104
in *Midlantic* case, 130–132
practices of, as information source, 224–225
Ron Pair in, 161–162
state sovereignty and power of, 174–175
Supreme Court distrust of, 233–234
bankruptcy law
administrative vacuum in, 193–196
in *Bildisco* case, 110–112
characteristics of Supreme Court cases involving, 37–38
Congressional power concerning, 39–41
constitutional doctrine and, 76–78
criminal law *vs.*, 146–157
cultural resistance to debt relief and, 234–235
environmental law *vs.*, 12, 98
evolution of Supreme Court on, 68–76
as information source, 221–229
legal academic perspective on, 11–13
qualitative analysis of judicial decisionmaking and, 21–23
relief provisions in, 28
Solicitor General and, 206–209
sovereign immunity and, 79
Bankruptcy Power
in Bankruptcy Act of 1898, 44–46
Bankruptcy Code interpretations of, 98
collective bargaining and, 99–100
constitutional scope of, 17–18
economic importance of, 197–198
government construction of, 198–199
ideology of Supreme Court justices concerning, 33–35
relief provided by, 31–32
Ron Pair case and, 168–170
sovereign immunity and, 79
Stern v. Marshall case and, 68–76
Supreme Court interpretation of, 42–43, 95, 208, 231–232
Bankruptcy Reform Act of 1994
Supreme Court rulings and, 12–13, 94–96
Bankruptcy Technical Corrections Act of 2010, 29
bankruptcy trade groups
amici filed by, 212–214, 216–218
Barton, Russell, 180–182
Bellingham Insurance Agency, 69–71
BFP v. Resolution Trust Corporation, 12, 20, 22–23, 98, 174–192
argument and decision by Justices in, 185–187
background details of, 174–175
bankruptcy proceeding in, 183
dispute details in, 180–182
dissenting opinions of justices in, 189–191
Durret case and, 178–180
federal *vs.* state law and, 177–179
foreclosure as fraudulent conveyance in, 175–180
lower court rulings on, 180–184
majority opinion of Justices in, 187–189
review granted by Supreme Court, 184–185
secured credit issues in, 190, 202–206
Supreme Court jurisprudence concerning, 184–191
Bildisco case, *see NLRB v. Bildisco*
Black, Hugo (Justice)

opinions in bankruptcy proceedings of, 45–46
Black, Ryan C., 13–15, 18
Blackmun, Harry (Justice), 2
arguments in *Marathon* case, 50
bench memoranda in Bildisco from, 108–109
BFP case, 185–187, 189, 190, 191
Bildisco case and, 107
Continental Airlines bankruptcy and *Bildisco* ruling and, 119
Granfinanciera case and, 59–61, 63–65
Hoffman case and memos of, 84–87
Hoffman opinion of, 87–91
initial *Bildisco* decision and, 110–112
Kelly v. Robinson and, 151–153, 155–156
Midlantic case and, 133–137, 140–142
Nordic Village case and, 91–94
opinions in bankruptcy cases of, 49–50
opinions in securities and tax rulings of, 35–36
retirement of, 94–96
Ron Pair case and, 165–170
state sovereign immunity opinions, 81–83, 87
Union Carbide opinion of, 58–59
Booth v. Maryland, 147
Brennan, William J. (Justice)
arguments in *Marathon* case, 50–56
Bildisco case and, 107, 117–118
constitutional issues and bankruptcy and, 76–78
Continental Airlines bankruptcy and *Bildisco* ruling and, 119
Granfinanciera case and, 61–65
Hoffman opinion of, 87–91
initial *Bildisco* decision and, 110–112
Midlantic case and, 138–140
onions in securities rulings of, 35–36
retirement of, 91–92
Ron Pair case and, 167–170
state sovereign immunity opinions, 82–83
Stern v. Marshall case and, 65–68
Union Carbide opinion of, 58–59
Breyer, Steven (Justice)
Katz case and, 95–96
opinions in bankruptcy rulings of, 35
Stern v. Marshall case and, 50–56, 73
Brookings Institution, 25, 26
Brotherhood of Railway, Airline and Steamship Clerks, Freight Handlers, Express and Station Employees, AFL-CIO v. *REA Express, Inc.*
Bildisco case and, 106
Brotherhood of Railway, Airline and Steamship Clerks, Freight Handlers, Express and Station Employees, AFL-CIO v. *REA Express, Inc.*, 104–105
Bildisco case and, 107–109, 111–113, 120–121
Brown v. Board of Education, 195
Brunstad, Eric, 212–214
Bullard v. Blue Hills Bank, 233–234
Bureau of Labor Statistics, 101–102
Burger, Warren (Chief Justice), 48–50
arguments in *Marathon* case and, 50
Bildisco case and, 107, 112–118
Kelly v. Robinson and, 150
Midlantic case and, 133–137
resignation of, 60
state sovereign immunity opinions, 81
business bankruptcies
bankruptcy law and, 28, 121–123
Bildisco case and, 120–121
Bussel, Dan, 1, 12, 29

Carter, Jimmy (President), 25
Casey, Anthony, 233–234
Catron, John (Justice), 39–41
Central Virginia Community College v. Katz, 94–96
amici filed in, 216–218
Bankruptcy Clause and, 96–97, 231–232
information sources in, 222
certiorari jurisdiction of Supreme Court
bankruptcy decisions and, 27
in *Ron Pair* case, 162–163
CFTC v. Schor, 67
Chamber of Commerce, 121
Chapter 7 (Bankruptcy Code of 1978)
consumer relief under, 28

Dewsnup v. Timm case and, 215
Office of United States Trustee cases and, 200–202
Chapter 11 (Bankruptcy Code of 1978)
in *BFP* case, 183
in *Bildisco* case, 112–118
business bankruptcies and, 28
debtors' control enhanced in, 29
Marathon case and, 48–56
in *Nordic Village* case, 91–94
REA Express case and, 104–105
Chapter 13 (Bankruptcy Code of 1978)
consumer relief under, 28
debtors discharge and, 156–157
Chase & Sanborn Corporation, 56–65
child support payments
Supreme Court rulings concerning, 146–148
Chisholm v. Georgia, 80–82
Christian Science Monitor, 120–121
Chrysler bankruptcy filing, 110–112, 121–123, 234–235
City of New York v. Saper, 160–161
claim/no-claim dichotomy
in bankruptcy jurisprudence, 67, 68
"clarity" requirement
in *Hoffman* case, 87–91
Clean Air Act, 126–127
Clean Water Act, 126–127
clear statement rule, *see* "unmistakable clarity" standard
Cohen v. de la Cruz, 164–165, 226–227
collateral in bankruptcy cases
amici filings concerning, 219–221
fraudulent conveyance and, 175–180
collective bargaining
Bankruptcy Power and, 99–100
in *Bildisco* case, 105–118
Continental bankruptcy and, 118
federal regulations concerning, 100–101
laws concerning, 102–103
in REA Express case, 104–105
Collier treaties, 137
Commerce Clause
bankruptcy proceedings and, 95
commercial law
bankruptcy proceedings and, 45
Commission on the Bankruptcy Law of the United States, 24–30, 232–233
Bankruptcy Code enactment and, 43–48
state sovereign immunity and, 83–84
Comprehensive Environmental Response, Compensation, and Liability Act (CERCLA), 82–87, 126–127
"Conference" (of Supreme Court Justices)
Granfinanciera case and, 59–61
Kelly v. Robinson deliberations, 153
Marathon case and, 48–56
in *Midatlantic* case, 136–137
in *Ron Pair* case, 165
Congress
Bankruptcy Code enactment by, 24–30, 43–48, 125–126
BFP case and, 178
Bildisco case and reaction of, 120–121
Eleventh Amendment and power of, 79
Granfinanciera case and authority of, 62–63
judicial appointments powers of, 43–48
jurisdictional reforms in bankruptcy process by, 46–48
Marathon case arguments over power of, 52–56
OSHA enforcement orders and, 57–59
power over bankruptcy law of, 39–41, 49–50, 61–65
quasi-judicial process in Bankruptcy Code and powers of, 42–43
Rake v. Wade case and, 171–173
sovereign immunity issues and, 79–83
state sovereign immunity and bankruptcy law, 83–84
Stern v. Marshall case and authority of, 66–68
Supreme Court bankruptcy rulings rejected by, 11, 29–30, 94–97
Congressional Quarterly

"salience" scores of Supreme Court rulings in, 33
consent
bankruptcy adjudication and role of, 68–76
in *Wellness* case, 75–76
constitutional doctrine
bankruptcy interests and, 48–56, 206–209
in *Hoffman* case, 87–91
as information, 222
irrelevance of bankruptcy to, 76–78, 96–97
Solicitor General's bankruptcy cases and, 206–209
state sovereign immunity and, 94–96
"constrained" decision-making, 8–11
The Constrained Court (Bailey & Maltzman), 11
consumer relief
in bankruptcy law, 28
Continental Airlines, bankruptcy of, 101–102, 118, 225
contract termination
in Bankruptcy Code, 100–101
in Bildisco bankruptcy filing, 105–107, 114–118
in *Kevin Steel* case, 103–104
in *Midlantic* case, 143–144
in REA case, 104–105
conveyances
in real property law, 175–180
"core" proceedings
EBIA case and, 69–71
creditors
Bankruptcy Code of 1978 provisions concerning, 28
fraudulent debtors and, 175–180
in *Midlantic* case, 135–136
non-statutory exceptors and, 159–161
oversecured creditors, 160–162
in *Ron Pair* case, 170–171
sheltering of, 217–219
criminal law
amicus briefs in, 195–196
bankruptcy *vs.*, 146–157
debtor discharge and, 151–153, 156–157
victims' rights *vs.* criminal restitution, 146–148
criminal restitution, *see also* restitutionary obligation
victims' rights *vs.*, 146–148
Criminal Victims Protection Act, 156–157
cross-jurisdictional insolvency, 95
current events
as information source in bankruptcy cases, 225
Cuyahoga River fire, 126–127

debtor discharge
in bankruptcy law, 28
in *Bildisco* case, 108–109, 113
in *Dewsnup v. Timm* case, 215
fraudulent debtors and, 175–180
in *Kelly v. Robinson*, 151–153, 156–157
labor law and bankruptcy and, 100–103
in *Midlantic* case, 135–136
"new entity" approach to, 105–107
Office of the United States Trustee cases, 198–202
as restitutionary obligation, 154–155
in *Ron Pair* case, 164–165
trustee's limits on, 142–144
debtor-in-possession
in *BFP* case, 194–195
in *Kevin Steel* case, 103–104
"new entity" principle and, 106
property transfers in foreclosure and, 174–175
debt relief
cultural resistance to, 234–235
Dellmuth v. Muth, 82–87, 90
Dembart, Lee, 12, 174
de novo review
EBIA case and, 69–71
Dewsnup v. Timm, 215, 224–225, 227–229
Dineen, Francis, 152, 153
district courts
bankruptcy proceedings and, 69–71
in *Kelly v. Robinson*, 149–150
Ron Pair in, 161–162
in *Wellness* case, 73
Douglas, William O. (Justice)

opinions in bankruptcy proceedings of, 45–46
Drexel Burnham Lambert, 182
due diligence
in *BFP* case, 182
Durrett v. Washington National Insurance Co., 178–180, 184
Dyk, Tim, 224–225

economic conditions
bankruptcy law and, 25, 121–123, 235–237
Education for All Handicapped Children Act (EAHCA), 82–83
Eighth Amendment
victims' rights and, 147
Eleventh Amendment
Bankruptcy Code and, 95
Hoffman case and, 84–91
non-monetary *vs.* monetary relief and, 226–227
in *Nordic Village* case, 92–93
sovereign immunity in bankruptcy and, 79–84, 87
environmental law
bankruptcy *vs.*, 12, 98
in *Midlantic* case, 143–144
Environmental Protection Agency (EPA), 126–127
Midlantic case and, 142–144
Union Carbide case and, 58–59
Equal Protection Clause, 195–196
ERISA retirement plans
bankruptcy cases involving, 198–199, 217–218
Ernst, Daniel R., 27
Executive Benefits Insurance Agency v. Arkison, 43–48, 69–71, 211
Executive Branch
absence of bankruptcy administrator in, 26, 193, 195, 206–209, 232–233
Ex parte Young, 80
expert knowledge
in amicus briefs, 194–195
external knowledge
judicial decision-making and role of, 13–15

fair equivalent value principle
foreclosure sales and, 178
fair market value
in *BFP* case, 187–191
fraudulent conveyance and, 175–180
federal agencies
bankruptcy law and, 98, 198–199, 206–209
Bildisco case and conflict between, 100–101
judicial decisionmaking and role of, 13–15
proposed bankruptcy agency, 26
secured credit bankruptcy cases and, 202–206
Federal Deposit Insurance Corporation (FDIC), 202–206
Federal Home Loan Mortgage Corporation, 178–180
federal judiciary system
bankruptcy judges proposal and, 26
independence and prestige of, 52
Federal Mediation and Conciliation Service, 102–103
federal regulatory legislation
bankruptcy law and, 98
fraudulent conveyance and, 177–179
as information source, 221–229
Midlantic case and, 137–138
Solicitor General and, 206–209
Federal Solid Waste Disposal Act, 127
federal sovereign immunity, 80–82, 202
fee bankruptcy cases
Solicitor General's role in, 200–202
Field v. Mans, 222–223
FIFRA, 58–59
Fitzpatrick v. Bitzer, 80–82
foreclosure proceedings
bankruptcy policy and, 235–237
in *BFP* case, 180–183
as fraudulent conveyance, 175–180
Justices' ignorance concerning, 224–225
Supreme Court arguments concerning, 185–187
Foreman, Sheldon and Ann, 180–182
Fourteenth Amendment

state sovereign immunity and, 80–82
fraudulent conveyance
in *BFP* case, 183, 189
foreclosure as, 175–180

game theory
strategic interactions of Justices and, 9–10
Gebbia-Pinetti, Karen M., 22–23
General Motors bankruptcy filing, 110–112, 121–123, 234–235
Gillman, Howard, 19
Ginsburg, Ruth Bader (Justice)
Affordable Health Care Act upheld by, 194–195
Bank of America v. Caulkett and, 223–225
BFP case and, 185, 187, 190–191
Katz case and, 95–96
onions in securities rulings of, 35–36
Stern v. Marshall case and, 67
Yates v. Hendon case and, 217
Goulet, Victor, 182
government loans
Chrysler and General Motors bankruptcy filings and, 121–123
Graber, Mark, 19
Granfinanciera, S. A. v. Nordberg, 43–48, 56–65
claim/no-claim distinction in, 68
constitutional issues and, 76–78
doctrinal principles in, 57–59
information sources in, 222
judicial deliberations over, 59–61
Stern v. Marshall case and, 66–68
Greenhouse, Linda, 120–121
Gregory v. Ashcroft, 187–188
Grogan v. Garner, 212
Grutter v. Gollinger, 195

Hall v. United States, 220
Hartford Underwriters Insurance v. Union Planters Bank, 219
Harvey, Anna, 9
Hirshman, Linda, 195–196
Hoffman v. Connecticut Department of Income Maintenance, 29–30
amici in, 216, 220–221
argument and decision in, 84–87
Congressional overruling of, 94–96
justices' opinions in, 87–91
Kelly v. Robinson and, 148
sovereign immunity issues in, 79, 82, 83, 202
Supreme Court jurisprudence in, 83–91
Holmes, Oliver Wendell (Justice), 159–161
Howard Delivery Service v. Zurich American Insurance Co., 220–221
hypotheticals, Justices' reliance on, 226–227

ideology scoring
statistical analysis of Supreme Court bankruptcy jurisprudence and, 31–36
Imperial Savings Association, 180–184
import, in amicus briefs, 195
injunctive relief
state sovereign immunity and, 80–82
in personam powers, 95
In re Bundles case, 180
In re Kerber Packing Co., 160
In re Klein, 40
In re Madrid, 178–180
in rem powers, 95
In re Quanta Res Corp., 130–132
institutional design
institutional capacity *vs.*, 13
lack of, in bankruptcy jurisprudence, 212–214
Supreme Court decisionmaking process and, 10, 31–36
internal papers of Supreme Court justices
qualitative analysis based on, 19–21
Internal Revenue Service (IRS)
bankruptcy cases and, 159–161
Ron Pair case and, 158–159, 161–162, 168–171
Supreme Court jurisprudence concerning, 35–36
tax-related bankruptcy cases, 200

investment property purchases
loan risk of, 182
involuntary transfers
foreclosures and, 177–179
IRAs
tax exempt status of, 198–199

judicial appointments
Congressional power over, 43–48
judicial opinions in Supreme Court bankruptcy cases, *see also* specific Justices
amici and, 193–196, 216–221
"attitudinal" *vs.* "constrained" approaches to, 8–11
BFP case and, 185–189
characteristics of bankruptcy cases involving, 37–38
Continental Airlines bankruptcy and *Bildisco* ruling and, 119
court-provided information in, 221–229
decision to hear Bildisco case, debate over, 107
division of Justices in *Ron Pair*, 168–170
external knowledge and, 13–15
Granfinanciera deliberations, 59–65
in *Hoffman*, 87–91
hypotheticals as basis for, 226–227
impact of amici in, 211–214
individual Justices' votes in bankruptcy cases and, 32
jurisdictional reforms to bankruptcy process and, 46–48
in *Kelly v. Robinson*, 153–156
in *Midlantic*, 137–142
in *Nordic Village*, 93–94
oral arguments as information source in, 223–225
preconceptions of Justices in, 227–229
role of internal papers in, 19–21
in *Ron Pair* case, 162–168
in sovereign immunity cases, 84–87
table of Justices' papers, 242–244
underenforcement of bankruptcy law in, 231–232
in *Union Carbide* case, 64
in *Wellness* case, 73
jurisdictional issues
Congressional bankruptcy reforms and, 46–48
in EBIA case, 69–71
Marathon bankruptcy case and, 48–56
in *Wellness* case, 71–76
jury trial
bankruptcy proceedings and, 45–46
Granfinanciera case and right to, 56, 59, 61, 65
Justice, Department of
Supreme Court decision-making and role of, 13–15, 45–46

Katchen v. Landy, 44–46, 50–56
Granfinanciera case and, 56–61, 63–65
Stern v. Marshall case and, 66–76
Katz case, *see Central Virginia Community College v. Katz*
Kearse, Amalya (Judge), 149–153
Keck, Thomas, 19
Keller, Bill, 120–121
Kelly v. Robinson, 1–3, 22–23, 29–30, 98
background on, 148–150
bankruptcy court litigation involving, 148–149
briefing and argument in, 151–153
Conference deliberations over, 153
Court of Appeals procedure in, 149–150
criminal law *vs.* bankruptcy in, 146–157
decision to review by Supreme Court, 150
hypotheticals used in, 226–227
legacy of, 156–157
opinions of Supreme Court justices in, 153–156
Supreme Court decision in, 150–156
victims' rights movement and, 147
Kennedy, Anthony (Justice), 61–65
Bank of America v. Caulkett and, 223–225
BFP case and, 185–189
on *Booth*, 147
Hoffman opinion of, 87–91

Katz case and, 95–96
Ron Pair case and, 165, 168–170
state sovereign immunity opinions, 81–83
Wellness case and, 73
Kennedy, Frank, 24
Stern v. Marshall case and, 65–68
Kevin Steel, supra case, 103–104
Bildisco case and, 105–109, 111–113

labor law
bankruptcy and, 99–110, 112, 121, 123, 124
Bankruptcy Code of 1978 and, 99, 100
in Bildisco case, 112–113
politics and, 101–102
REA Express case and, 104–105
Supreme Court interpretations of, 108–109
Larsen, Allison Orr, 211, 221
"later amendment trumps earlier" principle, 81
Lawless, Robert M., 12
Lawrence, Adam, 60–61
Lazarus, Richard, 18, 195–196
Lee, Rex, 50
legal academic perspective
on bankruptcy, 11–13
New Legal Realism and, 9–10
qualitative analysis of Supreme Court rulings and, 18–23
on Supreme Court rulings, 8
Lewis Jones case, 128–129
liability on a claim
in *Kelly v. Robinson*, 148–149
"likely to fail" standard
in Bildisco case, 112–113
Linda R. S. v. Richard D., 146–148
Littwin, Angela, 28
Lorenzo, Frank, 101–102, 119
Los Angeles Times, 171–173

magistrates analogy
in *Wellness* case, 73
Mahler, Russell, 126, 129–130
Maltzman, Forrest, 11, 14, 18
Mann, Bruce, 95–96, 217–218
Mansfield, Walter (Judge), 149–150
Marathon case, *see Northern Pipeline v. Marathon*
Markell, Bruce A., 12, 174
Marsh, Harold, 24
Marshall, J. Howard II, 65–68
Marshall, John (Justice), 39
Marshall, Pierce, 65–68
Marshall, Thurgood (Justice), 2
arguments in *Marathon* case, 50
Bildisco case and, 107
Granfinanciera case and, 61–65
Hoffman opinion of, 87–91, 216
initial *Bildisco* decision and, 110–112
Kelly v. Robinson and, 155–156
Midlantic case and, 136–137, 140
onions in securities rulings of, 35–36
opinions in bankruptcy rulings of, 35
retirement of, 91–92
Ron Pair case and, 165, 168–170
state sovereign immunity opinions, 81–83
Union Carbide opinion of, 58–59
Marshall, Vickie, 65–68
McCleskey v. Kemp, 1
means test bankruptcy cases
Solicitor General's role in, 200–202
Midatlantic National Bank, 130
Midlantic Bank v. New Jersey Department of Environmental Protection, 12, 98
amici in, 214
BFP case and, 190–191
clerks' opinions in, 133–135
Conference of Justices discussion in, 136–137
hypotheticals used in opinions of, 226–227
Kelly v. Robinson and, 150
legacy of, 145
lower court rulings on, 130–132
oral arguments before Supreme Court in, 135–136
political background, 126–127
property abandonment and, 128–129
Quanta Resources Corporation and, 129–130

Ron Pair case and, 165–170
Solicitor General and, 198–199
Solicitor General's role in, 142–144
Supreme Court jurisprudence in, 133–142
switched vote of Justice Stevens in, 140–142
Midwest International Standard Products, 158–159
Milavetz, Gallop & Milavetz v. United States, 220–221
Milken, Michael, 182
Moglen, Eben, 1
Motor Vehicle Pollution Control Act, 127
Murphy, Walter F., 9–10
Murray's Lessee v. Hoboken Land & Improvement Co., 52–53

Nadelmann, Kurt H., 39
National Association of Bankruptcy Trustees, 95–96
National Association of Manufacturers, 121
National Bankruptcy Review Commission, 25
National Conference of Commissioners on Uniform State Law (NCCUSL), 175–180
National Labor Relations Act
Bankruptcy Code and, 100–103, 123
Bildisco case and, 110–112, 120–121
Kevin Steel case and, 103–104
National Labor Relations Board (NLRB)
Bildisco bankruptcy filing and, 105–107, 143–144
"new entity" reconciliation
bankruptcy *vs.* labor law and, 103–104
in Bildisco bankruptcy case, 105–107, 113
New Legal Realism
Supreme Court decisionmaking process and, 9–10
news media
Bildisco case coverage in, 120–121
Ron Pair coverage in, 171–173
New York Times
"salience" scores of Supreme Court rulings in, 33
New York Times, 120–121, 129–130
NLRB v. Bildisco, 12, 33, 98
arguments before Supreme Court in, 109–110
background to, 100–101
bankruptcy *vs.* labor law in, 99–124
Chrysler and General Motors bankruptcy filings and legacy of, 121–123
company bankruptcy filing, 105–107
Congressional reaction to, 120–121
consequences of, 118–121
Continental Airlines bankruptcy and, 119
current events as information source in, 225
decision to hear case, Supreme Court debate over, 107
disparate views of clerks in, 108–109
initial Supreme Court decision in, 110–112
justices' opinions in, 112–118
labor politics and, 101–102
legal context of, 102–107
Midlantic case and, 137–138, 140–142
Solicitor General and, 198–199
Solicitor General's arguments in, 143–144
Supreme Court jurisprudence in, 107–121
NLRB v. Burns Internal Security Services, 108–109
Nobelman v. American Savings Bank, 227–229
"non-core" proceedings
EBIA case and, 69–71
nongovernmental elites
amici filed by, 212–214
Supreme Court decisionmaking and, 11
non-jury proceedings
bankruptcy process and, 45–46
EBIA case and, 69–71
Granfinanciera case and right to, 56, 59, 61, 65

Nordic Village, see United States v. Nordic Village
Nordic Village, Inc., 91–94
Northern Pipeline Construction Co., 48–56
Northern Pipeline v. Marathon, 29, 40
Bildisco case and, 120–121
Congress's power over judicial appointments and, 43–48
constitutional issues and, 76–78
information sources in, 222
Justice's perspectives on bankruptcy in, 48–56
Stern v. Marshall and, 65–68
Union Carbide case and, 58–59
Norton's Bankruptcy Law and Practice, 222
Norwest Bank Worthington v. Ahlers, 20–22, 212, 220

Occupational Safety and Health Review Commission, 57–59
O'Connor, Sandra Day (Justice)
on affirmative action, 195
BFP case and, 178–180, 185–189
Bildisco case and, 107, 113, 115, 123
Granfinanciera case and, 61–65
Hoffman opinion of, 87–91
initial *Bildisco* decision and, 110–112
internal papers of, 20–22
Katz case and, 95–96
Kelly v. Robinson and, 153–156
Marathon case and, 50
Midlantic case and, 135–136, 138, 226–227
opinions in securities and tax rulings of, 35–36
Ron Pair case and, 163–170
state sovereign immunity opinions, 81–83
Union Carbide opinion of, 58–59, 62–63
Office of the United States Trustee (OUST)
Midlantic case and, 142–144
Solicitor General and, 198–202
Off Road Vehicles - Recreation and Family Campground, Inc. (ORV), 181
Ohio v. Kovacs, 198–199
oral arguments, Justices' information gleaned from, 223–225
organized labor
Bildisco case and, 101–102, 120–121, 143–144
Chrysler and General Motors bankruptcy filings and, 121–123
Continental bankruptcy and, 118
Osborne, Russell, 181, 183–185
Ottenheimer v. Whitaker, 128–129
oversecured creditors
in *Ron Pair* case, 160–163
Owens, Ryan J., 13–15, 18
Owen v. Owen, 22
Owen v. Owen, 20

Pacelle, Richard, 11
Packwood, Robert, 121
Pair, Ron, 158–159
Palmore case, 50
Pardo, Rafael, 27
Patterson v. Shumate, 198–199
Payne v. Tennessee, 147
PBGC v. LTV Corp., 23
Pedersen, Wayne and Marlene, 180–183, 190
Pennsylvania Department of Public Welfare v. Davenport, 156–157
Pennsylvania Dep't v. Davenport, 29–30
Pennsylvania v. Union Gas Co., 82–91
Congressional overruling of, 94–96
per curiam opinion
Supreme Court bankruptcy rulings and, 40
Perez v. Campbell, 190–191
Pildes, Richard H., 13
Pioneer v. Brunswick, 23
plain meaning principle
in *BFP* case, 183, 187–191
Supreme Court bankruptcy rulings and, 12
Plank, Thomas, 40
plenary power

in Bankruptcy Act of 1898, 44–46
policy decisions
cultural resistance to debt relief and, 234–235
Midlantic Supreme Court deliberations involving, 140–142
Ron Pair case and, 168–170
secured credit bankruptcy cases and, 202–206
Supreme Court rulings and, 8–11
politics
individual Justices' votes in bankruptcy cases and, 32
judicial decisionmaking and, 16–17
labor politics and, 101–102
in *Midatlantic* case, 126–127
qualitative analysis of Supreme Court rulings and, 18–23
Supreme Court rulings and, 8–11
Posner, Richard, 4, 9
Powe, Lucas A., 10
Powell, Lewis (Justice), 1–3
Bildisco case and, 107, 113, 123
Continental Airlines bankruptcy and *Bildisco* ruling and, 119
on crime and victims' rights, 147
draft dissent in *Midlantic* of, 138–140
Grandfinanciera case and, 61–65
Kelly v. Robinson and, 150–156
Marathon case and, 50–56, 108–112, 119
Midlantic case and, 125–126, 133–137, 140–143, 214, 226–227
opinions in securities and tax rulings of, 35–36
Ron Pair case and, 168–170
Solicitor General and, 198–199
state sovereign immunity opinions, 81
pre-bankruptcy labor settlements, 121–123
preference actions in bankruptcy proceedings, 44–46
foreclosures and, 175–180
in *Nordic Village* case, 91–94
Pritchett, Herman, 8, 10, 22–23
private litigation
sovereign immunity and, 80–82
probate exception
bankruptcy rulings and, 65–68
property
abandonment by bankruptcy trustees, 128–129
creditors' possession of, 159–161
in *Dewsnup v. Timm* case, 215
foreclosure as fraudulent conveyance of, 175–180
priority claim concerns and, 135–136
public fisc
in *Ron Pair* case, 170–171
public rights doctrine
Granfinanciera and, 57–59, 62–63
Marathon case and, 52–53
purchaser status
in *Kevin Steel* case, 103–104

qualitative analysis of Supreme Court rulings, 18–23
Quanta Resources Corporation, 129–130, 134–135
quantitative analysis of Supreme Court rulings, 8–9
amici contributions, 211–214
coding of, 17–18
quasi-judiciary process, in Bankruptcy Code, 42–43, 61–65
Quinn-Martin ideology scores, 17–18
statistical analysis of bankruptcy jurisprudence and, 32

RadLAX Gateway Hotel, LLC v. Amalgamated Bank, 227–229
Railway Labor Act, 104–105, 108–109, 112–113
Rake v. Wade, 29–30, 171–173
Rasmussen, Bob, 11–13, 90, 94, 158
REA Express case, *see Brotherhood of Railway, Airline and Steamship Clerks, Freight Handlers, Express and Station Employees*, AFL-CIO v. *REA Express, Inc.*
Reagan, Ronald, 101–102
real estate industry
Durret case and, 178–180
price volatility in, 184–185
real property law

foreclosure as fraudulent conveyance in, 175–180
price volatility and, 184–185
reasonably equivalent value principle
in *BFP* case, 188
foreclosure sales and, 178–180
Rehnquist, William (Chief Justice), 33
BFP case and, 185–189
Bildisco case and, 107, 109–110, 112–118, 123
draft majority opinion in *Midlantic* by, 137–138
Granfinanciera case and, 61–65
Hoffman opinion of, 87–91
initial *Bildisco* decision and, 110–112
Kelly v. Robinson and, 153–156
Marathon case and, 50
Midlantic case and, 135–136, 138–140, 214, 226–227
Nordic Village case and, 92–93
opinions in bankruptcy rulings of, 33
opinions in tax and securities rulings of, 35
preconceptions in opinions of, 227–229
Ron Pair case and, 165, 168–170
state sovereign immunity opinions, 81
Resolution Trust Corporation, 174–175, 178–180, 183–184
BFP case and, 184–191
restitutionary obligation, 1–3
in *Kelly v. Robinson*, 148, 153
Roberts, John (Chief Justice), 66–68
Baker Botts v. ASARCO and, 223–225
Katz case and, 95–96
preconceptions in opinions of, 227–229
Wellness case opinions of, 73
Robinson, Carolyn, 146, 148–150
Rodino, Peter W., 120–121
Rodriguez, Alberto Duque, 56–65
Rogers, Jim, 40
Ron Pair case, *see United States v. Ron Pair Enterprises, Inc.*
The Roosevelt Court (Pritchett), 8
rule of statutory construction
in *Midlantic* case, 138–140
"salience" scores of Supreme Court rulings, 17–18
statistical analysis of bankruptcy jurisprudence and, 33
savings and loan crisis
secured credit bankruptcy cases and, 202–206
Scalia, Antonin (Justice), 12
BFP case and, 174, 185–191
constitutional issues and bankruptcy and, 76–78
Granfinanciera case and, 59–61
Hoffman opinion of, 87–91
internal papers of, 20–22
on judicial authority concerning bankruptcy, 42
Katz case and, 95–96
Kelly v. Robinson and, 153, 155–156
Nordic Village case and, 92–93
opinions in securities and tax rulings of, 35–36
preconceptions in opinions of, 227–229
Ron Pair case and, 164–165, 168–170
Seventh Amendment interpretation by, 64
state sovereign immunity opinions, 81–83, 85–86
Stern v. Marshall case and, 65–68
Timbers case and, 222–223
Wellness case and, 75–76
Yates v. Hendon case and, 217–218
Schuman, Carl, 151–153
Schwab v. Reilly, 217–218
Schwartz, Alan, 12, 18
secured credit bankruptcy cases
amici filed in, 219–221
Bankruptcy Act of 1841 and, 39–41
BFP case, 190
foreclosure as fraudulent conveyance and, 175–180
Midlantic case, 130–132
Rake v. Wade, 171–173
Ron Pair case and, 158, 159, 161, 162, 173
Solicitor General and, 202–206
Securities and Exchange Commission (SEC), 27, 29

Supreme Court jurisprudence concerning, 35–36
securities issues
Supreme Court jurisprudence concerning, 35–36
Segal, Jeffrey, 8–9
Segal-Cover ideology scores, 17–18
statistical analysis of bankruptcy jurisprudence and, 32
Segal-Spaeth Supreme Court Database, 8–9, 17–18
statistical analysis of bankruptcy jurisprudence and, 32
Seligson, Charles, 24
Seminole Tribe of Florida v. Florida, 95–97
separate but equal standard, 195
Seventh Amendment
bankruptcy law and, 45–46, 76–78, 81
Granfinanciera case and, 56, 59, 61, 65
Scalia's interpretation of, 64
sheltering, in bankruptcy rulings, 218–219
Simon, Paul, 120–121
Skeel, David, 4, 234–235
Solicitor General
amici briefs filed by, 211–214, 217–218
arguments before Supreme Court in Bildisco and, 109–110
bankruptcy interests and, 206–209
Bildisco case and role of, 107
in *Dewsnup v. Timm* case, 215
federal agency cases and, 198–199
Hoffman case and, 216
hypotheticals used by, 226–227
information sources for, 247–248
labor law *vs.* Bankruptcy Power and, 99–100
Midlantic case and role of, 142–144, 214
Office of the United States Trustee cases, 198–202
role in bankruptcy cases of, 197–198, 210–211, 232–233
in *Ron Pair* case, 163–165, 170–171
secured credit bankruptcy cases and, 202–206
sovereign immunity cases and, 202
tax-related bankruptcy cases, 200
weaknesses of, 193–196
Solorio v. United States, 42
Sotomayor, Sonia (Justice), 72
Wellness opinions of, 73
Souter, David (Justice)
BFP case and, 178, 185–187, 189–191
on *Booth*, 147
Katz case and, 95–96
Nordic Village case and, 91–92
opinions in bankruptcy rulings of, 35
sovereign immunity, *see also* state sovereignty, 200
bankruptcy law and, 79
in *Hoffman v. Connecticut Dep't*, 79–91, 216
in *Nordic Village* case, 91–94
Solicitor General and cases involving, 202
Spaeth, Harold, 8–9
stare decisis
Supreme Court decisionmaking process and, 10
state criminal procedure
federal interference with, 2, 147, 154–155
Kelly v. Robinson and, 150–153
Solicitor General and, 195–196
state environmental laws
Midatlantic case and, 127, 130, 132, 133, 135, 136, 142, 144
right of abandonment and, 138
state regulations
as bankruptcy information source, 222–223
fraudulent conveyance and, 175–180
state sovereignty
amici information concerning, 216–218
bankruptcy rulings and, 79–83
in *BFP* case, 174–192
Congressional rejection of Supreme Court rulings on, 94–96
federal sovereign immunity *vs.*, 92–93
statistical analysis of Supreme Court bankruptcy jurisprudence, 31–36
Statute of Elizabeth (1571), 176
statutory cases
Bankruptcy Code and, 98

statutory language, *see also* "plain meaning" principle
 Hoffman case interpretation of, 90
 in *Midlantic* case, 133–135
 systemic values *vs.*, 146
Stern v. Marshall, 43–48, 65–68, 218–219
 constitutional issues and, 76–78
 EBIA case and, 69–71
 Wellness case and, 71–76
Stevens, John Paul (Justice), 2
 arguments in Bildisco and comments of, 109–110
 BFP case and, 185–187, 190–191
 Bildisco case and, 107, 114–118, 123
 Granfinanciera case and, 61–65
 Hoffman opinion of, 87–91
 initial *Bildisco* decision and, 110–112
 Katz case and, 94–96, 216–218
 Kelly v. Robinson and, 150, 155–156, 226–227
 Marathon case and, 50–56
 Midlantic case and, 135–138
 Nordic Village case and, 91–94
 opinions in bankruptcy rulings of, 33
 preconceptions in opinions of, 227–229
 Ron Pair case and, 168–170
 state sovereign immunity opinions, 81–83, 85–86
 switched vote in *Midlantic* case of, 140–142
 Union Carbide case and, 59
"such claim" language
 in *Ron Pair* case, 163–165
summary jurisdiction
 in Bankruptcy Act of 1898, 44–46
 in Bildisco bankruptcy filing, 105–107
Sunstein, Cass, 14
Supreme Court bankruptcy jurisprudence, *see also* judicial decision-making
 amici contributions to, 193–196, 211–221
 "attitudinal" *vs.* "constrained" approaches to, 8–11
 Bankruptcy Code *vs.* Bankruptcy Power and, 98
 in *BFP*, 184–191
 in *Bildisco*, 107–121
 characteristics of cases involving, 37–38
 clerks' opinions in *Midlantic*, 133–135
 Congressional rejection of, 11, 29–30, 94–96
 constitutional doctrine irrelevance to bankruptcy and, 76–78, 96–97
 court-provided information in, 221–229
 distrust of bankruptcy judges in, 233–234
 doctrinal principles in *Granfinanciera* and, 57–59
 evolution of, 68–76
 external knowledge and, 13–15
 Granfinanciera case and, 56–65
 in *Hoffman*, 87–91
 hypotheticals as basis for, 226–227
 initial *Bildisco* decision, 110–112
 in *Kelly v. Robinson*, 150–156
 Marathon bankruptcy case and, 48–56
 in *Midatlantic* case, 133–142
 in *Nordic Village*, 91–94
 oral arguments as information source in, 223–225
 preconceptions of Justices in, 227–229
 quasi-judicial process in Bankruptcy Code and, 42–43
 in *Rake v. Wade*, 171–173
 references to cases, 245
 in *Ron Pair* case, 162–168, 171–173
 Solicitor General and, 197–198
 sources of Court's citations, 246
 sovereign immunity and, 79–83
 statistical analysis of, 31–36
 Stern v. Marshall and, 65–68
 table of bankruptcy cases, 239–241
 table of Justices' papers, 242–244
 underenforcement of bankruptcy law in, 231–232
 in *Wellness* case, 71–76

Tabb, Charles, 12–13, 25, 142
Takings Clause
 Midlantic arguments involving, 142–144
Task Force on Victims of Crime, 147

tax liens
in bankruptcy proceedings, 159–161
in *Dewsnup v. Timm* case, 215
Ron Pair case and, 158–159, 161–162, 168–171
tax litigation
bankruptcy laws and, 200
IRA status, 198–199
Supreme Court jurisprudence concerning, 35–36
Teamsters Union, 120–121
arguments before Supreme Court in Bildisco and, 109–110
Bildisco and, 100–101
"Term" of the Supreme Court, 56
textual guidance
avoidance of, in sovereign immunity cases, 202
in *BFP* case, 189
in Supreme Court bankruptcy decisions, 11–13
third party creditors
real estate purchase for debt settlement, 178–180
Thomas, Clarence (Justice)
BFP case and, 185–187
EBIA case and, 69–71
Katz case and, 95–96, 216–218
opinions in securities and tax rulings of, 35–36
preconceptions in opinions of, 227–229
Wellness case, 75
Thomas v. Union Carbide Agricultural Products Co., 58–59
Granfinanciera case and, 59–63
Stern v. Marshall case and, 67
Three Mile Island, 126–127
Thygerson, Kenneth, 182
Till v. SCS Credit Corp., 218–219
Timbers of Inwood Forest, 17
Timbers of Inwood Forest, 222–223
title insurance
BFP case and, 178–180
Toibb v. Radoff, 206–209
tortious interference
bankruptcy proceedings and, 65–68
trustees in bankruptcy proceedings, *see also* Office of the United States Trustee
in Bankruptcy Act of 1898, 44–46
Midlantic case and, 133, 135–136
property abandonment by, 128–129
property transfers in foreclosure and, 174–175
Tull v. United States, 61
TVA v. Hill, 155

unfair labor practices
in Bildisco bankruptcy filing, 105–107
in *Bildisco* case, 110–112
Uniform Fraudulent Conveyance Act (UFCA), 177–179
Uniform Fraudulent Transfer Act (UFTA), 177–179
Uniform Law Commission, 177
Union Carbide case, *see Thomas v. Union Carbide Agricultural Products Co.*
unions, *see* organized labor
United Autoworkers Union (UAW), 121–123
United States Bankruptcy Administration, 232–233
proposal for, 26
United States v Bass, 160
United States v. Nordic Village, 200
United States v. Nordic Village, 29–30
Congressional overruling of, 94–96
sovereign immunity in, 12, 79–83, 202, 226–227
United States v. Raddatz, 53
United States v. Ron Pair Enterprises, Inc.
secured credit issues in, 200
United States v. Ron Pair Enterprises, Inc., 98, 158–173
certiorari in, 162–163
Conference deliberations in, 165
dissenting Supreme Court opinion in, 167–168
division of Justices over, 168–170
factual setting, 158–159
information sources in, 224–225

legal setting for, 159–161
lower court rulings on, 161–162
majority Supreme Court opinion in, 165–167
oral arguments in, 163–165
Solicitor General, creditors, and public fiscal policy in, 170–171
Supreme Court jurisprudence in, 162–168
United States v. Security Industrial Bank, 204
United States v. Security Industrial Bank, 40
United States v. Whiting Pools, 200
"unmistakable clarity" standard, 87–91
Bankruptcy Code and, 125–126
in *Nordic Village* case, 91–94

Veenstra, Loring, 4, 99–145, 158–173
Victim and Witness Protection Act, 147
victim impact statement, 147
Victims of Crime Act, 147
victims' rights
criminal restitution *vs.*, 146–148

wage-earner plans
in bankruptcy law, 28
Wallace, Larry, 163–165, 224–225
Wallace's Bookstore, 94–96
Warburg Paribas Becker Inc., 130
Warner, Ray, 46, 57
Warren, Elizabeth, 25
Watts, Kathryn, 27
Weinfeld, Edward, 24, 25
Wellness International Network v. Sharif, 17–18, 43–48, 231–232
constitutional issues and, 76–78
information sources in, 222
White, Byron (Justice)
arguments in Bildisco and comments of, 109–110
Atlas Roofing opinion of, 57–59
bench memoranda in Bildisco from, 108–109
Bildisco case and, 107
constitutional issues and bankruptcy and, 76–78
Continental Airlines bankruptcy and *Bildisco* ruling and, 119
Granfinanciera case and, 61–65
Hoffman opinion of, 87–91, 216, 220–221
initial *Bildisco* decision and, 110–112
Kelly v. Robinson and, 155–156
Marathon case and, 50–56, 73
Midlantic case and, 136–138
opinions in bankruptcy proceedings of, 45–46
opinions in securities and tax rulings of, 35
retirement of, 94–96
Ron Pair case and, 165, 168–170
state sovereign immunity opinions, 81–83
Stern v. Marshall case and, 65–68
Whittington, Keith, 19
Whole Women's Health v. Hellerstedt, 195
Will, Hubert, 24
women's rights
amicus briefs concerning, 195–196
Women's Rights Project, 195–196

Yates v. Hendon, 217–218
Younger v. Harris, 154–155

Zera, Edward, 83–84